"Creating shareholder value in a global economy demands a well-calibrated strategy to compete and win across markets. David's insights will help leaders formulate that strategy and make the tough decisions and trade-offs necessary to successfully implement it."
Steven A. Kandarian, Chairman, President, and Chief Executive Officer, MetLife Inc.

"David has a great ability to combine academic theory with practical business insights, which he uses to translate complex issues into simple concepts and decision tools. In this book he comprehensively covers international strategy from theory to pragmatic application in a very readable form supported by practical examples from real life."
Nils S. Andersen, CEO, The Maersk Group

"In the avalanche of business books reaching the market today, David's *International Strategy* is a rarity – an informative and engaging overview of the best current research neatly interwoven with insightful accounts of leading edge management practice. Without getting bogged down in abstractions or generalizations, Collis guides the reader through an impressive range of academic findings, all the while grounding the theory in real-world examples. And while the book's title highlights its focus on strategy, it's not a view of strategy as abstract concepts or complex charts. Above all, Collis is a pragmatist who never leaves his reader understanding the 'what' but wondering about the 'how.' *International Strategy* is a book that deserves a prominent place on every executive's bookshelf and on every serious business student's desk."
Christopher A. Bartlett, Thomas D. Casserly, Jr. Professor of Business Administration Emeritus, Harvard Business School

"David Collis has a deep understanding of academic research *and* corporate practice. Both are on display in this comprehensive yet very readable text that combines insights from mainstream (domestic) strategy with those from international business and economics—and that spans both the external environments within which firms operate and their internal organizational structures and processes."
Pankaj Ghemawat Anselmo Rubiralta, Professor of Global Strategy at IESE Business School, and Distinguished Visiting Professor of Global Strategy, New York University Stern School of Business

"I came away from this book realizing how complex, how hard, international strategy is for any but the smallest and simplest organization. International executives really need this book, because it is both expert and realistic."
Richard Koch, author of the million-copy-selling *The 80/20 Principle*, and *The 80/20 Manager*

"David's work is first rate in terms of his ability to clearly explain concepts and to make them come alive in a practical way for students and leaders on the front lines. His observations, suggestions and concepts ring true based on my years of experience managing and sitting on the boards of large and complex international companies. *International Strategy* is a valuable resource that advances the field."
Kevin Sharer, former Chairman and CEO of Amgen, Senior Lecturer of Business Administration Harvard Business School

International Strategy
Context, Concepts and Implications

David Collis

Harvard Business School

WILEY

Registered office
John Wiley & Sons Ltd, The Atrium, Southern Gate, Chichester, West Sussex, PO19 8SQ, United Kingdom

For details of our global editorial offices, for customer services and for information about how to apply for permission to reuse the copyright material in this book please see our website at www.wiley.com.

Library of Congress Cataloging-in-Publication Data:

Collis, David J.
    International strategy : context, concepts and implications / David Collis, Harvard Business School.
        pages cm
    Includes index.
        ISBN 978-1-4051-3968-7 (paperback) – 1. International business enterprises–Management.   2. Strategic planning.   3. Strategic alliances (Business)   4. Competition.   I. Title.
        HD62.4.C626 2014
        658.4′012–dc23   2014017637

A catalogue record for this book is available from the British Library.

ISBN 978-1-405-13968-7 (pbk)
ISBN 978-1-118-74092-7 (ebk)   ISBN 978-1-118-74087-3 (ebk)

Cover design by Dan Jubb
Cover image from iStock

Set in 11/15 MinionPro by Aptara Inc., New Delhi, India
Printed in Great Britain by CPI Group (UK) Ltd, Croydon, CR0 4YY

To my family: past, present, and future.

CONTENTS

ACKNOWLEDGMENTS

Standing on the shoulders of giants that others may see further.

As the saying above suggests, my greatest debt of gratitude is to those who have gone before – some of whom I have learnt from personally, others of whom I only know through their work. It is my predecessors' research and insights that have enlightened my understanding of international strategy (and, more broadly, competitive strategy), and enabled me to capture and present the ideas expressed in this text. Collectively, the names of those who have developed the field are featured in the "Further Reading" sections of the book. I do, however, want to individually mention those who have had the greatest influence on this book. Chris Bartlett, Adam Brandenburger, Chris Carr, Dick Caves, Pankaj Ghemawat, Sumantra Ghoshal, Barry Nalebuff, Michael Porter, Mike Spence, Mike Yoshino, and, more recently, colleagues Juan Alcacer, Bharat Anand, Misiek Piskorski, Jan Rivkin, Jordan Siegel, Toby Stuart, and David Yoffie have all contributed in ways they probably do not know, let alone remember. I thank each of them.

Two other constituencies also deserve recognition for their contributions – intended or otherwise – to this book. The first are my former students whose comments and questions in class, although they often do not realize it, actually do influence my thinking. More important, the pressure to deliver something of more lasting value than just a fun 80-minute conversation pushed me to develop the frameworks for this book.

The companies I have worked with and written cases on over the years also deserve acknowledgment. If one is to understand how the world really works, and whether one's ideas can actually influence practice, it is vital to be in the field, interacting with, learning from, and observing the results of employing the processes and frameworks laid out here. As an academic I truly value these opportunities.

Thanks are also due to the institutions where I have had the privilege of being employed for the last 30 years and which have supported the research and case writing that underpins this book. The Harvard Business School must be first among those, but it was during a five-year stay at the Yale School of Management from 1997 to 2002 that I began writing the book as a complement to the new "Global Strategy" course I originally developed there. I am embarrassed to note that the original draft has a start date of December 1998! But it was my stay at Yale that provided the impetus for the manuscript.

As always a cast of characters supports the actual writing of the text. Rosemary Nixon, my original editor at what was then Blackwell, stuck with me until we pushed the manuscript over the line about 10 years after signing the contract. Mary Reed and Matt Shaffer provided research support in the last couple of years, and Cathyjean Gustafson has been the orchestrator of all things administrative, ensuring that everything gets done on time and to her flawless standards. As always, errors and omissions remain my responsibility.

Finally, as the dedication observes, prolific thanks are due to my family.

David Collis
MVY and Concord

PREFACE

PERSPECTIVE

This book is designed for executives in companies that compete across national borders who wish to make valuable contributions to every discussion about their company's international strategy.

The decision maker it is written for is a senior manager within a multinational. This does not imply that the ideas apply only to large firms. That decision maker could as easily be the CEO of an Internet startup who is interested in expanding overseas, as the head of Unilever, Sharp, or Ford.

While the unit of analysis might occasionally shift from the firm to the country, the book takes as given the differences we see around the world – differences of geography, culture, economic policy, and institutional structures. This book is less about how the world economy is becoming more interdependent or what social, political, and economic forces are at work.[1] Instead, the book is concerned with how managers can effectively create shareholder value in the world today given all these differences and drivers.

This book is not about international trade theory, although the economics of comparative advantage and international trade under imperfect competition underpin it. Nor is it about international business in the sense of "how to" open an office in a foreign country, or the legal requirements of doing business in different countries, although those idiosyncrasies and vagaries are the background for the text. Neither is it about the specific functional aspects of international business – international marketing and international finance, in particular – although it draws on and refers to those disciplines when necessary. The implications of exchange rate volatility and the financial instruments available to mitigate their effects, for example, are covered when they affect strategic decisions, but the book does not attempt to treat those topics on their own terms. This is not the text to learn about derivatives, or the benefits of exchange rate devaluations, but it will illustrate how those variables affect broader strategic questions. Less is said about joint ventures than in many other texts on international business. Alliances and other forms of partnerships are common in international competition for strategic reasons that will be made apparent in the text, but their specific form, and their operational management, are better dealt with as a subject in their own right.

This is, therefore, unashamedly a book about international strategy. Since so many authors claim to cover this ground when in fact they address tactical issues, an important early part of the text addresses the two definitional questions of what is distinctively international, and what is uniquely strategic about "international strategy"?

AUDIENCE

As a result of adopting the perspective of the manager in a firm active in international competition, the audience for this book should, first and foremost, be every executive concerned with the formulation and implementation of strategy in a company that competes internationally. For them it should provide a framework and a toolset to resolve the hard decisions they must make every day. It should also be relevant to executives who, even if they do not themselves operate outside a country, nevertheless face competitors from foreign countries.

The book has less to say to policy makers who have to address issues of trade, exchange rates, policies towards multinationals, etc., and who take the country and the welfare of its inhabitants as the focus of their concern. However, in designing those policies, government officials should benefit from understanding the managerial perspective – what concerns them, what motivates them, and what shapes their decisions. Only by empathizing with the incentives and choices that corporate executives face can policy makers effectively design programs that will achieve their desired ends.

Clearly, the book should be read not just by managers in multinationals, but also by those who work with, advise, or support multinationals. Investment bankers, consultants, investment analysts, suppliers, anyone who needs to know how companies are approaching international strategy and the profound ramifications that will have throughout their organizations, should read this text.

Because its content is designed for managers, the book will also be valuable to students who aspire to become such executives and who want to learn how companies can successfully compete internationally. Those are the two primary audiences – managers and students. Come to think of it, that covers just about everyone with an interest in international competition and strategy!

READING THE TEXT

This book has been designed for multiple uses and is, accordingly, divided into three parts: setting the context, introducing the conceptual framework, and providing pragmatic advice. Each has a specific purpose and a value for certain audiences, so a brief guide is in order.

The most obvious suggestion is for executives who are dipping into the text to provide real-time answers to a particular issue they currently face. For them, the solution is to jump to the relevant chapter in Part Three where tools and processes are presented that are immediately applicable to their situation. I would, of course, encourage them to spend time in the earlier parts of the book – particularly Chapters 5 and 6 – in order to improve their understanding of the concepts and theories of international strategy, but those parts are not required reading to get value from the pragmatic advice of Part Three.

For students, ideally MBA students with a grounding in competitive or business unit strategy, the converse is true. You should start at the beginning of the book in order to grasp the unique characteristics of international competition that practitioners already understand, and to absorb the intellectual foundations of the subject. For you, Part Three should be seen as an opportunity to apply what you have learnt and to begin to wrestle with the details of the topic that will confront the rest of your managerial careers.

For scholars, much of the early part of the book should be familiar, but the integrated presentation of ideas (with appropriate references and careful articulation of the links to well-known approaches) should be valuable. The text is intended to offer a coherent approach to international strategy that is derived from first principles: What is different about international strategy? What are the elements of such a "strategy?" And so on. Appropriate footnotes and a limited reading list of the most relevant and highly cited works accompany each chapter, so the intellectual support for the text is documented and supporting materials identified. There are also additional online resources available for instructors and students at www.wiley.com/go/internationalstrategy, which include a suggested syllabus, lecture support materials, case suggestions, assignment questions and additional links.

The flow of the text is, therefore, best represented as starting from the general and proceeding to the specific – from understanding context and theory to application, tools, and practice. Along the way, extended examples or well-known theories that are perhaps peripheral to the core argument, but are nevertheless worthy of discussion, are captured in text boxes. These add to the richness and depth of coverage of the material. There is some (limited) repetition of ideas among the chapters since each is designed to be understood on its own terms, or assigned separately. That redundancy has been kept to a minimum.

Whatever your purpose in reading the text, I wish you well on your journey.

On Definitions

Terminology has complicated many previous discussions of international strategy. In particular, the use of the term "global" strategy has led to enormous misunderstanding. Many observers have used the term to describe any strategy with cross-border implications. Indeed, many told me to name this book "Global Strategy" since that is how executives today think of international competition. However, others have applied the term to a particular type of strategy for dealing with international competition which assumes a standard approach to competition around the world.

Another term that has meant different things to different authors is the unit of analysis that is the focus of this book: companies that compete across international borders. Some authors refer to such companies as multinationals, or MNCs, others as transnationals or TNCs, and yet others as multinational enterprises or MNEs.

While I would not claim that the definitions adopted here are held by everyone, it is important that readers become familiar with how they are applied in this text:

- International – a generic term that applies to anything that involves activities across borders. International strategy, for example, has no normative connotations whatsoever (hence it is used as the title of the book); it merely refers to the fact that when firms compete across borders they need to approach strategy from an international perspective.

- Multinational – a generic term referring to any company that has activities in many countries. Multinational and its equivalents are used interchangeably with no normative connotations.

- Firm, company, corporation, enterprise, and organization are used interchangeably when referring to a hierarchical economic entity.

We describe and use a typology of different strategies in this book, and it is important to know that when referring to a particular strategy the terms below have specific meanings:

- Local – when used to describe a strategy this term implies that the firm's sales and activities are almost exclusively domestic.

- Export and import – transfer of goods or services across borders, but also refers to a particular choice of strategy that does not involve the firm in a substantial international presence.

- Multidomestic – identifies a strategy in which a multinational's activities in each country are managed independently.

- Global – a specific term that implies a company has adopted a uniform approach to competing around the world.

- Transnational – another specific term, popularized by Chris Bartlett and Sumantra Ghoshal, that identifies an ideal type of strategy and organization. The transnational strategy aims to transcend strategic tradeoffs and exploit a unique advantage through the coordinated management of a dispersed international network of activities.

These definitions imply that "international" is the umbrella term for activity that crosses borders, while "global," "multidomestic," "transnational," "local," and "export" have specific meanings when designating a particular strategy for competing internationally.

NOTE

1. Chapter 1 does, however, explain how those forces establish the contemporary context for international strategy.

INTRODUCTION: MOTIVATION AND DEFINITION – WHAT IS INTERNATIONAL STRATEGY?

CHALLENGE

Not so long ago, three books arrived on my desk on the same day. Each is by a well-respected academic author, and each is replete with endorsements from successful executives. All are zealous, almost messianic, in their advocacy of a particular approach to international strategy. One proclaims that the only successful international strategy is to be "globally dominant" (Govindarajan and Gupta, 2001). Another argues instead that there is an absolute requirement to transform corporations "from global to metanational" (Doz *et al.*, 2001). The third states in no uncertain terms that the other two are wrong, and that when dealing with "the end of globalization" the only viable strategy is "to profit from the realities of regional markets" (Rugman, 2005). What are reasonable managers supposed to think, let alone do, when faced with such vehemently argued, yet contradictory, advice?

The answer is simple. All three authors are correct. And all three authors are wrong. Each is promulgating a strategy that is sensible – that can lead to competitive advantage and international success under the appropriate circumstances. All are badly overstating their case by arguing that every company should pursue their particular recommendation. In the vernacular of the racetrack, the real answer is that there are "horses for courses." There is no one right international strategy that is best for every firm under every circumstance. Instead there is a set of strategies, each of which can be very powerful and successful, if chosen at the right time for the right industry, and if implemented effectively.

Indeed the lesson of this book is that implementing any one international strategy successfully is more important than blindly pursuing the "ideal" strategy that the current management guru is advocating. The challenge for most managers is not to choose the single best international strategy, but to align the answers to four fundamental questions that all firms which compete internationally confront: in which countries to compete; what product variation to allow around the world; where to locate activities; and how to organize the multinational to be consistent with the underlying advantage they are building around the world? It is the orientation of this book, first, around the underlying sources of advantage that firms can exploit by virtue of competing internationally, and then around the four critical choices that come up every day in every firm competing across borders, that differentiates this text from so many others. It is a pragmatic handbook for managers, not a manifesto for leaders. And that is its value.

MOTIVATION

A large global financial services firm recently acquired the international operations of a competitor for nearly $15 billion. The acquisition doubled the firm's international presence and brought with it operations in nearly 30 countries, an expanded product range, and an organization with a global headquarters in the USA and several regional offices.

As with all effective acquisition processes, the company required a detailed post-merger integration plan to address the myriad decisions involved in combining two entities, ranging from the choice of IT platforms to personnel appointments and compensation. Yet none of the individual integration projects could begin until the acquirer had articulated the overall international strategy for the company going forward. Without a strategic direction, teams would lack clear objectives and guiderails for their work, and might even propose conflicting plans.

Consider that the combined entity had a presence in 64 countries ranging from the tiny (Nepal and Jamaica), through the emerging (India and China), to the substantial (USA and Japan). Which of these countries should be exited, and how should resources be allocated among those retained? What should the company's final geographic footprint look like if it sought to balance mature but profitable markets with fast-growing but investment-needy developing countries? A 64-nation portfolio, for example, would have very different implications than a choice to focus on driving revenue to more than $1 billion in each of 10 nations.

As the provider of a range of financial products sold through multiple distribution channels, the firm also had to decide its future product portfolio. Retirement products with onerous capital requirements had been the core of sales in mature geographies. In contrast, simple life insurance products were in strong demand in rapidly growing markets. Distribution also varied around the globe from banc-assurance in Europe to owned agency in China. Which should be pursued where? And, more important, to what degree should those products and channels be allowed to vary between countries? Would there be strict limits on what could and could not be sold, and by which method, around the world? Or would country managers be given autonomy to select from a substantial product range those few appropriate to their own market?

Unlike a manufacturing firm for whom optimizing the location and configuration of factories is typically a major source of value creation, the location of most activities in the combined entity, such as sales, was not in question since they had to be performed close to the customer. Even the location of functions outsourced to low labor-cost countries, like call centers and software development, were not contentious as both entities had been pursuing similar approaches. Nevertheless, certain location choices did arise. Each entity had a well-recognized brand, but their geographic footprints now overlapped. Deciding which brand name should be chosen, and whether corporate marketing based in the USA would have sole responsibility for driving the new positioning and advertising worldwide, was, therefore, critical.

Finally, the acquired firm had been run as a series of country fiefdoms with each country manager held accountable for aggressive growth and profit targets, but allowed to pursue whatever actions were deemed necessary to deliver results. The acquirer had a more centralized structure, with a relatively large head office and more direct influence over each country. How should the combined entity be organized going forward? What role should the global headquarters play? Should the company perhaps be divided regionally, rather than, as historically, split between US and international units?

CRITICAL CHOICES

Hopefully these questions that this firm was wrestling with will resonate with the reader. It is the tough choices they raise that confront executives of every multinational every day. Importantly, they cannot be answered independently but must be resolved in a consistent fashion. That is the reason that companies need an international strategy, and laying out a framework for developing such a strategy and applying it to answer these choices is the task of this book.

Central to that framework will be the notion of how the firm creates value by virtue of its international activities – of what advantage it exploits in order to triumph in international competition. Without this guiding principle to align answers to those difficult strategic decisions, the firm is doomed to underperform.

Importantly, the international advantage that multinationals create is not the cost leadership, focus, or differentiation that many are familiar with from the competitive positioning approach to business unit strategy. That the firm has a favorable initial position in the marketplace is taken for granted. The question for international strategy is not whether we should be low cost or differentiated. It is how international activities contribute to the further realization of whatever advantage has already been chosen. If we seek to win in the marketplace by being low cost, how can the selection of products we offer around the world and the location of our manufacturing facilities contribute to furthering our low-cost position? If we have a unique product or capability in our home country, in which other countries can we successfully exploit that range of products or capabilities, and how do we structure the firm to continuously transfer our new innovations around the globe?

DEFINITION OF INTERNATIONAL STRATEGY

So what are the elements of an international strategy? Here goes ... But be aware that the full meaning of this definition of international strategy as specifying **how the multinational creates value across countries, and what principles and constraints guide decisions** in every part of the organization, will only become apparent as you read more of the text.

Every strategy must fulfill two purposes. The first is to identify how the firm creates value by capturing a strategic sweet spot where its capabilities satisfy a set of customer needs in a way that competitors cannot – external positioning. The second is to establish the boundaries and guiding principles for the organization, so that each and every individual and department know the choices they should make to support the chosen positioning – internal alignment. Setting these bounds empowers front line employees and allows the organization to delegate decisions, secure in the knowledge that they will work synergistically to achieve the global optimum.

Since the strategy needs to be effectively communicated in order to be implemented, these principles should be captured in a succinct statement identifying a firm's (O) objective, (S) scope, and (A) advantage (Collis and Rukstad, 2008).

The **O**bjective is (ideally) the **single metric** that will drive behavior throughout the multinational and for which senior management will be held accountable.

Scope defines the **broad domain** in which the firm will operate – typically a definition of the core business model that will be deployed throughout the world. It then describes the boundaries to the multinational's product market presence – the constraints on the range of products it will offer, and the limits to the geographies in which it will operate.

The **A**dvantage element is more complex. In the international context it is impossible to describe a customer-facing value proposition in detail because the exact manifestation of the business often differs between countries. Instead, the **international advantage** identifies the asset stocks which the firm leverages to create value across countries – what the international business literature calls firm-specific advantages

(FSAs), and the strategy field calls resources (from the resource-based view of the firm). To achieve the internal alignment of activities, the advantage then describes **how the firm is configured** to leverage those resources internally. This identifies the countries whose factor markets it will exploit, and how the firm will be organized to realize value from its resources.

Note that the four fundamental strategic decisions are answered by the scope and advantage elements of the strategy statement. Scope addresses the choice of what product to offer and in which countries to compete. Advantage covers where to locate activities and how to organize the firm.

If this sounds difficult, rest assured that it can be done. Reading the rest of this book will help you do so and will describe in detail the ideas just introduced. For the moment let us examine an **international strategy statement** that captures these ideas in 100 words or less and that could be applied to the company mentioned earlier (more examples and their deconstruction are given in Chapter 5). A complete version of the strategy includes a detailed deconstruction of this statement – typically a few pages long – that elucidates the full meaning behind each phrase and provides detail behind the cryptic summary of "a balanced set of larger countries." The short statement is, however, useful in clarifying management thinking and as the vehicle for organization-wide communication.

International Strategy Statement

Global Insurance Company

OBJECTIVE: To generate 40% of corporate earnings from international activities by 2016, with over $100 million of earnings from six markets.

SCOPE: Providing broad-based solutions for protection and savings needs to middle-income consumers with outstanding service levels

- through locally appropriate products and channels
- in a balanced set of larger countries where we can achieve competitive scale

ADVANTAGE: Leveraging our underwriting, asset/liability management, and multichannel distribution and marketing capabilities to build strong local market shares with

- local distribution and marketing, supported by global IT and product development, within
- a regional organization structure

If you think this statement offers valuable guidance to those working in the organization, then the strategy has served its purpose. I would like everyone who completes this book to be able to come up with a similar strategy statement for their multinational. That is my promise, and your challenge!

REFERENCES AND FURTHER READING

Bartlett, C.A. and Ghoshal, S. (2002) *Managing Across Borders: The Transnational Solution*, 2nd edition. Harvard Business School Press: Boston, MA.

Collis, D. and Rukstad, M. (2008) Can you say what your strategy is? *Harvard Business Review*, 86(4), 82–90.

Doz, Y.L., Santos, J., and Williamson, P. (2001) *From Global to Metanational: How Companies Win in the Knowledge Economy*. Harvard Business Publishing: Boston, MA.

Ghemawat, P. (2007) *Redefining Global Strategy: Crossing Borders in a World Where Differences Still Matter*. Harvard Business Review Press: Boston, MA.

Govindarajan, V. and Gupta, A.K. (2001) *The Quest for Global Dominance: Transforming Global Presence into Global Competitive Advantage*. Jossey-Bass: San Francisco.

Rugman, A.M. (2001) *The End of Globalization: Why Global Strategy Is a Myth & How to Profit from the Realities of Regional Markets*. American Management Association: New York.

Rugman, A.M. (2005) *The Regional Multinationals*. Cambridge University Press: Cambridge.

The Context Facing Multinational Firms

The daily demands of your job as a multinational executive are typically daunting and often overwhelming. Issues that require immediate attention can arise anywhere around the world at any time, so that you really do have to be on call 24/7. Travel requirements can be onerous and tiring, however well you believe you adjust to time zone differences and jetlag. Language differences and cultural nuances complicate life in foreign countries and intrude on the established routines of home life and office. Given these pressing challenges, it is often hard for managers to take time to reflect on the bigger picture (unless perhaps it is on a sleepless overnight international flight) and examine their own role and that of their company in contemporary society. And yet, if you are to develop a viable long-term international strategy, it is vital to be aware of the broader drivers of change in the global environment and the issues arising from those changes, however far removed from your current concerns they might appear.

Part One of the book therefore encourages readers to step back from the daily grind and provides an overview of the context facing multinationals – how integrated is the global economy, where is globalization going, and what issues the phenomenon generates? And why do firms even operate across borders in the first place? What is the rationale for the existence of a multinational?

Chapter 1 describes the extent and drivers of globalization in the contemporary world and the issues, both economic and, as important, social, that the process generates. Chapter 2 explains the theory of why multinational firms exist as a precursor to articulating the role that strategy plays in their management.

Both chapters are important, even if their content seems distant from the executive's daily concerns. Unless you understand the tectonic forces shaping our world, you will be oblivious to factors that determine long-term firm performance. This part of the book, therefore, provides an important grounding in the role of multinationals within modern society. Grasping its lessons should ensure that your international strategy is robust to whatever societal changes may be just around the corner.

The Ubiquity and Importance of International Competition

MOTIVATION

On my birthday, my wife, who usually buys most of my clothes, included among my presents several shirts. I admired the colors – bright, because she accuses me of dressing like an English schoolboy – and the styling, but, in all honesty, I was more impressed by the origin of the shirts. One was from Mexico. A second was from Malaysia. No surprises there. But the third was from Mongolia. Mongolia! With the alliterative three Ms, I knew I had the opening for this chapter. What more evidence do you need for the ubiquity of international competition than three shirts, purchased at the same US store, coming from three countries as different as Mexico, Malaysia, and Mongolia?

But that is not all. The UN currently lists 17 countries beginning with the letter M. As a quick test of your global awareness, can you list all 17?[1] Would it have surprised you if that third shirt had come from any one of those 15 other "M" countries? I think not. The fact that today a basic commodity could come from literally any of 17 countries beginning with the letter M is indicative of just how interconnected the world economy has become. To confirm this, do what I ask my students to do to their neighbors on the first day of class – look at their underwear! Where was it manufactured?[2] Point made.

But it is not just the products you buy that are affected by international competition. So is your job and the salary you receive in that position. How many of you can honestly say that your career has been untouched by foreign competition capturing the market for your products, or when a desirable job opportunity was either "offshored" or pursued by an internationally mobile applicant from another country?[3]

We are all familiar with the offshoring of over 2 million US manufacturing jobs that are estimated to have been relocated overseas since 1983,[4] but even in my sphere which is perhaps the last bastion of invulnerability to offshoring – academia – the threat is real. Already some IT support functions for higher education have been moved to India and contributed to the growth of an industry that now employs over two and a half million workers (Ghemawat, 2011). Some professors have left the USA for positions at foreign institutions: from Harvard Business School, professors have recently gone to be deans of business schools in China and the UK, and the President of Caltech left to run the King Abdullah University of Science and Technology in Saudi Arabia. Further, students have been voting with their feet by choosing to attend a university outside their home country. One in ten students at Scottish universities is now from England (not just hoping to study with a member of the royal family) even though they pay tuition fees their Scottish brethren do not. Australia is one of the largest educators of foreigners with over 500,000 overseas students, or about 25% of the student population in higher education.[5] And many countries, such as Malaysia, are building their own institutions to bring their students home from the UK and Australia.[6] When even academia is subject to the vagaries of international competition, we know it must be having an effect!

I began to draft sections of this book in the late 1990s, a period that saw diminished interest in issues of international competition. The threat from Asia, and Japan in particular, appeared to be over after the Japanese bubble burst in 1990 and the Asian tigers suffered the crisis of 1997. The Internet and the "new economy" took all the news, bursting onto the scene with the promise of huge and lucrative new markets. Yet international competition always remained a vital part of the economy. Even today, which is the more interesting business opportunity: another channel of distribution to reach existing customers called the Internet, which perhaps accounts for 5% of your sales;[7] or a huge foreign market that typically accounts for at least 80% of your global industry?[8] Put another way, the entire Internet economy today is only equivalent to the GDP of the fifth largest country in the world (Dean et al., 2012).

As I conclude this book in the second decade of the twenty-first century, international competition is back on the front burner. The bursting forth of China, and to a lesser extent the other BRIC countries and emerging markets, onto the world trade stage has brought about a new wave of concern about globalization – this time affecting professionals as well as manual workers. Offshoring has reappeared as a campaign issue in the US Presidential elections. China has grown at a compound rate of nearly 10% per annum for the last 20 years, putting to shame developed country growth rates even before their recent struggles. With that country's growth, along with the rise of India, it is as if nearly 2 billion new workers and consumers suddenly appeared on the world scene, adding one-third to the population integrated into modern economic activity. No wonder there have been huge repercussions from these events.

The "Great Recession" only heightened our awareness of global interconnectedness. What began as a subprime mortgage crisis in the USA in 2007 quickly became a global financial crisis and then a global recession as "financial contagion" spread around the world. Capital flows, both long-term investment and short-term speculative, dominate the world exchanges. Up to $5 trillion is traded internationally each day,[9] with profound consequences as exchange rates fluctuate unpredictably. As we strive to recover from that recession, it is concern about the viability of the eurozone – itself a construct that reveals how interconnected economies have become – that holds the US economy in thrall. No one can attempt to predict the future performance of the US economy without having some indication of EU and, of course, Chinese economic performance.

And it is not just the intertwining of economies that has increased. At last count in 2007, nearly 50,000 transnational corporations with 600,000 affiliates around the world were responsible for $11 trillion of output – more than the total value of trade.[10] The Fortune 500 firms now have, on average, about 30% of their profits from overseas and an even larger share of their sales.[11] Moreover, trade has been accompanied by an increase in international investment. Roughly 45% of the world's capital stock is owned by companies or individuals that are domiciled in foreign countries (Roxburgh et al., 2011), and in many developing countries, such as Mongolia and Mozambique, more than 10% of GDP is represented by foreign direct investment.

Companies have therefore globalized along with economies so that competition among multinationals with a presence in many countries is one of the most obvious features of the contemporary business landscape. In 1975 the top 10 auto manufacturers came from four countries and each had substantial production facilities only in their home markets. Today, the top 10 auto manufacturers come from five countries (two of them different than before), and many of these have nearly 50% of production outside their home markets. It is true that the absolute number of companies with international activities is limited – Ghemawat notes that only 4.6% of all US firms were exporters and only 0.1% had multinational activities – but their importance to the economy is substantial since they are typically the largest, most efficient firms in the economy. Those same 0.1% of firms, for example, account for a fifth of all private sector jobs in the USA, while including foreign multinationals operating in the USA raises that share to a quarter.[12]

At the beginning of the twenty-first century, therefore, only a very few businesses are completely isolated from foreign trade. Whether in the form of direct competitors, overseas customers, offshore suppliers, or global media, nearly all companies have economic relationships that cross borders. For such organizations, understanding how to compete internationally – how to capitalize on the opportunities presented by foreign markets and exploit favorable overseas factor costs; how to ameliorate the risks presented by volatile exchange rates and heterogeneous competitors and economic conditions; and how to cope with the complexity of managing global flows of products and information among people of diverse cultural backgrounds – will be critical to their future competitive success.

EXTENT OF GLOBAL ECONOMIC INTERDEPENDENCE

Once upon a time there was a world where over 40% of GDP involved trade across borders, where a single currency dominated the world monetary system, and where international flows of capital accounted for up to 5% of GDP even in the richest countries (Baldwin and Martin, 1999). If this description sounds like an optimistic scenario for the world in the middle of the twenty-first century, think again. This *was* a description of the world at the turn of the last century! In 1900, in many industries nearly 50% of manufactured goods were exported, while many raw material-producing countries exported 80% of their output. The pound sterling, backed by gold, was the world's only reserve currency, and, reflecting its dominance in the global economy, the UK owned more than half of foreign direct investment in many countries (including 46% in the USA as late as 1914).[13]

The basis of the economic system in 1900 was, of course, very different from today's global economy. The pattern of trade at that time swapped goods manufactured in the home country for raw materials extracted from colonies within the various empires then in existence, on terms favorable to the colonial powers. In spite of such obvious historic differences, the fact remains that since the establishment of sovereign states in Europe during the seventeenth century, and certainly since the Industrial Revolution in the early nineteenth century, international trade and competition has been a prominent feature of the world economy. The anomalous period in history was, in fact, the interwar years, particularly the Great Depression, when protectionist trade policies both reduced trade and substantially hindered economic recovery.

Similarly, for much of time, Western Europe, China, and India contributed roughly equal shares to global GDP (Exhibit 1.1). In the sweep of history, the anomalous period is not today, but actually between 1800 and 2000 when China and India by and large disappeared from the global economic landscape.

Viewed in this light, the increase in the level of trade since World War II and the emergence of the BRICs, which has led some observers to see the world as profoundly more interdependent than ever before, is, in fact, merely a return to a normal state of

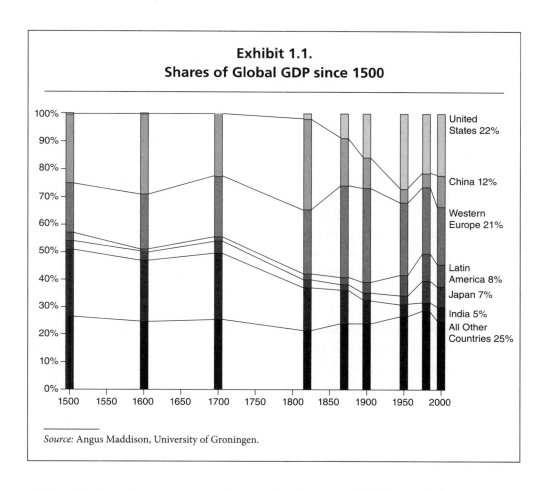

Exhibit 1.1.
Shares of Global GDP since 1500

Source: Angus Maddison, University of Groningen.

affairs. World trade increased at about twice the rate of GNP growth between 1955 and the impact of the first oil crisis in 1975. Since then, and in spite of lower world economic growth, trade has continued to expand 50% faster than GNP. As a result, the share of world production that is exported has indeed increased from about 7% in 1955 to nearly 25% in 2005, according to the Strategy, Policy, and Review Department of the International Monetary Fund in 2011. In the manufacturing sector, which is inherently more traded than the service sector, exports now typically make up nearly 80% of output in most developed countries. Even the USA has half of its manufactures leaving its borders[14] (more than five times the export share of its post-WWII trough in 1955). But it was only in the 1980s that these numbers surpassed their level in 1914.

Similarly, China's position as the second largest economy with a 12% share of global GDP is merely a recovery toward equivalence with its share of global population at 19%. The USA remains today the world's largest economy, but it is safe to say that its preeminence will erode until surpassed by China around 2020.[15]

TWENTY-FIRST-CENTURY DIFFERENCES

The really interesting question is whether the current degree of interdependence is substantively different to what has gone before, or is merely reverting to the long-run trend (see, e.g., Bordo *et al.*, 1999; Baldwin and Martin, 1999). I argue that it is substantively different because of the **pervasiveness** of its effect – in terms of both the numerous aspects of daily life that are now affected and the percentage of the population that is directly affected – and its **speed**. Unlike when most of the population lived and worked their entire lives within a few miles of where they were born and only rarely saw outsiders or purchased goods not made in the locality, there are few people in the world today truly excluded from international connections – as the T-shirts with strange English language phrases that seem to adorn even recently discovered indigenous tribes illustrate. Moreover, the speed with which events in one part of the world, such as the US subprime mortgage crisis, affect everyone around the world now matches the rate that only a natural disaster, like the eruption of Krakatoa, would have achieved in the past.

Some of the differences between the early twenty-first and early twentieth centuries are obvious. This time around global interdependence is primarily economic, and participation by countries is, by and large, voluntary. In contrast, historical interactions among countries were more often than not compulsory as militaristic regimes extended empires around the world.[16] In the past, the direction of trade in industrial or manufactured goods was from developed countries to the developing world in return for its raw materials. Now it is the developing countries that are exporting manufactured goods to the developed world.

Indeed, if today nation states are splintering rather than combining (six countries, for example, replaced the former Yugoslavia), the basic unit of economic policy is actually expanding. The establishment of the eurozone and the expansion of the EU to 27 countries, with a further six scheduled or keen to enter, demonstrate the trend toward economic integration. If the EU moves further toward fiscal integration to accompany that monetary integration, the trend will be extended. The creation of free trade zones like NAFTA, AFTA, and Mercosur also support the move toward global economic integration.

Other differences are more subtle, only appearing in retrospect but revealing a **second wave of globalization** in the twenty-first century. This succeeds the initial post-WWII wave which saw the growth of trade among, and movement of manufacturing jobs between, a select group of what became developed countries.

Perhaps the most important difference about the second wave of globalization is the appearance on the global stage of the **emerging markets**.[17] While measures can

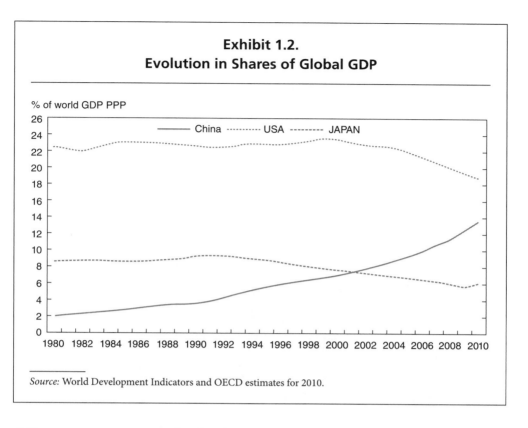

Exhibit 1.2.
Evolution in Shares of Global GDP

% of world GDP PPP

China ——— USA ·········· JAPAN

Source: World Development Indicators and OECD estimates for 2010.

differ, no one can argue with China's emergence as an economic superpower in the last 20 years (Exhibit 1.2). From only 2% of global GDP in 1982, it has become today the second largest economy in the world. By some definitions, emerging markets collectively are set to surpass the GNP of advanced economies in 2013 (Exhibit 1.3), and everyone predicts that the majority of world economic growth will occur in developing countries over the next 30 years (Exhibit 1.4).[18] The balance of economic power in the world is indeed shifting, as the CFO of GE, Keith Sherin, recognized when he stated, "We are shifting our centre of gravity to emerging markets" (Crooks, 2013).

Indeed, in 2012 over 350 million Chinese were considered middle income (achieving an income of between $6,000 and $15,000 dollars per annum) (quoted in Carlson, 2012), and the proportion of that population earning between $17,000 and $35,000 a year was expected to increase from 6% in 2010 to 51% by 2020 (quoted in Moody and Chang, 2013).

While the BRICs are the largest and most visible of the emerging markets, we should not overlook the role to be played by economies like Indonesia (with a population of 238 million currently contributing about 1.25% of global GDP), the Philippines,

Exhibit 1.3.
Evolution in Shares of Global GDP

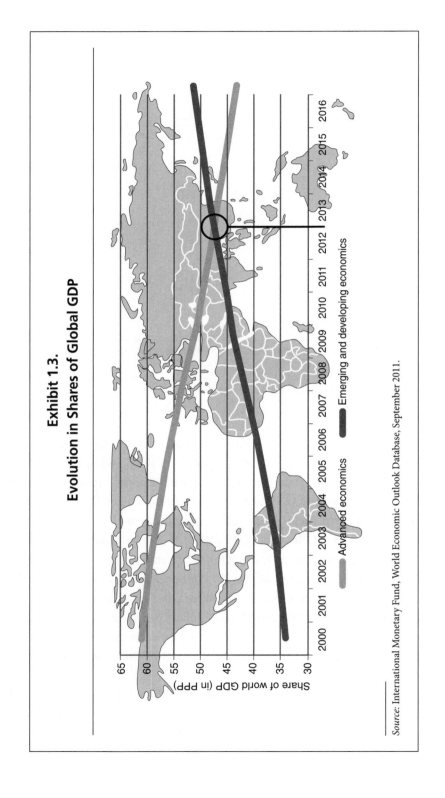

Source: International Monetary Fund, World Economic Outlook Database, September 2011.

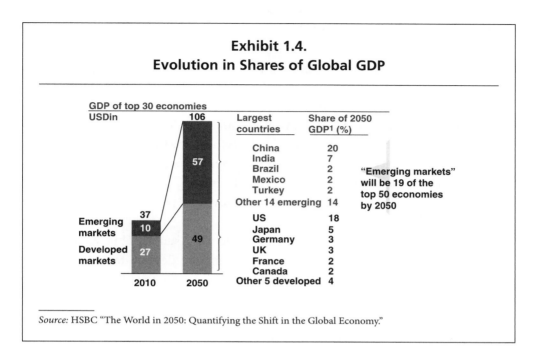

Exhibit 1.4.
Evolution in Shares of Global GDP

GDP of top 30 economies
USDin

Largest countries	Share of 2050 GDP[1] (%)
China	20
India	7
Brazil	2
Mexico	2
Turkey	2
Other 14 emerging	14
US	18
Japan	5
Germany	3
UK	3
France	2
Canada	2
Other 5 developed	4

"Emerging markets" will be 19 of the top 50 economies by 2050

Source: HSBC "The World in 2050: Quantifying the Shift in the Global Economy."

Turkey, or Nigeria. As these countries embrace the global economy and shift workers from subsistence agriculture into the industrial sector, another several hundred million workers will join the global labor force.

As they do so, they will contribute to another aspect of the second wave of globalization. In this phase, manufacturing jobs move to a **second generation of low labor-cost locations** – from Japan and Southern Europe to Madagascar and Mozambique (as the introduction to the chapter suggested). Footloose industries, like textiles, are already onto their third or fourth location as the crisis in Lesotho's textile industry illustrates. Primarily owned by Taiwanese companies, Lesotho relied on 55 factories employing 55,000 workers for about 20% of its GDP, until the Great Recession and the impending end of a preferential trade agreement with the USA saw much of that output shift to Bangladesh.[19]

But it is not just manufacturing jobs that are being offshored. Today it is **knowledge workers** that are leaving developed countries. The fear of call center workers, software developers, financial analysts, and even radiologists as their jobs move to the Philippines and India, or Hungary and Poland, is readily apparent. Forrester Research famously forecast that 3.4 million service jobs would be offshored from the USA between 2003 and 2015 (McCarthy, 2004). Even MBA students are feeling the hot breath of emerging market competition for their jobs. Companies like Grail Research and Office Tiger, established or used by consulting firms Monitor and BCG respectively, now employ 350 and 4,000 people in India and are performing tasks that were mine when a new management consultant in the 1980s.

Finally, the growth of the new economies is leading to the inclusion of their largest and most successful firms into the **global corporate elite**. In 2005 only 27 of the Fortune Global 500 came from the BRICs. Today 83 of the top 500 are from those countries and more than 100 are from developing countries. CEMEX and Grupo Bimbo (the world's largest baker) from Mexico, Mittal Steel and Tata Consulting Services from India, Haier in appliances, Lenovo in personal computers, and Huawei in telecommunications from China, to say nothing of LG and Samsung from Korea, have all penetrated the global elite – and not just as OEM providers, but as globally recognized brands in their own right.

We are now in a world of open economies, and to be successful in such an environment, companies must understand their role in, and develop their strategy for, international competition. But before we get there, we need to investigate whether the trend toward globalization has homogenized the world – or in the words of one of its more vocal advocates, Tom Friedman, "flattened" the globe – and if its continuation is inevitable. If those like Friedman are correct, perhaps we do not need the subject of international strategy since we are on the way to becoming a single integrated world!

IS THE WORLD REALLY THAT INTEGRATED?

Important observers of international competition, while not disagreeing with the data on increasing economic interdependence, disagree profoundly with the argument of a flattened world. Pankaj Ghemawat has even coined a phrase – the "10% presumption" – to reflect his belief that on most measures, whether economic or social, the world is only about 10% of the way toward complete integration (Ghemawat, 2007). Similarly, Alan Rugman provides evidence that only 3% of even the largest companies are truly global. Instead, nearly 90% retain a primarily regional footprint (Rugman, 2001).

The evidence they present is, in fact, central to a text on international strategy, since, as Ghemawat points out, it is only the fact that the world is "semiglobalized" that the subject exists (Exhibit 1.5)!

Ghemawat, for example, examines data on a range of variables from telephone calls and university students to patents (Exhibit 1.6). He argues that if the world was perfectly integrated, the distribution of these activities across countries would simply match populations or their share of GDP. With perfect integration, such that, for example, the distribution of the student body in an MBA class would match global populations with 19% Chinese, 18% Indian, and so on,[20] he finds that many measures fall well short even of his 10% presumption.

Exhibit 1.5.
Implications for Global Strategy

Zero (Complete
Localization)

Semiglobalization

Total (Complete
Globalization)

Cross-Border Integration of Markets

Source: Ghemawat, 2003.

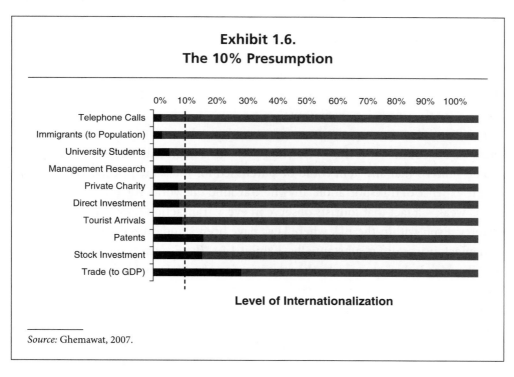

Exhibit 1.6.
The 10% Presumption

0%   10%   20%   30%   40%   50%   60%   70%   80%   90%   100%

Telephone Calls
Immigrants (to Population)
University Students
Management Research
Private Charity
Direct Investment
Tourist Arrivals
Patents
Stock Investment
Trade (to GDP)

Level of Internationalization

Source: Ghemawat, 2007.

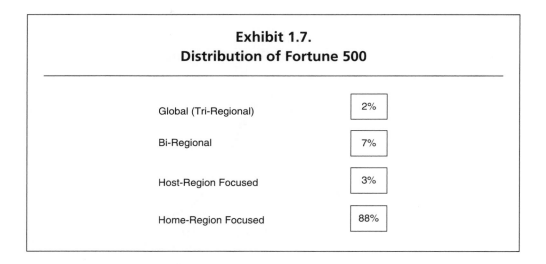

Exhibit 1.7.
Distribution of Fortune 500

Global (Tri-Regional)	2%
Bi-Regional	7%
Host-Region Focused	3%
Home-Region Focused	88%

Rugman and Verbeke (2004) support their contention that regional strategies are still the most appropriate for firms that face international competition by measuring the global footprint of large corporations (Exhibit 1.7). Defining presence in one of the three regions of the world – Americas, Asia, and Europe – as having at least 20% of a firm's sales there, they demonstrate that only 2% of the Fortune 500 have a truly global footprint, operating across all three regions, and 88% remain home region focused with, on average, 88% of their sales in that home region. While this is older data (2001) and a firm could have 39.99% of its sales outside its home region and still be called a "home regional," the data does show how limited the global footprint of even large multinational corporations remains.[21]

Another cut at the extent of economic interdependence is to examine price differences across countries. If the world were perfectly integrated, the "law of one price" should hold so that any item could be purchased for the same price, except perhaps for the expense of transportation, anywhere around the world. Again, the evidence for this is weak – a fact that tourists observe in every transaction they make in a foreign country. Even within the EU, where laws have been standardized and one currency is in effect, prices differ substantially (Exhibit 1.8). *The Economist* famously monitors the "Big Mac Index" that tracks the relative price of a McDonald's hamburger – chosen since the product reflects a good mix of inputs – across countries. This typically illustrates a 4:1 ratio in prices between the highest- and lowest-priced countries. Similarly, the price of a Starbucks latte varies from $2.50 in New Delhi to $9.83 in Oslo (at current exchange rates) (illustrated in the *Wall Street Journal* in 2013).

A more visual representation of the lack of global interdependence is the social network created by Facebook, in which the level of brightness reflects the density of

Exhibit 1.8.
Price Variations within the EU in 2002

Euro–area difference between highest and lowest price

	(Percentage)
Cinema ticket	170
Bottled water	115
Coffee in café	102
Milk	77
Levi 501 jeans	75
Nurofen	70
Pampers	57
CDs	40
Big Mac	22
DVD player	15
Computer game	13
Iron	7

Source: Dresdner Kleinwort Wasserstein (Economist 10/18/03).

"Friends" linkages.[22] The fact that the map looks like a picture of the world at night, with each country brightly illuminated but with the oceans essentially dark, shows how important nation states remain as units of social interaction.

Finally, we can simply take the data that is used as evidence for global integration to show the converse – the glass as half empty, not half full. While trade (imports plus exports) now accounts for 56% of global GDP, that number actually only proves that nearly three-quarters of economic activity still takes place within, not across, borders! While this share is decreasing, it is still the fact that the majority of transactions and interactions occur within, not between, countries.

We can, therefore, conclude that today we are in Ghemawat's "semiglobalized" world. After the disruptions in the first half of the twentieth century from two world wars and the Great Depression, the world has resumed its movement toward economic interdependence. As we surpass previous levels on some dimensions and reach equivalence on others, we nevertheless have to acknowledge that the majority of economic activity still occurs within the borders of the nation state and that it is the issues raised by the profound differences that remain between countries which confront firms in international competition.

FUTURE OF GLOBALIZATION

Is the world nevertheless set on an inexorable path of increasing integration that will bring with it an inevitable harmonization of economic and cultural life around the world? That is certainly the impression conveyed by the previous discussion and one that seems to prevail over concerns about violent conflict arising from entrenched religious or ethnic divides. Yet Niall Ferguson reminds us that prior to World War I many optimists were predicting the end of war as economic linkages between major powers, notably the UK and Germany, became so central to their economies that they simply could not afford to fight each other (Ferguson, 2005). Tom Friedman made a similar claim in 1996 when asserting that no two countries that had McDonald's had ever gone to war – unfortunately that claim fell apart in the Balkan conflict. Thus we should not be naive about the inexorability of continuing integration among economies, or the favorable outcomes arising from such interdependence.

Potential dangers to global harmony abound. Niall Ferguson, again, reminds us of the analogy to 1914 by pointing out that no one then believed a world war would start with a crisis sparked within one small European state and ultimately invoked by the neutrality of an even smaller state. Today, the risk of such a war could lie not in Europe, but in the Middle East or in Asia. And superpower conflict is not at an end. One Presidential candidate believed that Russia was the number one geopolitical enemy of the USA. Others see China's expansionism in South East Asia as the major geopolitical concern for the twenty-first century. Regardless, we cannot just hope that global interdependence continues. We must instead examine the forces that underlie such behavior in order to predict its future evolution.

Drivers of Globalization

The underlying causes of globalization are "the usual suspects" identified by many observers, although classified in different ways into a combination of technological and ideological drivers (Dreher *et al.*, 2008). Among these are the new **digital technologies** – the Internet, broadband communications, personal computers, etc., that enable the transfer of information at speeds and prices that were unimaginable only a few decades ago. In 1960 there were only 36 telephone circuits across the Atlantic[23] and investment banks had a room of telephonists whose only task was to come to work early and dial until they got one of those lines (which was then held by the company for the entire day). A transatlantic phone call at the time cost $30 per minute. When I arrived in the USA as a student in September 1976, I telephoned my parents once to let them know I was safe, and then not again until Christmas Day because the cost (about $5 a minute in 1976 dollars) was so high. Today, only 40 years later, there is close to infinite trunk capacity, both cable and satellite, across the North Atlantic, and a call costs 2 cents per minute, and is even free on Skype!

Other technological advances in air travel, shipping, and logistics (think 747s and A380s as well as container vessels and very large crude oil carriers) have driven down **transport costs** for people and physical goods. Transport, freight, and insurance costs more than halved to 3% of import prices between 1970 and 2002.[24] The gradually increasing size of container ships, for example, reduced shipping costs by about $50 per FFE (a 40-foot container) or 2.5% each year since 1975, and allowed for a dramatic expansion in traded goods. Indeed, the shipping cost for a pair of sneakers from Asia to Europe is now less than 25 cents. But technological advances have also created enormous possibilities for the exchange of social and cultural motifs. The ubiquity of *Who Wants to be a Millionaire?* or *American Idol* (with the substitution of your country's name in the title) on media as diverse as satellite television and streaming video represents only the extreme of a more culturally integrated world. The increasing standardization of languages around the world – English is the only language allowed for air traffic controllers anywhere in the world, 55% of all billion websites are in English, 4% in Chinese[25] – is another metric of cultural homogenization.

If it is technology, and the productivity improvements it has wrought, that have driven globalization, it has been facilitated, and in many ways legitimized, by the predominance of a **liberal democratic capitalist philosophy** that expounds the virtues of free trade, deregulation, and privatization. The success of the "free world" after WWII led to the acceptance by a majority of countries of the benefits of such an economic and political regime. The ending of communism and the breakup of the Soviet Union seemed to validate that belief. The adoption of the policy of "it is glorious to get rich" in China, and the creation of the EU, eurozone, and Pacific Alliance are other indicators of the political support for integration and liberalization of trade. Indeed, average tariff rates have fallen from 40% in 1947 to about 4% today.

To the extent that some countries have resisted the siren call of liberal philosophy, the hegemony that economic success brings has put enormous pressure on them to fall in line with those values and ideologies. Holdouts, like North Korea and Cuba, remain rare and increasingly desperate. This free trade philosophy has, in turn, produced a set of state and international institutions and policies that directly promote globalization since the benefit of increasing interdependence is one of its cornerstone tenets.

The agents that have translated the underlying drivers of globalization into reality have been multinationals and their operation in the product, capital, and labor markets. Without their actions in exploiting the potential of technology and market freedoms, globalization would not have progressed as far or as fast. Given these drivers, unless a major political or ideological change occurs, it is hard to see the extent of globalization reversing in the next decades. Perhaps the rate of increase will slow, but the level of integration will be unlikely to fall.

THE "GLOBALIZATION" DEBATE

The obvious effects of increasing international interdependence are economic. However, there are social and political consequences which create a more multifaceted context within which multinationals operate, and which have induced passionate responses from sections of society (see, e.g., Mickelthwait and Wooldridge, 2003).

While there are numerous strands to this reaction, from anarchistic rejections of any centralized power and libertarian paranoia about the New World Order, to environmental concerns about global warming and left-wing visions of a new global corporatism, it is worth examining the broader **social impact** of globalization. Since multinationals are the actors driving globalization, they are ready targets for those who oppose its outcomes. As a result, if you are an executive operating in an interrelated world, it is vital to understand societal responses to globalization, as Shell found when it tried to dispose of a production rig in the North Sea; when Nestlé was restricted in the marketing of infant formula to developing countries; when the WTO abandoned its meeting in Seattle because of violent street protests; and as banks discovered during the "Occupy" movement.

While other social trends, such as climate change and income inequality, are also forcing their way onto boardroom agendas, it is the fallout from the "globalization" debate that concerns us here. Indeed the prevalence of the word globalization (whose usage has quintupled in the last 10 years)[26] has almost made it a cliché. Yet the phenomenon remains poorly defined, which has led many commentators to confound it with contemporaneous trends, such as US hegemony, which are not inevitable consequences of globalization.

Definition

Perhaps the best definition of the term *globalization* is as "a process of increasing transactional interdependence across borders of nation states" (Held and McGrew, 2007). This definition has the merit of viewing globalization as a process rather than an end state, and of maintaining a more than purely economic perspective on what is occurring, since transaction is an intentionally broad term covering social interactions as well as market exchanges. Globalization is, then, a multidimensional process that captures not just the economic integration of product, labor, and capital markets, but also cultural, ideological, and institutional integration.

Benefits

The primary benefit of globalization is economic. It is accepted by rational thinkers that increasing trade and information flows increases aggregate global economic welfare. Even mainstream critics of globalization do not debate that conclusion.

Free Trade and Specialization

To clarify the benefits of free trade one need go no further than the Ricardian 1817 doctrine of **comparative advantage**. Even if one country has an absolute advantage in the production of every good, trade will still occur between countries according to the relative advantage each has in particular goods (see box). Similarly, if we believe that non-coercive exchange is mutually beneficial – no party will participate unless it gains – any trade must increase overall welfare. No sensible economist disagrees with the conclusion that, in aggregate, trade improves welfare. Even at the current, historically low levels of protectionism an ending of tariffs would raise global GDP by 1–2%.[27] And when Japan ended a period of almost complete autarky after 1853, it has been estimated that it benefited by 8–9% of GDP (Bernhofen and Brown, 2005).

Theory of Comparative Advantage

A simple exercise demonstrates that even if one country has an absolute advantage in the production of two goods, trade is still beneficial to both parties. Ricardo illustrated this using wine and cloth produced in England and Portugal. Note in the example below that Portugal can produce more per capita than England of both cloth and wine. If we assume two people live in each country, then in the absence of trade, Portugal can produce 8 units of wine and 4 of cloth, England 4 units of wine and 3 of cloth, for a total of 12 units of wine and 7 of cloth. If trade occurs and Portugal specializes in the production of wine, in which it has the comparative advantage (it can produce twice as much wine per capita as England, but only one-third more cloth per capita), and England in cloth, the two together can now produce 16 units of wine and 6 of cloth. Whether at Portuguese prices with wine being half the cost of cloth, or English prices when wine costs 75% of cloth, both countries are now better off.

Per capita output

	Portugal	England
Wine	8	4
Cloth	4	3

The benefit of free trade in goods also applies to the free movement of capital and labor. The former actualizes comparative advantage by ensuring that capital flows to the relevant sectors within each country and increases specialization. The latter provides another mechanism for improving global productivity by reallocating labor to more efficient producers. It also ensures equality of opportunity with all the spillover benefits that freedom of movement brings to education, careers, and personal fulfillment.

Intra-Industry Efficiency

An additional benefit of global competition is the reallocation of production to more efficient producers within each country. When we recognize that all firms in an industry are not equally productive, it is easy to see that trade will drive out the least efficient producers, some of whose output will be replaced by more efficient producers. This **infra-marginal reallocation of production** within the country has been shown to increase welfare by an additional 1–2% of GDP (Bernard *et al.*, 2007).

Increased Variety

The other important economic benefit of globalization is to increase **consumer choice**. This argument is less frequently made, but increases in variety are a real consumer benefit. Do not forget that while some may decry the globalization of McDonald's, no one is forced to buy McDonald's. In fact, Americans are happy to enjoy Italian and Mexican restaurants. Should we ban those because they are an outcome of globalization? Economists estimate that increased variety adds between 1 and 3% to GDP (Broda and Weinstein, 2006).

Drawbacks

Economic Inequality

Concerns about the economic effects of globalization on welfare focus not on whether there is an aggregate gain, but on the distribution of those gains. The argument is that **increasing inequality of income** can result from globalization, both **between countries** and **within countries**. Even if in aggregate countries are better off from free trade, not every country or individual is guaranteed to benefit from globalization.

Exacerbating this concern is the fact that the **losers are usually concentrated** so their loss is of first-order magnitude, while the **benefits of free trade are diffused** among all participants in the economy so their gain is only of second-order magnitude. It is, therefore, very easy for politicians and polemicists to publicize the detrimental impact of free trade, and hard for its proponents to justify. As an example, NAFTA immediately and visibly hurt the earnings and job prospects of several groups of workers, including car workers and those involved in electronics assembly. For them, the movement of manufacturing facilities to maquiladoras in Mexico did direct damage. The compensating benefits accrued to all consumers who each experienced very small savings on the price of their next new automobile. The "great sucking sound" of jobs moving south of the border was easy to identify; less evident was the marginal reduction in the CPI that resulted.

The within-country inequality argument falls straight out of international trade theory and states that winners are those who have skills or factors that are in relative abundance in a country, and that losers are those whose skills or factors are in relative scarcity in the country.[28] In the USA, since the country is relatively well endowed with capital, intersectoral shifts that result from free trade generally have the first-order effect of harming labor. This is particularly true for unskilled labor, which in the USA has lost share of GDP to capital and skilled labor over the last 30 years. In 1980, unskilled labor's share of national income was approximately 26%; by 2004 that had fallen to 18%, according to the IMF in 2007. Partly as a result, the Gini coefficient measure of the dispersion of income within a country has risen in the USA from .40 in 1980 to .48 in 2011.[29]

Indeed, opponents of free trade in the USA have pointed to the increasing wage disparity between skilled and unskilled workers as evidence of the adverse effects of free trade. Unfortunately it is not clear that the major cause of increasing US income inequality has been trade. As Paul Krugman has pointed out, since trade only affects just over 20% of the economy, it is hard to find an explanation there. Services now make up over two-thirds of the economy and it is difficult to see how international trade in fast food – of which there is none – contributes to the widening of the wage gap (see box).

What Explains Widening Income Inequality in the USA?

Plausible explanations beyond international trade for widening pretax income inequality in the USA since the 1970s include technology, a decline in unionization, immigration, and the one-time outward shift in the global labor supply resulting from the sudden integration of hundreds of millions of subsistence wage agricultural workers into the industrial sector from India and China. However, it has to be acknowledged that the latter two causes are indirect results of globalization, and that the findings remain controversial and await further research.

Technology can increase income inequality by substituting capital for labor – automating tasks previously performed by unskilled labor. More recently, analysis suggests that skill-biased technology, notably computerization, might be to blame for widening inequality. If computers complement high-skilled (i.e., college-educated) employees by enabling them to work more effectively, but substitute for the routine work of less educated workers, their widespread adoption – the main technological change since the 1970s – can produce a divergence in earnings between college and high school graduates in the USA (Autor *et al.*, 2008).

> Similarly, immigration of 20 million over the last 20 years (of whom perhaps 8 million were illegal immigrants) is a culprit that has been identified as depressing unskilled wages in the USA.
>
> More importantly, a dramatic expansion of the global workforce in the last 20 years has reduced the capital/labor ratio worldwide and driven down wages. Dick Freeman estimated that the addition of China, India, and the former Soviet bloc to the global economy doubled the global workforce and halved the capital labor ratio to a level from which it will take 30 years to recover (Freeman, 2005). This phenomenon would cause a drop in real wages, even though trade at every point in time still improves welfare.

Note that losers in developing countries, in contrast, are capital and skilled labor. Unskilled labor actually benefits from free trade – think of the millions of Chinese workers who have migrated from rural poverty to, at least, a better paid life in urban factories.[30]

Between countries the disparity in incomes is even more obvious. Today the wealthiest 225 individuals have assets that are greater than the annual income of the poorest 2.5 billion citizens. The three richest have assets larger than the combined GDP of the world's 47 poorest countries (Mittelman, 2000).[31] What is more, those inequalities are increasing and are concentrated on the north–south divide.

Race to the Bottom

Unfettered global capitalism, it is argued, will drive economic conditions to the lowest level. If there is any advantage to be gained from exploiting workers or degrading the environment, the harsh pressures of global competition will force **every country to copy the practices of the most exploitative corporation or nation**, or suffer the consequences. However hard individual governments try to raise such standards, the pressures of globalization condemn them either to join an inexorable race to the bottom, or to see their nation bypassed by global corporations.

This concern rose to prominence in the debate over the environmental impact of globalization, since it has been observed that in the race to the bottom, the environment is the first to suffer. Former Treasury Secretary Larry Summers even went on record when at the World Bank arguing that exporting pollution to developing countries would increase social welfare!

Theory of the Race to the Bottom

When different jurisdictions compete to attract firms by lowering taxes and regulatory burdens – such as environmental standards and labor protections – in ways that may have adverse social consequences, it is referred to as a "race to the bottom." This can be seen as a "prisoner's dilemma" of international political economy. Policy makers in each jurisdiction might prefer a world in which every country adopted regulations that limited harm to the environment and guaranteed certain protections to workers; but each jurisdiction has an incentive to "defect" by lowering its own regulations, thereby attracting foreign investors and boosting domestic economic growth. Thus, international competition can drive all countries to adopt weaker regulations than are ideal.

The race to the bottom has also been seen as a major barrier to coordinated international action to reduce carbon emissions and mitigate climate change. Fast-growing low-income countries, such as China and India, are loath to adopt costly environmental regulations as they attempt to catch up to their Western counterparts; and the USA and others, in turn, are loath to adopt costly environmental regulations lest more manufacturers leave their borders for China and India.

This phenomenon places multinationals in a difficult position as they too are drawn into the race to the bottom. Should they minimize their costs by relocating to or sourcing from countries with the weakest legislation, or should they adhere to a higher standard that is perhaps demanded by domestic consumers and shareholders?

As an example, in the 1980s and 1990s, Nike largely sourced from suppliers in South Korea and Taiwan. But as these countries developed, they raised working conditions and grew more expensive. Nike urged its suppliers to move their operations to lower cost regions, such as Indonesia. This was partly because the Indonesian government, under the Suharto administration, which was eager to attract foreign direct investment, was particularly harsh on unions in the country. By the mid-1990s, labor activist Jeff Ballinger drew attention to the crowded, hot, and often dangerous conditions in the "sweatshops" of Nike's Indonesian contractors, whose laborers earned less than $1 a day. These revelations, including persistent accusations that Nike's contractors employed child labor, made Nike the focus of student protest in the USA and elsewhere in the developed world (Spar, 2002).

In 2011, a study by McKinsey identified Bangladesh as the "next hot spot," to become the world's major ready-made-garment exporter within five years. But in 2012 and 2013, a string of factory fires and collapses killed more than a thousand garment-factory workers in the country. The fires and deaths instigated a wave of labor protests and demands within Bangladesh for legislation to improve working conditions and enforce existing laws. Indeed, in several cases, factory owners were prosecuted for "unpardonable negligence," highlighting lax oversight at the factories. It also caused a number of UK and US retailers, such as Tesco, to rearrange their sourcing contracts so as not to depend on Bangladeshi suppliers.

Similarly, in January 2012, *The New York Times* ran a series of reports on Chinese factories owned by the Foxconn Technology Group, where iPhones and iPads were manufactured. The reports described a series of worker suicides, deadly explosions, and details on worker conditions, such as dorm residence and long and unpredictable hours that shocked US readers and Apple customers. The tragedies and controversial conditions at these Foxconn factories could be seen as a product of the race to the bottom because China perhaps did not enforce safety regulations to win manufacturing jobs. Unfortunately, this laxity, allowed and even exploited by US firms, may also have endangered Chinese workers.

Winner Takes All

International trade theory demonstrates that, if there are increasing returns to scale, a firm with a substantial global market share will prevail over a smaller competitor in another country – even if that country has a factor cost advantage – simply because of its scale advantage. This locking in of early mover advantages, even if ultimately inefficient, historically justified "infant industry protection" in developing countries. In order to prevent a local Indian steel company being overwhelmed by imports, it was appropriate for India to impose tariffs that allowed the indigenous producer time to build globally competitive scale.

A variant of this "winner takes all" phenomenon resulting from global communications can also increase inequity. Consider the popular music business. Previously, local stars in each country would top the charts and make a good living. After MTV, the top of the charts in any country is likely to be the same in every country as Madonna, the Spice Girls, and Britney Spears in turn become global superstars. While Madonna can earn outrageous sums of money from her worldwide celebrity, a singer who might previously have been a local star finds herself squeezed out of the charts and off the earnings list. Since **the world converges on one winner**, the global concentration of income increases.

Loss of Political Sovereignty

These arguments presuppose that the integrated global economy erodes national economic sovereignty as local policies fall victim to the vagaries of "global economic forces." Indeed, one insidious drawback of globalization, which unites the Right and Left, is the idea that the nation state is losing its influence as **sovereignty is usurped** by "unaccountable" international institutions and the "invisible hand."

The right-wing version is found in the fears of survivalists and libertarians of a New World Order in which the UN flies unmarked black helicopters to impose its will on a free people. More mainstream conservatives have a sense that the USA is less able to control its own future (read, exert its power around the world) because of the power of international institutions, and resent this loss of sovereignty (exemplified by the US refusal to join the Court for Crimes against Humanity in case US soldiers get indicted). The solution they advocate is for the USA to pursue isolationist policies that limit free trade, immigration, and overseas involvements, and to withdraw from international affairs.

The left-wing version of these arguments concerns corporate capitalism and the ability of global capital markets to disrupt a country's development strategy. The first strand to this argument is a claim that **free trade condemns developing countries to remain underdeveloped**, since all they have to sell is cheap labor. Attempts to upgrade their economies will be thwarted by global product and factor market competition, in much the same way that colonialism subjugated local development. A variant of this argument is that economic development will be delayed when highly skilled labor is sucked out of developing countries to high-wage economies. This concern is often deeply felt by graduate students from developing countries who are guilt-ridden by their decision to stay in the USA, rather than return to help their domestic economy.

The second strand to this liberal argument is the "speculators can bring down an economy" argument that arose when George Soros made a billion dollars by betting against the pound in 1992, effectively forcing the UK to exit the currency peg. Volatile capital flows, it is argued, ensure that **governments have lost the ability to manage their own economies**. They are now subject to the vagaries of global capital markets and cannot isolate themselves from these pressures to pursue their own economic policies. A less extreme version blames the IMF for imposing a standard set of economic policies – ending government subsidies of basic foods and energy, curtailing government deficits, paying back international debts, etc. – and blackmailing countries to accept these policies (by threatening to withhold loans), however detrimental the policies might be to equity and the long-term economic development of the country.

Today the complaint by the PIIGS (Portugal, Italy, Ireland, Greece, and Spain) is that they have to bend to the requirements of their Northern European counterparts and adopt unpopular austerity measures if they are to remain in the euro. Monetary and fiscal unions and free trade agreements appear to limit any government's ability to assert its sovereignty by pursuing independent economic policies.

Cultural and Ideological Imperialism

A final drawback of globalization for many observers is the impoverishing effect of an homogenized culture. Where once there was a proliferation of lively and varied indigenous cultures and traditions, we are, it is argued, converging on a **monocultural world** whose values are consumerism, whose images are barely clothed androgynous teenagers, and whose representatives are Hollywood and Madison Avenue (Klein, 2002). The success of television shows like … *Idol* (with your country's name in the title) around the world seems to exemplify that homogenization. The sense is that local cultures are being overwhelmed by Western (or US) culture and that the reduced variety impoverishes the world. The "winner takes all" outcome, noted above, obviously contributes to this homogenization, as Taylor Swift replaces local stars in every country.

The more extreme version of this anti-globalization argument is that we are entering an age of US materialistic cultural hegemony. It is wrong, people argue, to measure welfare solely on quantifiable economic measures since people are impoverished when they are taught to value only material possessions. This is an argument not about the drawbacks of cultural homogeneity per se, but about the particular materialistic culture that is being adopted. And yet those citizens who bemoan the influence of the Kardashians as cultural icons are the very ones who are overjoyed when Greenpeace has a worldwide impact it could never have had before the advent of worldwide television and social media.

Responses to Globalization

Faced with the adverse consequences of globalization, sociologists observe three responses to the perceived powerlessness of the average citizen (Hirschman, 1970). One strategy represents an exit decision in despair at the loss of national sovereignty. Another is an attempt to make voices heard against the power of corporate capitalism. The third embraces the trend and seeks to turn it to citizens' own advantage.

Globalization could be leading to the **alienation** of the voting public from the political process. Even if individuals can influence national policies, when those policies are supplanted by international institutions and forces, they feel disenfranchised and withdraw their commitment to and involvement in politics. This could account for the decreasing percentage of the population now voting in general elections: participation rates are down to all-time lows around the world, and are barely above 70% in mature democracies.[32]

In contrast, there are growing numbers of **local political initiatives** and activities. Rather than embrace globalization, these responses attempt to escape its effects by shifting political activity to a sphere that individuals can still influence. It is as if, powerless in the face of anonymous global forces, people refocus on the neighborhood where they do have influence. The upsurge in community affairs – to stop development in my backyard, to halt traffic down my street, and so on – can be attributed to the desire to be involved politically at a level where participation still has impact.

The more troubling downside of this response is a retreat to parochialism and its subversion by nationalists and other extremists who seek to exclude alien elements and forces. Ethnic cleansing is the extreme of this philosophy. Appeals for insularity in US foreign policy and a return to the isolationist doctrine of non-intervention outside the hemisphere are a less vehement example of this response. Both turn their back on globalization and hope to keep its influence at bay by ignoring or physically excluding the broader world.

Lastly, there has been an increase in **global activism** to match the very globalization process it seeks to halt. As mentioned above, with the advent of global social media,

Greenpeace is able to coordinate a worldwide boycott of Shell Oil products and to launch a worldwide campaign to save the whale to which the youth of many countries generously contribute. If the relevant dimension of decision making has shifted from the nation state to the international arena, political movements have responded by matching the increase in scope. Ironically, even NGOs which resent the globalization process are, therefore, expanding globally to achieve their own ends.

Public Policy Implications

None of the above is meant to demean the suffering of those unfavorably affected by free trade in goods, capital, and ideas. What it does downplay, however, is that there are appropriate policy responses to globalization that do not resist or restrain the process, but do remedy its negative effects.

Within countries the solution for those adversely affected by globalization is adequately funded **transition programs**. Because there is a net economic gain from trade, such a policy can be implemented while still leaving a surplus. This is why free trade should be accompanied by retraining grants and unemployment benefits that promote and smooth the transfer of the disadvantaged into more productive sectors. Even at the level of intercountry inequality, redistributive policies can ensure that the eventual outcome is Pareto efficient (everyone is at least no worse off than before free trade). Initiatives like Bono's Justice 2000, which advocated debt cancellation for the poorest countries, are designed to achieve this goal.

Remedies for the adverse consequences of globalization do, however, argue for some form of global intervention and regulation. It was the emergence of regulatory standards that ended child labor and a host of other social problems brought on by unrestrained capitalism in the UK in the nineteenth century. The analog in the global arena is the need for **a supranational regulatory body** whose policies would be democratically determined.

In the domestic context, it is obvious who the actor should be. In the global context, it is less clear which are the appropriate agencies, and what their policies should be. Should there be a global agency with effective enforcement powers for labor and environmental standards? This is the dilemma that the WTO and other international bodies face today, and for which they are much vilified. The WTO, for example, has a goal to prevent countries from using social policies as non-tariff barriers, such as the USA unfairly protecting its fishermen by imposing a ban on non-dolphin-friendly tuna. The WTO, therefore, sets maximum standards for health and safety that countries can impose on goods and services sold domestically. Critics, like World Trade Watch, argue that with no minimum standards to meet, international competition can easily become a race to the bottom, while the imposition of a maximum prevents enlightened countries enacting policies that would be welfare improving. The maximum forces governments to level down their policies as they seek "harmonization," rather than having minima that force countries to level up policies. Such difficulties in the implementation of policies should not detract from the fact that there is a solution that involves international agencies establishing and enforcing global standards.

Implications for Managers

"Globalization" for good or bad is now a central feature of international competition. There clearly are powerful economic arguments in its favor, but there are also justifiable concerns about the impacts of the process, both economic and otherwise. In principle, many of the adverse consequences of globalization can be mitigated by appropriate policies, just as they were within countries in the nineteenth century. However, courage is required to adopt certain policies within countries, and to introduce or strengthen a set of international institutions. The challenge going forward is to design those institutions to be effective at remedying the ill effects of globalization while remaining truly democratic.

But does any of this discussion of globalization matter to CEOs and executives, or is it just for politicians and radicals? Importantly, as key actors in the process, multinational executives, while not needing to be at the forefront of the policy debate, at a minimum, need to take a position on certain issues, particularly as **corporate social responsibility** becomes incorporated into their strategies and behavior. Being clear, for example, about the extent to which their firm will capitalize on "the race to the bottom" or will instead embody a set of principles that might prohibit the firm from operating in certain countries, becomes vital.

And if we conclude that, in spite of the concerns and objections of large parts of the community, globalization is likely to continue barring some repeat of WWI-like escalation of national or religious conflict, executives still have to address its economic consequences.

The most important of these is that the **locus of economic growth is irrevocably shifting to the emerging markets and the southern hemisphere**. As mentioned earlier, there is disagreement as to when income in those countries surpasses that of the developed world, depending on which countries are categorized as emerging markets and the measure of GDP (current exchange rates or purchasing power parity). Nevertheless, everyone agrees that the majority of future economic growth will come from releasing the potential in markets with populations in the hundreds of millions in Asia, Latin America, and Africa. As a corollary, **south–south trade** will increase rapidly and offer opportunities to enterprises of all sizes that can create relationships across those geographies. Indeed, south–south trade in manufactures has tripled over the last 30 years and is already almost as big as north–north trade (Human Development Report, 2013; Charan, 2013).

Accompanying this shift in the location of economic activity is a **growth in the middle class**. Even if income inequality is increasing, economic growth in lower income countries is pushing an increasing share of the global population into the middle class. If that segment is defined as consumption of $10 per capita per day in purchasing power equivalent, it is projected that the middle-class population will be larger than that with low incomes by 2022, and that, by 2030, two-thirds of the globe will be middle income (Kharas and Getz, 2013). This segment typically seeks an **intermediate market positioning,** not the high-end multinational brands, nor the traditional local low-price products, but reliable and consistent value-priced products[33] – which highlights the novel opportunities available in emerging markets (Jullens, 2013).

Globalization will also lead to more interdependent economies which, ironically, will increase the degree of specialization in any one country. This implies that industry **value chains will be disaggregated** as each stage is relocated to the most efficient country. This is why a product as simple as the Slazenger tennis ball will have traveled 51,000 miles (81,600 km) and will be manufactured with materials from, or processes performed in, 13 countries before being played at Wimbledon.[34]

Interconnection of markets will extend from trade in goods to further integration of capital and labor markets. As a result, competition from new countries with novel approaches and business models will emerge. The **bottom of the pyramid** has already been identified as a market opportunity (Prahalad and Hart, 2002) which even established multinationals have turned into novel sources of innovation. GE Healthcare famously developed an ultra-portable ECG machine for China, which it then sold around the world at prices 80–85% below its existing models, while Levi's first introduced its Denizen brand jeans in Asia to retail at between one-third and one-half the price of the Levi brand. But the radically different factor market conditions in these countries support very **different "business models"** that pose very different competitive threats. There is, for example, an argument being made that Indian firms have a different approach to innovation – termed *jugaad*, "the gutsy art of overcoming harsh constraints by improvising an effective solution using limited resources" (Radjou *et al.*, 2011) – which allows them to succeed with minimal resources. Whereas these new forms of strategic variety could be called "disruptive" because they are likely to come in at the low end of the market, the more appropriate order of the day might be to **expect the unexpected** from previously disregarded or ignored geographies. In this sense, continuing globalization will **increase competition**.

Competitive Challenge from Globalization

One consequence of increasing global economic interdependence is that companies now experience "more" competition (defined in a specific way) than when they faced only domestic competition.

The sense in which companies experience "more" competition has nothing to do with the absolute number of competitors, for which we can make no valid predictions. Rather, the "more" refers to the variety of competitors. In a homogeneous world, certain competitive types will be supported in equilibrium, but with heterogeneity among economies, that set of strategic varieties expands. While a firm's strategy, customized for domestic idiosyncrasies, might initially appear ineffective outside its own economy, as economies globalize and become more integrated, exogenous changes, such as a shift in demand or exchange rate, can suddenly make the firm's product attractive in other countries. Companies from obscure, and possibly ignored, foreign countries then emerge with apparently novel strategies. Thus even if global concentration falls with the emergence of multinationals from new countries, the degree of competition does not decrease, but rather increases as the types of competitor expand.

One conclusion is that international competition, as we have suspected and experienced, is tougher than purely domestic competition.

CONCLUSION

Editors at the *Harvard Business Review* regularly poll their readers on the issues that concern them and would like to see addressed in the publication. Surprising to the editors is the fact that international competition and globalization often appear toward the bottom of the list. Given everything covered in this chapter, why is this? And is it appropriate, or should executives be more attuned to the challenges and opportunities presented by international competition?

I think there are two reasons for the relative lack of interest in international competition expressed by managers from, primarily, developed countries. The first is that, even though they face dilemmas in their international activities, executives are confident they can deal with them because their beliefs and assumptions about the world are unchallenged. The triumph of democracy, capitalism, and its accompanying institutions have allowed managers to become complacent as they observe little alien in the world – only a convergence on familiar domestic norms. Unfortunately, this is a very parochial argument, particularly since the majority of economic growth is now in emerging markets that do remain fundamentally different even when drawn into the global economy. How many of you would be truly comfortable operating in rural India?

The second explanation is hubris – that international competition is not an issue for winners. This is even more troubling since it is the unknown and disregarded that most often upsets the apple cart. If the buzzword in strategy today is "disruption" and the best response to its threat is, as Andy Grove of Intel famously noted, to remain paranoid, I hope that this chapter has done enough to convince even the most seasoned international executive that the repercussions of globalization deserve serious thought.

NOTES

1. The full list is Madagascar, Malawi, Malaysia, Maldives, Mali, Malta, Marshall Islands, Mauritania, Mauritius, Mexico, Micronesia, Monaco, Mongolia, Montenegro, Morocco, Mozambique, Myanmar. The Republic of Macedonia is currently seeking recognition as a separate nation state.
2. The two countries for whom exports of cotton underwear were their largest single apparel export in 2013 were El Salvador and Thailand! (US Department of Commerce, Office of Textiles and Apparel, reported in *Business Week,* July 1, 2013, p. 16.)
3. Or when you considered taking a job for a foreign firm, or in another country.
4. Korn, M. (2012) Outsourcing is good for America, July 23, accessed at http://finance.yahoo.com/ blogs/daily-ticker/outsourcing-good-america-cato-michael-tanner-141051681.html. This number refers to the direct movement of jobs abroad. It does not include jobs lost because products were imported instead of being manufactured at home.
5. Australia Trade Commission: International Student Data, accessed at http://www.austrade.gov.au/ Export/Export-Markets/Industries/Education/International-Student-Data/default.aspx.
6. In the 1990s, 20% of Malaysians in higher education studied outside the country. (http://www .guardian.co.uk/higher-education-network/blog/2012/jul/02/higher-education-in-malaysia).
7. The Internet currently constitutes 5% of US retail sales (http://www.census.gov/retail/mrts/www/da ta/pdf/ec_current.pdf) and accounts for between 3.4% of GDP in developed countries (McKinsey Global Institute (2011) Internet matters, May) and 4.1% of GDP in the G20 countries (Dean, D., DiGrande, S., Field, D., Lundmark, A., O'Day, J., Pineda, J., and Zwillenberg, P. (2012) The Internet economy in the G-20. Boston Consulting Group Perspectives, March).
8. McKinsey refers to the $30 trillion opportunity in emerging markets over the next 20 years (Atsmon, Y., Child, P., Dobbs, R., and Narasimhan, L. (2012) Winning the $30 trillion decathlon. *McKinsey Quarterly,* August).
9. The April 2013 average from Bank of International Settlements, reported in *The Economist* (2013) September 14, p. 97.
10. Orbis data as reported in http://www.forbes.com/sites/bruceupbin/2011/10/22/the-147-companies -that-control-everything/.
11. In 2010, 46% of the S&P 500 sales came from outside the USA, reported in Ghemawat, P. (2011) The globalization of firms. IESE Globalization Note Series, accessed at http://www.ghemawat .com/management/files/AcademicResources/GlobalizationofFirms.pdf.
12. Because they are more productive and pay higher wages, those 0.1% of companies contribute one-quarter of all employee compensation and value added, see Slaughter, M. and Tyson, L. (2012) A warning sign from global companies. *Harvard Business Review,* March.
13. Lewis, C.S. (1938) America's stake in international investments, Washington, DC, p. 546. Another source maintains that the UK accounted for 60% of long-term foreign investment in the USA at that date (Wilkins, M. (1994) Comparative hosts. *Business History,* 36, 20).
14. This number is similar to the percentage that the EU exports beyond its boundaries.
15. The OECD predicts that China will become the world's largest economy in 2016, reported in Moulds, J. (2011) China's economy to overtake US in next four years. *Guardian,* November 9. *The Economist* believes 2020 (Economist Special Report (2011) The global economy, September 24, p. 5). China is already the world's largest trader of goods, having surpassed the USA in 2012.
16. Although some would still argue that participation in today's global economy is far from voluntary and remains as exploitative as in previous centuries.

17. These were previously termed less developed countries (LDCs).

18. In fact emerging markets have contributed over 50% of global GDP growth since the turn of the century (Goldman Sachs (2013) The submerging economies. *The Economist,* August 12, accessed at http://www.economist.com/blogs/freeexchange/2013/08/emerging-markets).

19. See IRIN (2011) Lesotho textile industry gets a lifeline. November 24, accessed at http://www.irinnews.org/Report/94302/LESOTHO-Textile-industry-gets-a-lifeline.

20. MBA students should quickly calculate the integration level for their class by comparing the share of foreign students in the class to the share of world population outside the country.

21. More recent research supports this perspective: see Wolf, J., Dunemann, T., and Egelhoff, W. (2012) Why MNCs tend to concentrate their activities in their home region. *Multinational Business Review,* 20(1), 67–91; Dunning, J.H., Fujita, M., and Yakov, N. (2007) Some macro-data on the regionalisation/globalisation debate: a comment on the Rugman/Verbeke analysis. *Journal of International Business Studies,* 38, 177–199.

22. This may be viewed at http://dabrownstein.files.wordpress.com/2014/02/paul-butlers-map-of-fri endships.jpg?w=858&h=405

23. The first day of the TAT-1 cable installed in 1958 saw 558 telephone calls from London to the USA, reported at http://en.wikipedia.org/wiki/TAT-1.

24. Bank of England estimates, reported in Dean, M. and Sebastia-Barriel, M. (2004) Why has world trade grown faster than world output? *Bank of England Quarterly Bulletin,* Autumn, 310–320.

25. W3 Techs (2014) Usage of content languages for websites, accessed at http://w3techs.com/techn ologies/overview/content_language/all.

26. Collins English Dictionary, Word usage trends, accessed at http://www.collinsdictionary.com/dictionary/english/globalization.

27. Estimates that include more benefits to trade, such as scale economies and increased variety, suggest that free trade would increase global GDP by about 3% today (Anderson, K. (2012) Costing global trade barriers, 1900 to 2050. Working Paper No. 2012/08, May, Australian National University).

28. This is derived from the traditional Heckscher–Ohlin and Stolper–Samuelson theories.

29. US Census Bureau, accessed at http://www.census.gov/newsroom/releases/archives/income_wealth/cb12-172.html.

30. The driver of productivity growth in China is not so much catching up in productivity within the industrial sector, but simply labor movement from low-productivity agriculture in the west of the country to higher productivity industry along the coast.

31. Astoundingly, the richest 85 people in the world now possess as much wealth as the poorer half of the entire global population (Working for the few. Oxfam Briefing Paper, January 20, 2014, accessed at http://www.oxfam.org/sites/www.oxfam.org/files/bp-working-for-few-political-capture -economic-inequality-200114-summ-en.pdf).

32. See Pintor, R., Gratschew, M., and Sullivan, K. (2002) Voter turnout rates from a comparative perspective. Global Report, pp. 75–116, accessed at http://www.idea.int/publications/vt/upload/Voter%20turnout.pdf.

33. It is important to note that a "stuck in the middle" positioning can be successful if the product has the greatest gap between willingness to pay and cost (see Chapter 2).

34. This may be viewed at http://www.wbs.ac.uk/news/the-50000-mile-journey-of-wimbledons-tennis -balls/.

REFERENCES AND FURTHER READING

Autor, D., Katz, L., and Kearney, M. (2008) Trends in US wage inequality: revising the revisionists. *Review of Economic Statistics*, 90(2), 300–323.

Baldwin, R. and Martin, P. (1999) Two waves of globalization: superficial similarities, fundamental differences. National Bureau of Economic Research Working Paper, #6904.

Bernard, A., Redding, S., and Schott, P. (2007) Comparative advantage and heterogeneous firms. *Review of Economic Studies*, 74(1), 31–66.

Bernhofen, D. and Brown, J. (2005) An empirical assessment of the comparative advantage gains from trade: evidence from Japan. *American Economic Review*, 95(1): 208–225.

Bordo, M., Eichengreen, M., and Irwin, D. (1999) Is globalization today really different than globalization a hundred years ago? NBER Working Paper #7195.

Broda, C. and Weinstein, D. (2006) Globalization and the gains from variety. *Quarterly Journal of Economics*, 121(2): 541–585.

Carlson, B. (2012) Who belongs to the Chinese middle class? *Global Post,* September 10.

Charan, R. (2013) *Global Tilt: Leading Your Business Through the Great Economic Power Shift.* Crown Business: New York.

Crooks, E. (2013) GE lifted by strong emerging markets growth. *Financial Times,* January 18.

Dean, D., DiGrande, S., Field, D., Lundmark, A., O'Day, J., Pineda, J., and Zwillenberg, P. (2012) The Internet economy in the G-20. Boston Consulting Group Perspectives, March.

Dicken, P. (2007) *Global Shift: Mapping the Changing Contours of The World Economy.* 5th edition. Guilford Press: New York.

Dreher, A., Gaston, N., and Martems, P. (2008) *Measuring Globalisation.* Springer Science + Business Media: Berlin.

Ferguson, N. (2005) A bolt from the blue? The City of London and the outbreak of the First World War. In Wm. Roger Louis (ed.) *Yet More Adventures with Britainnia: Personalities, Politics and Culture in Britain.* I.B. Tauris: London, pp. 133–145.

Freeman, R. (2005) China, India and the doubling of the global labor force: who pays the price of globalization? *The Globalist,* June 3.

Friedman, T.L. (2005) *The World is Flat: A Brief History of the Twenty-First Century.* Farrar, Straus, and Giroux: New York.

Ghemawat, P. (2001) Distance still matters: the hard reality of global expansion. *Harvard Business Review*, 79(8), 137–147.

Ghemawat, P. (2003) Semiglobalization and international business strategy. *Journal of International Business Studies*, 34(2), 138–152.

Ghemawat, P. (2007) *Redefining Global Strategy: Crossing Borders in a World Where Differences Still Matter.* Harvard Business Review Press: Boston, MA.

Ghemawat, P. (2011) *World 3.0: Global Prosperity and How to Achieve It.* Harvard Business Review Press: Boston, MA.

Held, D. and McGrew, A. (eds.) (2007) *Globalization Theory: Approaches and Controversies.* Polity Press: Cambridge.

Hirschman, A. (1970) *Exit, Voice and Loyalty.* Harvard University Press: Cambridge, MA.

Human Development Report (2013) *The Rise of the South.* UN Development Programme: New York, p. 7.

Jullens, J. (2013) China's mid market: where "good enough" just isn't. *Strategy and Business Blog,* July 9.

Kharas, H. and Getz, G. (2013) The new global middle class: a cross-over from West to East. Brookings Institution.

Klein, N. (2002) *No Logo.* Picador: New York.

Krugman, P. (1992) *Geography and Trade*. MIT Press: Cambridge, MA.

Levitt, T. (1983) The globalization of markets. *Harvard Business Review,* May/June, 92–102.

McCarthy, J.C. (2004) Near-term growth of offshoring accelerating. Forrester Research, Inc., May 14.

Mickelthwait, J. and Wooldridge, A. (2003) *A Future Perfect: The Challenge and Promise of Globalization*. Random House: New York.

Mittelman, J. (2000) *The Globalization Syndrome: Transformation and Resistance*. Princeton University Press: Princeton, NJ.

Moody, A. and Chang, L. (2013) Global significance of China's middle class. *China Daily,* February 8.

Ohmae, K. (2002) *Triad Power*. Free Press: New York.

Prahalad, C.K. and Hart, S. (2002) The fortune at the bottom of the pyramid. *Strategy + Business*, 26(1), 2–14.

Radjou, N., Prabhu, J., and Ahuja, S. (2011) Use jugaad to innovate faster, cheaper, better. HBR Blog Network, December 8.

Roxburgh, C., Lund, S., and Piotrowski, J. (2011) Mapping global capital markets 2011. McKinsey Global Institute, August.

Rugman, A.M. (2001) *The End of Globalization: Why Global Strategy Is a Myth & How to Profit from the Realities of Regional Markets*. American Management Association: New York.

Rugman, A.M. (2005) *The Regional Multinationals: MNEs and 'Global' Strategic Management*. Cambridge University Press: Cambridge.

Rugman, A.M. and Verbeke, A. (2004) A perspective on regional and global strategies of multinational enterprises. *Journal of International Business Studies*, 35(1), 3–18.

Sirkin, H., Hemerling, J., and Bhattacharya, A. (2008) *Globality: Competing with Everyone from Everywhere for Everything*. Business Plus: New York.

Spar, D.L. (2002) Hitting the wall: Nike and international labor practices. Harvard Business School Case #9-700-047, rev. September 6.

Stiglitz, J. (2002) *Globalization and its Discontents*. W. W. Norton: New York.

Veseth, M. (2005) *Globaloney: Unraveling the Myths of Globalization*. Rowman & Littlefield: Oxford.

Vietor, R.H.K. (2007) *How Countries Compete: Strategy, Structure, and Government in the Global Economy*. Harvard Business School Press: Boston, MA.

Wolf, J., Dunemann, T., and Egelhoff, W.G. (2012) Why MNCs tend to concentrate their activities in their home region. *Multinational Business Review*, 20(1), 67–91.

Why Do Firms Go International?
The Justification for the Existence of the Multinational Corporation

MOTIVATION

Once upon a time there was a small but fast-growing furniture maker, based outside Barcelona, selling classical bedroom and dining room sets to the local Catalan market.[1] Part of its success came from offering a wide range of catalog designs to complement the very limited inventory carried in local retailers' tiny stores. Part of its advantage came from the short delivery times it offered, enabled by a combination of job lot craft production and a willingness to go over and above the call of duty to satisfy customers.

And then, when facing a fall in local demand, two things happened to disrupt the even flow of events in the company. First, an acquaintance introduced it to the relative of a minister in Uzbekistan who claimed to be interested in purchasing the equivalent of two months' output of a limited range of bedroom furniture. Second, rumors were heard that IKEA was looking at a site in Barcelona for its first Spanish furniture store. How should the company respond? Should it take the Uzbek order? Should it visit IKEA headquarters in Delft, Holland and try to become a supplier to IKEA stores in France as a precursor to supporting the Catalan entry? Should the firm now become a multinational?

This and many other similar stories are typical of the process by which firms confront the decision to step beyond their borders and become multinational. While many firms have years, if not centuries, of foreign experience, the question of whether or not to become a multinational – of how value is created by extending the geographic scope of the corporation – is the most basic for international strategy to address.

PRINCIPLES

Interestingly, when a firm begins to sell outside its home country, it will likely have been one of the more **efficient domestic producers**, but on average it will be less profitable beyond its home market (Exhibit 2.1) – the so-called **liability of foreignness**.

International trade experts have shown that exporting firms are among the most efficient in their industry.[2] This is perhaps not surprising since we argue that to be successful internationally a firm must start with a domestic competitive advantage. They also show that the profitability of firms' international activities is typically lower than in their domestic business. This does not mean that firms should not become multinational. Provided that the profitability of foreign activity is above the cost of capital, geographic expansion will still create shareholder value, even if the average profitability of the firm declines. Indeed, the most recent research suggests that geographic diversification does create shareholder value.[3]

Nevertheless, it is clear that foreign operations on average offer lower returns than domestic operations. Observers classify the causes of that inferior performance into three categories of tacit and social costs: unfamiliarity; relational; and discrimination (Denk *et al.*, 2012). The first gives rise to mistakes because the multinational lacks local information and knowledge. The second includes the additional costs of managing a foreign operation (e.g., expatriate and travel costs), and the lack of embeddedness and trust in local networks (e.g., the reticence of locals to do business with multinationals). The third is simply the, sometimes explicit, practice or policy favoring indigenous firms over foreigners, whether by governments or consumers.

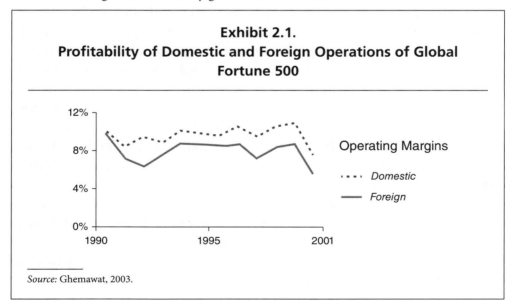

Exhibit 2.1.
Profitability of Domestic and Foreign Operations of Global Fortune 500

Source: Ghemawat, 2003.

It is important to recognize that the extent of liabilities varies with "distance" between the multinational's country and the subject country – a Saudi firm operating in Somalia, for example, might suffer less than a US firm in that country. The liability also appears to decline over time, implying that there is learning by the subject firm and by the country itself – think how you view Korean brands today compared to 15 years ago. The net effect, however, is that there is always a penalty that must be paid when a firm enters a new country. To overcome this, and still create shareholder value, is the challenge for international strategy.

Theory identifies **three conditions** that must hold if the multinational, defined as **an entity with hierarchical control over activities that cross borders,**[4] is to exist by creating value through geographic expansion:

- an intrinsic competitive advantage;
- an economic advantage to, and hence a motivation for, an international presence;
- a cost advantage to carrying out transactions inside the firm rather than through some form of market exchange or contract.

INTRINSIC COMPETITIVE ADVANTAGE

Activities and Flows

Every successful company that creates shareholder value has a competitive advantage. This statement is as true for international competition as it is for domestic competition. That is why international strategy follows the core business unit strategy course in nearly every business school, and why the underlying concepts and frameworks of business unit strategy are as relevant in the international as in the domestic context (see box).

Tools of Strategic Analysis

Although international strategy is a discrete field, it is important to recognize that **all the tools and techniques of strategic analysis** developed for domestic competition also apply in the international sphere.[5] International strategy takes the basic building blocks of strategic analysis – the definition of what is a strategy, industry analysis, competitive positioning, competitive dynamics and prediction, strategic option generation, sustainability, etc. – as given and applies them in the international context where they are assumed to be understood by practitioners and readers of this book.

Since the basis of any successful international strategy is a company's initial domestic **competitive advantage**, it is necessary to explain that concept. We cannot help a company develop an international strategy unless we know why domestic customers buy its product or service – what a firm does differently, uniquely, or better than its competitors. This can be as simple as being a low-cost producer of a commodity chemical, like Dow, or offering a distinctive product or level of customer service, like Apple or Enterprise car rental.

The essence of a competitive advantage is to create more value for customers than any competitor. This comes from offering a product or service with a **distinctive value proposition** that is defined as having the **widest wedge between customer willingness to pay and cost to produce** (see box). Willingness to pay represents the intrinsic value of the product to the consumer – in principle, given your income, the set of every other product available for sale etc., how much would you be willing to pay to be able to consume this product? Cost is formally the supplier opportunity cost – the best price that suppliers of all the inputs required to make the product are able to realize elsewhere – but which we can simply think of as the full cost incurred to produce the item.

Theory of Competitive Advantage

Competitive advantage is both defined by and measured as the firm possessing a wedge between customers' willingness to pay for its product and the cost it incurs to deliver the product that is larger than that of any competitor. While a proof of the theory is beyond this text, a simple representation illustrates the concept.[6]

Consider competition between two firms to sell a single product to one individual (Exhibit 2.2). Each competitor offers a different version of the product. Firm 2 offers some features that the customer values highly but is more expensive to produce than the basic version offered by Firm 1. Which firm will win the customer? Which firm has the competitive advantage?

Exhibit 2.2.
Value-Based Representation of Competitive Advantage

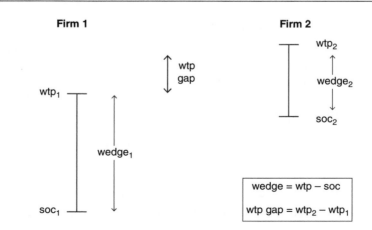

Exhibit 2.3.
Value-Based Representation of Competitive Advantage

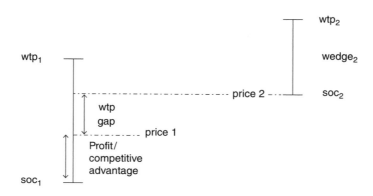

The answer is the firm with the bigger wedge between the customer willingness to pay for the particular product and its cost to produce. In the example (Exhibit 2.3), Firm 1 can reduce price to a level where the customer just prefers to buy its product – the value he or she gets from Firm 1 is slightly higher than from Firm 2 – and yet Firm 2 cannot price any lower because it would no longer be profitable. At that price Firm 1 wins the business and is profitable. Firm 1 therefore has the competitive advantage (see Exhibit 2.4 for a more formal proof).

Exhibit 2.4.
Value-Based Representation of Competitive Advantage

FORMALLY

Firm 1 has a competitive advantage iff: when $price_2 = soc_2$, $price_1 > soc_1$

iff $soc_2 - (wtp\ gap) > soc_1$

iff $soc_2 - (wtp_2 - wtp_1) > soc_1$

iff $wtp_1 - soc_1 > wtp_2 - soc_2$

iff $wedge_1 > wedge_2$

If it is the size of the wedge between willingness to pay and cost that determines competitive advantage, why is it that strategists often talk about pursuing either a low-cost or a differentiation strategy? The answer is that they are both wrong and right to do so. They are wrong in that any successful strategy is "differentiated" in the sense of being different from competitors. The "differentiation" strategy being described is really a "high willingness to pay" strategy.[7] They are also wrong in that every effort must be made to widen the wedge, regardless of whether that requires driving cost

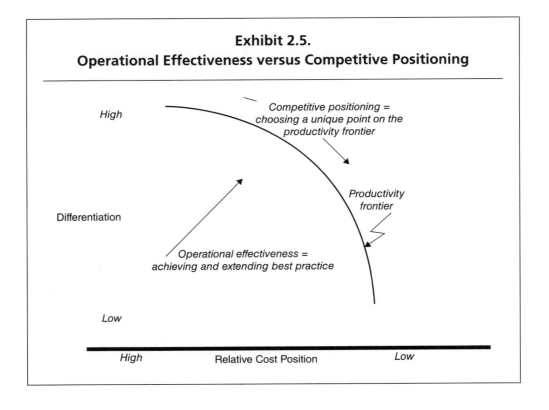

Exhibit 2.5.
Operational Effectiveness versus Competitive Positioning

High

Competitive positioning =
choosing a unique point on the
productivity frontier

Productivity
frontier

Differentiation

Operational effectiveness =
achieving and extending best practice

Low

High   Relative Cost Position   Low

down or increasing customer willingness to pay. In Porter's terms, every firm should strive to reach the efficiency or production frontier by driving cost as low as possible subject to delivering its chosen value to customers, or making its product as attractive to customers as possible subject to a certain level of cost (Porter, 1996) (Exhibit 2.5).

Strategy gurus are, however, right in that organizational demands typically require companies to focus their employees around a single goal – cost reduction or customer value – in order to ensure internally consistent actions. They are also right that cost must be reduced subject to the constraint of delivering a certain value to customers, or that willingness to pay be driven as high as possible subject to a certain cost (that is the definition of reaching the productivity frontier). But it is the "subject to" which is central to strategy. Indeed, strategy is this prior selection of "hub decisions" which then determine how all are set to optimize performance (Rivkin and Collis, 2008; Van den Steen 2012; Ghemawat and Levinthal, 2008). In Exhibit 2.5, a firm has to choose the vector it wishes to pursue and then pushes to reduce cost and increase willingness to pay along that vector. The vector is the strategic choice that can loosely be thought of as gaining competitive advantage primarily by reducing cost or increasing customer willingness to pay.

This definition of competitive advantage is a **static representation** of current position. It can be directly measured by comparing the revenue and expenses that are generated by, or accrue to, the set of activities that the firm undertakes to deliver the product or service to customers. It therefore focuses on **activity flows** so that, for example, a firm will have a competitive advantage because it spends less on advertising than competitors. Indeed, a substantial part of the strategy consultants' revenue comes from performing relative cost analysis, and quantifying willingness to pay advantages for clients.

Multimarket Transfer of Resources and Stocks

With international strategy we must be concerned with more than just short-term advantage in a single market. We want to know what, if anything, stops competitors copying or even exceeding the size of our wedge tomorrow, and how we can transfer that advantage to other geographies. We want to understand what underlies **sustainable competitive advantage across markets**. This concern introduces the **dynamics** of strategy and requires us to consider a complementary perspective to the activity-based view of the firm popularized by Michael Porter. This perspective focuses on **asset stocks** rather than flows because it is their level that is both hard to adjust and which determines the flow expenditures or revenue associated with the performance of an activity. The reason the firm noted above spends less on advertising (a flow or activity measure of current performance) is that it has a stronger brand name than competitors (a stock measure of the underlying asset). Competitive advantage is best measured by the flows associated with each activity, but the sustainability and transferability of that advantage comes from the level of the relevant stock or asset.

Notice that stocks and flows are **duals** of one another, so that both are required for a complete understanding of competitive advantage. The strength of a brand name determines the level of advertising spending required this period. But the accumulation of those expenditures over time (and any depreciation of the brand in consumers' minds) in turn alters the stock level of the brand. The metaphor is of bathwater. The water level at any time represents the stock. The flows are the water coming into the bath through the taps and out of the plug hole.

The approach which emphasizes the importance of stocks to the explanation of durable intra-industry differences in performance (the economists' term for sustainable competitive advantage) and which has taken its place in the field of strategic management in the last two decades is the **resource-based view (RBV)** of the firm (Wernerfelt, 1984; Petaraf, 1993). As with the activity-based view of the firm, we cannot do justice to the full set of ideas embedded in the RBV, but will just introduce the key ideas (see box).

Resource-Based Theory of the Firm

What Are Resources?

Resources are the set of assets owned or accumulated internally by a firm which can be classified into tangible assets, intangible assets, and organizational capabilities (more commonly referred to as "core competences" (Prahalad and Hamel, 1990) although better thought of as "distinctive competences").[8] Tangible assets are plant and equipment, buildings, and other physical items, like the fiber optic cable entering your house that has replaced the twisted copper wire of the phone company. Intangible assets are those that involve intellectual property, like mastery of a technology, or customer perceptions, like brand names. Organizational capabilities are the result of a firm's routines and processes and determine the efficiency and effectiveness with which a given set of inputs is converted into outputs (they determine the firm's production function). Pragmatically, organizational capabilities can be thought of as the adverbs that characterize how a firm operates relative to its peers, namely, faster, higher quality, and so on, and give rise to a "capability" such as "taking regional brands into national distribution."

What Makes a Resource Valuable?

A number of conditions must exist for a resource to underpin sustainable competitive advantage. An earlier article outlined three conditions for a resource which produced something that customers valued to be a source of competitive advantage – demand, scarcity, appropriability (Collis and Montgomery, 1995) (Exhibit 2.6). Jay Barney, in what has perhaps become the accepted list of conditions, identifies four conditions of a resource

Exhibit 2.6.
Conditions for a Resource to be Valuable

- The Test of Demand
  - Utility
    - Does the resource produce something that customers want (at a price they are willing to pay)?
  - Competitive Superiority
    - Is the resource really better than what competitors have?
- The Test of Scarcity
  - Imitability
    - Is the resource hard to copy?
  - Substitutability
    - Does a competitor possess an alternative resource that has more value for the customer?
- The Test of Appropriability
  - Distribution of Profit
    - Who gets the value created by the resource?

that underpin sustained competitive advantage: valuable, rare, inimitable, and non-substitutable. The two lists essentially define a valuable resource as one which is (a) better at providing something customers value, (b) hard to imitate, acquire independently, or substitute with an alternative, and (c) vested within the organization rather than an individual so that the firm can extract the rents it accrues.

The basic idea behind the RBV is that every firm can be thought of as a heterogeneous bundle of resources (or assets) that are hard to change or acquire. Differences in those resource bundles lead to differential firm performance.

We introduce the RBV not only because it is the standard strategy tool for understanding the durability of competitive advantage, but also because international competition requires some form of interrelationship across countries. In some multinationals it could be activities, such as a manufacturing facility, that are shared between countries. However, in many other multinationals, few activities are directly shared between countries, and even the product itself might be different. In this case, looking to understand how one country's operation benefits from activities in another country is difficult. If the advantage in country A is lower advertising expense, but country B does not share media markets with A, where is the benefit to operating in both? Rather than looking to map activities that are shared between countries, most multinationals transfer skills, capabilities, and assets – the resources represented by the brand positioning, not the lower advertising expenditures; the plant operating management expertise, not the output of a shared factory across countries. In these cases it is resource stocks that underpin value creation both through time (sustainability) and across markets.

We can therefore assert not only that successful domestic firms possess a competitive advantage, but also that they possess a valuable set of resources that can be leveraged into new markets, or enhanced by activity in the new market. Indeed, every theory of the multinational starts from an assumption that the firm possesses a durable competitive advantage by virtue of its ownership of valuable resources.

WHAT IS A FIRM'S INTERNATIONAL ADVANTAGE?

Once a firm successfully builds a domestic competitive advantage and a distinctive bundle of resources, it can consider becoming an active international player. Why does such a firm choose to go international and become, for the first time, a multinational? What are the motivations that lead companies to become internationally active?

The economist's trivial answer to the question is that there have to be some **scope economies** that reduce cost, or increase volume or willingness to pay when entering new markets, and that these economies are sufficient to offset the liability of foreignness noted at the beginning of this chapter. But that is just restating the obvious. We want to know where those scope economies come from. What are the sources of value creation from geographic diversification? What can be the source of a firm's **international advantage**?[9]

Leverage an Existing Advantage

The classic explanation of why firms become multinational is that they choose either to exploit or to enhance an existing domestic competitive advantage.

Exploit

The first of these motivations is simply the **market-seeking** desire to become larger and more profitable. If my company is a profitable manufacturer of bone china in England, why not also sell that china in Europe? When a firm believes that its original competitive advantage will translate into a new market, extending its geographic footprint will increase its profits. Foreign market entry in this case is a **product market** diversification that happens to cross borders.

The initial competitive advantage, discussed above, that is leveraged into the new market is called a **firm-specific advantage or FSA** (Rugman, 1981), or an **ownership advantage or O** (Dunning, 1998) in the international business literature. This advantage can be any of the traditional competitive advantages that business unit strategy describes. It could be that the firm has a unique and differentiated product, like an Apple iPad. It could be that the company has built a low-cost position in the manufacture of simple LEDs, like the Chinese firm Sana Optoelectronics. Or it could simply be that the firm has a set of capabilities or competences that are superior to the competition in the market it enters. When the former Soviet Union and other Eastern European countries opened up to Western firms after 1989, many companies, like the Italian utility Enel, acquired formerly state-owned enterprises that had been poorly run and improved their performance by the application of modern management techniques and heavy capital investment. Similarly, firms from developed countries often have operational skills that are superior to local companies in emerging markets. In this regard, they can be seen as possessing FSAs that create value when applied in those new markets.

Note that FSAs only have value in markets where they are competitively superior to indigenous producers. English tea bags might find a ready market in the USA, but fail to find a space in sophisticated tea-drinking cultures where there are already many quality tea offerings. If a country has a poorly developed capital market, a multinational that has access to capital can be a success, whereas it might struggle in a country with a well-developed capital market.

As an important aside, which we will return to in a moment, it is also necessary to explain why the firm itself needs to become multinational – that is, to operate its own activities in another country. Why must the firm extend its scope to the new country, rather than just export its goods or license a firm in that country to sell its products? Or, in the case of Enel, perhaps act as a consultant to the local utility?

Enhance

The second explanation for becoming multinational does not involve the company becoming a competitor in foreign markets. Rather than selling beyond its home country, the international activity involves overseas production. An Internet startup company employs Indian programmers to reduce cost. Nucor opens a direct reduction iron ore plant in Jamaica to supply its US steel mini-mills. Neither of these examples results in the firm entering new product markets, it merely relocates some of its activities to foreign countries.

The second classic explanation for becoming multinational therefore focuses not on the product market, but on the **factor market**. In this, the firm enters a foreign country with a **resource-seeking** intent in order to capitalize on lower factor costs in that location. A chocolate manufacturer decides to establish its own cocoa plantations in Ghana in order to reduce its input costs. Notice that rather than leverage the FSA into another country, this strategy seeks to exploit a **country-specific advantage or CSA** (Rugman, 1981) or **locational advantage or L** (Dunning, 1998) in order to enhance its competitive advantage in the domestic market.

Again, the same proviso applies. Why does the firm itself need to expand its boundaries across countries? Why cannot it simply source these cheaper factor inputs from a company based in the appropriate country?

Theory of Country-Specific Advantages

This is not a text about international trade or economic development, so we will not dwell on how countries develop their advantages. We do, however, need to offer some pragmatic observations about the evolution of CSAs since multinationals should have an awareness of how these factors, which to them appear exogenous, play out over time. We start by noting four factors that drive CSAs (Exhibit 2.7).[10]

The first follows the traditional explanation of comparative advantage that CSAs arise from differential **factor market endowments** – countries with a relative oversupply in a factor will have an advantage in products that use those factors more intensively. This explains why Saudi Arabia exports oil, Ukraine wheat, and China exports any easily

---

Exhibit 2.7.
Drivers of Country-Specific Advantages

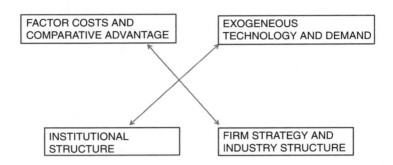

manufactured item requiring large amounts of unskilled labor. While, traditionally, the factors of production were land, labor, and capital, today we think about a more fine-grained set of factors that include intellectual property and types of skilled labor. Clearly, there is a limit to how far this disaggregation can go, since we can always explain why a country wins in global competition in gold-plated faucets because it possesses the most advanced factors of production for gold-plated faucets! But the notion of understanding comparative advantage based on relative endowments of more than just three factors of production clearly makes sense.

The second factor is the **institutional structure** within the country. This includes a list of government policies, such as liberalization and privatization, the property rights regime in force, the political system, and so on. Without an appropriate set of structures, the inherent potential in an economy's factor endowments might not be realized. Consider that China before 1970 had a huge low-paid population (i.e., a comparative advantage in unskilled workers), but a barely noticeable share of world trade. It was only after the institutional changes embedded in the "it is glorious to get rich" policies of the Deng Xiaoping government after 1978 that China began to exploit its comparative advantage.

Third, there are **technology and consumer tastes** that determine, and so can exogenously shift, an industry production function and demand curve. If, for example, young Asians start to drink wine, and if expensive wine becomes a status symbol in China, the alteration in consumer demand can lead to a rearrangement of country advantages. Indeed, the growth in relatively ill-informed, Asian demand contributed to the shift in wine production from the "Old World" (Europe) to the "New World" (USA, and the southern hemisphere producers, Australia, New Zealand, Argentina).

Finally, there are **firm strategy and industry structure**. The wine industry is instructive in this regard. Australia has been at the forefront of the New World producers grabbing a nearly 10% share of global wine exports, up from less than 1% in 1990, as France's share fell from 20% to about 10% (by volume) over the same time (Morss, 2012). Australia's success has come from a limited number of producers – the combined market share of the top four Australian wine companies is 90% – who, copying the transition in the beer industry, moved the industry from a craft-based agricultural business, where the art of the vintner and the quality of the terroir and the season's weather were paramount, to a typical fast-moving consumer packaged-goods industry with heavy advertising, a limited number of brands described by grape, and a scientific approach to growing grapes (drip irrigation, mechanical harvesting) and products (adding sugar to appeal to younger drinkers, screw caps). The French, in contrast, were handicapped by thousands of tiny producers, each with a vested interest in maintaining the uniqueness of their own chateau, and with institutional restrictions of the "Appellation Controllée" prohibiting the adoption of many innovations.

The importance of identifying firm factors is to stress that the firm is not a passive agent in the evolution of comparative advantage. Rather, firms are vital actors as their strategies, both competitive and non-market, have enormous impact on what can often seem like an inexorable, if glacial, process.

Evolution of Comparative Advantage

How does comparative advantage evolve? Is there a predictable pattern explaining how the preferred location for an industry shifts between countries over time?

First, it is **not the case that a single country completely wins** in any given business. There are always niches and segments within an industry that are subject to different economic drivers. Product variety (horizontal and vertical differentiation) and value-added slices allow different countries to succeed in different parts of "an industry." The UK continues to produce Land Rovers, even though mass market car firms have, by and large, left the country (and Rover is now owned by the Indian firm, Tata Motors). Indeed, the operation of comparative advantage leads to increasing country specialization and the emergence of complex global supply chains within many industries.

Second, **no shift of location is irreversible**. The USA is now winning back some manufacturing jobs, previously lost to Asia. As the manufacturing process is refined, and as product designs simplify the process and reduce the number of parts, the direct labor content of a product, like an iPhone, decreases. This reduces the cost advantage of low labor-cost countries and supports the return of manufacturing closer to the domestic market and development teams.

Third, **countries pass through stages** as they develop and upgrade their advantages over time (Porter, 1998; Vietor, 2007). While no path is deterministic, and no two countries look exactly the same, there is a sense that the typical progression begins by exploiting low labor costs,[11] and moves to investment in heavy industry and manufacturing process skills before, ideally, reaching an advantage based on innovation. This is the path Japan, then Korea, and now China appeared to pursue. Indeed, countries are always pressured to upgrade their advantages by the next generation of emerging markets that have the labor cost advantage – as China is now feeling the heat from Vietnam and Indonesia. If they fail to do so they can get caught in the "Middle Income Trap" and may never make it to the ranks of high-income countries (Vietor, 2007).

Fourth, there is **convergence** toward the highest income countries' standard of living – at least for countries that are able to get traction with their economic development. That is to say, it is easier for countries to grow faster when behind and emulating leading countries, than when having to innovate and push the production frontier themselves. The USA caught up to the UK, Japan caught up to the USA, and so on. Indeed, in a world with the free flow of capital, labor, technology, and ideas we would expect a gradual convergence of GNP per capita.

Data shows that the expected convergence is more muted than might be expected. The Asian dragons are almost the exception in this regard. What is clear is that convergence only happens if economies adopt appropriate institutional arrangements to support development, and that convergence is toward a level that is conditioned by the initial factor endowments of the country. Notably, the original level of education in a country appears to have a substantial impact on the level of income to which a country asymptotically converges (Jones, 1997).

Create a New Advantage

Both of the above motivations to extend the scope of the firm across borders involved the exploitation of an existing advantage, whether firm or country specific. Two additional motivations involve the multinational, for the first time, **creating an advantage by virtue of its international activities.** That is to say, rather than leveraging an existing advantage, these motivations create a competitive advantage as a consequence of the firm's international activity.

Global Scope

The first of these motivations is to increase **global scope** in order to exploit supply side economies of scale and experience. Perhaps the firm is based in a small domestic market, like Nokia, the Finnish mobile (cell) phone giant. By becoming multinational such a firm is able to build an advantage through increased scale of operations. Notice that the firm still has to begin with a domestic competitive advantage; the scope expansion simply brings an additional advantage. Honda, for example, was a leading Japanese producer of motorbikes before it exploited global economies by entering US and European markets.

Increasing geographic scope not only reduces cost but can also create unique products or services. This can be thought of as creating a demand side advantage through international activities. FedEx, for example, can offer **global coverage** for express delivery to customers by virtue of its global network. If it did not have stations in nearly 200 countries, it simply could not provide that service to customers. Similarly, the Hult International Business School is able to provide a unique MBA experience by offering students a rotation between its six campuses in Boston, London, Dubai, Shanghai, Buenos Aires, and San Francisco. The global offering that appeals to students is only possible because the school has a presence in many countries.

Global Coordination

The second motivation creates a dynamic advantage through the **coordination of a geographically distributed set of activities**. A global footprint provides the unique ability to continually optimize operations across countries, and leverage learning from anywhere to everywhere in the world. Whether it is the ability to rapidly shift production between countries in response to fluctuations in exchange rates, interest rates, or inflation (supply side), or the possibility of taking a product innovation or a fashion breakthrough from one country to another (demand side), a firm that actively and effectively coordinates a dispersed network of activities can create a unique **dynamic advantage**.

An interesting note about these two motivations is that they are not *a priori* either FSAs or CSAs. Rather, the advantage is created *ex post* out of the combination of the FSAs and CSAs, particularly when CSAs are defined to include product market characteristics, such as size and growth.

Offensive and Defensive Motivations

Each of these motivations can be applied offensively or defensively. The **offensive** argument implied in the above examples is to become multinational in order to gain an advantage over those who are not active internationally. The typical story of an entrepreneurial firm that begins selling in another country; the multinational that becomes the first to set up operations in a new low-cost country, like Laos; or the strategy pursued by Honda or Caterpillar to create global economies of scale: each suggests expanding before international competition.

However, since all motivations to internationalize are predicated on scope economies, firms might have to match competitors with a global footprint if they are not to be overwhelmed. Examples of this **defensive** motivation abound. When, during the time of "Mad Men" in the 1960s, the advertising agency business was becoming prominent, all of today's large firms (with the exception of the Japanese leader, Dentsu) created a global network of offices. For each, the motivation was the fear that if they did not do so, clients would leave them for a "one-stop shop" global competitor. Even worse was the concern that a country in which the incumbent agency did not have an office could allow a multinational competitor a "foot in the door" back home. This fear was made real when Leo Burnett won the Ford global account after first serving Ford in Argentina, where J. Walter Thompson, previously the Ford agency, had no office.

Similarly, the need to prevent competitors gaining an advantage by exploiting global scale or arbitraging factor costs has driven many companies to match competition by shifting manufacturing overseas. Newell-Rubbermaid was late to move its manufacturing to China and so lost market share to Walmart and other high-volume retailers when Asian-sourced production became acceptable to those chains. Airbus had to build a global sales network to match Boeing, or run the risk of losing everywhere, even in its home European market, because of a scale disadvantage. If firms do not respond to competitive moves they will be overwhelmed by multinationals. CEMEX, for example, the Mexican firm that is currently the third largest cement company in the world, would almost certainly no longer exist but would have been acquired by a global competitor during one of the Mexican economic crises, had it not chosen to become multinational in the early 1990s.

More generally, therefore, one of the reasons to become international is to match competitors' moves. Indeed, the notion of **multimarket competitive interaction** originated in the international field (see box). This highlights the notion that when firms meet each other in more than one market, it is necessary to incorporate oligopolistic interaction into firm strategy.

Theory of Multimarket Contact

Strategists have noted the possibility for firms that meet each other in many markets (whether across geographies, over time, or across businesses) to fashion some sort of agreement out of their repeated interactions (Knickerbocker, 1973; Scott, 1982; Karnani and Wernerfelt, 1985; Bernheim and Whinston, 1990). The extended scope of interaction allows competitors to signal each other and so reach an equilibrium that leaves all better off. By observing each other's behavior over an array of different markets, companies can be confident that others "play by the rules," which justifies less aggressive and more profitable, although still competitive, behavior. This "equilibrium" need not be collusive, since it does not require illicit behavior, merely the recognition of mutual interdependence.[12]

The formal theory supporting this behavior is beyond this text. The intuition behind it is the threat of mutually assured destruction. If one multinational has a small presence in a competitor's home market, it can threaten to destroy profitability in that market by cutting prices. This will have a substantial impact on the competitor, but only a small effect on the firm itself. Similarly, the competitor can build a small presence in the multinational's home market. The recognition that each now possesses the potential, at relatively low cost, to ruin the other's home market leads to a truce in which neither aggressively cut prices; both respect the other's market position; and both make good returns.

In particular, global competitive interaction can improve **industry structural attractiveness**. The cement industry is an example where increasing global concentration improves profitability. Because the same competitors frequently meet each other in different markets, they have learnt how to manage prices through the business cycle without detriment to their performance.

WHY INSIDE THE FIRM? INTERNALIZATION ADVANTAGE

With an underlying competitive advantage, and a motivation to exploit some form of geographic scope economies, there is one last condition that must hold for a company to become multinational. It should be cheaper to undertake the international activity inside the firm than to simply transact with a foreign company for the performance of the activity. This is important because we can always identify a market alternative to expanding the boundary of the firm across borders.

Disney, for example, earns profit from many countries in which it does not itself have a presence by licensing the use of its animated cartoon characters to companies that do compete in those markets. Any company with a successful product, in principle, always has this option of earning profits elsewhere through licensing, or other contractual arrangement, rather than by becoming an active participant in those markets.

This same condition must also be true if other motivations are to give rise to the multinational. If a retail gift shop can more effectively access foreign products by buying from an importer at a domestic trade show, than by setting up a purchasing office in Milan to buy directly from an Italian manufacturer, it will not become multinational. Similarly, if Nucor could convince a local company to invest in direct reduction technology in Jamaica and supply it on a long-term contract at terms better than if it made the investment itself, then Nucor would have no desire to become multinational.

In the formal terms of transaction cost economics, for the multinational to exist the **governance cost** of keeping the transaction inside the company – the hierarchical alternative – has to be lower than the cost of completing that transaction through some sort of exchange – the market alternative. It is only when Disney can more cheaply or effectively sell its own plush toys in the Congo, than it could by licensing Mattel to do so, that it should extend its geographic scope to include the Congo. There has to be an **internalization or I advantage** (Dunning, 1988), for the firm to become multinational – to actually operate outside its borders.

Unfortunately, this explanation merely begs the question of why the governance cost of one form of organizing transactions is lower than another; we need to provide an intuition that aids strategists in understanding when to keep activities inside the firm and when they can be outsourced or accessed through contractual relationships.

Although there are costs and benefits to both the internal and external organization of transactions (see box), the explanation for internalization typically comes from some form of **market failure** that inordinately raises the cost of market transactions. Instances when transfer through market exchange is expensive or impossible involve either intangible assets or informational resources, or those that require relationship-specific investments, such as the classic story of Fisher Body supplying auto bodies to General Motors (Casadesus-Masanell and Spulber, 2000). It is relatively easy for finished goods and commodities to be sold at arm's length in spot markets, which is why many such products sell through importers or agents. It is a lot more difficult to arrange a contract that covers all the eventualities surrounding the use of technical knowledge that resides not in blueprints, but in the minds of engineers, or to write a contract for the life of an alumina mine that can only supply a single processing facility. In the international context, for example, perhaps the multinational is concerned that a foreign licensee might steal the product design, or worries that the foreign supplier might not make adequate investments in equipment customized to the multinational's unique requirements.

Transaction Costs and Internalization Theory

Transaction cost theory seeks to explain when activities are efficiently retained within a corporate hierarchy and when they can better be accessed through market exchange. Indeed, it addresses one of the fundamental economic questions whose original formulation won Ronald Coase the Nobel Prize for Economics (Coase, 1937) – what is the limit to the scope of the firm?

The analysis starts by recognizing that there are costs and benefits to both types of organizational arrangement for the governance of transactions (Table 2.1). The efficient arrangement simply depends on the balance of these costs and benefits.

Table 2.1 Costs and Benefits of the Market and Hierarchy

	Market	Hierarchy
Benefits	High-powered incentives	Authority
	Informational efficiency	Coordination
Costs	Contracting costs	Agency costs
	Market power	Bureaucracy

Source: Collis and Montgomery (2005)

In many ways, the benefits of the market are what the hierarchy fails at and vice versa. The market gives decision-making authority to those closest to the current information, and rewards them directly for their performance. The resulting high-powered incentives for those who essentially run their own business are perhaps the greatest strength of markets. The failings of the market are its inability to coordinate behavior among self-interested parties, and the cost of writing complete contracts that cover all eventualities over the lifetime of the agreement.

In contrast, the benefit of the hierarchy is the authority to tell employees what to do and so directly coordinate their actions. However, the hierarchy suffers from agency costs – the self-interested behavior of employees (agents) who act in ways, such as shirking, that favor themselves rather than the firm. While remedies to reduce agency costs, such as monitoring and control systems, exist, they have their own costs (Jensen and Meckling, 1976). In addition, the delay and reduced freedom of operations within a hierarchy impose bureaucratic costs on the firm.

We typically make the pragmatic presumption that the benefits of high-powered incentives and specialization make the market the preferred arrangement. If that is the case, the hierarchy will only triumph when transaction costs are very high, and it is to the conditions that cause such obvious market failures that much theory has been directed.[13]

Market failures typically arise in two situations. First, when the valuable asset being transferred is intangible, tacit, or informational so that it cannot be accurately described in a contract or has no further value once revealed (Akerlof, 1970). Second, when there are repeated transactions requiring dedicated investment by either or both parties (i.e., relationship-specific assets). Examples of the former are contracts for using a new technology that cannot be accurately described – how can the purchaser know whether it was told everything about the technology? Examples of the latter are a mine supplying a refinery that can only use that grade of ore – once the refinery has been built, the mine can renege on any contracts as the refinery has no alternative but to use that mine's output. Williamson (1985), for example, argues that opportunism in the presence of relationship-specific assets is the primary cause of market failure.

This discussion has simplified the choice of organizational form. In reality there is a widely used set of intermediate organizational forms – joint ventures, franchises, and so on – which a full treatment of transaction cost addresses (Hennart, 1993).

The important idea is the necessity to challenge every decision to extend the geographic scope of a firm's operations with the question: why not just contract for this activity?

Deconstruction of the Multinational?

An argument has been made that technology, particularly the Internet, will lead to the disintermediation and deconstruction of multinationals. Cheaper communication and easier, richer interactions between firms that are facilitated by new technologies will, it is argued, allow companies to become the hub of a network of shifting alliance partners, subcontractors, and temporary employees. The result will be the ending of the multinational as we know it, replaced by a virtual organization that supplants the corporate hierarchy with a set of contractual agreements among a vast number of independent entities.

This argument misunderstands the forces that determine the scope of the multinational. Multinational companies exist when the cost of organizing a particular transaction is lower when coordinated inside the firm's hierarchy than when conducted through a market exchange or contract. It is true that the new digital technologies lower the costs of market transactions, which would suggest that more activities can indeed be carried out on the market. However, those same technologies also make it substantially easier and cheaper for firms to manage a geographically dispersed organization! Email makes it more efficient for headquarters to deal with a country manager in Brazil, just as it also makes it more efficient for that firm to deal directly with a customer in Brazil.

Whether technology reduces the cost of market or hierarchical transactions more is an empirical question that can only be answered on a case-by-case basis. There is no *a priori* theoretical reason to believe that the Internet disproportionately cuts the cost of doing business with third parties rather than inside the firm. Many multinationals can attest to the way that email, teleconferencing, and intranets have made enormous improvements in their ability to effectively coordinate dispersed operations. In the auto industry, for example, design can now be concurrently undertaken at centers in different countries by sharing a common server and three-dimensional design programs.

Technology is everywhere reducing communication costs and facilitating the remote conduct of business in ways that have enormous repercussions for international activity, but that revolution does not necessarily lead to the demise of the multinational in the form that we have known it for the last several hundred years.

Theories About the Existence of the Multinational

We now have the complete set of conditions needed to explain the existence of the multinational corporation. These factors have been combined by different authors in slightly different theoretical descriptions of the multinational, and the box briefly characterizes those approaches. Although essentially similar, they each use different language and it is important that readers understand how they relate, as each has had broad adoption by scholars.

International Economics

The first formalization of the theory of the multinational occurred within international economics. Dick Caves in his classic text *Multinational Enterprise* defined the multinational as an enterprise that "controls and manages plants located in at least two countries," and explained its existence as requiring *locational forces* to justify spreading production around the world, and a *transactional advantage* to justify placing the plants under common administrative control (Caves, 1982). This he attributed to the MNEs' ownership of intangible assets in the case of horizontal multinationals, and to excessive bargaining costs when vertical relationships involved costs to switch to another partner.

Dunning's Eclectic Theory

The second formalization of a theory for the existence of the multinational came from international business and is best captured in John Dunning's so-called eclectic or OLI theory (Dunning, 1988). He identified the three conditions required for the existence of the multinational: O (ownership advantage) that is the underlying source of the firm's competitive advantage; L (locational advantage) that provides an explanation for the benefit the firm gets by choosing this country as a location for some of its activities; and I (internalization advantage) that explains why the firm itself operates in the foreign country. This was essentially the approach outlined above.

FSAs and CSAs

More recently a variant of the eclectic theory has been proposed that condenses Dunning's three factors into two – FSAs and CSAs (Rugman, 1981). The mapping of FSA to ownership advantage and CSA to locational advantages is obvious. There is, however, one extension to CSAs in this version that gives them a more general relevance than I have perhaps given credit so far. CSAs as I have described them have focused on factor market conditions. A country is desirable as a location for activities because of its lower factor costs etc. and CSAs appear to motivate only resource-seeking strategies. In this version, CSAs also apply to product market conditions and so are required for market-seeking strategies as well. CSAs in the full version therefore include market size, income level, and so on – factors that make the country attractive as a market.

The question is why the internalization advantage is deemed no longer necessary to explain the existence of the multinational. The answer lies in a more restrictive definition of an FSA than the ownership advantage that Dunning advocated. This definition effectively incorporates the resource-based view of the firm by arguing that an FSA has to be a source of sustainable advantage and so must be hard to acquire, accumulate, or transfer. In that case, FSAs have been defined with an inherent O component.[14]

Internationalization Process

The Uppsala school importantly introduced dynamics into the process of becoming multinational (Johanson and Vahlne, 1977; Melin, 1992). Rather than view the firm as a static entity with a certain equilibrium geographic scope, they showed how the enterprise evolved over time as its activities and past commitment decisions altered its market knowledge and future commitment. The result was a gradual escalation of a multinational's geographic scope and depth of presence in any market as it learnt how to operate internationally and overcome any liability of foreignness.

PRAGMATIC EXPLANATION

Theories explaining the existence of the multinational exist in the fields of international economics, international business, and international strategy (see previous box). One or other of them underpins treatment of the multinational in every textbook and article. Below I offer a more pragmatic explanation of the justification for becoming multinational that is valuable to strategists trying to determine whether expanding geographic scope will increase shareholder value.[15]

The underlying justification for an expansion of the scope of the firm into any new market requires passing two tests that can be characterized through the interplay

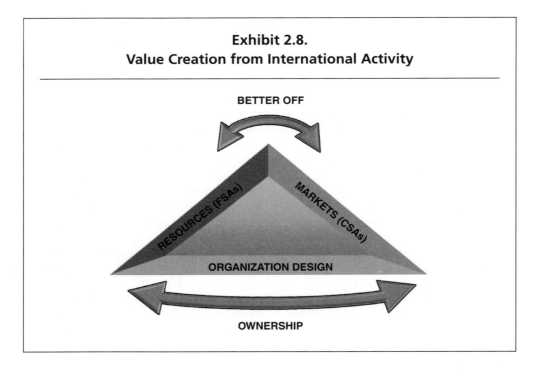

Exhibit 2.8.
Value Creation from International Activity

BETTER OFF

RESOURCES (FSAs)

MARKETS (CSAs)

ORGANIZATION DESIGN

OWNERSHIP

of firm resources (FSAs), country factors (CSAs), and organizational design (Collis, 2012; Piskorski, 2005) (Exhibit 2.8):

- **"Better off,"** which explains how economic value is created through geographic expansion.
- **"Ownership,"** which explains why it is cheaper to conduct the activity inside the firm hierarchy than through a market transaction.[16]

Better-off Test

The better-off test argues that a multinational must create value (sufficient to outweigh the liability of foreignness) through its international activities. That value comes from improving the competitive advantage of its operations in one market by virtue of leveraging products, inputs, operations, or capabilities from elsewhere. As suggested earlier, the direction of that improvement can come from deploying some unique firm resources in a new market (exploit from left to right), or from taking advantage of country factors within the firm (enhance from right to left). The former is the utility improving plant operations in Russia. The latter is establishing a factory in a low labor-cost country. In addition, extending scope to new markets can itself create new resources – the scale of Boeing or the global coverage of FedEx.

Exhibit 2.9.
The "ADDING" Value Framework as Applied to CEMEX

LEVERS	CEMEX
Adding Volume	Became world #3 in volume
Decreasing Costs	Post merger integration and best practice transfer
Differentiating/Increasing Willingness to Pay	Consumer brand building and rapid delivery
Improving Industry Attractiveness	Consolidate industry among multinationals
Neutralizing Risk	Geographic diversification
Generating and Using Knowledge	Local innovation and best practice transfer

Source: Ghemawat, 2007.

A pragmatic way to measure whether international activity creates value translates the resource-based approach into flow terms. Pankaj Ghemawat has introduced such an activity-based framework and applies the acronym **ADDING** to six categories of ways that extending geographic scope creates economic value, while using the example of CEMEX to flesh out the ideas (Exhibit 2.9) (Ghemawat, 2007). This framework can serve as a systematic checklist for strategists confronting a specific decision to expand geographic scope.

Below I give examples of each of the six categories and show how they relate to the underlying scope economies discussed earlier (Table 2.2). Although categories overlap and the same examples can be relevant to more than one category, a rigorous application of the ADDING value framework enables you to identify all potential sources of value creation through international activity; exactly what category you put any particular source in is less important.

Adding Volume

The obvious example of adding volume is the multinational extending its sales territory into a new country, the way that the UK bone china company began to sell in

Lever	Market seeking	Resource seeking	Global coverage	Coordinated global activity
A	Additional market	na	Scale	na
D	na	Static arbitrage	Scale	Dynamic arbitrage
D	Augment local products	na	Global customers	Continuous innovation
I	Multimarket contact	Multimarket contact	Match competitors	Match competitors
N	Diversification?	Match competitors	Match competitors	Dynamic arbitrage
G	Augment local products	na	Global insights	Continuous innovation

Table 2.2 Adding Value and Scope Economies

na = not applicable.

Europe. Doing more of something that is profitable domestically and in which you already have a competitive advantage makes obvious sense. Similarly, the additional volume that Intel gains by selling computer chips in Asia allows it to exploit scale economies and reduce cost.

Decreasing Cost

International activities can reduce cost by sourcing from foreign locations in order to arbitrage current factor cost differences. Expanding geographic scope to increase volume and exploit scale and experience economies is another example. Similarly, the continuous optimization of arbitrage opportunities among a dispersed global network of activities can reduce cost.

Differentiating/Increasing Willingness to Pay

The traditional market-seeking multinational "differentiates" itself by introducing a new and differentiated offering to augment those currently available in a country. Establishing a global network to provide truly global coverage for the first time, like FedEx, is another example of multinational activity generating an offering with a high willingness to pay. Being always able to bring the latest product innovations to markets around the world also allows the multinational to continuously refresh its differentiated product offerings to customers.

Improving Industry Attractiveness

Any expansion of geographic scope that extends competitive overlap can improve industry attractiveness through the restraint of competition that multimarket contact brings. In this regard, matching competitors by (a) expanding to one of their product markets or sourcing from an additional market where they have a presence, (b) building global scale or offering a global network to customers, and (c) using a coordinated global network to match competitive footprints can all be advantageous.

Neutralizing Risk

Managers often justify international expansion by arguing that geographic diversification reduces risk. If our domestic business is cyclical, entering a foreign market whose demand is not perfectly correlated will smooth earnings and make our stock less risky. Indeed, this was one of the motivations that CEMEX had for diversifying outside Mexico.

Unfortunately, this is not necessarily a valid argument. Efficient capital market theory explains that shareholders can diversify risk themselves – there is no value to the firm doing it for them. If the Mexican cement business is very cyclical, I, as a shareholder, can just buy assets in a business that is uncorrelated with those returns. Moreover, if risk reduction is the only value created by the scope expansion, maybe the firm should actually enter the furniture business in Turkey because that is perfectly negatively correlated with the Mexican cement business!

There are two rebuttals to this argument. The first point is that while efficient capital markets do not exist, informational asymmetry does – shareholders do not have full transparency into all aspects of a multinational's business. This would imply that shareholder value can be created by reducing a company's earnings volatility. I leave judgment about the efficiency of capital markets to the reader's discretion.

The second is that other non-financial forms of risk can be reduced by geographic expansion. Multimarket contact, for example, reduces the incentive for firms to engage in destructive competition. Similarly, risk from the volatility of international economic performance can be turned into an opportunity as continuously reoptimizing output between plants turns volatile exchange rates into an advantage. However, this creates shareholder value not as a reduction in financial risk, but through real improvements to competitive advantage.

Generating and Using Knowledge

The value created by generating and using knowledge is exactly the argument made for the dynamic arbitrage of ideas and innovations from anywhere to everywhere around the world. The same argument even applies to the one-time transfer of expertise that occurs when a multinational sells its traditional products in new markets.

Ownership Test

Ownership is economic when the cost of administering a cross-border transaction within the multinational is lower than the cost of writing, monitoring, and enforcing a market contract. The ownership test therefore compares the cost of the market transaction to the internal organizational cost.

Key to the cost of a transaction is the **valuable resource** – whether the firm's own capabilities, or the country's unique endowments – involved in the cross-border activity. Two factors determine whether a resource can be cheaply used by another party through a market contract – **current clarity** and **future protection** – and these provide a framework for deciding whether the firm needs to incorporate it inside the hierarchy (Table 2.3).[17]

Current clarity refers to how well understood is the resource to be transferred or the activity to be performed. When both sides know exactly what is involved, can specify exactly what each side will do, and can verify after the fact whether the other party performed what it said it would do, then a contract can be relatively **easily written**. The resources and activities that have this clarity and so can be exchanged or transferred with market contracts include technological blueprints, the design of a Mickey Mouse toy, a commodity, like oil, or the molecular formula of a pharmaceutical – anything that can be formally specified and written down in advance. Resources that fail in this regard and so must be kept inside the firm hierarchy include tacit and intangible

---

Table 2.3 Resources and the Ownership Test

		Resource clarity	
		High	Low
Resource protection	High	Mickey Mouse toy CONTRACT	Plant operating knowhow HIERARCHY
	Low	Unique ore mine HIERARCHY	Early stage technology HIERARCHY

---

knowledge, such as the art of making the gallium arsenide-based wafers for LED chips, or the expertise of a professional services firm.

Future protection concerns the longer run and the extent to which, because the contract is hard to **monitor and enforce**, a contractual partner can exploit the relationship to its advantage. While every multinational has to assume some degree of trust in its foreign partners and have some confidence in the legal enforcement of the contract, there are some types of relationship which are more vulnerable to exploitation after the contract is written. These involve either continuing investment by the partner, or when the multinational has no credible alternative once it has committed to this particular partner. In either case, an unscrupulous partner can behave opportunistically by respecting the terms, but not the spirit, of the contract. A local supplier, for example, might not invest in sufficient worker training. A distributor with an exclusive territory might ask for additional marketing support in return for continuing to push the product. In these cases, the multinational has no recourse unless the contract specifies everything in advance,[18] and the failure to fulfill the terms of the contract is readily observable and will be enforced by the courts.[19]

The transaction cost of a cross-border market exchange therefore varies by type of resource and is exogenous to the firm. Costs inside the hierarchy, however, are the other half of the scissors determining which form of governance has the lowest cost. Thus, the design of the administrative context of the multinational – its organization structure, systems and processes – is critical to justifying geographic diversification. This is why the ownership test also relates to **internal organizational design**.

Indeed, the geographic scope of the multinational is ultimately constrained by its organizational capacity. This is why factors that increase managerial coordination costs constrain geographic scope just as much as transaction costs. Endlessly expanding to evermore heterogeneous markets, for example, will, at some point, stress the organization to such an extent that it cannot cope, even if the incremental transaction is the same as one that has already been successfully internalized in other countries.

Passing the ownership test therefore depends on the balance of the costs of market transactions and the internal hierarchy that result from the resource being leveraged and the internal organization design.

NOTES

1. This example is based on the case by Enright, M., Ballarin, E., Terre, E., and Rodriguez, M. (1995) Antmobel A. Harvard Business School Case #795-100.
2. Research has shown that the causal relationship runs from efficiency to exports, and not from the logic that exports increase output which, in turn, improves efficiency.

3. Creal, D., Robinson, L., Rogers, J., and Zechman, S. (2013) The multinational advantage (February 1). Chicago Booth Research Paper No. 11-37; Fama-Miller Working Paper. Previous research has reached more negative findings: some find an inverted U in the relationship between profitability and geographic diversification; others find an "international discount" analogous to the "conglomerate discount" in multibusiness companies (Denis, D.J., Denis, D.K., and Yost, K. (2002) Global diversification, industrial diversification and firm value. *Journal of Finance,* 57(5), 1951–1980). Methodological and measurement issues abound in this research and a discount does not imply that geographic expansion destroys value provided that Tobin's q remains above 1 (although many studies find this is not the case).

4. Defining the firm is a non-trivial task. What is the defining characteristic of a firm? Is it simply the presence of employees? But where does that leave my own consulting firm that has no employees other than myself – the owner? Is it a legally defined corporate entity? My consulting firm would certainly qualify, but then what delineates a firm from any other legal entity, such as the Boy Scouts? Is it just that one is for-profit and the other is not?! Another definition is "a private institution devised to organize, through employment contracts, interdependencies between individuals based in more than one country" (Hennart, J. (2009) Theories of the multinational enterprise. In A. Rugman (ed.) *The Oxford Handbook of International Business,* 2nd edition. Oxford University Press: Oxford).

5. Readers unfamiliar with basic strategic analysis should consult one of the standard texts on the subject. An extensive, but by no means exhaustive, list of such books (see References and Further Reading) includes Porter's *Competitive Strategy* and *Competitive Advantage,* Grant's *Contemporary Strategic Analysis,* Oster's *Modern Competitive Analysis,* Saloner *et al.'s Strategic Management,* Besanko *et al.'s Economics of Strategy,* and Ghemawat's *Strategy and the Business Landscape,* as well as the classic *Business Policy* by Andrews *et al.*

6. The general theory is detailed in Brandenburger, A. and Stuart, H. (1996) Value based strategy. *Journal of Economics and Management Strategy,* 5(1), 5–24.

7. The terminology comes from industrial organization economics which distinguishes horizontal differentiation, when companies offer products with different attributes to appeal to different consumers (think SUV versus sports car), from vertical differentiation where one product is universally preferred by all customers but costs more (think BMW versus Chevrolet).

8. Core competence suggests that whichever activity the firm performs well relative to all its other activities is valuable. In that sense, every firm must have a core competence. The idea we want to capture is that the resource is competitively superior or distinctive. In this sense, most companies will not have a distinctive competence (Collis, D. and Montgomery, C. (1995) Competing on resources: strategy in the 1990s. *Harvard Business Review,* July/August, 140–150).

9. International advantage is analogous to competitive advantage in a business unit and corporate advantage across product markets for diversified corporations.

10. Chapter 9 examines the Porter "Diamond" which also explains the evolution of comparative advantage.

11. If the country possesses abundant natural resource, like oil, diamonds, or iron ore, the path will look different.

12. Nothing in this section should be taken as an endorsement of illegal behavior to conspire to fix prices or otherwise manipulate markets. Unfortunately, too many instances of such behavior have been proven in recent years.

13. Related theories that provide alternative perspectives on the scope of the firm have been advanced to explain market failure, such as incomplete contracts: Grossman, S. and Hart, O. (1986) The costs and benefits of ownership: a theory of vertical and lateral integration. *Journal of Political Economy,* 94(4), 691; Aghion, P. and Holden, R. (2011) Incomplete contracts and the theory of the firm: what have we learned over the past 25 years? *Journal of Economic Perspectives,* 25(2), 181–197.

14. Don Lessard extended the framework, arguing that FSAs must be relevant, appropriable, and transferable (RAT) to new countries if they are to be exploited, and that CSAs must be complementary,

appropriable and transferable (CAT) to the company if they are to enhance the multinational's competences (Lessard, D., Lucea, R., and Vives, L. (2012) Building your company's capabilities through global expansion. *Sloan Management Review,* Winter).

15. The framework advanced here is similar to that introduced in corporate strategy. This should be the case since international and corporate strategy both address the topic of the scope of the enterprise across markets – with markets defined as businesses in one instance and geographies in the other case.

16. A firm creates value when the net advantage of being "better off" minus the cost of "ownership" is positive. Thus a firm could not be "better off" operating a mine in Chile than a local mining company, but would still choose to do so if the contractual alternative were too expensive.

17. This follows Capron, L. and Mitchell, W. (2012) *Build, Borrow or Buy.* Harvard Business School Press: Boston, MA.

18. If it did, it would be so long as to make the *ex ante* cost of writing the contract prohibitive.

19. Importantly, this suggests that the institutional structure of a country has a substantial impact on ownership.

REFERENCES AND FURTHER READING

Akerlof, G.A. (1970) The market for "lemons": quality uncertainty and the market mechanism. *Quarterly Journal of Economics*, 84(3), 488–500.

Andrews, K., Bower, J., Christensen, C., Hamermesh, R., and Porter, M.E. (1973) *Business Policy: Text and Cases.* Richard D. Irwin: Homewood, IL.

Bernard, A.B., Jensen, J.B., Redding, S.J., and Schott, P.K. (2011) The empirics of firm heterogeneity and international trade. National Bureau of Economic Research Working Paper, #17627.

Bernheim, B.D. and Whinston, M.D. (1990) Multimarket contact and collusive behavior. *RAND Journal of Economics*, 21: 1–26.

Berry, H. (2006) Shareholder valuation of foreign investment and expansion. *Strategic Management Journal*, 27(12), 1123–1140.

Besanko, D., Dranove, D., and Shanley, M. (1996) *Economics of Strategy.* Wiley: New York.

Brandenburger, A.M. and Stuart, H.W. (1996) Value-based strategy. *Journal of Economics and Management Strategy*, 5(1), 5–24.

Buckley, P.J. and Hashai, N. (2009) Formalizing internationalization in the eclectic paradigm. *Journal of International Business Studies*, 40(1), 58–70.

Cantwell, J.A. (2009) Location and the multinational enterprise: a neglected factor? *Journal of International Business Studies*, 40(1), 5–19.

Capron, L. and Mitchell, W. (2012) *Build, Borrow or Buy.* Harvard Business School Press: Boston, MA.

Casadesus-Masanell, R. and Spulber, D.F. (2000) The fable of Fisher Body. *Journal of Law and Economics*, 43(1), 67–104.

Casillas, J.C. and Acedo, F.J. (2013) Speed in the internationalization process of the firm. *International Journal of Management Reviews*, 15(1), 15–29.

Caves, R. (1982) *Multinational Enterprise and Economic Analysis.* Cambridge University Press: Cambridge.

Coase, R. (1937) The nature of the firm. *Economica*, 4(16), 386–405.

Collis, D. (2012) Global strategy. Harvard Business School Publishing Note #712-489.

Collis, D. and Montgomery, C. (1995) Competing on resources. *Harvard Business Review*, 86(7/8), 140–150.

Collis, D. and Montgomery, C. (2005) *Corporate Strategy: A Resource-based Approach*, 2nd edition. McGraw-Hill Irwin: Boston, MA.

Collis, D. and Rukstad, M. (2008) Can you say what your strategy is? *Harvard Business Review*, 86(4), 82–90.

Creal, D.D., Robinson, L.A., Rogers, J.L., and Zechman, S.L.C. (2012) The multinational advantage. Chicago Booth Research Paper No. 11–37, Fama-Miller Working Paper.

Denis, D.J., Denis, D.K., and Yost, K. (2002) Global diversification, industrial diversification, and firm value. *Journal of Finance*, 57(5), 1951–1979.

Denk, N., Kaufmann, L., and Roesch, J.-F. (2012) Liabilities of foreignness revisited: a review of contemporary studies and recommendations for future research. *Journal of International Management*, 18(4), 322–334.

Dos Santos, M.B., Errunza, V., and Miller, D. (2008) Does corporate international diversification destroy value? Evidence from cross-border mergers and acquisitions. *Journal of Banking and Finance*, 32(12), 2716–2724.

Doukas, J.A. and Kan, O.B. (2006) Does global diversification destroy firm value? *Journal of International Business Studies*, 37(3), 352–371.

Dunning, J.H. (1980) Toward an eclectic theory of international production: some empirical tests. *Journal of International Business Studies*, 11(1), 9–31.

Dunning, J.H. (1988) The eclectic paradigm of international production: a restatement and some possible extensions. *Journal of International Business Studies*, 19(1), 1–31.

Dunning, J.H. (1995) Reappraising the eclectic paradigm in an age of alliance capitalism. *Journal of International Business Studies*, 26(3), 461–491.

Dunning, J.H. (1998) Location and the multinational enterprise: a neglected factor? *Journal of International Business Studies*, 29(1), 45–66.

Dunning, J. and Lundan, S. (2008) *Multinational Enterprises and the Global Economy*, 2nd edition. Edward Elgar: Cheltenham.

Eriksson, K., Johanson, J., Majkgard, A., and Sharma, D.D. (1997) Experiential knowledge and cost in the internationalization process. *Journal of International Business Studies*, 28(2), 337–360.

Gande, A., Schenzler, C., and Senbet, L. (2009) Valuation effects of global diversification. *Journal of International Business Studies*, 40(9), 1515–1532.

Ghemawat, P. (2006) *Strategy and the Business Landscape*, 2nd edition. Pearson/Prentice Hall: Upper Saddle River, NJ.

Ghemawat, P. (2007) *Redefining Global Strategy: Crossing Borders in a World Where Differences Still Matter*. Harvard Business Review Press: Boston, MA.

Ghemawat, P., Collis, D.J., Pisano, G.P., and Rivkin, J.W. (1999) *Strategy and the Business Landscape: Text and Cases*. Addison-Wesley: Reading, MA.

Ghemawat, P. and Levinthal, D. (2008) Choice interactions and business strategy. *Management Science*, 54(9), 1638–1651.

Grant, R., (2010) *Contemporary Strategic Analysis*, 8th edition. John Wiley & Sons: San Francisco.

Grossman, S. and Hart, O. (1986) The costs and benefits of ownership: a theory of vertical and lateral integration. *Journal of Political Economy*, 94(4), 691–719.

Hennart, J.-F. (1993) Explaining the swollen middle: why most transactions are a mix of market and hierarchy. *Organization Science*, 4(4), 529–547.

Hennart, J.-F. (2009) Theories of the multinational enterprise. In A. Rugman (ed.) *The Oxford Handbook of International Business*, 2nd edition. Oxford University Press: Oxford.

Hitt, M.A., Tihanyi, L., Miller, T., and Connelly, B.L. (2006) International diversification: antecedents, outcomes, and moderators. *Journal of Management*, 32(6), 831–867.

Jensen, M.C. and Meckling, W.H. (1976) Theory of the firm: managerial behavior, agency costs and ownership structure. *Journal of Financial Economics*, 3(4), 305–336.

Johanson, J. and Vahlne, J.E. (1977) The internationalization process of the firm—a model of knowledge development and increasing foreign market commitments. *Journal of International Business Studies*, 8(1), 23–32.

Johanson, J. and Vahlne, J. E. (1990) The mechanism of internationalisation. *International Marketing Review*, 7(4), 11–25.

Johanson, J. and Vahlne, J. E. (2009) The Uppsala internationalization process model revisited: from liability of foreignness to liability of outsidership. *Journal of International Business Studies*, 40(9), 1411–1431.

Jones, C. (1997) On the evolution of the world income distribution. *Journal of Economic Perspectives*, 11(3), 19–36.

Karnani, A. and Wernerfelt, B. (1985) Multiple point competition. *Strategic Management Journal*, 6, 87–96.

Knickerbocker, F.T. (1973) *Oligopolistic Reaction and Multinational Enterprise*. Harvard University Press: Boston, MA.

Lessard, D., Lucea, R., and Vives, L. (2012) Building your company's capabilities through global expansion. *Sloan Management Review*, 54(2), 61–67.

Malhotra, N. and Hinings, C.R. (2010) An organizational model for understanding internationalization processes. *Journal of International Business Studies*, 41(2), 330–349.

Marshall, A. (1898) *Principles of Economics*. Macmillan: London.

Melin, L. (1992) Internationalization as a strategy process. *Strategic Management Journal*, 13(S2), 99–118.

Morss, E. (2012) The global wine industry: where is it going? American Association of Wine Economists.

Oster, S. (1994) *Modern Competitive Analysis*, 2nd edition. Oxford University Press: Oxford.

Peteraf, M.A. (1993) The cornerstones of competitive advantage: a resource-based view. *Strategic Management Journal*, 14(3), 179–191.

Piskorski, M. (2005) Corporate strategy. Harvard Business School Publishing Note #705-449.

Porter, M. (1980) *Competitive Strategy*. Free Press: New York.

Porter, M. (1985) *Competitive Advantage*. Free Press: New York.

Porter M. (1996) What is strategy? *Harvard Business Review,* November/December, 61–78.

Porter, M.E. (1998) *The Competitive Advantage of Nations*. Free Press: New York.

Prahalad, C.K. and Hamel, G. (1990) The core competence of the corporation. *Harvard Business Review*, 68(3), 79–91.

Qian, G., Li, L., and Rugman, A.M. (2013) Liability of country foreignness and liability of regional foreignness: their effects on geographic diversification and firm performance. *Journal of International Business Studies*, 44(7), 635–647.

Rivkin, J. and Collis, D. (2008) Strategic renewal. Harvard Business School Publishing #708-503.

Rugman, A.M. (1981) *Inside the Multinationals: The Economics of Internal Markets*. Columbia University Press: New York.

Saloner, G., Shepard, A., and Podolny, J. (2001) *Strategic Management*. John Wiley & Sons, Inc.: New York.

Scott, J. (1982) Multimarket contact and economic performance. *Review of Economics and Statistics*, 64, 368–375.

Van den Steen, E. (2012) A theory of explicitly formulated strategy. Harvard Business School Working Paper, No. 12-102, May.

Vietor, R.H.K. (2007) *How Countries Compete: Strategy, Structure, and Government in the Global Economy*. Harvard Business School Press: Boston, MA.

Wernerfelt, B. (1984) A resource-based view of the firm. *Strategic Management Journal*, 5, 171–180.

Williamson, O. (1975) *Markets and Hierarchies: Analysis and antitrust implications*. Free Press: New York.

Williamson, O. (1985) *The Economic Institutions of Capitalism: Firms, Markets, Relational Contracting*. Free Press: New York.

Zaheer, S. (1995) Overcoming the liability of foreignness. *Academy of Management Journal*, 38(2), 341–363.

Conceptual Framework: What is Different about International Strategy?

If we answered the question of *why* the firm should extend its presence internationally, we now have to understand *how* the firm should extend its presence around the world. This is the domain of international strategy.

Part Two lays out the conceptual frameworks underpinning the book's treatment of international strategy. First, it introduces the **Rule of Four** to highlight the unique factors that arise when competition crosses borders, and so explains what is different between international and domestic strategy. It then introduces a set of **generic international strategies** that provide direction to the multinational and ensure the consistent alignment of every difficult choice such firms confront.

Since the firm itself does not change dramatically when it becomes multinational – no phase change occurs when it ventures outside its domestic market – why do we need international strategy as a separate discipline with a new set of concepts and analytical techniques? The answer is that when a firm enters a new country, whether to sell or locate activities, it has, for the first time, to balance the challenges with the advantages of integrating activity across differentiated markets. On the one hand, multinationals seek to capitalize on differences among markets to create value by arbitraging factor or product market differences and their variation over time. On the other hand, the presence of those differences throws doubt on the appropriateness of the original competitive advantage, and questions how to accommodate those market differences. It is this tension between the costs and benefits of operating across differentiated markets that is unique to multinationals.

Chapter 3 therefore highlights the vast **differences between countries** that make international strategy a study unto itself. The seemingly trivial fact that competition takes place across national borders is actually the crucial explanation of its distinctiveness. The chapter then observes that in a semi-globalized world, the considerable differences remaining between countries give salience to four strategic **decisions**: what product to offer and how much variation to allow around the world; in which countries to compete and how to allocate resources across geographies; what should be the global configuration and specific location of each activity; and how to structure and manage the multinational.

Chapter 4 identifies the **strategic tradeoffs** underlying each of those decisions that make their resolution so difficult. It then shows how pursuit of a single advantage brings coherence to those choices by providing a unifying objective around one of the four **international advantages** that multinationals can craft by virtue of their global footprint.

Chapter 5 lays out the set of generic international strategies, each of which pursues a unique international advantage. Chapter 6 suggests how firms can decide, given the underlying economics and conditions of their business, what is the best strategy for them to pursue. Although the international strategies described are archetypes rather than exact prescriptions for answering the four key decisions confronting multinationals, their default prescriptions offer the requisite direction to executives and ensure that everything the multinational does around the world is mutually reinforcing and internally consistent.

What is Distinctively International about International Strategy?

PRINCIPLES

If we accept the ubiquity and importance of international activity in the contemporary business world, it is still incumbent on an author of "international strategy" to explain what is different about international strategy – to define what is both distinctively international and uniquely strategic about the topic. This will establish that the ideas and frameworks introduced in the text are not addressed by other disciplines. Since this is achieved by identifying four characteristics of international strategy, each of which features four explanatory factors, I refer to the framework as the "Rule of Four."

This chapter highlights the first of the two factors that make international competition distinct from domestic competition – differences and decisions.

The Rule of Four

The distinctively international characteristics of international strategy arise when competition crosses national boundaries. Thus, they must derive from **differences** between countries either in current product or factor market conditions, or in the scale or rate of change of those conditions. I have identified four such fundamental differences.

But all such differences will be strategically irrelevant unless they require multinationals to alter aspects of the original domestic strategy. Thus, geographic heterogeneity must lead firms to reexamine certain **decisions** that drove their success within a single market. Many operational decisions can be delegated, and allowed to vary between countries because they can be locally optimized and readily altered. It is only decisions with long-lasting repercussions, and whose resolution affects other choices, that have to be made consistently around the world. It is these decisions that must be reexamined when the firm moves beyond the domestic market and confronts the need to both accommodate and exploit differentiated market conditions. I have identified four such strategic decisions.

Those decisions are particularly difficult to make because they involve **tradeoffs** between different competitive advantages and so cannot be answered on operational efficiency grounds alone. Multinationals must balance the advantages arising from differentiation between and integration across geographies, and each strategic decision reflects that tension in a unique way. I have identified four such underlying tradeoffs.

To align every decision and to resolve their tradeoffs in the internally consistent manner that is the hallmark of an effective strategy requires each choice to be made according to the underlying advantage that the firm seeks to exploit or create by virtue of its international activity. I have identified four such sources of **international advantage**.

While it would be tempting to link each of the four differences of international competition to a specific decision, which in turn raises a tradeoff that is answered by the underlying source of advantage (and believe me, I tried for years to do so!), I think that is stretching logic too far. There are overlaps in the linkages between factors which make that task impossible (Exhibit 3.1).

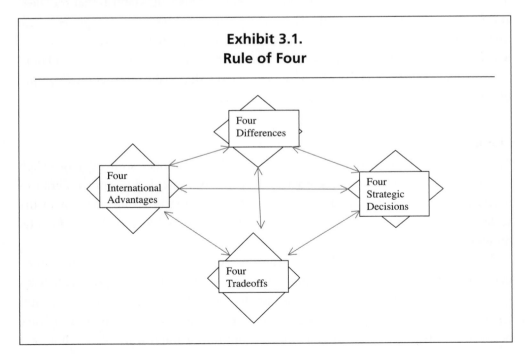

Exhibit 3.1.
Rule of Four

MOTIVATION

We are all familiar with the purple FedEx truck, and its guaranteed overnight delivery service that Tom Hanks so memorably made "absolutely, positively" sure to get to its recipient in the movie *Castaway*. And what could be more ubiquitous than a premium service delivering documents and small packages from anywhere to everywhere in the world? However, what superficially looks like the same FedEx truck going about the exact same task in Shanghai and San Francisco is, in fact, a very different operation.

The service in China is not even the same as the global version. FedEx is restricted by the government in its domestic Chinese operations. As a result, there are only a few cities from which FedEx can offer an intra-China delivery service. Thus, almost all its business in China is in and out of the country – imagine trying to make a US operation profitable without being able to offer intra-America service! Customer service levels are also very different. In the USA, a pickup and delivery driver is expected to be in and out of a location as quickly as possible. In contrast, drivers in China are allowed five minutes at each pickup in order to provide the assistance shippers expect in filling out the global shipping form.

While the location and appearance of its handling facilities are similar to those in developed countries, FedEx's actual operations in China are different. Local law prohibits FedEx from using the commercial vans that are familiar on the streets of Western cities. Instead, FedEx has to use converted passenger vehicles for ground operations in China. The level of automation in the facilities is substantially lower than in the USA since lower Chinese wage rates support a lower capital/labor ratio. Indeed, there are extraneous security personnel at the airport facility – part of, to put it politely, local political pressure to maintain certain employment levels.

Finally, until recently FedEx operated in China through a joint venture with a domestic logistics firm – an organization structure rarely employed by the company in the rest of the world. And yet, FedEx operates a global service to nearly every country in the world!

This example illustrates that when operations cross borders, no matter how "globally standardized" the product or service offering, a multinational has to confront fundamentally different local environments that call into question a set of decisions which are given when operating domestically. Within a single country it is usually possible to implement a business model in almost the same way. Yet internationally a firm has to somehow arrange every aspect of its operations to accommodate local conditions. How it does this, while maintaining an international advantage, is the fundamental challenge of international strategy.

DIFFERENCES IN INTERNATIONAL COMPETITION

Despite increasing convergence among the world's economies and cultures, huge differences between countries remain that are readily apparent to any international traveler. A list of those differences would begin with language and dialect (there are over 7,000 distinct languages in the world today, and yet the sixth most common language only has 183 million speakers, or 3.2% of the global population)[1], include food, humor, history, politics, and religion, and end up taking in just about every aspect of daily life.

There are many examples, some obvious, others more subtle, that illustrate these deep-seated phenomena. One of my favorites is the orange popsicle that is prominently advertised in French bars and cafés as "Zit" – a product that no self-respecting American would ever eat. Just to make the point, the product itself is called an ice lolly in England (and the US version of Word underlines lolly in red because it does not recognize that as a valid noun!).[2] The annoyance of having to carry a portfolio of adapters for different voltages and plug configurations is well known to business travelers. And so on . . . . Indeed I am sure every reader can plug in their own favorite example of incongruities and incompatibilities they have suffered abroad.

No schema has been found to categorize these overt differences in any systematic way. The list offered below is in no way a mutually exclusive and exhaustive typology, but is a pragmatic classification that readers can amend in ways they find valuable.

Product Market Heterogeneity
Consumer Taste and Culture

Perhaps the most obvious difference between countries is that consumers' tastes are as varied as the cultures they reflect (Exhibit 3.2). From food to fashion, and from holidays to housing, no aspect of daily life is untouched by local preference and interpretation. While each idiosyncratic variation might, by itself, seem to be of little consequence, variations cumulate and interact to create truly distinctive environments.

Mid-Westerners visiting Spain may be amazed to find that no restaurant opens for dinner before 9 p.m. – a time when many of them would be in bed. Asians are easily offended when their sense of personal space is invaded by Latins who approach too close or show appreciation in overtly physical ways. The subordinate role of women in the Middle East causes endless problems for European businesswomen active in those cultures. And so on.

Of course, global product categories from cola and burgers to bottled water and basketball shoes exist, and tastes are becoming more homogenized. We need look no further that the worldwide presence of Thai restaurants, the *Titanic* movie, Tom Cruise, and YouTube, to see how widespread cultural phenomena can become and how

Exhibit 3.2.
European Differences in Preferences for Tomato Soup

Country	Creamy vs Puree	Thick vs Liquid	Smooth vs Pulp	Sour vs Sweet	Dark vs Light Color	Herb impact
Austria	creamy	thick	smooth	sweet	dark	medium, Italian
Bulgaria	creamy	liquid	smooth	sour	dark	medium
Denmark	creamy	thick	smooth	sour	light	herbs, fruity
France	puree	liquid	smooth	sweet	light	medium, Italian
Germany	puree	thick	pulpy	sour	dark	medium, Italian
Hungary	creamy	liquid	smooth	sour	dark	Italian
Italy	puree	liquid	pulpy	sour	light	
Poland	creamy	liquid	smooth	sour	light	Italian
Russia	creamy	liquid	smooth	sour	dark	Italian
Spain	puree	liquid	smooth	sour	dark	
Sweden	creamy	thick	smooth	sweet	light	mild notes
Switzerland	puree	liquid	smooth	sour	light	
UK	puree	liquid	smooth	sour	dark	

Source: Adapted from an Exhibit in HBS case # 713-418

differences between cultures have narrowed enormously over time. I remember being struck during a visit to the old Imperial Palace in Kyoto, Japan, that recreates the visit of a foreigner to the Imperial Court at the end of the nineteenth century, how different Japan was from the West in 1900 – the court still wore traditional costumes, floors were designed to creak so that intruders could be heard, guards armed with samurai swords stood behind concealed doors, visitors had to remove their shoes, and so on. And yet I had just come from days of meetings with Japanese businessmen distinguishable from their Western counterparts only by their language and by their smoking.

Commonalities are, however, more typical in some products and for some customer groups. Youth culture is more global than the tastes and preferences of older generations. High-income consumers around the world are more similar in their tastes than lower income consumers. Is it any wonder that the brands which are quoted as exemplars of global homogenization – Rolex watches, Levi jeans, and Coca-Cola – cost multiples of the local equivalent? Or that the diet of the working classes varies far more between countries than the menus at the most fashionable and expensive restaurants – all perhaps featuring "molecular" cuisine.

Commonalities in consumer demands are closer among countries that share historical similarities. English-speaking countries share many traits and foibles. Countries with a similar geography are also alike. Chile, New Zealand, and South Africa share roughly the same latitude. They are all wine exporters of note, they all grow kiwi fruit, and Chile even prides itself on being the "England of South America," a claim that South Africa could make with respect to the African continent, and that New Zealand might – with Australia – make for South East Asia.

Nevertheless, intrinsic differences among countries abound because culture is so deep rooted and systemic. The common memory, which constitutes a culture, is made up from the cumulative vagaries of a country's history, climate, geography, language, politics, etc. Their joint development depends on every element of culture at each point in time, so that the resulting evolution is what economists term "path dependent" – it can only be duplicated by complete repetition of the entire preceding history (Arthur, 1994). As a result, even when the exact same phenomenon, such as the Kardashians, hits different countries, its impact varies because the context in which it is interpreted is different. Thus, even as the world becomes exposed to many more common phenomena, the all-embracing nature of cultures up to that point in time will maintain substantial differences among countries.

It is hard to quantify many of the differences described above. Nor is there any useful metric of cultural variety. We can find some ad hoc measures such as the number of religions in the world today (Exhibit 3.3). Perhaps all we need to do is to refer to these select examples and argue that because those differences are substantial and yet constitute only a fraction of the entire set, any aggregate measure of heterogeneity would indeed be enormous.

Factor Market Heterogeneity

Business Infrastructure

The business infrastructure includes all the logistical elements involved in carrying out activities within a country from the voltage of the electrical system and the density of the railway network to the physical structure of the retailing environment. Differences on these dimensions are not only trivial, like having to build transformers into electrical and electronic equipment for voltage conversion or adopting the local standard for paper size, but also more substantive, such as when distribution goes through power retailers, like Walmart and Home Depot, rather than traditional Japanese mom and pop stores, and when earthquake construction codes only affect building design in some countries.

Importantly, these differences not only affect factor markets, but also carry over to attributes perceived by customers. The order processing and credit verification system for a country where power retailers are the major channel of distribution will look very different than a system designed for a plethora of small mom and pop operations.

Exhibit 3.3.
Atlas of Faiths

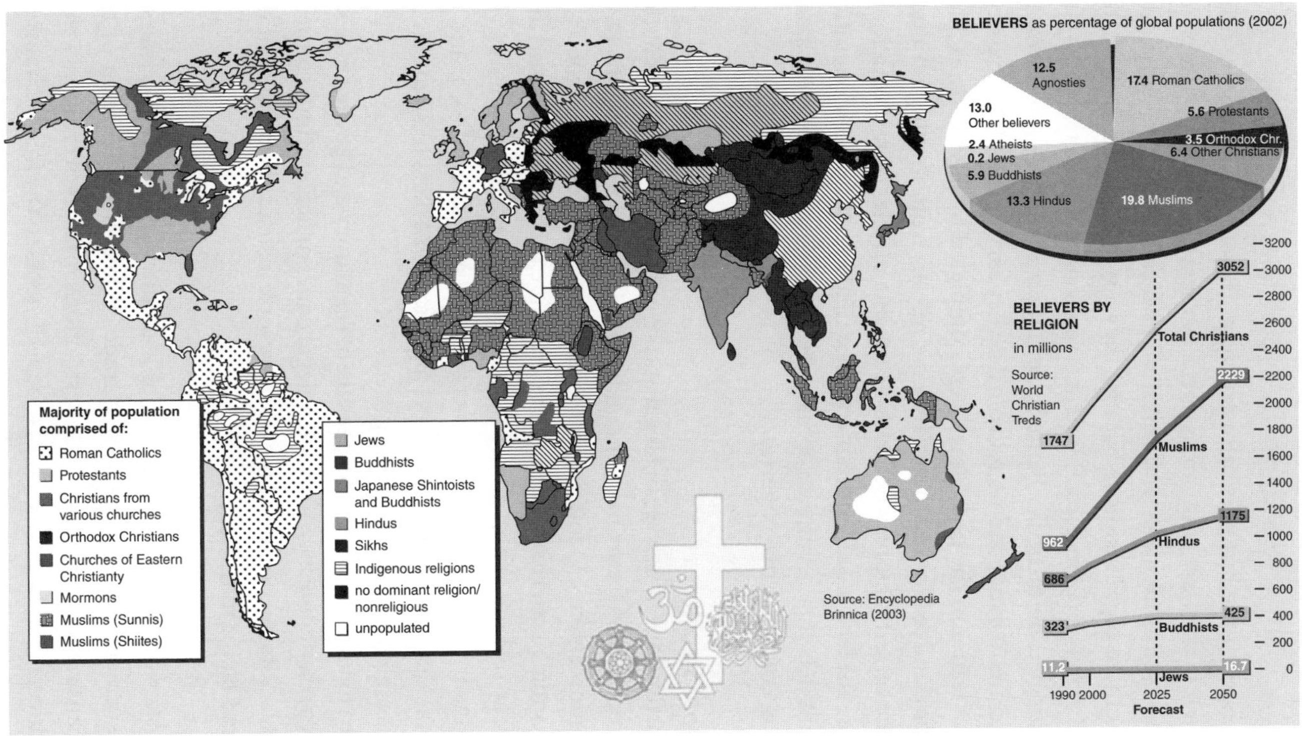

BELIEVERS as percentage of global populations (2002)

17.4 Roman Catholics
5.6 Protestants
3.5 Orthodox Chr.
6.4 Other Christians
19.8 Muslims
13.3 Hindus
5.9 Buddhists
0.2 Jews
2.4 Atheists
13.0 Other believers
12.5 Agnostics

BELIEVERS BY RELIGION
in millions

Source:
World
Christian
Treds

Total Christians   3052   2229   1747
Muslims   1175   952
Hindus   686
Buddhists   425   323
Jews   187   172

Forecast   1990 2000   2025   2050

Source: Encyclopedia Britannica (2003)

Majority of population comprised of:
- Roman Catholics
- Protestants
- Christians from various churches
- Orthodox Christians
- Churches of Eastern Christianty
- Mormons
- Muslims (Sunnis)
- Muslims (Shiites)
- Jews
- Buddhists
- Japanese Shintoists and Buddhists
- Hindus
- Sikhs
- Indigenous religions
- no dominant religion/ nonreligious
- unpopulated

Relying on a remote centralized service operation might be inappropriate in a country where the telephone system, let alone the interactive broadband highway, is poor or non-existent.

Differences in the business infrastructure, therefore, can require just as profound an alteration in the ways companies operate across various countries as more apparent differences in customer taste and culture. The fact that they are less immediately obvious makes them more insidious because they are unexpected. DeRemate, the original copy of eBay in Latin America, found that replicating the auction site was the easy part of the strategy. The difficulty came in settling transactions in economies where few people had credit cards and no reliable delivery service, like UPS, existed. Instead the majority of trades in the early years were completed by physically exchanging money for the item! Indeed, many manufacturers refrain from moving production offshore because the infrastructure, whether it be reliable utilities, transportation and communication, or the lack of skilled technicians, is inadequate for their operations. Similarly, business models that require a sophisticated infrastructure, like Amazon, will simply not work in countries like Nigeria.

Institutional Structures

It is the institutions which set the legal and regulatory structure of a nation that create unique product and factor market conditions. Rules and regulations (and the accompanying enforcement capabilities) governing the operation of the goods, capital, labor, and intellectual property markets both determine their efficiency, and the market failures and rent-seeking opportunities that drive firm strategies and FSAs.[3] Indeed strong domestic institutions support the emergence of successful MNCs, and those institutions interact and co-evolve with firms and factor markets to shape a country's competitiveness (He and Lin, 2012; Peng *et al.*, 2009).

It is hard to identify any single measure of regulatory and governance structures. We can find representative metrics, such as legal codes or accounting regimes (Ghemawat, 2011), but lacking an aggregate measure we look instead at examples of their effects in product and factor markets.

Product Market   One consequence of a country's institutional framework comes from government interference in free trade. Whether in the form of tariff barriers, import licensing, or non-tariff trade restrictions, many governments choose to favor local producers over imported goods. Impediments to the free exchange of goods also exist in the form of bribery and physical intimidation, and the absence of cash that adds friction. Their influence is obvious since they limit the ability of foreign firms to compete on an equal footing.

Several interesting contemporary institutional examples fall under the environmental rubric. One of the key drivers of the adoption rate of LED lighting is legislation outlawing sales of traditional incandescent light bulbs. In the USA, Congress has gone back and forth on the idea. In Europe, in contrast, incandescents were to be effectively phased out by 2012. In fact, the most extensive use of LED lighting is in China, where the engineer-run Communist Party is mandating its adoption in all new infrastructure projects. Laws on emissions by ships (responsible for about 3% of global carbon dioxide emissions) to reduce the sulfur content of their fuel from the current 1.5% of low-grade bunker fuel to 0.5% by 2020 are about to change the design of container vessels so that they might feature liquid natural gas as fuel, or possibly even a return to sail!

Capital Markets   In Western economies we are accustomed to, if not inculcated with a belief in, the efficiency of capital markets. Whereas the focus of this hysteria has been on the efficiency of asset pricing, for our purposes the important dimensions of efficiency concern the availability and cost of capital. In particular, in developed economies, inefficiencies due to the absolute size of capital requirements are not believed to exist. Any project, whether a nuclear power station or an individual entrepreneur's dream, is supposed to find appropriately priced funding. In contrast, in developing countries, access to capital may be a huge deterrent to economic activity. The emergence of microfinance initiatives in developing countries only illustrates how most inhabitants of the globe have limited access to even the small amount of capital necessary to buy a sewing machine or a cow. When such conditions exist for at least half the world's population, it is easy to see how preferential access to capital, whether from nepotism, bribery, or explicit government policy, can be a valuable source of rents and an important determinant of firm strategy and industry structure. The existence of family-run groups in emerging markets can, for example, be partly attributed to this market failure (Khanna and Yafeh, 2007).

Labor Market   Labor market inefficiencies arise when there are social or legal impediments to the free movement of people that produce shortages or surpluses of particular skills or occupations. In developing countries, for example, there is believed to be a deficiency in the supply of well-trained managers. As a result, companies internalize the labor market – training their own employees, providing career paths inside the firm, and leveraging this scarce resource to enter a range of otherwise unrelated businesses. Other inefficiencies arise when adequate affordable housing is unavailable in labor-short locations, such as urban areas of China today, or when a government does not provide basic literacy education for its population. In contrast, regional concentrations, such as software engineers in Silicon Valley and animators in Hollywood, can create a self-generating pool of highly skilled workers.

One interesting example is the role of women in the workforce. In many Muslim and Asian countries, women play a limited part in employment – though not in all countries: Malaysia features a nearly 50% female workforce participation rate. Much of this is driven by women in those cultures choosing not to have careers, but some is due to overt discrimination and/or practices that restrict opportunities for women in the workforce. If it is the case that such discrimination exists in domestic firms, multinationals that either choose not to discriminate, or are prohibited from such behavior by legislation in their home country, should be able to exploit the inefficiency by hiring talented women at lower wages. Indeed, this is exactly what Jordan Siegel found in Korea (Siegel *et al.*, 2013).

Intellectual Property   The institutional regime that governs intellectual property can have a dramatic influence on competition. In the pharmaceutical industry, for example, patent laws vary enormously between countries. In some nations, patents are granted for a period of time after the drug first reaches the market. In other countries, products are patent protected from the date of discovery of the compound. In yet other countries, products are not patent protected at all. The best that pharmaceutical manufacturers might hope for in those locations is that the production process has some degree of patent protection. Even here, however, laws governing manufacturing drugs vary enormously, from stringent requirements for the licensing of any new production process to no oversight of facilities. The result is enormous variation in the quality and prices of the same pharmaceutical around the world, and in the structure of the industry in different countries.

In other cases it is the lack of protection that is a concern. China is notorious for the absence of laws concerning the enforcement of intellectual copyright. While improving, horror stories abound in this regard. Microsoft once estimated that it was missing 95% of the revenue it should be receiving from that country given the number of Windows programs installed in computers there (Khannah and Choudhury, 2008). Apple has similarly suffered from a spate of fake Apple retail stores. And Google even felt obliged to exit China because the Chinese government demanded access to accounts that Google felt was inconsistent with its protection of individual rights. Similarly, Twitter is not officially available in China because it refuses to comply with mandated censorship.

Firm Goals

Even the objective function of companies can differ between countries. To some extent such variation reflects underlying differences in the institutions governing the factor markets mentioned above – the ability of firms to pursue objectives other than pure profit maximization, for example, is contingent on a freedom permitted by their governance structure and the capital markets. To some extent the differences reflect underlying differences in culture – the 300-year time horizon adopted by certain Japanese firms, for example, is probably matched by a similarly low household discount rate. But the differences are so profound that they deserve separate mention.

In the Anglo-American capitalist system, firm objectives lie with shareholders and capital markets seeking the short-term maximization of profits. While observers may quibble with the precise definition of short term, and debate whether the USA or the UK is the most "short-termist," any differences between them are minor when compared to the Asian system. In Japan, South Korea, Taiwan, and the Chinese enterprises based in Hong Kong and Singapore, the primary objective has been long-term survival and prosperity. Whether the Continental European system lies between these two extremes can be debated. Certainly the system of worker co-determination must influence the firm's objective function, as does the bank-centered, rather than market-centered, approach to capital funding.

The classic interpretation of the difference in objective functions is that US firms maximize current return on investment (ROI), whereas Asian companies maximize long-term market share. This was used as the explanation for the relative performance of the USA and Japan in many industries, like machine tools, toward the end of the twentieth century. Owned by conglomerates, which allocated capital and incentivized divisional management on the basis of ROI, or by private equity, US machine tool manufacturers, such as Burgmaster and Bridgeport, by default gradually withdrew from the business after adopting a strategy of premium prices and limited investment. In contrast, Japanese manufacturers, such as Yamazaki and Mori Seiki, were prepared to invest at low rates of return for decades to build the sizable US market shares they saw as critical to their long-term strategy (Holland, 1989).

A deeper cultural explanation of the difference, once shared with me by a seasoned Japanese executive, harks back to the agricultural bases of the two economies. The USA, he said, had a history of "slash and burn" agriculture backstopped by vast untapped Western territories. Farmers could overexploit a region, confident that they could "go West" to settle virgin land. This produced a business mentality of short-term maximization and a willingness to exit businesses, secure in the belief that there would always be somewhere else to move to. In contrast, Japanese rice farmers always lived with the knowledge that the Japanese islands contained only a finite amount of arable acreage and so pursued a policy of intensive agriculture to continuously improve each parcel of land. Such a heritage, the executive argued, carried over into the philosophy of industrial enterprises and created the Toyota Production System of continuous improvement and the 300-year planning horizon of NEC.

Whether such explanations are true is less important than that they do reflect perceived differences in the ways that companies from different countries compete. Any multinational has to recognize that the strategies of its foreign competitors will not be the same as those of domestic competitors.

Firm Resources

The particular capabilities of firms that emerge within a country will be shaped by all the other factors mentioned above. Thus, different FSAs will arise from countries with different CSAs as domestic firms develop strategies to take advantage of their specific local opportunities. Firm and country characteristics therefore interact.

In the first place, the complete set of resources – physical, financial, intellectual, and organizational – available to firms in their home country differs. India, for example, is recognized as a source of low-cost computer programmers because of a surplus of well-trained, English speaking, technical university graduates. Less well known is that Ukraine also has an abundance of skilled computer programmers. The UK, which has a 50-year tradition of high-quality television programming at the BBC, is now a major source of talent for independent television production. And so on.

Second, to capitalize on favorable domestic factor market conditions and capture the rents available from inefficiencies and failures in those markets, firms develop distinctive capabilities. Today, India is claiming that indigenous firms are skilled at "jugaad" because their need to get by with inadequate resources while selling to low-income consumers has made them masters of "making do." Similarly, observers point to the dabbawalas of Mumbai, who deliver 130,000 lunches a day with six-sigma accuracy while using no technology, as an example of a unique combination of process and culture emerging as a response to that country's circumstances (Thomke, 2012).

The list of factors outlined above is not definitive. In fact, such categories overlap, and astute readers will have noted factor market phenomena appearing in multiple places. The co-evolution of all these factors makes sorting out their relative importance or attributing causal effects too ambitious. We merely note their complex interrelationships, and acknowledge how profound national differences are in product and factor markets.

Volatility

National differences are not only large, but also **unpredictable**. The heterogeneity noted above was a description of cross-sectional differences – and yet any differences we observe today will not be the same tomorrow. There are longitudinal changes that alter differences between countries in uncertain and yet substantive ways. As a result, multinationals face considerably more volatility than companies which only compete

Table 3.1 Variance Among Countries

Magnitude		Large	HEDGE	VOLATILE
		Small	STABLE	IGNORE
			High	Low

Predictability (inverse of uncertainty)

domestically. As the CFO of Yum Brands observed, "given how volatile the global markets have been, it's really difficult to forecast things" (quoted in Schoenberger and Hong, 2012).

Volatility covers two dimensions of change in phenomena such as exchange rates and GDP growth rates and the adoption rate of product and process innovations – the **magnitude** and **predictability** of their variation (Table 3.1).

Consider, for example, inflation rates. The variation over time within one country can be small: in the USA over the last 15 years, the average change in annual inflation has been less than 1%; or large: in Latvia over the last 10 years, annual inflation has fluctuated between minus 1.2% and plus 15.3%. Similarly, the predictability of that change ranges from low to high. The consensus analyst forecast for next year's growth rate in the USA is usually accurate to within 0.5%. In contrast, there is real uncertainty about whether growth in Vietnam will be 3% or 9%.

If variability in the measure is small and predictable, we are in a stable environment where today's differences will be the same tomorrow. If the variability is large but predictable, firms can typically hedge that uncertainty at relatively low cost. If, for example, it is broadly agreed that the Swiss franc will appreciate at 6% pa against the US dollar for the next two years, firms can offset the change with an appropriate financial hedge. If the variability is limited, even if it is unpredictable, we can safely ignore its influence on competition as its effect will be small. It is, therefore, only large and unpredictable variations in economically important variables that we need be concerned with, and such strategically relevant volatility between countries occurs in three domains: economic, technological, and political.

Economic

The most obvious source of volatility in international competition is the consequence of economic conditions differing among countries. When we see exchange rate shifts of 20% within a day, or the rapid deterioration in economic performance that compels fundamental alterations in macroeconomic policies, as recently in Spain, Greece, and

Cyprus, it is obvious we are faced with economic uncertainty. Nation states setting policies for reasons internal to their own economies and politics will always pursue some degree of uncoordinated actions. Until we have entities that determine economic policies on a level higher than the nation state – like the European Central Bank and the euro – we will always have economic volatility between countries.

The US trade-weighted exchange rate, for example, has shifted by more than 7% within the year in 9 of the last 24 years, and by more than 10% in 3 of those years. There are very few companies that can improve overall productivity by more than 7% in a year, and yet that is the effect that exchange rate volatility has had on US firms' costs in more than one of every three years. Clearly, the shift against single currencies within a year has been much more dramatic – the Thai baht, for example, devalued by 17% in one day in 1997, and Japan has seen a 25% yen devaluation against the dollar in the six months from November 2012 to May 2013. That uncertainty takes its toll. CEO Ian Cook, noting the threat posed to Colgate's earnings by the speed of the change in foreign exchange rates, observed, "You can't just go to the market on Monday morning and take your prices up with the retailer, never mind the competitor comparison" (Schoenberger and Hong, 2012). Studies in the auto industry, for example, suggest that only about 40–50% of exchange rate movements are passed through in price changes (Copeland and Kahn, 2012).

Interest rates exhibit even greater volatility. The simple average of the domestic interest rates of the largest 25 economies in the world regularly varies by more than 20% each year, and can vary by as much as several hundred percent. Indeed, since 2008 interest rates in all advanced economies have halved from over 4% to less than 2%.

Technological

It is often argued that the pace of technological change is accelerating. The introduction of digital technologies, and the emergence of the Internet and the broadband interactive superhighway are supposed to be giving birth to the New Economy – a third Industrial Revolution – and the development of an infrastructure that will have as revolutionary an impact on business as railways, the telegraph, and electricity did in their time. While this is debatable, it is clear that we have seen many radical technological innovations in the last 20 years, from the PC and DVDs to fuel cells and wind turbines. What concerns us, however, is not the absolute speed of technological change, but the unpredictability of that technical change between countries.

Different factor costs, tastes, culture, business infrastructure – all the sources of market heterogeneity we discussed above – lead to substantive differences in the direction and pace of technical change across countries. The rate of adoption of numerically controlled machine tools, the success of Internet banking, and the appeal of the new Fiat 500, for example, all vary between countries.

France led the world in interactive television with the government support of Minitel, but this, in turn, slowed adoption of the Internet. Penetration of mobile phones in the USA initially lagged some other markets because of conflict over the choice of a new technological standard. In Europe, where agreement to use GSM was reached easily and early, adoption was more rapid. One of the more interesting examples is that the most rapid adopter of mobile payment technology has not been the USA or Germany, but Kenya, where more than two-thirds of adults use money transfer by mobile phone (M-PESA), and one-quarter of GDP flows through the system (*The Economist,* 2013; Quelch and Jocz, 2012)!

Uncertainty refers to both product and process technology – to demand side and supply side shocks. On the demand side, sudden jumps in consumer demand for smart phones, or the emergence and equally rapid disappearance of the Pokemon craze, can be thought of as technological volatility. On the supply side, the development of CSP chips, fuzzy logic, and laser welding are all innovations that have been adopted with greater or lesser speed in different countries.

Political

Political changes have, in the last 25 years, altered the geopolitical landscape beyond recognition. The fall of the Iron Curtain and the breakup of the Soviet Union, through the liberalization of developing countries, like India and China, to the end of dynasties and dictators in the Arab Spring, remind us of the enormous political risk involved in international competition. The fate of countries like Sudan, Somalia, the Congo and Yugoslavia only reinforces the lesson.

In spite of pundits and consulting firms, to say nothing of the exorbitantly expensive efforts of the world's security agencies, it has proven next to impossible to predict political unrest, even at the grossest level of coups and government changes. Even predicting election outcomes within a stable country, like the UK, is difficult. Thus, we have to recognize that competing internationally brings enormous political uncertainty.

It is impossible to create a single measure of political volatility. One illustration is that the average duration of a regime in a democratic country is 12 years, a semi-democratic country 12 years, and an authoritarian regime 8 years.[4] These numbers imply that, on average, each year there will be about 20 regime changes around the world.

All these suggest that the unpredictability of international competition inevitably brings additional strains and complexity to the multinational organization.

Scale

The size of firms that compete internationally can be orders of magnitude larger than their domestic competitors. Even the world's largest economy, the USA, accounts only for 20% of global GDP, the top 10 countries 65%, so that broadening a firm's domain beyond national boundaries allows for the exploitation of scale economies and cumulative experience that are infeasible in a single market.

At the company level, world market shares are relatively fragmented, and in many cases declining. In pharmaceuticals the world's largest company, Pfizer, accounts for less than 10% of total industry output. The top 10 firms together do not make up half of world output. Even industries that typically come to mind as global are not highly concentrated. GM has only a 12% world market share. The top 10 auto manufacturers together account for less than two-thirds of world demand.[5] In semiconductors, Intel has a value market share of world production of 16%, but the top 20 manufacturers still only account for less than two-thirds of total output.[6] All of these numbers illustrate the potential scale that remains to be exploited by companies if they can replicate their domestic market shares (e.g., GM 29%), internationally.

But numbers on the shares of world production do not capture all the limitations facing firms that do not compete internationally. The distribution of patent filings demonstrates that innovation is spread around the world. Of the half-million patents filed in the USA each year, more than half now come from outside the country. Moreover, the sources of invention are becoming more geographically dispersed over time. The percentage of US patents granted to foreign individuals or companies has risen from below 40% over the last 30 years.[7]

Similarly, the distribution of the country of origin of the world's top consumer brands illustrates that no one country has a monopoly on creativity and marketing. In 2011 the top 50 brands in the world came from 12 different countries, with US brands only just making up half.[8] Of the world's top advertising agencies, as many come from the UK, France, and Japan as from the USA.

To achieve global scale now requires multinationals to compete in even more countries than before, and this increases their exposure to country heterogeneity. The number of countries that together constitute 90% of world GDP has increased from 21 in 1966 to 38 by 2012. More importantly, the absolute number of countries with annual consumption over $100 billion (in 1987 dollars) has risen from 8 in 1966, to more than 50 by 2012. Indeed, over the last 30 years the list of the largest 25 economies in the world has included, for the first time, countries as diverse as Iran, Indonesia, and South Korea. No longer can a UK firm operate in the comfort of the Commonwealth and expect to be at an efficient global scale.

WHY DO BORDERS MATTER?

It is only fair to acknowledge that there are profound differences *within* countries as well as between countries. Regions within the UK have their own dialects, as an English person listening with difficulty to a Scottish accent can assert. The influence of Hispanics in New England has been much less visible than in Miami. Regional differences like these abound, even within seemingly homogeneous countries like France and Chile. As a result, product and factor market differences do not correlate with national boundaries, and companies recognize this. Campbell's, for example, flavors its soups differently to accommodate regional tastes, with more salt used in the US Southwest than elsewhere. McDonald's allows its fast food outlets to offer regional items, such as a lobster roll during the summer in New England.

This begs the question of why the set of differences described above affect competition across countries, while still noticeable differences within countries do not have profound implications for competition. Why is inter-country competition fundamentally different from intra-country competition?

The answer is relatively straightforward. First, differences do occur within countries as the advocates of regional devolution in Spain, UK, and Italy would argue, but such differences are less substantive than those occurring across borders. The question of heterogeneity is really one of magnification. When examining a small part of a region within one country at very high magnification, there might appear to be much heterogeneity, but as the perspective zooms out those differences begin to disappear. When the magnification is set to take in the entire globe, the only visible heterogeneity is between countries.

In fact, differences that occur within a single country become only a **matter of degree** at the global level of magnification. In particular, as we will see in Chapter 6, adaptations to domestic differences do not incur dramatic penalties, and therefore do not rise to the level of strategic tradeoffs but remain as questions of operational efficiency. The example of salt in Campbell's soup makes the point. In the Southwest consumers prefer more spice and zest in their food. However, extra salt can easily be added to soup made for the Southwest. Campbell's does not need a discrete production facility, or even production line for that product. It can be sold through exactly the same channels of distribution, under the same brand, and with the same national advertising campaign as in New England.

It is when the magnification is adjusted to show only strategically relevant differences that we see how critical national borders become. In spite of seemingly contradictory moves to the extremes of regional devolution (as in the UK and Spain) and regional integration (as in the eurozone), it is the **nation state** that still plays the most significant role in establishing the institutional structures described earlier. Emerging after the Treaty of Westphalia in 1648, the nation state as a sovereign entity is traditionally defined by two characteristics: a distinctive cultural or ethnic population; and a unified political entity.

The first characteristic, as the representative of a **distinct population or community,** becomes a shorthand representation of commonalities across all the complexities of heritage, culture, ethnicity, religion, race, etc. In fact the overlap between country and self-identified nationality varies between 99% in Japan (that is to say, 99% of the population of Japan are ethnic Japanese and 99% of all Japanese live in Japan) and the United Arab Emirates where 84% of the population were expatriates in 2012 and only about were 12% ethnic emiris.[9] Nevertheless, to the extent that one of the profound causes of differences around the world is deep-seated cultural attitudes, the nation state becomes (an inadequate) mapping of those underlying phenomena.

The second defining characteristic of a nation state is political sovereignty and the establishment of a **common legal jurisdiction and state apparatus** within a country's boundaries. The existence of this shared political entity leads to a common institutional structure – of legal system, government bureaucracy, etc., within a country. It is that structure which we saw as a key driver of market differences around the world.

Substantive differences therefore lie between countries rather than within countries. If wage rates and taxes are lower in Texas than in Ohio, it is operationally efficient to relocate plants to the US South. In contrast, building a plant in Indonesia because it currently has the lowest wages among all countries with a certain minimum level of infrastructure might be extremely shortsighted. Within a few years the country might be in the midst of political turmoil, wages could have risen, or foreign companies expropriated.

CRITICAL DECISIONS

These effects of venturing beyond one's own nation state mean that any long-lived commitments have to be viewed very differently when undertaken across borders. In particular, four decisions become critical to a firm's success as it becomes multinational.

What Product?

In domestic competition a firm typically develops a product and market positioning that is appropriate for the entire country. It might be that the strategy is initially implemented in one region – as, for example, was Southwest Airlines' low-cost, short-haul, point-to-point domestic airline strategy – but the same strategy can be rolled out to the rest of the country. In contrast, in international competition, a product that sells well in one country might be rejected in another country.

Europeans prefer front-loading washing machines that are energy and water efficient but less durable than the US-preferred top loaders. The content of chocolate in Europe is, at minimum, 20% cocoa solids and often as high as 40%, whereas in the USA cocoa solids often account for only 10% of chocolate.[10] The flavor of Nescafé, Nestlé's global brand of instant coffee, differs around the world. Paper sizes differ around the world.

Should a firm, therefore, offer a uniform product around the world, or should it adapt the product offering to the specific needs of different markets? This first strategic decision confronting multinationals can be summarized as the choice between **one product or many products**. With a broad definition of "product" that includes all the marketing Ps – Positioning, Promotion, Place, Price – how standardized will be the global product? How much local variation will be allowed?

To answer this and, as we will see, the other critical decisions, we need to know the advantages accruing to each choice and the tradeoffs between them. Here we merely note that product choice reflects the tension between pursuing the advantages of global simplicity and efficiency, and those of local adaptation and responsiveness which have been at the heart of international business since the 1960s.

Where to Locate?

The second strategic decision arises when multinationals configure their global footprint and can be summarized as whether to locate each of their activities in **one location or in many locations** (and in which specific countries). Given that factor market conditions vary between countries, whether in terms of wage rates, tax rates, infrastructure availability, supply of advanced factors of production, etc., where a multinational chooses to locate its activities, and even whether it seeks to arbitrage those factor market differences, has a profound impact on performance.

While many activities, such as selling, are immobile because they have to be conducted within the final market, many others are footloose and offer the multinational a choice of location. Simplistically then, should a firm place its manufacturing in the one, currently low-cost country, or should it distribute those facilities across a number of countries in order to diversify risk and exploit the option value of multiple locations? Again, this statement of the choice (and the associated question of which is the single best location) hints at the strategic advantages and tradeoffs which are addressed in the next chapter.

Which Country?

When a firm extends its domain from the domestic to the global arena, it can exploit a new dimension of scale. The important decision in this regard concerns the scope of the multinational – should it compete in **one market or many markets**? While increased scope trivially allows the multinational to exploit scale economies, it also allows the skillfully managed company to capitalize on the intrinsic variation among countries. However, competing in more countries exposes multinationals to increased market heterogeneity.

Heterogeneity exacerbates the complexity of international management when simple things, like hours of operation, rise from the 8-hour work day to the 24-hour operations of a truly global organization, and when the number of languages in which executives are expected to be fluent reaches three in many European multinationals. In particular, the number of linkages between countries $[(n) \times (n - 1)/2]$ increases geometrically with the number of countries (n). If a firm expands its activities from five to just six countries, it therefore has 50% more exchange rates to monitor, 50% more interactions among country executives to manage, and 50% more trade routes to control. From this it is easy to see a tradeoff between expanding geographic scope and the managerial demands of increased market heterogeneity. Perhaps it is better to forgo the benefits of global scale for the simplicity of competing in fewer, more similar countries?

How to Organize?

Doing business across borders creates fluctuations and uncertainties that purely domestic companies do not face. It also adds the geographic dimension of heterogeneity to the challenge of integrating differentiated units. This raises the fourth strategic decision – how to organize international activities to effectively manage a set of geographically dispersed operations in a volatile environment.

To design the requisite administrative context requires a sophisticated application of organization tools beyond just boxes on the organization chart, to include personnel, resource allocation, management information systems, reward and incentive systems and processes, and so on. However, we can characterize the choice as between having a single global business unit or many geographic subsidiaries – between **one organizational unit or many organizational units**.

Even in domestic companies there is a tension between specializing units by function and integrating activities by product. Geography triples the interactions among

Table 3.2 Distinctive Characteristics of International Competition			
Differences			**Decisions**
Product market heterogeneity	→	PRODUCT	one or many products?
Factor market heterogeneity	→	LOCATE	one or many locations?
Scale potential	→	COMPETE	one or many countries?
Volatility and unpredictability	→	ORGANIZE	one or many units?

organizational units that have to be controlled and managed. A unified structure may be good at coordinating common activities across products and geographies but fails to optimize for those dimensions. In contrast, multiple discrete units have the benefit of clear accountability but at the expense of duplication of activities across those specialized units.

CONCLUSION

We started from an observation that countries differ on a whole host of dimensions: some obvious, others less visible; some trivial, others consequential. These differences affect many aspects of competition but we chose to represent them in four categories: **heterogeneous product markets** and **heterogeneous factor markets**; the increase in potential **scale** of activity; and the substantial **volatility and unpredictability** between countries.

Each of these differences suggests one of the fundamental strategic decisions that all firms facing international competition must resolve (Table 3.2), and which together create the strategic challenge facing the multinational.

Every multinational will have wrestled with these four thorny decisions. I am sure many readers can provide their own examples of tough debates on these questions – which, I suspect, rarely concluded to your satisfaction! But why cannot these decisions be easily resolved? And why do they reappear over and over again in every multinational? That discussion is the subject of the next chapter which demonstrates what is uniquely strategic about international competition.

NOTES

1. Ethnologue, Languages of the World, accessed at http://www.ethnologue.com/world.
2. Word also highlights the spelling traveller as incorrect!
3. Morgan, G., Campbell, J., Crouch, C., Pedersen, O., and Whitley, R. (2012) *Oxford Handbook of Comparative Institutional Analysis.* Oxford University Press: Oxford. Tarun Khanna, for example, makes

much of these differences in explaining international differences in the structure of industrial organization within countries (Khanna, T. and Palepu, K. (2011) Winning in emerging markets: spotting and responding to institutional voids. *World Financial Review,* May–June, 18–20).

4. Mundt, R. J. Is democracy stable? Compared to what? A preliminary exploration, accessed at http://www.stier.net/writing/demstab/stability.htm.

5. Organisation Internationale des Constructeurs D'Automobiles (2012) Production statistics, accessed at http://www.oica.net/category/production-statistics/.

6. HIS isuppli, Market research semiconductor rankings, accessed at http://www.isuppli.com/Semiconductor-Value-Chain/News/pages/Fourth-Quarter-Reprieve-Brings-Little-Relief-to-Semiconductor-Makers-in-2012-but-Spurs-2013-Rebound.aspx.

7. World Intellectual Property Organisation, reported in *The Economist,* January 5, 2013, p. 52.

8. Brandirectory, Ranking the world's most valuable brands, accessed at http://brandirectory.com/league_tables/table/global-500-2012.

9. United Arab Emirates, accessed at http://www.worldstatesmen.org/United_Arab_Emirates.html.

10. As reported in Pusuer, E. (2009) The great transatlantic chocolate divide. BBC News, December 15, accessed at http://news.bbc.co.uk/2/hi/uk_news/magazine/8414488.stm.

REFERENCES AND FURTHER READING

Acemoglu, D. and Johnson, S. (2005) Unbundling institutions. *Journal of Political Economy,* 113(5), 949–995.

Arthur, W. (1994) *Increasing Returns and Path Dependence in the Economy.* University of Michigan Press: Ann Arbor, MI.

Bloom, N., Genakos, C., Sadun, R., and Van Reenen, J. (2012) Management practices across firms and countries. *Academy of Management Perspectives,* 24(1), 203–224.

Cantwell, J., Dunning, J.H., and Lundan, S.M. (2010) An evolutionary approach to understanding international business activity: the co-evolution of MNEs and the institutional environment. *Journal of International Business Studies,* 41(4), 567–586.

Copeland, A. and Kahn, J. (2012) Exchange rate pass-through, markups, and inventories. Federal Reserve Bank of New York, Staff Report No. 584, December.

Ghemawat, P. (2011) The globalization of firms. IESE Globalization Note Series.

Hall, P.A. and Soskice, D. (2001) An introduction to varieties of capitalism. In P.A. Hall and D. Soskice (eds.) *Varieties of Capitalism: The Institutional Foundations of Comparative Advantage.* Oxford University Press: Oxford, pp. 1–68.

He, X. and Lin, C. (2012) Can strong home country institutions foster the internationalization of MNEs? *Multinational Business Review,* 20(4), 352–375.

Holland, M. (1989) *When the Machine Stopped.* Harvard Business School Press: Boston, MA.

Khanna, T. and Yafeh, Y. (2007) Business groups in emerging markets: paragons or parasites? *Journal of Economic Literature,* 45(2), 331–372.

Khannah, T. and Choudhury, P. (2008) Microsoft in China and India: 1993–2007. Harvard Business School Case #708-444.

Morgan, G., Campbell, J., Crouch, C., Pedersen, O., and Whitley, R. (eds.) (2012) *Oxford Handbook of Comparative Institutional Analysis.* Oxford University Press: Oxford.

North, D.C. (1990) *Institutions, Institutional Change, and Economic Performance.* Cambridge University Press: Cambridge.

Peng, M.W., Sun, L.S., Pinkham, B., and Chen, H. (2009) The institution-based view as a third leg for a strategy tripod. *Academy of Management Perspectives*, 23(3), 63–81.

Quelch, J. and Jocz, K. (2012) *All Business Is Local*. Penguin: London.

Rugman, A.M. and Collinson, S. (2010) *International Business*, 6th edition. Pearson Education: Harlow.

Schoenberger, C. and Hong, N. (2012) Dollar's surprising strength eats into the bottom line. *Wall Street Journal*, July 30.

Siegel, J., Pyun, L., and Cheon, B.Y. (2013) Multinational firms, labor market discrimination, and the capture of competitive advantage by exploiting the social divide. Harvard Business School Working Paper, 11-011.

The Economist (2013) Cash be cowed. September 14, p. 70.

Thomke, S. (2012) Mumbai's models of service excellence. *Harvard Business Review*, 90(11), 121–126.

What is Uniquely Strategic about International Strategy?

MOTIVATION

To continue an example introduced in the previous chapter, consider the following recent headline: "No Soup For You: Campbell Closes Its Oldest Factory in America".[1] In a stated need to "improve supply chain productivity," Campbell's announced in September 2012 that it was shutting down its oldest factory in the USA, and laying off about 700 workers. The Sacramento California soup plant had been in operation since 1947, but was apparently less efficient than Campbell's plants in North Carolina, Texas, and Ohio. The company said that the plant "had the highest production costs on a per-case basis" in its manufacturing network and therefore was no longer cost effective. North America President Mark Alexander noted, "we expect the steps we're announcing today to improve our competitiveness and performance by increasing our asset utilization, lowering our total delivered costs and enhancing the flexibility of our manufacturing network. These actions also will eliminate the capital investments needed to maintain the Sacramento plant."

What is interesting about this event (other than the unfortunate loss of jobs) is that this decision was made solely on the basis of supply chain effectiveness. While the optimal location of Campbell's US soup factories might be contentious, might require much analysis, and might even have a noticeable, if small, effect on margins, the decision bears on what Porter refers to as operational efficiency, and does not reach the level of a truly strategic decision. It can typically be made on its own terms with limited reference to decisions being made elsewhere in the organization. Indeed, over the long term, choosing North Carolina over California is not likely to make or break the business or fundamentally affect choices of product offering, served markets, or organization design. It is a discrete choice that can be made independent of other decisions.

In contrast, consider the decision by Cessna in 2007 to build its low-end 162 Sky-catcher light sport propeller plane (priced at around $100,000) in a new joint venture with Shenyang Aircraft Corporation (SAC) in China.[2] This was not a decision that was taken lightly, but was made in parallel with decisions about the geographic markets Cessna would serve and the product range it would offer.

By manufacturing the aircraft in China, Cessna reportedly saved an amount between 40% of the production cost and $71,000 per aircraft. Indeed, Cessna President Jack Pelton said that without China's participation, Cessna probably would not have started the Skycatcher program, noting that "if you are going to field a low-end product, this is about the only way you can do it."

Cessna immediately received much negative feedback from customers and potential customers. Complaints centered on the quality of products manufactured in China, the country's human rights record, the exporting of US jobs, and China's less than friendly political relationship with the USA. The backlash surprised Cessna and pro-voked a PR campaign explaining the decision from a business perspective and assuring customers that aircraft quality would not be compromised. However, even Doug Morales, the Cessna executive with overall responsibility for the project, expressed dismay at SAC's lax quality control procedures, noting that SAC employees routinely substituted cheap construction fasteners for higher quality aircraft fasteners.[3]

In 2012 Cessna extended the agreement in a new partnership with Avic Avia-tion Techniques and the Chengdu government. According to Mike Shih, Cessna Vice President of Strategy and Business Development, "the agreements pave the way for a range of light and mid-size business jets to be manufactured and certified in China." Brad Thress, Senior Vice President of Cessna Business Jets, noted that in this case the move into China "is not about cost, it's about market access and fostering the develop-ment of business aviation here." Indeed, CEO Scott Ernest downplayed the cost advan-tages of China by noting that labor accounted for only 15% of the total cost of a business jet, although he acknowledged that manufacturing in China had tax advantages since imported business jets were subject to a value-added tax of 17% and import duty of around 5%.

Two instances of plant location decisions: one domestic, the other international. In the former, the choice could be made on operational efficiency grounds alone. The lat-ter became strategic because of its broad-ranging repercussions and interdependencies with the opening of new product segments and entry to new geographic markets.

The Rule of Four

Here we continue the Rule of Four (Exhibit 4.1), and argue that each of the four criti-cal decisions which multinationals confront when their operations cross borders raises

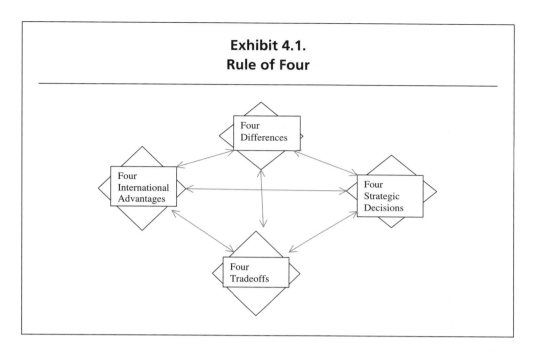

Exhibit 4.1.
Rule of Four

a tradeoff that cannot readily be reconciled. Unlike actions that improve operational efficiency, resolving those tradeoffs so that decisions are reinforcing rather than conflicting requires capitalizing on a single underlying advantage. These two factors, **irreconcilable tradeoffs** and their consistent resolution by reference to a **unique source of international advantage**, are, in fact, what make these decisions strategic (see box).

What Is Strategy?

Since the beginning of the field at the Harvard Business School, one of the basic premises of strategy has been the need to provide direction and consistency to a firm's activities. Captured in the notion of the strategy wheel, where strategy is the hub aligning the different activity spokes of the wheel, the internal value of strategy as providing fit and alignment to the firm's activities in support of a unique external positioning has become a mantra of the field (Christensen *et al.*, 1973).

Michael Porter distinguished this notion of strategic positioning from operational effectiveness by observing that strategy involved a unique configuration of activities, while operational effectiveness just performed the same activities better than competitors (Porter, 1996). For him, a strategic position was sustainable if the activity choices that combined to yield a competitive advantage involved tradeoffs with other strategic positions. As Porter wrote, "tradeoffs are essential to strategy."

These ideas identify the essence of strategy as realizing a distinctive competitive position by making an aligned set of choices for key activities from among alternatives, each of which involves a tradeoff between different competitive advantages.

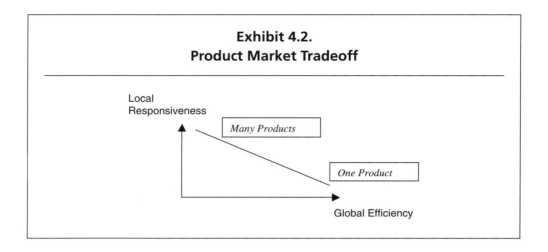

Exhibit 4.2.
Product Market Tradeoff

Local
Responsiveness

Many Products

One Product

Global Efficiency

STRATEGIC TRADEOFFS

What makes international competition so difficult is that there is no dominant or obvious answer to any of the four strategic decisions because each surfaces an underlying tradeoff.

What Product?

Local Responsiveness Versus Global Efficiency

The choice of one or many products raises the tradeoff between local responsiveness and global efficiency that has been at the heart of the international business literature. At one extreme we can imagine the efficiencies of a single product sold the same way everywhere around the world, like Intel chips or Rolex watches. At the other extreme, we can imagine a retail chain that adopts different formats and brand names in different countries so that it exactly meets customer requirements in every country.[4]

It is important to acknowledge this classic tradeoff, and recognize its validity within the product market where country differences require the optimal offering to differ around the world. If each country is allowed to customize products to the local market, limited efficiencies can be exploited and few activities shared across markets. Conversely, if firms choose to drive global scale and experience by offering a single standardized product, they will lose to local competitors whose offerings more closely match customer preferences in any geography (Exhibit 4.2). The **product market tradeoff** is therefore between increasing willingness to pay by adapting products to local market needs and reducing cost through the global efficiency of one product – between **local responsiveness** and **global efficiency**.

International business historically operated with only this one tradeoff and extended it beyond product choice to other aspects of the firm's activities. It therefore became a stand-in for the other tradeoffs which are examined independently in this text. The tradeoff between local responsiveness and global efficiency was, for example, applied to location choice, with the implication that responsiveness favored many locations, and efficiency a single location. Similarly, it was applied to organization design by arguing that if each country optimized products for its local market and had authority over a full set of activities, the logical organization structure was to have discrete geographic units, while if a standard product was being sold worldwide, the optimal structure was a single global product organization. Finally, the tradeoff was applied at the strategy level, where the decisions were rolled up into generic strategies – labeled multidomestic and global (see box) (Porter, 1986).

Generic International Strategies

The multidomestic and global generic strategies became a shorthand way of summarizing a number of related, but conceptually separate decisions, and provided the default answer to at least three of the key decisions facing multinationals within the local responsiveness/global efficiency framework (Exhibit 4.3). The multidomestic strategy increases customer willingness to pay by catering to local needs, which requires many products, many locations, and many discrete organizational (geographic) units. The global strategy lowers cost through offering one product, produced in one location by a unified (business unit) organization.

Exhibit 4.3.
Product Market Tradeoff and Generic International Strategies

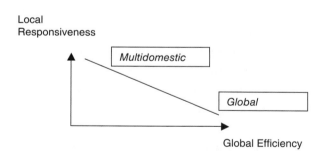

In fact, the local responsiveness/global efficiency framework was so powerful that authors were able to represent additional international strategies that pursued different advantages on the same chart (Exhibit 4.4) (Segal-Horn and Faulkner, 1999). The export strategy, which exploited country factor cost advantages, was placed in the lower left since the product was a commodity that did not need to be adapted to local requirements and

---

did not offer global scale economies. Success from locating in the country with the lowest factor cost simply transcended the responsiveness/efficiency tradeoff.

Exhibit 4.4.
Product Market Tradeoff and Generic International Strategies

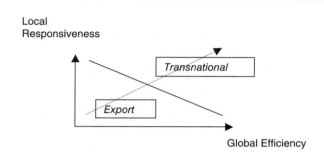

Bartlett and Ghoshal (1989) also argued that the tradeoff could be transcended, but this time by achieving the best of both worlds – being at the same time locally responsive and globally efficient! With their so-called transnational strategy, firms would disaggregate activities and differentially allocate responsibility for each activity in order to reap global efficiencies where those were important, and respond to local needs when that paid rewards.[5]

This representation of four generic international strategies captures the state of the art up until the turn of the century. One underlying tradeoff between two sources of international advantage gave rise to a representation that appeared to capture the essence of four fundamentally different ways of competing internationally.

However, with only one strategic tradeoff, this representation is sorely lacking. First, it collapses a set of independent choices about product, scope, location, and organization, each of which confronts a different tradeoff, into two dimensions. It is, therefore, too simplistic and suggests too little strategic variety. Porter, for example, introduced completely different tradeoffs concerning configuration and coordination into his treatment of global competition (Porter, 1986) – two dimensions that map directly into the locational and organizational decision features, and which a purely product market representation misses (see box).

Configuration and Coordination

Michael Porter's representation of generic international strategies focused on the configuration of a firm's activities – geographically concentrated versus dispersed – and the extent of organizational coordination of those activities – loose versus tight (Exhibit 4.5). The four generic strategies representing different combinations of location and organization can then be placed in that matrix.

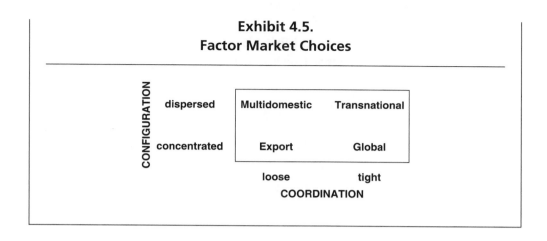

Exhibit 4.5.
Factor Market Choices

	loose	**tight**
dispersed	Multidomestic	Transnational
concentrated	Export	Global

CONFIGURATION (vertical axis) — COORDINATION (horizontal axis)

Second, the single tradeoff ignores other sources of international advantage. Bartlett and Ghoshal (1989) added a third advantage – the ability to leverage learning and innovation around the world – which brought a novel sense of dynamic efficiency to the discipline. Ghemawat (2003) then reminded us of the importance of the factor market, and criticized the responsiveness/efficiency tradeoff for not explicitly acknowledging factor cost arbitrage as a source of international advantage.

Thus, while the local responsiveness/global efficiency tradeoff is still valid in the product market analysis of competitive advantage, it has been asked to do too much. Essentially a tradeoff that applies to the product decision has been asked to stand in for locational, scope, and organizational decisions, each of which has different tradeoffs impinging upon different international advantages. As a result, the two-dimensional representation cannot effectively capture the full set of choices that underpin international competition. We, therefore, retain it as one, but only one, of four strategic tradeoffs.

Where to Locate?

Static Versus Dynamic Efficiency

The choice of one or many locations shifts attention from the product market to the factor market. The dimensions of this **factor market tradeoff** represent the additions of Ghemawat, and Bartlett and Ghoshal, to the international strategy canon in the context of advantages, whose joint exploitation is incompatible – **static versus dynamic efficiency** (Exhibit 4.6).

Consider the location of a multinational's manufacturing facilities. If a firm maximizes static efficiency, it will concentrate all its activities in the single country that is currently the optimal location. If sourcing from Malaysia yields the lowest total delivered cost, then Foxconn will concentrate all its computer assembly operations in

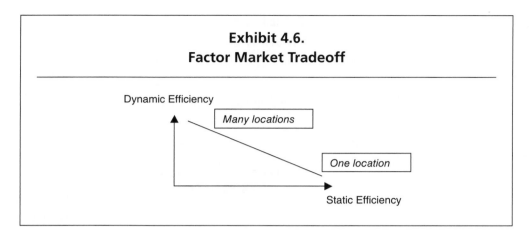

Exhibit 4.6.
Factor Market Tradeoff

Dynamic Efficiency

Many locations

One location

Static Efficiency

Malaysia. But a firm with a single location will not be able to arbitrage shifting factor costs and so retain dynamic efficiency as can a firm which is able to switch production between different locations. However, such a multi-location configuration cannot maximize the static efficiency of concentrating production in the optimal location.

Notice that a single location also allows the firm to exploit the scale economies which drive static efficiency. However, in the presence of global uncertainty and unpredictability, concentrating investment in one country becomes risky. In that case, multiple locations that hedge risk might be preferred. This reinforces the option value of many locations and highlights the tension between the static efficiencies of concentrated commitments and the dynamically efficient diversification offered by multiple sites.

A further aspect of the tradeoff concerns learning and knowledge transfers. Consider product development. If the firm has a single location, it will locate that activity in the country that is currently best for innovation. A cosmetics company might, for example, choose to locate its research and development center in Japan because Japanese women have the most demanding requirements for facial cosmetics. While this would be ideal for static efficiency, what if a breakthrough pops up in Australia? While it is true that ideas originating there could be transferred back to the Japanese development center, organizational constraints and impediments typically delay or even reject outside ideas and initiatives. If, however, Australia had its own R&D facility and was free to develop its own products, the breakthrough would have a much greater chance of being brought to market. Operating multiple locations therefore allows multinationals to leverage innovations throughout the entire organization from wherever in the world they are generated This, after all, is what Bartlett and Ghoshal (1989) meant as the learning advantage of the transnational corporation. With multiple locations for an activity, the multinational will be an insider in different countries and

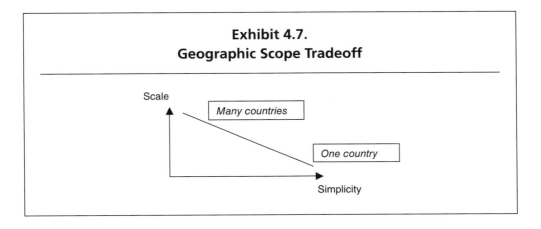

Exhibit 4.7.
Geographic Scope Tradeoff

Scale

Many countries

One country

Simplicity

can capitalize on innovations arising in any of those markets to ensure its dynamic efficiency.

Which Country?
Scale Versus Simplicity

The third strategic tradeoff concerns the number of countries in which to compete, or more generally how to allocate resources between countries. The underlying trade-off engendered is between the scale advantages of a broad geographic footprint and the simplicity of competing in fewer, more similar countries. The heterogeneity that accompanies expanded **geographic scope** means that the choice depends on the trade-off between **scale and simplicity** (Exhibit 4.7).[6]

The advantage of limiting geographic presence to countries that are inherently similar to each other (on economically important measures ranging from language and legal structure to physical distance and retail infrastructure) is the simplification of the management task and the efficiencies of repeating standardized tasks throughout the multinational.

In contrast, expanding geographic scope brings the benefits of scale economies. However, and unlike the implicit assumption in the responsiveness/efficiency tradeoff, as geographic scope expands, so market heterogeneity increases. The resulting complexity makes coordination difficult and leads to inefficiencies that, ironically, make it increasingly hard to achieve the intended scale economies.

How to Organize?
Coordination Versus Motivation

The fourth strategic tradeoff arises out of the **organizational challenge** of managing across borders. In the presence of heterogeneity and volatility, the struggle is to

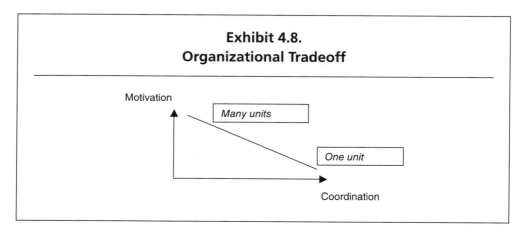

Exhibit 4.8.
Organizational Tradeoff

Motivation

Many units

One unit

Coordination

achieve the benefits of integration across countries – whether static scale efficiencies or dynamic arbitrage opportunities – without sacrificing the benefits of high-powered incentives in differentiated entities with full authority for their own activities.

The simplistic representation of this tradeoff between **coordination** and **motivation** is the choice between establishing one unit for the entire world (a global business unit) and many units (each representing a country subsidiary) (Exhibit 4.8).[7] Coordination across countries by a central unit takes away authority from geographic subsidiaries, while the more interdependent countries become, the less accountable each subsidiary is for its own performance. This loss of high-powered incentives reduces the motivation of country managers and lowers performance.

Conversely, if each country is given full responsibility for its own activities, it can be hard to achieve the benefits of global coordination. Incentivizing performance and fostering entrepreneurship in country subsidiaries are desirable, but that very freedom makes it difficult to achieve the benefits of integration, such as scale economies and learning transfer between countries.

Conclusion

Perhaps the two most powerful representations of international strategy are the original local responsiveness/global efficiency framework and Porter's configuration and coordination matrix. The argument made in this text is that each identified two of the four key strategic decisions. Thus, while both representations are valuable, to be complete we need to independently consider all four decisions and their accompanying tradeoffs:

Local responsiveness   **product market variety**
Global efficiency   **geographic scope**

| Configuration | **factor market location** |
| Coordination | **organization structure** |

SOURCES OF INTERNATIONAL ADVANTAGE

Each of the tradeoffs identified above arose because of the incompatibilities pursuing different sources of advantage. And it is to the underlying sources of advantage that the multinational seeks to exploit by virtue of its international activities that we turn. In Chapter 2 we introduced their essence as providing the motivation for international expansion by enabling firms to pass the "better-off" test. Here we represent them alliteratively, following Ghemawat, as four sources of international advantage:[8]

Motivation for international expansion	International advantage
Exploit existing FSA	Augment
Enhance with new CSA	Arbitrage
Global scope	Aggregate
Global coordination	Agglomerate

Augment

The first international advantage comes from **augmenting the product offering** in additional geographies. There was no US hamburger chain in Vietnam until Carl's Jr. arrived in 2010; Burger King entered in 2012; and McDonald's only announced its intention to expand into Vietnam in 2013. Consumers were therefore denied that experience until Carl's Jr. filled the gap in Vietnamese product space.

Notice that the intrinsic competitive advantage of the firm – its FSA – embedded in the product offerings can be of any type. The advantage could be a low-price version of locally available products, such as Lenovo PCs in the USA. It could be a unique product unlike anything already available in the country (which might be the explanation for the global success of an artist like Lady Gaga!), or it could be a vertically differentiated product, like BMWs in the USA. What matters are not the particulars of why the product is unique, but simply that an exact competitor does not already exist in the new market.

This international advantage can be interpreted as product market arbitrage. The firm already sells its product in country A and simply arbitrages that offering into country B. Many firms have succeeded with just this strategy, most notably, and to much scorn, the German Internet firm Rocket whose success comes from quickly copying Internet business models originating in the USA within Europe and emerging markets. This has led it to become a leader in Turkey and South East Asia with businesses like Wimdu, Pinspire, and Zenpay (that are, respectively, direct copies of Airbnb, Pinterest, and Square).

This strategy also refers to a company that brings skills or capabilities that are superior to those of local firms. In that sense, the firm augments the set of FSAs in the target country with a superior set of resources. When, after the fall of the Soviet Union, the Nordic brewer Carlsberg entered Eastern European countries through acquisition, it applied its knowhow to outdated and inefficient breweries in those countries, and introduced modern consumer marketing techniques. As a result, it was able to augment the existing capabilities in those countries, and build leading shares and a market capitalization of $20 billion. Similarly, the global expansion of MetLife is based not necessarily on a unique product but on **leveraging a set of capabilities** – asset/liability management, underwriting, multichannel distribution, and so on – that are weak or lacking in emerging markets. The product, typically life insurance, might not be missing in those countries, but the skill set is absent.

Ghemawat (2003), with a nod to local responsiveness, refers to this strategy as adaptation. However, this is incorrect. The first-order competitive advantage that the multinational brings is to augment local product space. The multinational must offer something that local firms do not or cannot provide. Adaptation is actually the strategic challenge that the multinational has to address as it struggles to alter the original product or capability to satisfy local needs. Thus, adaptation is actually a strategic disadvantage for the multinational, not a competitive advantage.

Arbitrage

The arbitrage advantage follows the traditional explanation for the multinational which begins overseas operations to exploit the **factor cost advantage** of a foreign country. It therefore reflects the advantage from exploiting CSAs resurrected recently by Ghemawat (2003).

The arbitrage advantage as defined here only considers the static exploitation of CSAs in a single location – Chinese steel companies buying low-cost iron ore mines in Western Australia. It therefore represents the firm-level exploitation of comparative advantage. Australia has a comparative advantage in iron ore, so a steel producer invests in sourcing raw materials from there. There is no sense of dynamic optimization in this international advantage. Nor is it intended to cover the dynamic learning and innovation aspects of international advantage. Arbitrage simply exploits current differences in factor market conditions around the world.

The advantage does, however, apply to more sophisticated versions of arbitrage than simply exploiting raw material and labor cost differences. Indeed, one important driver of firm location (as we will see in Chapter 9) is differential tax rates. This leads companies to raise capital in countries with favorable access to capital markets, or to relocate legal headquarters to domiciles with lower tax rates on profits and dividends (Desai *et al.*, 2006; Desai, 2009; Birkinshaw *et al.*, 2006).

Aggregate

The third source of international advantage is created by virtue of international activity, rather than by capitalizing on an existing firm or country advantage. It can involve either the supply or demand side advantages of a broad global scope.

The supply side advantage comes from capturing the **scale and experience** economies that global scope offers. By selling the same chip everywhere around the world, Intel is able to surpass minimum efficient scale in the extremely capital-intensive manufacturing process. Aggregation was the traditional advantage associated with Japanese success in the 1970s and 1980s as, successively, its motorbike, television, and automobile industries came to global dominance. While firms like Honda, Matsushita, and Toyota initially built substantial domestic businesses (crafting their original FSAs), it was their global expansion that secured their cost advantage as they reached production volumes that were multiples of local demand by selling extensively in Europe, the Americas, and, to a lesser extent, elsewhere in Asia.

The demand side advantage of aggregation comes from the ability to offer a product or service that is simply impossible to provide without global coverage. Classic examples would be the express delivery or freight forwarding businesses. It is only when a provider has a global presence that it can offer a service that appeals to customers wanting to ship products and urgent documents from anywhere to everywhere around the world. Global coverage is the value provided to customers, and that offering can only be provided by a multinational with **global scope**.

Agglomerate

The fourth international advantage that can be created by a multinational firm is what I have called, possibly ungainly, but certainly alliteratively, agglomeration. The dictionary definition of agglomerate as a verb[9] is "to form into a mass or cluster." I want it to mean the process of bringing structure to chaos – of adding value to a formless mass. I apologize if the term does not quite have that resonance or nuance for the reader. Believe me, I studied all the "a" words in the dictionary in search of a better term and could find nothing else.

The advantage I want to convey with the term is integrating a set of disparate entities – I have in mind a city that is an agglomeration of railroad stations, offices, shops, restaurants, and other buildings. The connotation that I want is of creating value from an assembly of different things. Agglomeration as an advantage capitalizes on differences among countries, by seeing opportunity not threats in those differences, and creates value by coordinating activities across their disparate product and factor markets.

Specifically, agglomeration refers to the advantages created by **a coordinated network of dispersed activities**. The dispersed activities part of the definition represents the distributed and differentiated nature of locations. The coordinated network part of the definition captures the organizational challenge for this advantage. The whole identifies the ability to capitalize on ever-changing CSAs and becomes more than the sum of the parts as product and knowledge flows to countries around the globe.

Agglomeration involves two related, but different mechanisms. The first is the continuous transfer of idiosyncratic **learning**. On the customer-facing side, ideas and innovations can be found anywhere in the world and rapidly transferred throughout the world. If the dulce de leche flavor of ice cream is a hit in Argentina, then introduce it in the USA and Europe. If Japan has huge success with Korean girl and boy bands, replicate them in Latin America. If Kate Middleton's preferred dress designer Sarah Burton of Alexander McQueen's label is from the UK, take those clothes and that brand to the Middle East. Wherever new trends, fashions, ideas, or fads originate, a coordinated network can quickly notice, identify, and rapidly replicate them throughout its global enterprise.

With respect to the supply side, learning refers to production process improvements. CEMEX, for example, makes much of the fact that many of its important productivity improvements came from outside Mexico. These process innovations, such as the discovery in Spain that old tires can be a fuel, were then leveraged throughout its global production system (Exhibit 4.9).

Similarly, FedEx discovered a cheap scanner for pickup and delivery in its local Chinese delivery company which operated at much lower cost than the traditional express business. The value of local variation is the proliferation of different experiments, each a response to slightly different conditions around the world, that generates innovation variety.

The second mechanism by which agglomeration creates advantage is by having a distributed network continuously respond to **current information**. The classic example is Becton Dickinson, the global manufacturer of blood container tubes. It has plants in more than 50 countries, many of which manufacture a standard tube. With manufacturing controlled centrally, if the exchange rate favors country X at a point in time, volume will be switched to that plant. When labor rates in country Y increase, volume can be switched from there to another country. The result is a multinational that can arbitrage ever-changing factor cost differences. Other examples were ABB Relays that had production centers in four countries, GE Medical Systems with dual

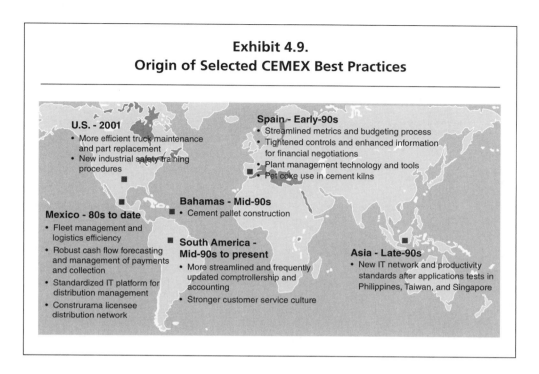

Exhibit 4.9.
Origin of Selected CEMEX Best Practices

U.S. - 2001
- More efficient truck maintenance and part replacement
- New industrial safety training procedures

Spain - Early-90s
- Streamlined metrics and budgeting process
- Tightened controls and enhanced information for financial negotiations
- Plant management technology and tools
- Pet coke use in cement kilns

Bahamas - Mid-90s
- Cement pallet construction

Mexico - 80s to date
- Fleet management and logistics efficiency
- Robust cash flow forecasting and management of payments and collection
- Standardized IT platform for distribution management
- Construrama licensee distribution network

South America - Mid-90s to present
- More streamlined and frequently updated comptrollership and accounting
- Stronger customer service culture

Asia - Late-90s
- New IT network and productivity standards after applications tests in Philippines, Taiwan, and Singapore

production centers, and NCR with dual production locations for all its key products and components. Proactively shifting activities among countries continuously optimizes performance and so goes beyond simple static factor market arbitrage.

Indeed, the value of agglomeration is the option value created from investing in many countries. And **option value** is the best way to think of this international advantage. Perceived as a threat or a risk, all of the complications and complexities of international activity are usually interpreted as a negative for multinationals. Yet that challenge can also be an opportunity as multinationals which master its complexities gain a competitive advantage.

CONCLUSION: THE RULE OF FOUR REVISITED

We are now in a position to pull together the four factors that make international strategy a distinct subject and relate them in a single representation (Exhibit 4.10). To this end, it is helpful to build the picture sequentially to show the logic of the relationships among the framework's elements.

We begin with the underlying resources or **FSAs** that enable the company to win in domestic competition. Any successful international expansion has to be built on capabilities that yield a traditional competitive positioning advantage, and these remain at the core of the multinational.

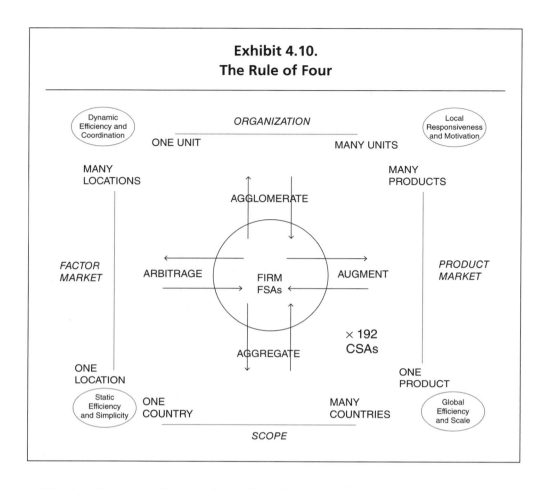

Exhibit 4.10.
The Rule of Four

We then locate the firm in the midst of 192 other countries, each of which has its own **CSAs** that give rise to *heterogeneity in product markets* (size, population, income level, etc.) and *factor markets* (labor cost, capital infrastructure, tax rates, etc.). The *volatility* in CSAs among countries and the *scale* potential across countries then become the other distinctive differences of international competition.

It is in this context that a multinational must choose among four **international advantages** that make it better off by virtue of international activity and allow it to overcome the liability of foreignness. The multinational can exploit product market differences by deploying its home market FSAs in order to *augment* product market offerings in additional countries. It can *arbitrage* factor market differences and so exploit the CSAs of foreign countries. It can build a presence in multiple product markets to *aggregate* demand and create scale advantages. Or it can *agglomerate* activities across locations in many countries in order to consistently innovate and continually optimize production.

Table 4.1 The Rule of Four

International differences	Competitive advantage	Critical decision	Tradeoff
Product market	Augmentation	One vs. many products	Global efficiency vs. local responsiveness
Factor market	Arbitrage	One vs. many locations	Static efficiency vs. dynamic efficiency
Geographic scope	Aggregation	One vs. many markets	Simplicity vs. scale
Volatility/ unpredictability	Agglomeration	One vs. many org. units	Coordination vs. motivation

And yet in diversifying geographically, the multinational has to confront the four strategic **decisions** and their accompanying **tradeoffs**. When augmenting product sets around the world, the multinational has to decide whether to offer *one product or many products*. The former capitalizes on *global efficiencies but trades off the local responsiveness* advantage of the latter. When arbitraging CSAs the multinational must decide whether to *locate each activity in one or many countries*. The former achieves *static efficiency, but at the cost of the dynamic efficiency* offered by the latter. If the multinational aggregates demand, it has to choose whether to *compete in one (a few similar) or many markets*. The former offers the *simplicity of competing in homogeneous markets, but misses the scale* advantages of the latter. Finally, if the multinational agglomerates across markets, it must decide whether to have *one organizational unit which can effectively coordinate the network, or many organizational units that better motivate their leaders* (Table 4.1).

SUMMARY: NEED FOR AN INTERNATIONAL STRATEGY

Individually the strategic questions raised by competing internationally are complicated to resolve, as we will see in the chapters dedicated to each decision. Resolving them consistently, so that decisions reinforce rather than conflict with each other, is more difficult. To achieve this goal, it is vital to adhere to a single strategy from among the set of generic international strategies introduced in the next chapter.

The potential is certainly there for **multiple sources of international advantage** to be present in one multinational at the same time. In the 1970s and 1980s, for example, the success of Japanese auto manufacturers in the USA and Europe was partly due to augmentation – the export of high-quality small cars unavailable locally; partly to arbitrage – Japan at that date had lower steel and labor costs; and partly aggregation – the experience and scale benefits of the global scope. In fact, if it is to be operationally efficient, the modern multinational almost certainly should be looking to all four advantages: it could take an existing product to a new country; enhance its cost position by relocating some manufacturing to a low labor-cost region; use its global scope to develop a unique product offering; and perhaps try to coordinate product innovation across countries.

A firm might, therefore, be creating value through any combination of the four advantages. However, as with domestic competitive advantage, we argue that a firm must ultimately **choose one international advantage as the driver of its strategy**. It is true that many decisions can be made on the basis of operational efficiency – when, for example, operations research analysis demonstrates that the cost-effective location for a new Benelux distribution center is in Amsterdam. In that case, economic necessity provides a clear answer to the location decision with limited reference to the overall strategy. However, the four key interdependent decisions can only be consistently resolved by defaulting to a strategy that pursues a single source of advantage.

The next chapter lays out the set of international strategies that exploit those different advantages. The question of whether a company can choose a strategy that is able to exploit all four advantages at the same time, rather than succumbing to organizational demands to focus on only one international advantage, is deferred until the last chapter.

NOTES

1. Accessed at http://www.inquisitr.com/346945/no-soup-for-you-campbell-closes-its-oldest-factory-in-america-700-lose-jobs/"pUM1JSykA2aDExqb.99.
2. Reported in Wikipedia, accessed at http://en.wikipedia.org/wiki/Cessna_162.
3. A US embassy document posted on Wikileaks, accessed at http://cables.mrkva.eu/cable.php?id=135132.
4. Note that the notion of product implied here is broader than simply the physical characteristics of the product or service. It also includes all aspects of marketing the product, such as brand positioning, that are subsumed in the traditional 4Ps of product, place, price, and promotion.
5. They also added a third dimension to this representation since the single tradeoff could not capture their new source of competitive advantage – the dynamics of knowledge, learning, and innovation transfer.
6. This tradeoff is impossible within the responsiveness/efficiency framework. The presumption is that global efficiency comes from exploiting a broad geographic scope. Unfortunately, this does not acknowledge that as scope expands, product markets become more heterogeneous and the management task becomes more complex, which makes it unlikely that a standard global approach will be successful.
7. As we will discover in Chapter 10, there are more sophisticated ways of approaching organization design and many more levers than simply the formal structure, but using structure as a shorthand representation captures the essence of the tradeoff.

8. The use of the "A" alliteration follows Ghemawat who identifies three strategies to address international differences: adapt to them (Adaptation); override them (Aggregation); and exploit them (Arbitrage). We build on those advantages and fully acknowledge his contribution in this, and many other, regards.

9. Unfortunately, the definition of agglomeration as a noun gives exactly the wrong connotation. It is defined as "a confused mass, or jumble."

REFERENCES AND FURTHER READING

Andrews, K., Bower, J., Christensen, C., Hamermesh, R., and Porter, M.E. (1973) *Business Policy: Text and Cases*. Richard D. Irwin: Homewood, IL.

Bartlett, C.A. and Ghoshal, S. (1989) *Managing Across Borders: The Transnational Solution*. Harvard Business School Press: Boston, MA.

Birkinshaw, J.M., Braunerhjelm, P., Holm, U., and Terjesen, S. (2006) Why do some companies move their headquarters abroad? *Strategic Management Journal*, 27(7), 681–700.

Christensen, C., Andrews, K., and Bower, J. (1973) *Business Policy*. Richard D. Irwin: Homewood, IL.

de Meza, D. and van der Ploeg, F. (1987) Production flexibility as a motive for multinationality. *Journal of Industrial Economics*, 35(3), 343–351.

Desai, M. (2008) The finance function in a global corporation. *Harvard Business Review*, 86(7/8), 108–112.

Desai, M. (2009) The decentering of the global firm. *World Economy*, 32(9), 1271–1290.

Desai, M., Foley, C.F., and Hines, J.R. (2006) The demand for tax haven operations. *Journal of Public Economics*, 90(3), 513–531.

Devinney, T.M., Midgley, D.F., and Venaik, S. (2000) The optimal performance of the global firm: formalizing and extending the integration-responsiveness framework. *Organization Science*, 11(6), 674–695.

Ghemawat, P. (2003) The forgotten strategy. *Harvard Business Review*, 81(11), 76–84.

Ghemawat, P. and Levinthal, D. (2008) Choice interactions and business strategy. *Management Science*, 54(9), 1638–1651.

Kogut, B. (1985) Designing global strategies: comparative and competitive value-added chains. *Sloan Management Review*, 26(4), 15–28.

Kogut, B. (1985) Designing global strategies: profiting from operational flexibility. *Sloan Management Review*, 27(1), 27–38.

Kogut, B. and Kulatilaka, N. (1994) Operating flexibility, global manufacturing, and the option value of a multinational network. *Management Science*, 40(1), 123–139.

Kogut, B. and Zander, U. (1993) Knowledge of the firm and the evolutionary theory of the multinational corporation. *Journal of International Business Studies*, 24(4), 625–645.

Lawrence, P.R. and Lorsch, J.W. (1967) *Organization and Environment: Managing Differentiation and Integration*. Harvard Business School Press: Boston, MA.

March, J.G. (1991) Exploration and exploitation in organizational learning. *Organization Science*, 2(1), 71–87.

Mudambi, R. and Swift, T. (2011) Leveraging knowledge and competencies across space: the next frontier in international business. *Journal of International Management*, 17(3), 186–189.

Porter, M.E. (ed.) (1986) *Competition in Global Industries*. Harvard Business School Press: Boston, MA.

Porter, M.E. (1996) What is strategy? *Harvard Business Review,* November/December, 61–78.

Rangan, S. (1998) Do multinationals operate flexibility? Theory and evidence. *Journal of International Business Studies*, 29(2), 217–237.

Rivkin, J.W. (2000) Imitation of complex strategies. *Management Science*, 46(6), 824–844.

Rumelt, R., Schendel, D.E., and Teece, D.J. (eds.) (1996) *Fundamental Issues in Strategy*. Harvard Business School Press: Boston, MA.

Saloner, G., Shepard, A., and Podolny, J. (2001) *Strategic Management*. John Wiley & Sons, Inc.: New York.

Segal-Horn, S. and Faulkner, D. (1999) *The Dynamics of International Strategy*. International Thomson Business Press: London.

Tushman, M. and O'Reilly, III, C.A. (1996) Ambidextrous organizations: managing evolutionary and revolutionary change. *California Management Review*, 38(4), 8–30.

Van den Steen, E. (2012) A theory of explicitly formulated strategy. Harvard Business School Working Paper, 12-102.

Verbeke, A. (2009) *International Business Strategy: Rethinking the Foundation of Global Corporate Success*. Cambridge University Press: Cambridge.

Generic International Strategies

MOTIVATION

At the beginning of this century a major European energy utility made two large acquisitions.[1] It bought a US electric utility based in North Carolina to diversify its country risk and enter a faster growing market. Then it acquired a large European power company with a complementary geographic presence in order to gain scale within Europe. And yet within eight years, the CEO had left, the US operation was up for sale, and a decentralized country organization had replaced the matrix structure put in place after the acquisitions.

Perhaps John Wells could have foretold the future when he slept badly flying over the Atlantic for the eighth time in a calendar year. He knew that his presence in the upcoming meeting in London would add nothing to the discussion, nor would he learn anything of value for his own operation. Indeed, as head of generation for the US utility, John had no interest in the heated debate about which design of nuclear power plant should be chosen for Europe, which was the meeting's focus, and yet his attendance as the US representative on the global utility's generating business operating committee was mandatory. Even then he wondered why his company had been purchased since it shared so little with its European counterparts.

Similarly, Pietro Garibaldi could have predicted the outcome when he struggled to get information from the UK purchasing group about its fuel purchases. Accountable for reducing the group's European-wide fuel costs by 5%, Pietro was responsible for creating a European-wide purchasing group out of the centralized purchasing group of his former company and the country-based purchasing departments of the acquired utility. And yet he had no direct authority over the geographic purchasing units. As a result, each country was refusing to cooperate with his initiatives as they strove to protect their own fuel-trading operations.

Struggling to generate returns to pay the billions of dollars of debt raised to finance the purchases, dispirited executives were torn between getting on the corporate bandwagon of more coordination and ignoring those initiatives in the hope of delivering results in their own businesses. Executives on the management committee were even going behind each other's backs as they privately told their own parts of the organization to ignore the "One Utility" strategy being promulgated by a headquarters staff grown to over 2,000 employees.

In this case it was clear that the utility's acquisitions were doomed to failure because it could not articulate or implement an effective international strategy. Was the company diversifying across discrete geographies? Building global scale? Sharing learning and activities? Ghemawat introduces his book on global strategy with a similar example of Coca-Cola's poor performance as it vacillated between local autonomy – launching 40 local brands in the 16 years between 1981 and 1997 (Ghemawat, 2007) – and centralization – building a global headquarters of over 6,000 in Atlanta as of 1996 (Schwartz, 1996). Both examples illustrate that the key to success in international competition is to choose and then implement a coherent international strategy.

PRINCIPLES

Need for an International Strategy

If we understand the notion of generic strategies in a single market, is there an analog in international competition? Are there generic international strategies that simplify delegated decision making inside multinational corporations and ensure activity choices are mutually reinforcing rather than as dissonant as those described above? Such generic strategies might not provide the definitive answers to all four strategic decisions but they will provide a strong bias as to how each should be answered.

There are six **generic international strategies** described below. It is important to recognize at the outset that these strategies are archetypes – representations of reality that capture key aspects of a "pure form" strategy. They are not necessarily practiced in exactly this fashion in any real-world multinational. They are characterizations of ideal-type strategies that simplify and accentuate their differences. Their merit lies in establishing boundaries for real companies to operate within, and providing a benchmark against which actual strategies can be compared.

In particular, such strategies outline the default answer to the four fundamental decisions confronting multinationals: What product? Which country? Where to locate? How to organize? As such, they enable firms to make aligned choices that are

Exhibit 5.1.

Exhibit 5.1.
Generic International Strategies

	International Advantage	Product?	Compete?	Locate?	Organize?
Local	Market Specific	Idiosyncratic	Local	Domestic	Functional
Export / Import	Arbitrage Factor Costs or CSAs	Commodity	Opportunistic	Domestic	International
Multidomestic	Augment Product Set or FSAs	Waterfall	Standalone Profitability	Most Activities in Each Country	Geographic
Global	Aggregate For Scale and Efficiency	Standard	Worldwide	Optimal for Each Activity, Concentrated	Business Unit
Transnational	Agglomerate For Dynamic Efficiency	Platform	Key Markets	Dispersed and Flexible	Purpose, People, Process

consistent with a chosen source of international advantage. In this chapter we outline the generic international strategies, the international advantage they exploit, and the default answers to each decision (Exhibit 5.1). In Part Three we examine the critical decisions in detail.

GENERIC INTERNATIONAL STRATEGIES

Local

Definition and Description

The local strategy, as its name suggests, is not an international strategy. Instead, the strategy to remain a purely domestic player simplifies all the questions of international activity by deciding to do none. It is a strategy to avoid the complexities and challenges of international competition by not becoming a multinational.

This is an important option to include in the armory of strategies. Not all companies need enter the international arena. For some the best choice is to remain local. Not all industries or sources of competitive advantage require firms to be international, and for many firms the best option might be the quiet life of the purely domestic competitor. Heresy though this may seem in an era of globalization, there are numerous examples of industries and firms that are more profitable because they decline to enter international competition.

There are few residential construction or plant hire firms, for example, that operate beyond national boundaries. I do not know of a dry cleaning firm that competes in multiple countries. If these examples are in industries which are inherently fragmented, it does not prevent the local strategy being successful in otherwise global industries. Hershey, the chocolate company, has only 9% of its sales outside the USA, and yet it has remained one of the most profitable chocolate manufacturers in the world – a set that includes such global powerhouses as Nestlé, Kraft (now Mondelez), and Mars. In major appliances, where global participants like Whirlpool and Electrolux might garner all the press, GE's operating unit, which has the vast majority of its sales in the USA, has been just as profitable. And for a long time in Europe, the most profitable strategy for major appliance manufacturers appeared to be to remain local (Baden-Fuller and Stopford, 1991). Adoption of the local strategy is, in many cases, perfectly viable, even if it does restrict the absolute size the firm can attain.

International Advantage

The local strategy succeeds against international competition when it has a bigger wedge between buyers' willingness to pay and cost than foreign firms (Chapter 2). This suggests that local strategies work best when there is some form of impediment to trade or "protection" for the local firms, either on the demand or supply side, so that international competitors do not overwhelm them.

Demand   One obvious advantage of the local strategy is catering to **idiosyncratic needs** by designing products to meet unique demands within the country or even sub-region. Customers buy the local product because it precisely fits their needs and shun internationally traded products that fail to satisfy local purchase criteria.

Businesses in which there are substantial differences in consumer preferences between countries are supportive of the local strategy. Sausages are the food I think of as being the most varied around the world. German sausages are very different to English sausages, which are different again to Italian sausages, and so on. In fact, regional variations of black sausages, blood pudding, and haggis even make it tough to know what you are getting when you choose sausages from a menu in England. Indeed, research by Unilever found that sausages were the product that had the least potential for homogeneity within Europe (Christensen and Zobel, 1997). This suggests that a purely local producer of sausages, such as the British Premium Sausage Company in Bradford, will be as successful, if not more so, than a multinational like Unilever, which sells sausages Europe-wide through its Walls subsidiary.

Supply   If there are **diseconomies**, rather than **economies of trade**, such as when transport or other costs of doing business internationally are extremely high, the local strategy retains a competitive advantage. One reason we do not see global dry cleaners is that it is simply too expensive to ship dry cleaning around the world. Most services, like hairdressers, plumbers, and roofers, fall into this category, since the provision of the service, almost by definition, has to take place in the country of purchase.

Similarly, if it is illegal to import a product, or if the tariff rate or other non-tariff barriers make importing infeasible, a local producer can survive happily, regardless of how inefficient it may be. This was undoubtedly the case for producers in developing countries that were for many years protected by their governments. Thus, **trade protection** favors the local strategy. When Latin America, Eastern Europe, and India liberalized trade, domestic firms faced enormous disruption (Khanna and Palepu, 1999). No longer protected from international competition, such firms had to make one of three choices: recognize their inefficiency and exit the business; become efficient and perhaps then expand internationally, as CEMEX, the Mexican cement producer, has done; or find some way to capture the value of incumbency by forming a joint venture or selling valuable assets – typically a locally recognized brand or access to distribution – to a multinational.

For the local strategy to be viable in the absence of protection, it must be true that producing for the domestic market alone allows the firm to reach the global **minimum efficient scale** (mes). Again, dry cleaning is an obvious example of the local strategy when mes is probably a single storefront.[2] In contrast, it is hard to imagine that an aircraft manufacturer serving only Argentina is likely to be near the world mes.

The likelihood that a purely domestic firm will be internationally competitive increases with the **share of value added that is either incurred locally or a globally traded commodity**. In those cases, which again include most service businesses, any advantage of global scale or access to lower factor costs outside the country will be limited since the share of the cost structure on which the multinational has the advantage will be small. This implies that businesses which are more amenable to the local strategy will be industries, such as construction, that rely on local value added, or oil refining, for which a globally traded commodity is a huge component of cost.

None of these instances guarantee success for the local strategy. Even if operations must take place locally, a multinational can still transfer its superior knowhow or brand to the local operation, in the way that McDonald's transfers the Golden Arches and its operating procedures to its fast food restaurants. This vulnerability remains a real risk to firms pursuing local strategies, so they must continually **upgrade FSAs** to deter entry by a multinational. Even a local sausage company would be vulnerable to a multinational food company that perhaps learnt how to vacuum-pack a sausage so that it stayed fresh for weeks and applied that technology to a locally flavored sausage. Diageo, the global spirits company, for example, reinvented beer in Kenya to produce a cut price local product excused from excise duty. Brewed from local barley and sorghum and served in kegs, not bottles, the East African product "Senator Keg" reached $150 million in sales within six years of launch (*The Economist*, 2012).

Strategic Alignment

The answer to all the strategic decisions – of product, geographic scope, location, and organization – is obvious once the competitive advantage of the local strategy has been validated. By definition, the scope of the firm is restricted to its domestic market; the product offered is that which fits the idiosyncrasies of the local market; and all activities have to be located in that market.[3] There might well be questions concerning each of these decisions within the single country: Do we accommodate regional taste differences? Where do we locate the plant within the country? And so on. But as we argued earlier, these questions, while relevant, are less pressing in the domestic context since all occur within national borders under the same institutional structures.

Export

Definition and Description

The export strategy is also not a multinational strategy, in that it primarily uses contracts to coordinate international activity, rather than internalizing foreign activity inside the firm hierarchy. In this strategy a firm sells a product through distributors or other third parties which take on the complexities of operating in foreign countries. As such, it is fairly straightforward to manage since international activity is minimal.

There are, however, limitations to this strategy. First, because the firm has restricted access to the consumer in foreign markets, it cannot easily adapt the product to meet local needs. Second, because the firm does not control the final delivery and sale of the product, it is hard to coordinate global activities, or even control actions on its behalf around the world. The result is that the export strategy is best adopted when the company does not require its own international advantage, but simply exploits its country's comparative advantage. In essence, the advantage of the export strategy, apart from the simplicity of operation, involves a firm exporting its country's unique or advantaged factor of production.[4]

Foxconn Technology, the operating brand name for the Taiwanese firm Hon Hai, is a good example of the export strategy. You might be familiar with the brand name from the various accusations that have been leveled against it for poor working conditions in its Chinese plants, but you are certainly familiar with the products it manufactures – even if they are not sold under the Foxconn name. Among other well-known brands the company manufactures are Apple, Intel, and Sharp. In fact, the iPhone 5 you have in your pocket almost certainly came from one of Foxconn's Chinese plants where it was made by one of their 1.4 million local employees. Primarily located now in China (although claiming also to be the second largest exporter from the Czech Republic), Foxconn has become the largest third-party assembler of electronics in the world by exploiting low-cost Chinese labor.

International Advantage

The export strategy is predicated on a country having a comparative advantage that an indigenous firm can **arbitrage**. Examples therefore include companies involved in raw material businesses, like oil and wheat. It is no surprise that Saudi Arabia exports oil, and that US Midwest farmers export wheat, since both benefit from their country's natural endowments.

Other export strategies involve goods that are not themselves factors of production, but which embed the factor of production with which the country is advantageously endowed. The obvious example is selling a country's low labor cost.

It often amuses me to think of factory workers in rural parts of western China making the plastic toys that go into Kids Meals at fast food restaurants. Those knick-knacks often represent the latest movie-related character, which I am sure the young female assembly workers have never seen. And yet they turn out millions of Beetlejuice characters or Robocops, and I cannot help wondering what they think of these obscure and often ugly toys! But that ignorance is actually the essence of the export strategy. The firm need know nothing of what it is making, who the ultimate customer is, or what the purpose of the item is, since all it is doing is selling the labor content of the toy.

Each season, the owner of the Chinese factory will contract with a distributor or a purchasing agent to produce so many of a certain item. Indeed, Hong Kong and Singapore are home to thousands of such intermediaries whose only job is to link up low labor-cost manufacturing facilities with US or European firms looking for contract manufacturing. Nike, for example, sources from up to 618 different Asian factories in 46 countries each season, as it hunts the best price for assembling shoes.[5] For any given product, like footwear, it might use 13 factories in the Americas, 2 in EMEA (Europe, Middle East and Africa), 38 in North Asia and 18 in South Asia.

The notion that firms with an export strategy are selling a factor of production, either directly or indirectly embedded in a particular item, can be extended to developed countries and more advanced factors of production. The NFL and the NBA, for example, have export strategies. Each exports its particular sport around the world – exploiting the unique American endowment of athletes who weigh over 250 pounds and yet can run 40 yards in less than 5 seconds, or are over 7 feet tall and can vertical jump 40 inches! Similarly, Bollywood exports movies based on the relative abundance of the factors of production needed to make Indian entertainment movies – screenwriters, directors, celebrity actresses, etc., clustered in Mumbai.

While it might surprise you to think of the NFL and Bollywood as pursuing an export strategy, the distinguishing characteristic of such strategies is their lack of operations outside the home market and their relative inattention to customers in foreign countries. Those are exactly the same features of the Chinese factory owner's strategy.

The export strategy does not just apply to factor markets. If the local market features unique products – think of the items you buy as a tourist, such as Murano glass, or carnival masks in Venice – then the export strategy can augment the product space in foreign markets, as when Murano glass is sold by retailers around the world. Again, the distinguishing feature would be the absence of international operations – no retail stores, for example, but contracts to sell through select retail outlets – and the exploitation of Murano's comparative advantage in decorative glass blowing.

Note that the export strategy is only successful when there are **limited interdependencies among countries**. Because an exporter does not have a coordinated presence around the world, it cannot compete in businesses where there are substantial scale economies. The risk of being excluded from a large market, and the inability to price aggressively for market share in key countries without the cooperation of a local distributor, also leave an exporter vulnerable to a coordinated attack by a global competitor. Natural resource businesses, for example, have limited interdependencies between countries, since the cost of growing wheat, or the production cost of oil, is relatively unaffected by the sale of another bushel or barrel. Similarly, Chinese labor costs are unaffected in the short term by the sale of products in additional foreign markets.

Strategic Alignment

Product   The first distinguishing feature of the export strategy is that it sells the **same product around the world**. The product is barely altered to meet the needs of foreign markets. Oil, for example, is not treated differently when it is exported to the UK rather than Argentina. The NBA does not adapt the rules of the game for shorter players in Europe. Nor does it change the program when selling television rights overseas to accommodate the fewer television commercials that are shown during games. What you see in the USA is what you get overseas. Nor does the NFL even (other than the unheard of NFL Europe that was terminated in 2007) have teams in other countries. Movie studios are similar, in that Hollywood makes the movies it is known for – big-budget action blockbusters with "A" list stars – and does not change the script or locations for foreign tastes.[6] Warner Brothers, for example, historically exported the movie that had been designed for domestic audiences.[7]

Firms pursuing the export strategy rely on intermediaries for their overseas operations and have no direct access to the end consumer, so find it difficult to adapt their products to heterogeneous international needs. The export strategy therefore requires universal demand. Obviously raw materials fit this definition, as does the embodiment of low labor costs in a product (although the actual product can look very different). Successful export strategies of more specialized factors of production, like the NBA or Hollywood, do, however, depend on **homogeneous international demand**.

Location   With the export strategy the firm itself has very **limited activities outside the home country**. Instead, nearly all international activities are undertaken by third parties. The NBA, for example, merely sells television rights to its games to European broadcasters. Nike's suppliers contract to sell fob their facilities and have no involvement once the product leaves their factory. The most that a firm with an export strategy might undertake is limited foreign sales, establishing its own importing subsidiary or distributorship in some foreign countries, but even then it will most likely not have a direct retail operation. Disney, for example, has established Buena Vista International for the distribution of its movies, but it does not own movie theaters. Over time the firm might change its strategy and become more active in foreign countries, perhaps establishing its own sales subsidiary, but then it would be moving away from the export strategy.

Scope   A firm pursuing the export strategy can choose whether or not to offer its goods for sale in any given country and can be selective about the foreign markets in which it sells. In this sense the export strategy is **opportunistic** with regard to its scope of operation. Selling for a while in one country, then exiting the market for a period, is acceptable since the strategy is not contingent on exploiting interdependencies between countries.

An exporter should, therefore, only be active in countries where and when it is profitable. For the Catalan furniture company mentioned in Chapter 2, for example, the Uzbek order should be accepted if the company is confident in the order's profitability on a standalone basis. If additional orders were never received, it would not matter to the long-term success of the company's export strategy.

Structure   The export strategy is often the first international strategy that companies pursue because of its simplicity and the limited demands it places on management time and resources. Indeed, many companies which are today successful multinationals began their international activity pursuing the export strategy. Timken, the century-old world leader in tapered roller bearings, relied on exporting through foreign distributors for the first 20 years of its international operations. Only in 1928, 17 years after it first sold in France, did it internalize the distribution function in France. And only in the 1950s did Timken establish more than a simple import and sales function in that country.[8]

Firms that initially follow the export strategy therefore tend to be immature or smaller companies with limited resources relying on contractual partners in foreign markets. They begin by organizing foreign activities with a siloed **international department** which handles relations with foreign distributors but has little influence on the core domestic activities, and which receives product that has been "thrown over the wall" separating international from domestic operations. The international department usually pays a transfer price to the domestic unit which is typically set to ensure that unit's own profitability.

Import
Definition and Description
For completeness, we need to identify the complement of the export strategy – the import strategy. This involves a firm which only competes in one country, accessing products through an international sourcing strategy. As a result, the company will have no international activities – other than perhaps an international purchasing operation – but it can take advantage of international activities to pursue the arbitrage advantage of reduced cost foreign production, or augmenting product space by offering a distinctive product in its local market. The epitome of the import strategy would be a gift shop that imports a variety of items – china, glassware, textiles, paintings – from all over the world. Note, however, that the import strategy involves more than purchasing raw material inputs from abroad. Rather, it requires the firm to buy the finished product so that the local value added is relatively small.

The import strategy **arbitrages foreign CSAs**, whether in the product or factor markets, through contracts rather than by establishing its own operations overseas. As such, it is symmetric with the export strategy, which sells in foreign markets through market contracts rather than inside the firm hierarchy. As a result, it can only be employed when demand in the home market is similar to that in other countries because the firm imports a product that has not been customized to its tastes. And it will only succeed if there are few interdependencies between countries, since the importer has no control over the geographic scope of its suppliers.

As with the export strategy, if the firm begins to add overseas activities – perhaps setting up its own manufacturing facilities internationally – the company moves away from the pure import strategy and needs to rethink the consistency of its four strategic decisions.

The Vertical Multinational

The extension of the pure form export and import strategies gave rise to the very first multinationals. These were the trading companies that **internalized foreign transactions** by appointing their own representatives in foreign countries. In Europe, leading merchants from the Italian city states, like Venice and Florence, established their own international activities between the tenth and fifteenth centuries. In Great Britain it was the Hudson's Bay Company and East India Company that were among these early multinationals, sourcing and importing beaver pelts, and spices and silk, respectively by the seventeenth century (Jones, 2005). In Japan, the "soga sosha," progenitors of the current trading houses Mitsui, Sumitomo, and Mitsubishi, were operating by the middle of the nineteenth century.

The common features of all these companies were their activities as trading companies that both **augmented the product set** available in their home country and overseas, and **arbitraged factor cost differences** across countries. In this regard, although they had limited value added beyond physical transportation and distribution, they really were progenitors of modern multinationals.

Their existence stemmed from the enormous challenges of international trade in those centuries and the difficulties, even impossibilities, of operating in unpopulated geographies or among civilizations that could not sustain reliable contractual relations. Put simply, in the pre-Industrial Revolution era no one could be trusted in a foreign country, so activities requiring any degree of investment had to be internalized within the firm. Advancing money to fur trappers in North America, or building a trading fort in India, could only safely be monitored within the firm itself or through trusted relations. The trading companies, therefore, created overseas offices, staffed by their own personnel to supervise these operations and minimize risk. In this regard, they grew beyond the archetype of the import strategy by having their own activities in foreign countries. By 1647, the British East India Company, for example, had 23 factories in India, each under the command of a factor or master merchant and governor, with 90 employees.[9]

These multinationals still exist in the modern **vertical multinational** that internalizes a global supply chain within the corporate hierarchy. The oil companies, like BP, Shell, and Exxon, with exploration and production arms in oil states, and refining and marketing operations in their traditional domestic markets, are one example. The vast agribusiness firms, like Cargill and ADM, that own land and plantations, source and process crops in many countries before transporting them to larger markets for sale to consumer packaged-goods companies, are another example.

Similar to the original trading companies, these vertical multinationals have internalized transactions along the global raw material supply chain in order to exploit country factor cost advantages. The issue confronting such contemporary vertical multinationals is that which almost went unchallenged in the historic version: Why does the supply chain need to be administered within the firm hierarchy? If today's technological and institutional infrastructures support intermediate markets, facilitate contractual relationships, and reduce transport and communication costs, what benefits accrue to a firm that internalizes those transactions within the hierarchy? Most of the oil companies, for example, encourage their upstream arms to sell at arm's-length market prices to their downstream activities. What then is the remaining benefit of being vertically integrated?

One possible answer lies in a competitive advantage that these modern versions have added to the traditional vertical multinational – the **informational advantage** that twenty-first-century communications technology confers on a coordinated global network of activities. With a presence in over 66 countries, Cargill, for example, has proprietary knowledge about the upcoming world wheat crop that allows it to generate profits trading the commodity and arbitraging sales between countries.

In this contemporary version of the vertical multinational, the historic justification for internalizing a global supply chain has, in some sense, disappeared. Exxon need not have a US gas station business to be successful as a discoverer of deep-sea oil. Market contracts can easily lead to the dismemberment of the vertical multinational, unless some other, informational, advantage justifies internalizing product transfers between production stages within the firm hierarchy. As such, although looking like a classic vertical multinational that is exploiting country advantages (CSAs), the modern vertical multinational is actually closer to a transnational that leverages the agglomeration benefits of a coordinated global network.

Multidomestic

Definition and Description

The multidomestic strategy is the first generic international strategy that involves the firm operating across borders as a true multinational. The distinguishing characteristics of this strategy are twofold. The first is taking an existing competitive advantage – traditionally embodied in a product set or capability that is successful in the domestic market – and replicating that within additional geographies. The second characteristic is that after an initial transfer of knowhow from the domestic entity, each foreign subsidiary is given the autonomy and the full range of activities to adapt its offerings to meet local market requirements.

The classic examples of multidomestic strategies were those followed by consumer packaged-goods companies, from Unilever and Procter & Gamble, to Gillette and Nestlé. These began as purely local companies, Dutch and British in the case of Unilever, which after establishing competitive advantage in the domestic market for a particular product line, such as margarine or soap powder, went international in order to increase sales and profitability. In doing so they merely transferred the product and the marketing approach originated in the home country to an independent foreign subsidiary which was free to adapt that product to local needs.

International Advantage

As we argued in Chapter 2, leveraging advantages around the world places emphasis on resources, not activities. This is particularly true for the multidomestic strategy where there is limited activity sharing and each country's product offering can diverge over time.

The emphasis for the multidomestic therefore has to be on building a **distinctive set of capabilities**, skills and knowledge that are transferable across national boundaries. Unilever, for example, sells its leading soap powder, Omo, in 62 countries under several different brand names, including Wisk in the USA, using many different formulations. In spite of this seeming variety and incompatibility, Unilever exploits a common set of skills in customer insight, consumer marketing, product innovation, etc., that enable the company to satisfy the universal consumer demand for clean clothes, even if the actual form the product takes varies according to the specific needs of each country.

Thus, enterprises pursuing the multidomestic strategy typically exploit superior abilities and knowhow (see box). With those resources, Unilever can **augment** existing product offerings in many countries around the world. Note that the intrinsic advantage can be found in production or customer capabilities, and can be either superior to, or just different from, that found in any of its new markets.

After completing an acquisition, CEMEX engineers and plant operatives are assigned to the new facilities as part of a SWAT team to reengineer processes, rearrange supply contracts, and identify investment projects that quickly bring the plant up to CEMEX's operating standards. While CEMEX encourages local managers to continuously draw on the company's best practices to ensure that it remains the most efficient local producer, it allows plant executives to choose the optimal local fuel source, which aggregates to use, and so on.

CEMEX's model, therefore, exemplifies both the initial transfer of competitive advantage from the parent company to the country subsidiaries and the subsequent local adaptations which are the distinguishing features of the multidomestic strategy. The benefit of this is obvious, as CEMEX has been able to increase operating margins at acquired plants by up to 7%.

Strategic Alignment

Product   The classic multidomestic strategy begins by transferring a firm's skills and capabilities, embodied in a set of product offerings and their associated market positioning and branding as well as the key manufacturing processes, to foreign countries. Unilever, for example, began its international activities by exporting products such as "Sunlight Soap Made in England by Lever Brothers." This was first exported to India in 1888 through local distributors before local manufacture was begun, after acquiring those distributors and setting up the company's own subsidiaries (Jones, 2005). Those products were the most successful domestic brands, Sunlight Soap in the case of Unilever, and advertisements at the beginning of the 20th century show how similar the product – "The Canadian make of Sunlight Soap is equal in every respect to that made in England" – and positioning was across countries in the early days. Both British and Canadian print advertisements from that time, for example, feature a bar of soap open to the left with a picture of a woman in an apron doing the wash and a similar claim – "largest sale in the world" and "fastest selling bar soap".

After this initial transfer of knowledge, and with the full set of activities, including manufacturing and engineering in place in a country, each subsidiary was then able to adapt that (broadly defined) product offering to local market conditions. The defining attribute of the multidomestic strategy is therefore **local adaptation**. Every subsidiary may leverage the parent's capabilities, but their implementation becomes customized to the unique demands of each country. In this way the multidomestic maintains an advantage over firms pursuing standard global product strategies and over local players that do not have access to the global corporate resources and capabilities.

Over time the product offering in each country will diverge from that of the home country. Lux, for example, the original Unilever flake soap product, is the leading soap brand in Brazil, Thailand, and India. In Japan, however, Lux is the market leader in hair care products! Unilever allows its Benelux companies to sell a carbonated "Lipton Ice

Tea" because the product has traditionally sold well there, even when that brand is "still" elsewhere.

A question then arises as to why the foreign subsidiary needs to continue to be owned by the original parent – if the child has been let loose, what is the ongoing value of parental reins? The contemporary answer is found in the continuous and multidirectional transfer of ideas, innovations, and capabilities across the global network that becomes the transnational strategy (see box). The historic answer was that most foreign subsidiaries continued to rely on a stream of innovations from the domestic operation. It was true that each country could choose what to do with any innovation – whether a new product, a new advertising campaign, or new production process – adopting it if it worked for them, possibly under a local brand or local positioning, but all major innovations still came from the domestic headquarters. As a result, the foreign subsidiary had to remain linked to the parent organization or it would lose its competitive advantage over time. Thus, each subsidiary had a limited role to play in the global entity. Rather than being active contributors to the global network they were merely passive recipients of headquarter's innovations.

Difference Between Multidomestic and Transnational Strategies

There is a suggestion that at present the multidomestic strategy verges into the transnational strategy with its reliance on the ongoing transfer of skills and knowledge across countries. Indeed, the two strategies are becoming more similar, particularly since the most prominent exponents of the transnational strategy are consumer packaged-goods companies that historically pursued the multidomestic strategy.

We can still usefully identify a difference between the two strategies. The classic multidomestic strategy involved a **one-time transfer of knowledge from headquarters** to individual countries, while the transnational strategy involves the **continuous transfer of capabilities between each and every country** (Exhibit 5.2). To the extent that the multidomestic continues to transfer knowledge, it is always hierarchical and **one directional –** from the headquarters to the subsidiaries – whereas the transnational is

Exhibit 5.2.
Transfer of capabilities

Classic Multidomestic   Transnational

multidirectional. Thus, while the multidomestic could be structured with autonomous country subsidiaries, the transnational requires a **coordinated** global network of interrelated geographic entities, each of which has its own capabilities that can make a contribution to continuously improving the multinational's performance.

Indeed, CEMEX demonstrates this behavior today as data on the relevant operating characteristics of all plants – from aggregate person hours per ton, to the grades of aggregate consumed – is readily available for comparison and benchmarking. Plant managers strive both to optimize their own operations and to continuously learn from their peers' advances. A triennial review of every plant's operations also ensures a regular transfer of learning that does not only originate from corporate headquarters.

This philosophy gave rise to the **product lifecycle** or **waterfall** approach to product development in the multidomestic (Vernon, 1966; Wells, 1972). In its archetypal form this began with the home country developing a new product to meet leading edge demand. Since most advanced skills, such as basic R&D, were retained in the domestic parent organization, and since the home country typically featured bleeding edge customers, new products would initially be developed for, and then introduced first in, the home country. Close links with corporate officers – always based in the home country – enabled innovations to be rapidly approved, and the physical adjacency of all functions allowed for easy experimentation. As most multinationals were based in developed countries, high-quality outsourced services, such as advertising agencies, were also available to support the product launch.

If the product was a domestic success, it would then be rolled out in a sequenced launch around the world. Initially, the introduction would be in advanced economies that were physically close and economically similar to the home base. This maximized the likelihood of repeating the success with minimal adaptation. Over time the product would be cascaded down to successively more distant countries – distant both in geography and stage of development – as the multinational learnt how to accommodate differences to the basic design and positioning, and as income in those countries increased to a level that could support sale of the product. By the time the product was available worldwide – a time that might be decades – new products would have been launched in the home market, beginning the product lifecycle all over again.

In this model, it was even possible on occasion to prolong the life of outdated manufacturing facilities by shipping them to countries that were at the beginning of the model generation. In the 1980s Crown Cork and Seal, for example, shipped its old crown lines (metal caps for bottles) to the Third World even as it was investing in two-piece canning lines in the USA. And before WWI, Singer ran the largest single factory in Tsarist Russia – a sewing machine factory utilizing equipment that had been discarded by its New Jersey and Glasgow factories.[11]

Location Because the multidomestic strategy encourages local adaptation, it requires the replication of **most of the firm's activities in every country** in which it competes. There might not be basic research undertaken in every country, but each must have some engineering and development capability to support local product variants. All will have local sales and marketing organizations, including their own market research capability, to sense and respond to the country's idiosyncratic consumer needs. And in many cases, countries will have manufacturing operations that are capable of, at the very least, final assembly and packaging, and more often are fully fledged plants perhaps lacking only some scale-sensitive component manufacturing.

The replication of activities in many countries is obviously expensive, and therein lies the drawback of the multidomestic strategy. In the search for local adaptability, the multidomestic sacrifices global efficiency. The natural evolution of the strategy in this regard has therefore been toward the **regionalization** of activities to realize efficiencies across countries that are close geographically (to minimize transport costs) and economically and culturally (to minimize the cost penalty of adaptation and product variation). Indeed, on their path toward the transnational strategy, many FMCG companies spent a decade in the 1980s or 1990s regionalizing many of their functions. Instead of having every activity in every country, major activities, such as manufacturing and product development, were concentrated in a regional center, or at least were placed under a single regional authority and optimized on a regional basis (see later).

Structure Multidomestic companies must allow geographic subsidiaries a substantial degree of **autonomy**, if they are to be able to respond to local needs. Only executives on the ground who are in touch with the local market can make effective decisions about how to adapt headquarters initiatives to their unique needs. This implies that **geography** is the most powerful dimension within the multidomestic organization and that important decision rights lie with country managers. Indeed, multidomestic companies were historically noted for the power of country managers who operated fiefdoms of their own. HSBC, for example, which operated this way, had until the 1980s a rule that any headquarters executive had to have the written permission of the country head to visit the latter's country. Once, when an up and coming executive, now the CEO of the company, was charged with developing a regional trading platform, his request to visit a certain large country was denied!

Giving each country authority over its own operations and holding it accountable for its own performance simplifies the management of multidomestic companies. The clear reporting arrangement also maximizes the incentives for entrepreneurial behavior by local management. These benefits are added to the basic thrust of the multidomestic strategy – local customization of central innovations and capabilities – to build a powerful set of advantages.

The role of the corporate parent within a multidomestic is necessarily minimized, since headquarters is not directly involved with the actual operation of the local plants and marketing organizations. Historically, physical impediments on communication made it impractical for headquarters to make local decisions with any timeliness, but, even today, the essence of the multidomestic strategy is to allow for country autonomy. The parent will monitor the results of operations and reward local executives on that basis, but their greatest contribution will be to identify, invest in, and then leverage from corporate headquarters to each geographic subsidiary the **core capabilities** of the organization. Headquarters acts as the corporate center developing and transferring the company's unique competences throughout the world. In this role, multidomestic companies were practitioners of "core competence" long before the term was coined.

As these competences and skills are often vested in individuals' tacit knowledge, the only way to deploy them throughout the company is to move those individuals around the world. Multidomestic organizations, therefore, typically have a **cadre of international executives** who are parachuted into a country to become expatriate country managers. Indeed, only recently have multidomestic firms begun to hire indigenous managers as country heads.

Scope   As a result of the autonomy of every country unit, the multidomestic enterprise is best viewed as a **portfolio of discrete country units**. While all leverage the common skills and capabilities of the home country organization, each operates independently and its performance is unaffected by the fate of sister countries.

As a portfolio of separate investments, resource allocation decisions within the multidomestic are made by treating each country on its own terms. Since there are limited interrelationships among geographies, investment decisions in one country have no repercussions on other entities. Thus, **each country stands on its own** with investments approved or rejected according to the potential returns within that country alone. In the extreme, if operations in a country are unlikely to ever be profitable, that country can be exited since its absence will have no effect on performance in other countries. When Union Carbide's industrial gases business was deciding what to do with its unprofitable European operations, the argument that it was pursuing a multidomestic strategy was compelling support for the divestment of those subsidiaries. Losing European operations would have no effect on its performance in other geographies and yet would save the losses the entity was generating. Thus, a multidomestic's geographic scope is driven by identifying in which countries it can cover the full cost of producing, selling, and delivering the product in that country on a standalone basis.

Global

Definition and Description

The archetypal global strategy involves making the opposite tradeoff from the multidomestic strategy, favoring global efficiency over local responsiveness, and achieves this by offering "the same product sold the same way everywhere around the world." While today the global strategy can feature a complex configuration of activities around the world – sourcing globally among dispersed manufacturing locations – implementing the global strategy is simplified because of its single-minded focus on optimizing the production and delivery of a standard product or service throughout the world. The advantages of such a strategy are the combination of simplicity and standardization that yields efficiency, and exploits scale and learning.

In the global strategy, countries are not independent but interdependent, and decisions cannot be made in any country without regard to their repercussions on other parts of the global organization. As a result, the global strategy requires the active **coordination** of activities around the world with the dominant axis of management being the global product division and with decision rights vested in those responsible for global activities, not individual geographies.

A classic example of the global strategy was Caterpillar in the earth-moving equipment business. Following the "Seabees" – the US Army engineers who built airstrips throughout the Pacific during WWII – Caterpillar established a global presence selling the exact same yellow bulldozer around the world through an exclusive dealer network similar to that in the USA. Initially, the bulldozers were built in US plants, mainly in Peoria, Illinois, which were responsible for over 80% of output into the 1980s. The equipment was exactly the same when sold in Thailand as when bought in the USA, satisfying a common global need for rugged and durable earth-moving equipment. Given the relatively high R&D costs and the scale economies involved in manufacturing engines and key components (approaching 100,000 units mes), Caterpillar's strategy of concentrating production in a single country was cost effective when annual global demand was only about 1 million units.

International Advantage

The viability of the global strategy is predicated on two conditions. First, the existence of a global customer who will buy a standard global product. Second, the existence of scale economies, or other interdependencies among countries that provide an advantage to a firm that can exploit them globally. These allow the global firm to exploit the benefits of **aggregation**.

Global Customers   The success of the archetypal global strategy requires the existence of a set of customers around the world who have essentially the same needs.

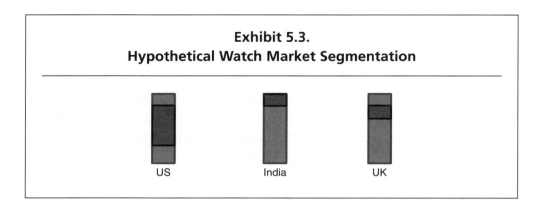

Exhibit 5.3.
Hypothetical Watch Market Segmentation

US India UK

Such **global customers** can be either the customer who wants the exact same product around the world, or different customers in each country who nevertheless value the same product attributes. In the former category are car companies wanting the efficiencies, consistency, and convenience of dealing with a single sheet steel supplier around the world, regardless of where its assembly plants are located. In the latter category are the airlines, each of which is domiciled in a different country, but which all value the exact same attributes of fuel efficiency, safety, and low capital and maintenance costs.

The existence of global customers does not necessarily imply the homogenization of global demand – that consumers everywhere are alike – rather it requires the existence of the same **global segment** in each country. The size of that segment and its position within each local market can vary substantially, provided a set of customers in each country values the same product attributes. Take a hypothetical example of Rolex watches (Exhibit 5.3).[12] In the USA it might be that consumers who buy Rolexes are middle class, so that Rolex is a mass market item. In India, it might be only the very wealthy who can afford Rolex watches, so that only a tiny tranche of customers buy the watch. In the UK, in contrast, it could be that Rolex watches are perceived as naff, or déclassé, so that it is only the nouveau riche who indulge in that ostentatious display of wealth. In each country the segment of the watch market that Rolex captures is very different. But in every country there is a segment that values the attributes of wealth and luxury for which Rolex stands.

The global customer need not be in existence before a global strategy is put into operation. Rather, the best examples of global strategy are those that create a global customer. As Ted Levitt, whose famous article "Globalization of markets" evoked interest in the global strategy, suggested (Levitt, 1983), creative strategies with "imagination" can conjure up a global customer out of a potpourri of seemingly different country demands. His example of washing machines in Europe envisaged the standardization of demand through the introduction of a small, automatic, front-loading washer with a heater. While market research suggested that consumers in individual European countries had idiosyncratic preferences, the introduction of such a washer at low prices would capitalize on underserved common needs. It is this notion of "seeing the unseen," of transcending apparent differences to satisfy the unifying underlying consumer need, that is the essence of creating the global customer.

We defer the detailed issues of global marketing – branding, pricing, advertising, etc. – until Chapter 7 and merely note here that the definition of global product covers these aspects of positioning and marketing.

Interdependencies Across Countries   The second condition for the existence of the global strategy is the presence of some form of economic interdependence across markets. In their absence, firms would be advantaged pursuing a local or multidomestic strategy that responded to local demands. Only if there are economic benefits to aggregation across markets can the global strategy be viable.

SUPPLY   The obvious interdependencies across markets are **scale economies.** The Boeing 787, for example, cost at least $16 billion to develop and another $16 billion to outfit manufacturing facilities (Gates, 2011). Such a large fixed expense can only be justified by selling that same plane everywhere around the globe. Developing a different model for developing countries would simply not be cost efficient. Similarly, semiconductors, operating system software, and LEDs have such large R&D costs, or require such large (billions of dollars) investment in manufacturing facilities, that only a player serving the global market with a standard product will be able to recover these upfront fixed costs.

Dynamic economies, such as **learning and experience,** can also support global strategies. The experience curve demonstrated in aircraft production, in which doubling accumulated output decreases production cost by about 20%, is a driver of global strategies in that industry and others, like semiconductors and shipbuilding.

In all these cases it is when the mes of operation is large relative to the global market size that the global strategy becomes relevant. If a local producer can reach the mes within the domestic market, there is no advantage to becoming global. In major appliances, for example, individual European countries were, for a long time, able to support indigenous producers because they reached the efficient scale of about 200,000 units within their local market (Baden-Fuller and Stopford, 1991). It must also be the case that **low transport costs** relative to the product's value make it economic to ship the standard product from a limited number of plants around the world. In cement, for example, perhaps a single huge facility would reduce manufacturing cost.

Unfortunately, distribution cost outweighs any production cost advantage once cement is shipped more than 300 miles (480 km) over land.

Notice that most examples of inherently global businesses are those in which a large share of cost lies in the fixed cost of **upstream activities**, like R&D and manufacturing. There are inherently less scale economies in downstream activities, like marketing and sales, while many of those activities have to be physically undertaken in every market.

DEMAND   Interdependencies across markets can also be found on the demand side. This is more than simply serving a similar customer around the world that we identified earlier; this is capitalizing on interrelationships among markets, such as when there are **network** effects – whether direct or indirect.

Direct network effects are present when a consumer is better off because another consumer also owns the product. In the international context, examples would include the express delivery business and adoption of fax machines. If FedEx only picks up from customers in the USA, its global delivery cost will be much higher than if it also picks up letters where it delivers them. Similarly, the more fax machines that are bought in Japan, the more connections are available to US fax owners.

Indirect network effects are those that work through a complementary product, hardware and software being the classic example. The profusion of iPhone applications developed for US customers, like "Angry Birds," encourages consumers in Asia to buy iPhones to access those same applications. Similarly, Japanese or Korean game developers prefer to develop for the video-game system that has the largest number of global customers. In each case, a global installed base induces supply of the complementary product, which in turn leads to additional global sales of the original product. The result is pressure to adopt a global strategy to capitalize on global network effects.

Strategic Alignment

Product   To realize economic interdependencies among markets, the product offering has to be relatively **standardized** around the world. The product does not have to be identical – even Boeing customizes the interior of its planes for each national carrier, and Intel will use local languages in its accompanying literature – but to get the most benefit from the underlying economies there have to be constraints on the variability of the product.

The term product means **more than just the characteristics of the physical product**. It includes the marketing-related aspects of brand positioning and the ancillary activities delivering and servicing the product, such as packaging, distribution, and aftersales support. To truly benefit from efficiencies and simplify the management task, the entire set of activities has to be similar everywhere. That is why the global strategy is described as "the same product, sold the same way everywhere around the world." Again, every activity does not have to be exactly the same everywhere, but the business system surrounding the product writ large has to be similar.

Scope   To fully exploit the economies that underpin the global strategy, a firm has to sell the product **globally.** More fundamentally, the strategy has to treat the world as a single market because of the economic linkages between countries. Unlike the multidomestic strategy, even if a global company is losing money in a particular country, it might remain in that country because those sales reduce costs or increase demand in the countries where it is profitable. When the marginal cost is lower than the average cost because of scale economies, the pressure on companies pursuing the global strategy is to sell wherever they can around the world.

Location   The choice of location for critical activities in the global strategy is more complicated. In principle, since the strategy is predicated on efficiencies and scale economies, it should **concentrate** activities in a limited number of locations that have the most **favorable factor costs** for the performance of that activity. This is why the classic global strategies were based in a single country. Caterpillar, until the late 1980s, had over 80% of its manufacturing in the USA. The Japanese motorbike and car companies only started producing outside their homeland when they had built substantial global market shares. Similarly, the Japanese consumer electronics companies only began to invest in US and European manufacturing facilities after dumping suits restricted imports from Japan.

Indeed, when the global strategy was first identified, it was associated with the threat from Japan to "hollow out" US manufacturing. As such, the strategy was seen as the natural extension of the export strategy, since manufacturing remained concentrated in the country with favorable factor costs. Magaziner and Reich, for example, estimated that Japanese auto manufacturers had at least a 15% cost advantage over US producers in the 1980s because of steel and labor cost differences (Magaziner and Reich, 1982).

Today, the global strategy can be more nuanced in its location choices (Chapter 9). First, unlike the classic strategy, **different activities can be located in different countries** to exploit the current factor cost advantages relevant for each. While Caterpillar used to make everything in Peoria, today it makes engines in China and India as well. Second, concentration in a single location is not required if the minimum efficient scale supports more than one facility. Intel, for example, now has nine major fabs in four countries including Ireland, Israel, and China, since its global scale allows it to operate this number of plants, while distributing them around the globe reduces risk.

The rule for the contemporary global strategy, therefore, is to ensure that every facility is at least at **mes** with locations for the resulting number of facilities diversified across countries to reduce risk and potentially exploit dynamic arbitrage possibilities (see box).

Difference Between Global and Transnational Strategies

If the multidomestic strategy blurs into the transnational strategy with respect to arbitraging knowhow, the global strategy can blur into the transnational with respect to arbitraging locational advantages (Exhibit 5.4). Again, the fundamental difference between the two is a hierarchical versus coordinated network approach. The global strategy hierarchically allocates activities to a limited number of locations; the transnational strategy continuously reoptimizes between a broader set of locations.

Exhibit 5.4.
Locational Arbitrage

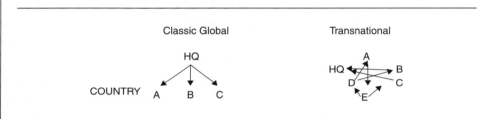

Structure   Since the global strategy is looking for simplicity and efficiency on a global basis, the organization design has authority vested in decision makers rewarded for global performance. Pragmatically, this means a **global product or line of business** structure with a global business head having ultimate decision rights. Often this is accompanied by a functional structure within the global business unit so that a head of manufacturing, for example, controls all plants and can decide locations, capacities, production volumes, etc., around the world. While country managers remain in charge of local activities, like sales, responsibility for even those activities will ultimately lie with a global functional head.

Regional

There is an intermediate international strategy that was pursued by many of the consumer packaged-goods (CPG) firms as they tried to get the best of both multidomestic and global strategies. It is, in fact, a strategy that appears to be relatively common in practice, in which the multinational configures itself by region (Rugman and Verbeke, 2004).[13]

Description and Definition

There are two variants of this strategy, both of which suggest that the regional strategy is a stage on a progression from local toward a more coordinated international strategy. The first variant is when the firm chooses **only to compete in a single region.** This might be as it expands away from the domestic market and naturally chooses its home region first. Natura, for example, the Brazilian beauty company, has focused on Latin America as it has grown to be a $3 billion company (Jones, 2012). It could, however, also reflect a conscious choice to limit the firm's geographic scope to the home region where its advantage is most likely to be transferable. Peugeot-Citroën, for example, is the second largest European car maker but struggles outside the region because, as its Director General noted, "The European market is unique. We buy hatchbacks, but most other markets buy sedans. Europe is big on diesel. Almost every other market prefers petrol. Europeans like manual gearboxes. Most other markets prefer automatics .... We have concentrated successfully on Europe and European tastes."[14] In this way, limiting geographic scope has been used to simplify the challenge of competing internationally.

The second and more recent incarnation of the regional strategy – the **Triad strategy** – sees the firm competing globally but operating with three regional businesses: Americas, Europe, and Asia (with Africa and the Middle East usually placed, somewhat ungainly, within Europe). This variant can best be thought of as being **global within a region** and **multidomestic between regions**. The multinational can then capitalize on economies and similarities within regions, but acknowledge and accommodate differences between regions. As this suggests, it is therefore predicated on the notion that regions exhibit more commonalities than occur globally, or that commonalities first appear within regions.

The Triad strategy is particularly popular with companies which have differing market positions in the three regions. Typically a multinational will be strong in its domestic region, perhaps has a reasonable share in a second region, but will have a small, if growing, share in the third region. Having each region able to behave independently gives the flexibility to behave according to its regional market share. This is therefore a natural path for firms to follow as they expand geographically and build positions beyond their home region.

Note that a variant of the regional strategy is to group countries not by continent, but by **stage of development**. Thus, a multinational might have a structure of developed and emerging countries. The benefit of this grouping is that similarities within emerging markets can be exploited, while differences with developed countries do not have to be directly addressed.

Strategic Alignment

Strategic alignment for the regional strategy follows the multidomestic between regions, global within regions, mantra. That is to say, within a region there are likely to be standardized products, with activities, such as manufacturing, concentrated in a limited number of locations and managed by a regional business leader who has authority over country managers. Each region will, however, operate relatively independently, balancing supply and demand internally within the region, and with limited oversight and authority from the global headquarters. Regions will continue to draw on the expertise of headquarters, and perhaps rely on it for product and process innovations, but there will be little in the way of sharing across regions.

Companies like Unilever and Procter & Gamble looked much like this in the 1980s and 1990s as they struggled to overcome the limitations of their previous multidomestic strategies which were costly and preventing effective product innovation as development fragmented into minor country-specific initiatives. The first step on the path to becoming more globally integrated was to rationalize their activities within each region, since a more dramatic move to global integration would have been resisted by the organization.

On this journey a regional coordination was put in place with authority over country managers and a set of changes initiated to foster regional integration. These included brand rationalization so that small, country-specific brands were dropped and local names replaced by the regional brand name. Packaging was standardized, which brought substantial cost savings, and production, now brought under a regional head, was concentrated within a few facilities. All of this occurred within the region, with little communication with other regions and certainly with no global sharing of activities or global rebranding. Unilever, in Europe, for example, never looked to the USA for ideas when innovating within the margarine (yellow fats) business in spite of its success there with "I Can't Believe It's Not Butter." Nor was there any material transfer of product between regions – each balanced supply and demand within the region.

The move to coordination within regions facilitated the next step on the journey by allowing these companies to consider more extensive global integration in the transnational strategy.

Transnational

Definition and Description

The transnational strategy (named by Bartlett and Ghoshal in their seminal book *Managing Across Borders*) was applauded as being state of the art for all multinationals in the 1990s as it appeared to offer the elusive goal of being "Glocal" – of being able to "Think Global. Act Local." It would realize this nirvana by incorporating the virtues of both strategies to transcend the tradeoff between the inefficiency of the multido-mestic strategy and the homogeneity of the global strategy, and even added a unique advantage through the ongoing transfer of learning between countries!

Pitched this way, the strategy appears compelling, since it seeks to get the best of all possible worlds – who would not want to be local and global, efficient and responsive? There were even a number of companies that were identified as exemplars of the transnational strategy, including, most notably, ABB (Asea Brown Boveri) under Percy Barnevik. And yet today, the excitement and hype around the transnational has dimmed.

As we discuss how the strategy is constructed and what must be in place for it to work effectively, perhaps we can understand why the transnational is not the solution for every multinational organization. In particular, we can see how the challenge of building a coordinated global network can founder on the pragmatic difficulties of managing such an organization. The goals of the transnational strategy remain aspirational, even if their realization remains problematic. We postpone until Chapter 11 the question of whether, if appropriately designed, the transnational is still the dominant international strategy.

International Advantage

The idea behind the transnational advantage is to build (and then manage) a coordinated, but dispersed, worldwide network of markets and activities. In principle, that network can be **locally responsive** and **globally efficient**, and can exploit both **static efficiency** opportunities by sourcing in low-cost locations and **dynamic efficiencies** by leveraging its insider status and worldwide flexibility to transfer knowledge and ideas around the world, while continually reoptimizing production in the light of changing factor costs. Put in terms of our sources of international advantage, the transnational strategy can have it all – **augment** product sets, **aggregate** across markets, **arbitrage** factor cost differences, and **agglomerate** activities for continuous innovation. The intent of the strategy is clear. Yet exactly how this could be achieved remains unclear – after all, the premise of international strategy is that fundamental tradeoffs exist!

In practice transnationals have begun to develop ways to at least **balance the tensions** in the strategic decisions, even if not to completely supersede those tradeoffs. The platform product strategy that will be outlined in Chapter 7 suggests one approach. Discrimination in the allocation of firm decision rights described in Chapter 10 is another. Below we indicate what approaches can help achieve the desirable balance on the key tradeoffs for each decision. The theme for all is to realize more nuanced approaches than a blunt "one size fits all" treatment by carefully disaggregating and discriminating among activities. As such, it is more difficult to describe strategic alignment for this generic international strategy, and much of the solution is articulated in the separate chapters on the individual strategic decisions.

Strategic Alignment

Product   The choice of product is a prime example of the difficulty of being prescriptive about strategic alignment as it requires balancing the similarities around the world with the differences between countries – the epitome of being "Glocal." The similarities allow activities and costs to be shared, and ensure that when a new idea is developed anywhere in the world it can be applied everywhere. At the same time the product must be allowed to differ between countries in order to support variations that drive local willingness to pay and generate local innovation.

The solution lies in being **selective about what is shared and what is altered** between countries. Rather than viewing the choice as applying equally to every activity, a more discriminating approach to the distribution of authority is adopted. The result is that aggregation occurs across activities where there are real benefits to standardization, while decision rights are delegated to support adaptation in those activities that yield a substantial advantage to the localized offering. It is by **disaggregating** the balance of local responsiveness and global efficiency that the transnational solution is established. Financial services companies today, for example, standardize back office functions and IT systems since there are scale economies in their operation, while allowing those global platforms to support a profusion of local product offerings. The same credit card might be offered everywhere, but the customer it is marketed to, the terms and conditions that come with it, and the distribution method by which it is sold can be infinitely varied.

While the intent is clear and appealing, the challenge, as always, is how to implement this practice. Chapter 7 provides much more detail. Here we want to introduce the notion of the **platform** as the state-of-the-art solution adopted by companies in a range of industries from manufacturing to services.

The platform, which can apply to the physical product or the brand positioning that is an integral part of the customer purchase behavior, is designed around a standard core that supports a locally variable appearance. The auto industry is a prime example of the platform approach that most readers will be familiar with.[15] Those aspects of the product that are scale sensitive and/or fundamental to the overall performance of the vehicle, like the engine, powertrain, and the physical platform on which the body is built, are standardized and become the "platform." These can be thought of as the common upstream core. Features that can be cheaply altered, that come at the end of the production line, or that have a substantial impact on local demand are allowed to vary. Whirlpool, the major appliance manufacturer, even went to the extent of drawing a green line on the shopfloor to distinguish the shared core of its product from the part of the production line where geographic variety was introduced.

The platform concept can be applied more broadly than to just manufactured items, but the intent remains the same. In services, like fast food restaurants, it is the kitchen processes and brand positioning that are the platform – the actual food items vary locally. In financial services, the platform is the standardized back office IT systems which support localization of the customer-facing product attributes, like the interest rate on a loan or the asset that can be collateralized.

Unfortunately, this description only begs the question of where to draw the line. It is easy to see how having some activities localized and some standardized solves the problem. The difficult question remains: Which activities fall in which category? In the case of bank accounts, for example, should the most basic of all activities – account opening – be standardized or allowed to vary by country? If it is standardized then all the data coming into a bank's systems will be the same, with common data fields supporting analysis and standardized cross-marketing opportunities. And yet financial regulations concerning account opening differ so much between countries – some require photographic identification, some accept electronic signatures, some do not, and so on – that designing a single system that can accommodate all those variations ends up losing the scale economies on which the case for standardization was based. Drawing the line between local adaptation and global standardization remains one of the key managerial challenges of the transnational (see Chapters 7 and 9).

Scope   The tradeoff between the scale offered by broad geographic scope and the simplicity and efficiency of limiting scope to fewer, more homogeneous countries is achieved by categorizing countries. Countries which are critical for global scale and innovation, perhaps China, are included in the portfolio even if they are different from the domestic market. More alien and smaller countries might be excluded.

In practice, this means that a transnational has to maintain a **presence in leading countries** – leading in terms of consumer demand, and product and process innovation – and where its key international competitors are located. P&G, for example, learnt that it could not succeed in the cosmetics industry without a presence in Japan, where women have the most demanding personal cleaning and makeup regimens, and where one of its important global competitors, Shiseido, was based. Indeed, the agglomeration advantage requires a presence in every country where important customers are located – Milan, Paris, and London for fashion, Hollywood and perhaps Mumbai for movies, for example.

This means that, unlike the multidomestic strategy, transnational firms might compete in countries in which they are unprofitable because insider status there gives them access to unique consumer, competitor, or process insights. Unlike the global strategy, however, the transnational strategy does not demand a presence in every country, because global scale is only part of the competitive advantage it exploits. A transnational can choose not to compete in some countries if they are either unprofitable or if product demands are so different that a platform product cannot support their idiosyncrasies. By choosing to **avoid outlier countries**, the transnational narrows its geographic scope relative to the global strategy.

Again, this is simple to say, but what if China is a radically different market than the multinational's core markets? Should it be included or excluded?

Location   The transnational strategy disperses activities in order to exploit dynamic arbitrage opportunities. This allows the transnational to turn what most companies see as a risk and a threat – international differences, volatility, and uncertainty – into a source of advantage. The tradeoff, of course, is with maintaining the static arbitrage advantage of concentrating activities to exploit scale economies and current factor cost advantages.

The transnational strategy therefore seeks to strike a balance between a concentrated global configuration (one location) and a dispersed network of activities (many locations). This is achieved, in the first instance, by **differentiating among activities**, so that manufacturing plants might be concentrated, but R&D dispersed. Second, for those activities in which there are multiple locations, the **individual importance of each location will wax and wane** as circumstances within and between countries alter.

In addition, the transnational has to be a **true insider in the leading countries** in which it locates, with a substantive and empowered presence in those countries having a real influence on global decisions, rather than being a branch office staffed by expatriates who do not understand the local culture. The role of foreign subsidiaries in this strategy is therefore very different than for other strategies. Indeed, the transnational has to have a **full set of activities in key countries**. If it does not, it will lack the capability to respond to new local ideas and develop its own innovative products and processes. If product development remains centralized in the home country, foreign trends will be overlooked, ignored, or overridden. If no manufacturing is based in foreign subsidiaries, there will be no reason to improve or de-bottleneck the processes which face unique factor constraints in different countries. The result will be inadequate variation in the firm's experiments. Consequently, the transnational has to give **authority and influence to foreign subsidiaries**. If domestic headquarters dominates international activities, it is likely to override ideas from overseas and prevent their innovations being adopted globally. Instead, the transnational strategy gives weight to foreign subsidiaries in a way that the classic multidomestic did not when subsidiaries remained subordinate to headquarters (see box).

How many such locations are required for each activity remains an issue. But it is probably the case that today the transnational should have at least one location in each Triad region.

Role of Subsidiaries in the Transnational Strategy

Importantly, pursuing the agglomeration advantage expands the role of international subsidiaries. They cannot be inert recipients of headquarters initiatives, but must develop their own capabilities to become active contributors to, and implementers of innovations. The intent is to craft an integrated entity from a set of appropriately differentiated subsidiaries.

Much recent research has addressed the question of how subsidiaries can contribute to the global enterprise. The thrust of their findings is that centers of excellence will emerge in those geographies that have CSAs relevant for the desired competences, and which have been granted a degree of autonomy within the transnational's integrated global network (Bouquet and Birkinshaw, 2008; Frost et al., 2002; Alcacer and Zhao, 2012).

Indeed, Bartlett and Ghoshal identified four roles that any geographic subsidiary could perform for a given activity, such as R&D (Exhibit 5.5). According to the CSA in the performance of the particular activity (the vertical dimension), and the inherent capability of the subsidiary (the horizontal dimension), each subsidiary would play a different role within the multinational. This could vary from leading the way to being merely a passive implementer of ideas and innovations. In skin care, for example, even before it relocated its headquarters, P&G allocated its Japanese subsidiary a leading R&D role because that market was characterized by very demanding customers. The off-diagonals capture quadrants that either should not happen – the black hole where the multinational wants to exploit the CSAs of that country but the subsidiary does not have the skills to do so – or where the subsidiary does not drive the activity because its CSAs are not relevant.

Exhibit 5.5.
Subsidiary Roles

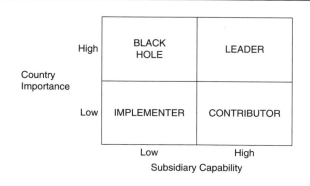

Source: Drawn from Bartlett and Ghoshal (2002).

Notice that all subsidiaries must have not only the ability to contribute to the rest of the organization, but also the absorptive capacity to continuously assimilate and incorporate global learning into their own activities (Song, 2014). This requirement reinforces the demands placed on, and expectations for, subsidiaries within the transnational.

Structure   The organization design of the transnational is hard to describe simplistically because it has to balance decision-making authority between the global business and function, and geographic subsidiaries – between one and many units. Indeed, the primary impediment to implementing the transnational strategy is just this organizational challenge of achieving the motivational advantage of high-powered incentives in many self-contained units (differentiation), and the global optimization that coordination (integration) provides.

One solution to the transnational's organizational challenge that was readily adopted by many multinationals – the matrix structure – is no longer seen as the salvation it was once believed to be. By having managers report to multiple bosses, the matrix pressured every executive to internalize, and so balance, the conflicting demands of country, business, and function themselves. In practice, the ambiguity only made executives more unclear about how to act, and more uncertain as to how to balance the different dimensions.

Instead of formal organization structure – the boxes and lines on the organization chart – the transnational now employs many **different organization design levers** (Chapter 10). These layer onto whatever formal structure is chosen; a series of horizontal processes and socialization tools that offset the vertical reporting lines and produce a more **nuanced allocation of decision rights** – perhaps R&D is managed centrally, but service and sales are managed locally – than in other strategies. More fundamentally, the solution to the transnational management challenge is seen not as lying in formalization of structure or even process, but in the **socialization of people and purpose**.[16]

While appealing, it is clear that incentives for and pressures on managers in such an organization are more complex than when vertical structures clearly define authority and responsibility. The result is conflict and tension within each and every manager so that the motivation/coordination tradeoff is, in some sense, just pushed down to the individual level.

Evolution of International Strategies

One observation that should be apparent from the above descriptions is how international strategies have evolved over time (Exhibit 5.6). One path started with the development of firm-specific capabilities for the local market and evolved into the horizontal multinational by leveraging those capabilities into independently operated subsidiaries (the multidomestic strategy exemplified by Unilever). The other path started by exporting country-based advantages to create a vertical multinational and then globalized by adding scale advantages to the original factor cost advantages (the route pursued by Japanese car companies). Later each converged toward the transnational strategy via the disaggregation (for previously global) or aggregation (for previously multidomestic) required of regional strategies.

Exhibit 5.6.
Evolutionary Paths

Export/Import — Vertical Multinational — Global

Local — Horizontal Multinational — Multidomestic

Regional — Transnational

A second observation is that the legacies of these differing paths shape a multinational's current culture and organization – the notion of an administrative heritage. As companies from different geographies tended to follow different evolutionary paths, Bartlett and Ghoshal even suggested there were substantive regional differences in multinational cultures and behaviors (Chapter 10).

IMPLICATIONS OF GENERIC STRATEGIES

Having introduced the generic international strategies, it is important to reiterate that they are archetypes. As ideal type representations we will not necessarily find any firm pursuing the pure form of each strategy described above in the real world. Rather, the generic strategies are caricatures that simplify reality by exaggerating certain aspects of their design, while glossing over or ignoring other aspects that might be similar between strategies. Real companies will often be found employing elements of several of the strategies. The question of whether such a combination can produce the "One Best Strategy" will be addressed in the final chapter.

Nevertheless, the generic strategies present a coherent way to align the four fundamental decisions that every multinational confronts, by identifying default solutions that are internally consistent. That alignment is driven by the need to support the international advantage that the firm seeks to exploit by virtue of its international presence, and is why the summary description of the generic strategies (Exhibit 5.7) begins with that advantage.

International Strategy Statement

We are now in a position to revisit the definition of an international strategy described in the introduction and provide additional examples of effective international strategy

Exhibit 5.7.
Generic International Strategies

	International Advantage	Product?	Compete?	Locate?	Organize?
Local	Market Specific	Idiosyncratic	Local	Domestic	Functional
Export / Import	Arbitrage Factor Costs or CSAs	Commodity	Opportunistic	Domestic	International
Multidomestic	Augment Product Set or FSAs	Waterfall	Standalone Profitability	Most Activities in Each Country	Geographic
Global	Aggregate For Scale and Efficiency	Standard	Worldwide	Optimal for Each Activity, Concentrated	Business Unit
Transnational	Agglomerate For Dynamic Efficiency	Platform	Key Markets	Dispersed and Flexible	Purpose, People, Process

statements. These cover the objective of the firm, its scope, and, most importantly, the advantage that it deploys in its international activities.[17]

Objective

The objective of the strategy is best thought of as the (ideally) single metric that management holds itself accountable for. That measure might be financial (30% of sales from international activities, revenue of $1 billion in six countries), or strategic (a 15% global market share, global sales over 1 million units). It could be cardinal (a 15% share), or ordinal (#1 in market share), but should represent an aspirational goal that motivates the organization and represents the **best milestone on the path to long-term shareholder value creation**. Whatever objective is chosen, it should be simple, measurable, proximate (i.e., has a date by which it must be achieved), and represent a stretch for management.

Scope

The scope of the strategy first describes the broad business domain of the multinational and its intrinsic competitive advantage – the competitive positioning advantage of low cost/differentiation. This element of scope establishes boundaries to the **product offering** in any country, typically at a high level of abstraction (e.g., low-cost, fast food restaurants), since the exact form the business takes in each country can vary substantially.

Scope then defines boundaries to the **set of countries in which the firm will compete**. Identifying these geographies is obviously a critical part of providing strategic direction to the multinational. However, the concern is not so much with identifying exactly which markets will be entered, but in clearly establishing limits to which markets should not be entered, so that they can be removed from all further consideration.

Advantage

The international advantage that the multinational will exploit across countries is perhaps the most difficult aspect of the strategy statement. While the intent is clear – to capture which of the four advantages the company is exploiting by virtue of its international activities – its representation, as for a business unit strategy, is best split into two parts.

The first is a description of the **resources** or FSAs that underpin the firm's value creation across geographies. These can either be preexisting capabilities (e.g., consumer insights); those created by virtue of the firm's international activity (e.g., accumulated global experience); or those CSAs the firm exploits by accessing a country's factor markets.

The second is a description of how those advantages will be realized within the firm by adopting an organization structure, systems, and processes that leverage and deploy resources throughout the firm. This part of the statement, therefore, describes the overall **organization design** and locus of decision making.

Each of these elements of strategy is more concerned with defining what the multinational will not do (i.e., the boundaries to its operations), rather than precisely defining what it will do around the world. Being explicit and complete about everything the enterprise does is impossible. Instead, the purpose of the strategy is to be clear about what executives should never consider. With those boundaries established, managers can be as entrepreneurial and creative as they like, secure in the knowledge that their activities and choices will be consistent with their global colleagues.

Examples

The examples of international strategy statements below illustrate each international advantage rather than repeat the generic strategies.[18] This shows how the valuable firm resources (FSAs) shape the strategy, but lead to slightly less distinction between the statements because they are not pure form examples.

Note that, as the consultants say in their slide decks, it is impossible to do justice to the strategies without a complete "deconstruction" of the statement – the detailed commentary that explains the nuanced meanings of each carefully selected word in the statement. As an example, the use of the word "key" in P&G's strategy statement obviously needs to be accompanied by a definition establishing the criteria by which countries qualify under this rubric. These details will be covered in Part Three where we address each key decision in turn. A full international strategy statement is therefore several pages long, but with the succinct summary forcing management clarity and providing a vehicle for communication inside the firm.

We start with an annotated example of Walmart's strategy statement that conveys some of the richness lying behind the bald summary.

Walmart (Augment)

To remain the largest volume discount retailer in the world in 2020.

Delivering the lowest prices for a broad range of regularly purchased discount retail and grocery goods that are always in stock in convenient locations, with an 80/20 rule for products in retailing environments similar to the US where we can quickly build a leading market share within an attractive market.

Leveraging our global scale, and supply chain, retail IT and merchandising capabilities,

by sourcing globally and localizing delivery, supported by centers of excellence in supply chain, merchandising and IT, but managed locally.

O: *"To remain the largest volume discount retailer in the world in 2020"*

A straightforward ordinal strategic goal that verges into a more motivational vision for the company.

S: *"Delivering the lowest prices for a broad range of regularly purchased discount retail and grocery goods that are always in stock in convenient locations"*

The first element of scope describes Walmart's intrinsic competitive advantage as a combination of a distinctive value proposition to customers and the business domain in which it operates. Walmart operates everywhere with everyday low pricing and a low-cost strategy; restricts itself to discount retailing and grocery (which actually covers a broad set of product possibilities); and relies on an efficient supply chain to support its well-located stores.

PRODUCT: *"with an 80/20 rule for products"*
COMPETE: *"in retailing environments similar to the US where we can quickly build a leading market share within an attractive market"*

- The second element of scope establishes the product and market boundaries for the firm. It acknowledges that some proportion (20%) of every store's offering will be localized, but that the majority will be goods available globally (Chapter 7 explains the 80/20 rule).
- With respect to geographies, Walmart has learnt that success in a new market requires achieving competitive scale rapidly – usually by acquisition or in a joint venture – not from organically building its own stores. It also requires the structure of retailing environment in the new country to be inherently profitable. Indeed, Walmart exited Germany, Indonesia, South Korea, and Hong Kong after failing to achieve the desired critical mass and when confronted, as with German store opening hour restrictions, by an institutional structure that restricted the Walmart business model.

A: *"leveraging our global scale, and supply chain, retail IT and merchandising capabilities"*
- This part of the advantage identifies the distinctive resources that add value to each country. Walmart obviously has global scale, but it has also built a set of capabilities around supply chain management (cross-docking, automation), IT (it has the second largest private database in the world), and merchandising.

LOCATE: *"by sourcing globally and localizing delivery"*
ORGANIZE: *"supported by centers of excellence in supply chain, merchandising and IT, but managed locally"*

Walmart's unit of management is the store, and store managers are delegated some responsibility for merchandising and pricing. They are supported by a supply chain that sources globally, even though a substantial share of product might actually be bought locally, and by headquarters functions that run IT, purchasing, and merchandising.

Next we offer three strategy statements that capture the other international advantages. Then we recast all four statements to compare and contrast their differing implications for the four strategic decisions.

Maersk Oil (Arbitrage)

O: Become a sustainable producer of 500,000 barrels of oil per diem by 2016
S: As one of the lowest cost producers
- Discovering both oil and gas
A: Leveraging exploration and production capabilities in deep sea and other tough environmental operating conditions to deliver complex projects on time and on budget as a trusted partner to governments, particularly in emerging markets
- from low cost reserves in difficult locations
- under a single global organization supporting "captains" for each project

---

Federal Express (Overnight Delivery) (Aggregate)

O: To become the largest global express delivery company by 2020

S: providing the fastest and most reliable service to every destination
- for overnight package delivery within and between countries
- to any location in the world

A: with the most comprehensive global coverage and largest scale of operations
- through a global network infrastructure (planes, hubs)
- managed by the global business unit

P&G (Agglomerate)

O: To remain the world's most valuable consumer packaged goods company through 2020

S: Offering branded consumer products that capitalize on unique customer insights and research to deliver distinctive consumer experiences.
- selling globally branded products
- in every key market

A: leveraging unique customer insights from around the world, and distinctive consumer marketing and multi-channel management skills
- with local implementation and delivery of globally developed products and brand positionings
- through global business units and shared services organizations supporting local market-facing executives.

To illustrate the power of the strategy statement to provide direction to the organization, we compare and contrast their implications below. Hopefully, the differences among the strategies will become apparent as we see how they lead to very different choices for each of the four strategic decisions.

Product   The product element of the strategy statement defines the degree of local product adaptation that is permitted. Here, the distinction between strategies should be readily apparent. Arbitrage and aggregate establish a default of no local variation. Agglomeration allows the physical features of the product to vary but not its brand positioning, while augment delegates authority over 20% of the product offering to local management.

Augment: 80/20 rule to allow for local adaptation;
Arbitrage commodities (oil and gas);

Aggregate standard global product which is the same everywhere around the world;
Agglomeration globally branded, even if the physical characteristics of the product itself might vary.

Compete   The boundaries around the markets in which the different strategies will compete are also fundamentally different. Aggregate will seek to be selling everywhere, as will arbitrage on an opportunistic basis. In contrast, augment will only compete where it can be profitable on a standalone basis, while agglomeration steers the middle course by competing in "key" markets.

Augment: standalone market profitability (which is the result of specifying retail environments where Walmart can quickly build a leading market share within an attractive market);
Arbitrage: markets are not specified since the product is a commodity that can be sold opportunistically wherever there is demand;
Aggregate: every market in the world;
Agglomeration: key markets (which obviously needs clarification to identify the characteristics of "key" markets but which, for P&G, would include parameters such as market size, domicile of main competitors, and regional diversification).

Locate   Boundaries to the location of the multinational's activities are more difficult to capture as they vary by activity and should identify specific countries. As a result, this part of the statement is more ambiguous, but nevertheless conveys important differences. Aggregate simply seeks to optimally locate facilities around the world, while agglomerate and augment have a balance between operations that must take place in countries in which they compete, and certain global functions that will be more geographically concentrated. Arbitrage is the easiest to identify since it will be present only in those countries that have the appropriate factor market characteristics.

Augment: global supply chain but local delivery, with global centers of excellence (whose location should be specified, but today probably lie in Bentonville and Asia);
Arbitrage: countries that have low-cost reserves in difficult locations (i.e., exploiting certain CSAs), and emerging markets where Maersk's willingness and ability to become a trusted partner for governments are more valuable;
Aggregate: global infrastructure with network facilities efficiently located around the world;
Agglomerate: local implementation and delivery of globally developed products and brand positionings.

Organize   The basic allocation of decision rights should be apparent from the organizational aspect of the strategy statement. Both arbitrage and aggregate have authority
lying with the global business unit while holding local management accountable for
implementation according to local conditions. Augment has reporting lines the other
way around, with local management being supported by global services. Agglomeration is the most complex organizationally, with a matrix attempting to balance the
three dimensions of country, business, and function.

Augment: managed locally, but with global sourcing;

Arbitrage: a single global organization with "captains" serving as project managers for
each exploration site held responsible for delivering results;

Aggregate: global business unit in charge of all strategic decisions even if local
management had the flexibility to seek out local operational efficiencies;

Agglomeration: global business units and shared services organizations supporting
local market-facing executive (i.e., a complex matrix organization).

*   *   *

I hope these statements serve as a guide to crafting a strategy for your company. Hopefully they illustrate how different multinational strategies can be; in particular, how different their answers are to the four strategic decisions. It is by specifying and communicating those boundaries that a multinational's international strategy provides much
needed direction to executives when confronting any of these contentious issues.

NOTES

1. This example is a disguised composite of events at a number of European utilities. Names and positions are fictitious.
2. At least in the retail business. Most seemingly independent dry cleaners actually utilize a shared cleaning facility.
3. This does not mean that the local firm does not import inputs. Such a firm will, however, not have
   any operations outside its borders.
4. Although the firm still needs some competitive advantage (FSA) against local rivals who can also
   exploit the country's comparative advantage.
5. Nike currently produces more in Vietnam than in China: 37% vs. 34% (Rein, S. (2012) *End of Cheap
   China*. Wiley: San Francisco, p. 35).
6. The studios do now take foreign tastes into account in developing movies since the foreign box office
   is 68% of total movie industry sales. The recent movie *Battleship*, for example, was altered so that the
   threat posed by aliens was not just to the USA but to the entire world!
7. Apparently this is not quite correct. Warner Bros did alter its movies in Germany in the immediate
   postwar period to avoid hurting German sensibilities. *Casablanca*, for example, was edited to contain
   no references to Nazis.
8. Timken website, accessed at http://www.timken.com/en-us/about/Pages/Timeline.aspx.

9. East India Company Wikipedia entry, accessed at http://en.wikipedia.org/wiki/British_East_India_Company.
10. CEMEX has built other capabilities, for example, in marketing, that complement those in manufacturing.
11. Potkina, I. (2006) The Singer Company in Russia 1897–1917. Paper presented at XIV International Economic History Congress, accessed at http://www.helsinki.fi/iehc2006/papers3/Potkina.pdf.
12. I trust this fictitious example does not offend owners of Rolex watches!
13. Rugman identified 88% of multinationals pursuing a regional strategy.
14. M. Picat, Director General of Peugeot, quoted in *Business Life* (2013) Business Life meets Maxime Picat, January, p. 11.
15. GM, for example, had 30 platforms in 2010, but intends to have only 10 global platforms by 2020 (Colias, M. (2011) GM to slash global vehicle platforms by more than half, to 14, by 2018. *Automotive News,* August 9, accessed at http://www.autoweek.com/article/20110809/CARNEWS/110809876). Similarly, Ford intends to drive sales of over 6 million units from 5 platforms by the middle of this decade (Ramsey, M. (2010) Ford SUV marks new world car strategy. *Wall Street Journal,* November 20, p. B2).
16. This was the contribution of Bartlett and Ghoshal in their notion of the individualized corporation, which is covered in more detail in Chapter 10 (Ghoshal, S. and Bartlett, C. (1999) *The Individualized Corporation.* HarperBusiness: New York).
17. See Collis, D. and Rukstad, M. (2008) Can you say what your strategy is? *Harvard Business Review,* 86(4), 82–90, for a fuller description of the framework applied to business unit strategy.
18. These are not necessarily the actual international strategy statements of the companies in question.

REFERENCES AND FURTHER READING

Alcacer, J. and Zhao, M. (2012) Local R&D strategies and multi-location firms. *Management Science,* 58(4), 734–753.

Ambos, T.C., Andersson, U., and Birkinshaw, J. (2010) What are the consequences of initiative-taking in multinational subsidiaries? *Journal of International Business Studies,* 41(7), 1099–1118.

Andersson, U., Forsgren, M., and Holm, U. (2001) Subsidiary embeddedness and competence development in MNCs — a multi-level analysis. *Organization Studies,* 22(6), 1013–1034.

Andersson, U., Forsgren, M., and Holm, U. (2007) Balancing subsidiary influence in the federative MNC: a business network view. *Journal of International Business Studies,* 38(5), 802–818.

Baden-Fuller, C. and Stopford, J. (1991) Globalization frustrated: the case of white goods. *Strategic Management Journal,* 12(7), 493–507.

Bartlett, C.A. and Ghoshal, S. (2002) *Managing Across Borders: The Transnational Solution,* 2nd edition. Harvard Business School Press: Boston, MA.

Birkinshaw, J.M. and Hagstrom, P. (2000) *The Flexible Firm: Capability Management in Network Organizations.* Oxford University Press: Oxford.

Birkinshaw, J.M., Hood, N., and Jonsson, S. (1998) Building firm-specific advantages in multinational corporations: the role of the subsidiary initiative. *Strategic Management Journal,* 19(3), 221–241.

Birkinshaw, J.M. and Pedersen, T. (2008) Strategy and management in MNE subsidiaries. In A.M. Rugman (ed.) *The Oxford Handbook of International Business,* 2nd edition. Oxford University Press: Oxford, pp. 367–388.

Bouquet, C. and Birkinshaw, J. (2008) Weight versus voice: how foreign subsidiaries gain the attention of headquarters. *Academy of Management Journal*, 51(3), 577–601.

Calori, R., Atamer, T., and Nunes, P. (2000) *The Dynamics of International Competition*. Sage: London.

Cantwell, J.A. and Mudambi, R. (2005) MNE competence-creating subsidiary mandates. *Strategic Management Journal*, 26(12), 1109–1128.

Christensen, C. and Zobel, J. (1997) Unilever's butter beater. Harvard Business School Case #698-017 (Exhibit 6).

Collis, D. and Rukstad, M. (2008) Can you say what your strategy is? *Harvard Business Review*, 86(4), 82–90.

Frost, T., Birkinshaw, J.M., and Ensign, S. (2002) Centres of excellence in multinational corporations. *Strategic Management Journal*, 23(11), 997–1015.

Gates, D. (2011) Boeing celebrates 787 delivery as program's costs top $32 billion. *Seattle Times*, September 24.

Ghemawat, P. (2003) The forgotten strategy. *Harvard Business Review*, 81(11), 76–84.

Ghemawat, P. (2007) *Redefining Global Strategy: Crossing Borders in a World Where Differences Still Matter*. Harvard Business Review Press: Boston, MA.

Ghoshal, S. (1987) Global strategy: an organizing framework. *Strategic Management Journal*, 8(5), 425–440.

Ghoshal, S. and Bartlett, C. (1999) *The Individualized Corporation*. Harper Business: New York.

Hagen, B., Zucchella, A., Cerchiello, P., and De Giovanni, N. (2012) International strategy and performance—clustering strategic types of SMEs. *International Business Review*, 21(3), 369–382.

Inkpen, A. and Ramaswamy, K. (2006) *Global Strategy: Creating and Sustaining Advantage across Borders*. Oxford University Press: Oxford.

Jones, G. (2005) *Merchants to Multinationals*. Oxford University Press: Oxford.

Jones, G. (2012) The growth opportunity that lies next door. *Harvard Business Review*, July/August, 141–145.

Khanna, T. and Palepu, K. (1999) The right way to restructure conglomerates in emerging markets. *Harvard Business Review*, 77(4), 125–134.

Levitt, T. (1983) The globalization of markets. *Harvard Business Review*, May/June: 92–102.

Magaziner, I. and Reich, R. (1982) *Minding America's Business*. Harcourt Brace Jovanovich: New York.

Peng, M. (2006) *Global Strategy*. Thomson/South-Western: Mason, OH.

Porter, M.E. (ed.) (1986) *Competition in Global Industries*. Harvard Business School Press: Boston, MA.

Rugman, A.M. and Verbeke, A. (2004) A perspective on regional and global strategies of multinational enterprises. *Journal of International Business Studies*, 35(1), 3–18.

Schleimer, S.C. and Pedersen, T. (2013) The driving forces of subsidiary absorptive capacity. *Journal of Management Studies*, 50(4), 646–672.

Schwartz, J. (1996) Earning It: a marathon of disruption for corporate Atlanta. *New York Times*, July 21.

Segal-Horn, S. and Faulkner, D. (1999) *The Dynamics of International Strategy*. International Thomson Business Press: London.

Song, J. (2014) Subsidiary absorptive capacity and knowledge transfer within multinational corporations. *Journal of International Business Studies*, 45, 73–84.

Spulber, D. (2007) *Global Competitive Strategy*. Cambridge University Press: Cambridge.

Tallman, S. (2009) *Global Strategy*. John Wiley & Sons, Ltd: Chichester.

The Economist (2012) Intoxivation: how a new market is producing a wave of innovation in an old industry.

Vernon, R. (1966) International investment and international trade in the product cycle. *Quarterly Journal of Economics*, 80(2), 190–207.

Wells, L. (1972) *The Product Life Cycle and International Trade*. Harvard Business School Press: Boston, MA.

Yip, G.S. (2002) *Total Global Strategy*, 2nd edition. Prentice Hall: Englewood Cliffs, NJ.

Choice of Generic International Strategy

We stated that there is rarely "one right" strategy to pursue in international competition. There are many industries where firms are able to succeed while pursuing different international strategies. Major appliances, confectionery, and fast food restaurants are examples where one firm has succeeded with a global strategy (Whirlpool, Mars, and McDonald's, respectively); another with a multidomestic or regional strategy (Electrolux, Cadbury, and KFC); while others have flourished with a local strategy (GE, Hershey, and Taco Bell). Even in the beer industry, Anheuser-Busch InBev has a global strategy, SABMiller is multidomestic, and local brewers, like Samuel Adams, also prosper.

Indeed, our little Catalan furniture manufacturer probably had a free choice between the export strategy by accepting the Uzbek order and a more regional strategy by seeking to become an IKEA supplier. Either choice, if implemented effectively by aligning the four strategic decisions appropriately, would probably have succeeded for an extended period.

We do, however, need to provide a way for companies to choose among the generic international strategies. Although it is rare that economic determinism compels the adoption of a specific international strategy, there certainly are some industries, like semiconductors or aircraft, where the underlying economic structure can only support one strategy. Conversely, not every strategy will work in every industry. Thus, even if international strategy is a choice in many industries allowing each company to decide according to its heritage and capabilities and management preferences and judgment, it is important to outline the economic determinants of successful international strategies.

PRINCIPLES

Any successful international strategy will build off the company's original business model and competitive advantage. That is why the decision about which international strategy to pursue must start from an analysis of the **firm's valuable resources**. It is also why clarifying the firm's advantage is a critical part of the international strategy statement. FSAs differ in the extent to which they can exploit the four sources of international advantage. A low-cost competitor winning on scale is more likely to consider aggregation and would therefore look to verify that was viable, before considering other sources of international advantage. Conversely, a frequent innovator depending on novel consumer insights would be more likely to pursue agglomeration and would initially look to the feasibility of that advantage.

More generally, it is the relative strength of the **factors that support or limit the ability of a firm to exploit each of the four sources of international competitive advantage** that determine which of the generic international strategies are feasible in any industry (Exhibit 6.1).

The drivers for each of the strategies can be summarized as follows:

- Augment: extent of differences in the business system (writ large) among countries that create gaps in product and capability space but favor locally adapted products.

- Aggregate: degree of economic interdependence between markets that generate efficiencies across geographies.

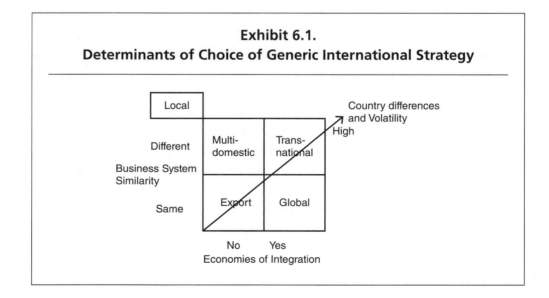

Exhibit 6.1.
Determinants of Choice of Generic International Strategy

- Arbitrage: extent of current factor cost differences that generate static arbitrage advantages.
- Agglomerate: volatility and unpredictability of differences between countries that generate dynamic arbitrage and innovation opportunities.

The relevance and impact of each of these drivers has to be assessed and a judgment made about their relative importance. This will identify industries that only support one strategy and provide insight into which are the most powerful sources of advantage in any industry.

BUSINESS SYSTEM SIMILARITY

The reason that companies cannot simply replicate their domestic strategies globally is that countries differ. And yet there is substantial variation in the degree to which businesses differ around the world. The container shipping business is similar everywhere around the world. The roadside vendor business is very different: in South Africa it is hawking mobile phone cards; in Greece fake luxury goods; in Malaysia food products; while in Singapore it is actually illegal to operate without a license. The first determinant of which international strategy will be most effective in a business is therefore the **extent of differences in the business system** around the world (Exhibit 6.2). Answering

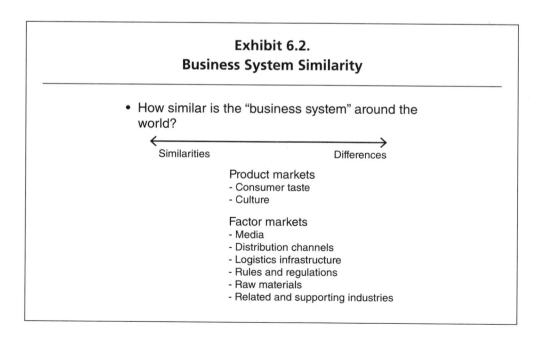

Exhibit 6.2.
Business System Similarity

- How similar is the "business system" around the world?

Similarities ← → Differences

Product markets
- Consumer taste
- Culture

Factor markets
- Media
- Distribution channels
- Logistics infrastructure
- Rules and regulations
- Raw materials
- Related and supporting industries

this captures the degree to which the product must vary among countries and thus the extent to which a strategy of local responsiveness is required. Similarities tend to support global and export strategies with standard products. Differences support multidomestic and transnational strategies that augment products or FSAs available locally, and allow for the requisite local adaptation. If, however, the differences are too extreme, there are no opportunities to augment the domestic offering, and only the local strategy will succeed.

We can characterize country differences in many ways. Here we follow the distinction between product and factor markets and simply observe that industries fall on a continuum from similar to different in their variation across countries. There is no simple way to quantify these differences (but see Chapter 8 for one method), so this analysis is more qualitative than quantitative.[1]

In the product market, differences arise among any of the determinants of consumer demand – income, cultural heritage, fashion, etc. – that we are all familiar with (Chapter 3). Factor market differences are as, if not more, important to the degree of business system similarity. Can the same media mix and marketing strategy be supported in countries where there are differing restrictions on television commercials affecting children, sexual content, and so on? Can a distribution strategy that focuses on big box retailers work in a country, like Japan, that protects small retail outlets? Can the product be physically distributed the same way if there are no railroads or vehicular infrastructure to support containerized shipping?

Just because differences exist between countries does not mean that they are strategically significant. As we will see in Chapter 7, differences only become significant when they cannot be overridden or accommodated at minimal economic cost. Thus, significant and immutable differences tend to be those embedded in a country's heritage. Small houses and apartments in Japan and Hong Kong, for example, are more likely to have a permanent influence on demand than the nationality of film stars. Differences concerning activities that are a large share of the total cost of a product or service are also more likely to be strategically relevant than those concerning small items. Manuals being printed in different languages, for example, will have much less impact than differing requirements for pollution controls, such as catalytic converters on cars.

EXTENT OF INTERDEPENDENCIES AMONG COUNTRIES

The second determinant relates to the extent of economic interdependence between countries. Essentially the question is that posed by Porter, "**Am I better off in**

```
┌─────────────────────────────────────────────────────────────────┐
│                          Exhibit 6.3.                             │
│                    Country Interdependencies                      │
├─────────────────────────────────────────────────────────────────┤
│                                                                   │
│        • "Am I better off in country A by virtue of               │
│            my presence in country B?"                             │
│                                                                   │
│                    Pro                         Con                │
│        Fixed R&D cost              High Transport Costs, Tariffs  │
│        Economies of Scale          Government Restrictions        │
│        Experience Curve            Different Customer Needs       │
│        Factor Cost Differences     Incompatible Standards         │
│           and Volatility           Management Costs               │
│        Global Customers               - time/expense              │
│        Network Externalities          -autonomy                   │
│        Common Worldwide            Business System Differences    │
│           Competitors                                             │
│        Imitative Innovations                                      │
│                                                                   │
└─────────────────────────────────────────────────────────────────┘
```

country A by virtue of my position in country B?" If competitive position in one country is improved because of a firm's presence in another country, then there are economic interdependencies that require treating the entire globe as a single entity rather than as a set of separate markets (Exhibit 6.3). The more interdependence, the more viable is a strategy of global efficiency. The less interdependence, the more selective a multinational can be about its geographic scope.

There are many sources of interdependencies, as well as factors that create diseconomies which limit the degree of economic interdependence. It is the balance of these scope economies and diseconomies that determines whether a successful international strategy needs to aggregate and agglomerate in order to exploit those interdependencies, or whether the local strategy can survive.

On the **supply** side the set of economic drivers that create scope economies include:

• High fixed costs that can be amortized across multiple markets. Typically, these are the upstream fixed costs, such as R&D or manufacturing plants. The reason that the semiconductor industry is only populated by firms pursuing global strategies is the multibillion dollar investments required in R&D and fab plants.

• Substantial economies of scale operating on large parts of the cost structure. The large minimum efficient scale for auto manufacturers demands at least a regional strategy for success, and perhaps even a global presence, as the remaining regional European players like Renault and Peugeot-Citroën appear to be discovering.[2]

- Experience or learning curve economies that bring costs down as accumulated output increases. These economics characterize the semiconductor and aircraft industries, contributing to their global nature.

- The existence of substantial factor cost differences among countries can require a firm to disperse activities and suggests that an international strategy reliant on a few locations will be unsuccessful.

On the negative side is a set of factors that limit or restrict trade itself:

- High transport costs and tariffs that restrict the flow of goods and services between countries. The reason that most service businesses do not show economic interdependencies is the prohibitive cost of providing a service, like hairdressing, across borders.

- Government restrictions on activity by foreign firms that prevent their operation in certain countries.

- Incompatible standards, such as historically prevailed in mobile telephony, which prevent products suitable for one standards regime being used elsewhere.

And more generally:

- The full list of business system differences identified above that impede the naive replication of activities across countries.

On the **demand** side factors creating interdependencies across markets include:

- Global customers demanding consistent provision of the product or service they purchase around the world. For example, several consuming industries for industrial gases feature firms with a global footprint, such as Mittal Steel and Intel, which prefer to do business with one provider everywhere around the world.

- While global customers, such as multinationals that use the same employee benefits vendor around the world, are typically B2B, there are also global consumer brands. High-end luxury goods, like Prada, benefit from having their cosmopolitan consumers show up in celebrity hot spots around the world – think movie stars in Aspen and Portofino. In these locations other wealthy people (and probably as important, less wealthy people watching reality television and entertainment news programs) are impressed by their clothes and accessories. The desire to emulate them then creates global status or aspirational brands, like Kate Spade.

- Network externalities, whether direct or indirect, that increase demand for a product, like Xbox, in one country because more consumers own it in another country.

- The presence of global competitors can also force a firm to acknowledge linkages between markets. If not, the company with a global footprint might, for example, be able to subsidize an attack on the home of a single market competitor. Only by defensively building its own global presence to create a threat of retaliation can the firm prevent this (Chapter 4).

- Innovations that are regularly adopted around the world or imitated by competitors in different countries. For example, fracking – the practice of fracturing shale rock to recover natural gas – has been quickly adopted around the world. Schlumberger was able to leverage that new technology to quickly build a position in Asia. In contrast, innovations in construction do not get copied broadly. The US, for example, is replacing wooden siding with PVC, a material that is barely used in Europe.

On the negative side are demand characteristics that limit global economic interdependence. These can be thought of as factors favoring simplicity over scale and that make it hard for a multinational to extend across heterogeneous markets to benefit from aggregation:

- Business system differences that prevent a multinational offering the same product everywhere, including fundamental differences in customer needs across countries.

- Management costs – direct and indirect – that accompany the attempt to coordinate activities across countries.

As with business system similarity, we cannot precisely quantify the extent to which economic interdependencies exist across countries. Accordingly, the intent of this analysis is to identify a set of relevant characteristics and assess for each the net effect of positive and negative economies. The presence of negative economies supports the local strategy because it could actually be harmful to be present in more than one country; few economies support the export and multidomestic strategy since there are no compelling economic arguments to be present in many countries; and positive economies suggest a bias to the global or transnational strategies whose broad geographic presence can capitalize on their presence.

Exhibit 6.4.
Static Arbitrage Opportunities

Arbitrage Opportunities

PRO	CON
• SUPPLY	• SUPPLY
– Factor cost differences on large parts of the cost structure	– Activities are not footloose
– Stability in factor cost differences	– Limited share of cost in mobile activities
– Shorter term commitment to a location	– Limited factor cost differences
	– High transport costs
• DEMAND	– Barriers to trade
– Product market differences of intermediate level	• DEMAND
	– Substantive product market differences

One tool that can be useful as a guide to the analysis of economic interdependencies is the value chain. Typically, it is activities that lie upstream in the value chain, such as R&D and component manufacturing, that are more scale and learning sensitive and give rise to interdependencies between countries. In contrast, businesses where more of the value added accrues in downstream activities, such as services, are less appropriate for global strategies. While not definitive, a quick check of where the larger chunks of value added in an industry lie can be a useful guide to the extent of interdependencies among countries.

CURRENT DIFFERENCES IN CSAs

The third determinant is the extent to which differences between countries create static arbitrage opportunities (Exhibit 6.4). These arise when factor costs in the business differ between countries on important parts of the cost structure. They also arise when product market differences are of an intermediate level so that a novel or fashionable product introduced from another country can augment domestic product space.

Substantial factor market differences favor a strategy that operates in countries with a comparative advantage (favorable CSAs) and undercuts the feasibility of local and multidomestic strategies that are predicated on satisfying local demand from within each country.

Two criteria shape the importance of factor cost differences. The first criterion is simply the **magnitude of factor cost differences** between countries. If the factor is a globally traded commodity, like semiconductors, it is unlikely that there will be much of a locational advantage to be gained. In contrast, if countries, for example, impose very different tax regimes on domestically consumed oil, the cost of energy can be a major determinant of location. Currently, while there is a global price of a barrel of oil that is captured in well-known commodity indices, such as Brent Crude, the actual price of oil within a country varied in May 2012 from Norway at $9.69 gallon to Venezuela at $0.09 gallon because of differential tax and subsidy treatments.[3] Electricity prices similarly differ by a factor of more than three and so shape the locational strategies of energy-intensive producers, like aluminum companies.

To commit to exploit the arbitrage advantage, a multinational must be confident that any current factor cost differences will be stable for the length of the investment period. That is why purchasing a component or raw material on a spot market can be more readily arbitraged than investing in an R&D facility. Over the life of the asset, volatility in factor costs can invalidate the decision to commit to arbitrage from a single location.

The second aspect affecting the potential for static arbitrage opportunities is **the size of the cost element**. The search for low labor costs has driven manufacturing from developed to developing countries. However, as design and process innovation reduce the labor content of an item, the need to chase the lowest labor cost erodes. Indeed, this dynamic played out in one of the first "advanced" industries when Japan, and then Taiwan, replaced the USA as the largest manufacturer of television sets in the 1970s and 1980s. Even at that time, as automatic insertion replaced manual insertion, and as the number of components in a finished set fell from over 1,200 to over 200, direct labor assembly hours fell from nearly 10 to less than 1. At this level, the advantages of offshoring began to erode, and the number of television sets manufactured in the USA has actually increased since 1975, passing the previous peak (and Japanese output!) by the early 1990s (Gao and Tisdell, 2004).

The same thing is happening today with Apple products and other advanced technology items. By 2012 the direct labor content of an iPhone was down to 2.4% of the retail price (Exhibit 6.5). At those levels, even if Chinese labor is substantially cheaper than in the USA, pursuing savings on 2–3% of the cost structure becomes less worthwhile. As a result, Apple is now returning some manufacturing to the USA where it benefits from being closer to the end consumer.

Product market differences among countries are also drivers of arbitrage opportunities. That is, after all, the underlying principle behind the augmentation strategy.

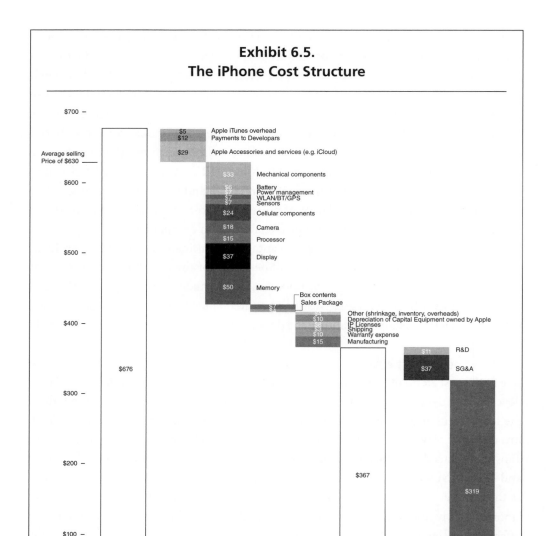

Exhibit 6.5.
The iPhone Cost Structure

- $5 Apple iTunes overhead
- $12 Payments to Developars
- $29 Apple Accessories and services (e.g. iCloud)
- $33 Mechanical components
- $6 Battery
- $7 Power management
- $7 WLAN/BT/GPS
- $7 Sensors
- $24 Cellular components
- $18 Camera
- $15 Processor
- $37 Display
- $50 Memory
- Box contents
- Sales Package
- Other (shrinkage, inventory, overheads)
- $10 Depreciation of Capital Equipment owned by Apple
- IP Licenses
- Shipping
- $10 Warranty expense
- $15 Manufacturing
- $11 R&D
- $37 SG&A

$700

Average selling Price of $630

$600

$676

$500

$400

$367

$300

$319

$200

$100

Amount deferred: $16

$16

$0

□ Revenues | Ancillary Revenue | BOM | Package | Assembly, Licensing, Depreciation, other | □ Gross Margin | Operational Expenses | ■ Operating Margin

Source: Bill of materials (BOM) estimates from iSupply; others are estimates by Horace Dediu of Asymco

As was noted above, countries have to have somewhat differing product markets to give rise to this initial arbitrage opportunity, but not such vast differences that there is insufficient demand to support the foreign product. Trying to sell air-conditioners to Iceland, for example, will probably be unsuccessful.

Working against the arbitrage strategy are the usual impediments to trade – transport costs, tariffs, non-tariff barriers, etc. – that simply prevent locating an activity anywhere but in the final consumption market. In addition, there are cases where footloose activities constitute an insignificant part of the cost structure, or do not feature large variations in factor costs around the world.

EXTENT OF VOLATILITY

The fourth determinant of choice of international strategy is the presence of factors creating an advantage from continuously arbitraging activities and learning across dispersed locations. There is an important difference here between static arbitrage – Vietnam is today the low-cost production location for textiles – and dynamic arbitrage – the ability to continually reoptimize production among locations, and take learnings from anywhere to quickly deploy them everywhere around the world. The former can be done once and then left alone. The latter requires ongoing coordination, and becomes more valuable when there are unpredictable variations between countries.

Indeed, the value of agglomeration is the option value created from investing in many countries. And **option value** is the best way to think about the determinants of whether such a strategy is worthwhile. It is therefore factors that increase uncertainty and unpredictability that make dynamic optimization worthwhile (Exhibit 6.6). In the palm oil business, for example, an industry one might assume is stable and predictable, many of the large South East Asian plantation companies based in the current low-cost locations of Malaysia and Indonesia are making investments in Africa – namely, Liberia and Ghana – and in South America. The value of such investments lies not just in the risk reduction of country diversification, nor even in the possibility that large exchange rate movements might shift relative factor costs, but also in market demand uncertainties. Environmental sustainability concerns, for example, might limit consumer demand for palm oil produced in plantations carved out of uncut forests in South East Asia, rather than those that replaced other crops on existing plantations in Africa. Health concerns can shape demand as palm oil is relatively low in saturated fats, but has a high percentage of monounsaturated fats and few really bad polyunsaturated fats; genetic engineering advances in seed technology might then affect the optimal location for growing palm oil; and so on. Even a mature agricultural business, like palm oil, can be subject to sufficient uncertainty and volatility – particularly given the 15-year time span to bring a new plantation into full production – to justify the pursuit of dynamic arbitrage.

The first set of drivers of volatility and unpredictability relates to economic conditions:

- Exchange rate volatility is the most obvious source of dynamic arbitrage opportunities – the annual average change in the dollar against other currencies, for example, is over 7%. Acknowledging that most industries cannot achieve that level of annual productivity improvement implies that (what to a single firm seem to be) exogenous fluctuations in exchange rates have more impact on competitiveness in any given year than the firm's own actions! However, as was noted in Chapter 3, it is not the volatility of exchange rates alone that matters, but also the unpredictability of those exchange rate movements. If exchange rate changes are large but predictable – perhaps because they correlate with differences in inflation rates – the anticipated movement can be hedged. It is only the unpredictable component of exchange rate fluctuations that creates an arbitrage opportunity.

- It would be easy to assume that all industries are impacted by exchange rate volatility in the same way. However, the competitively relevant set of countries differs by industry. In the copper industry, for example, key producers are Chile, China, Peru, and the USA. It is therefore the volatility of exchange rates between these countries that determines the potential for dynamic arbitrage in the copper business. In contrast, for LCD screens, the major producing countries are Korea, Japan, and Taiwan. Exchange rate volatility among those countries is very different than that between Chile and China.

- Similarly, unpredictable differences in GDP or industry-specific growth rates create the opportunity to shift production between locations. CEMEX, for example, exploits the fact that the construction cycle is imperfectly correlated among countries to export cement from countries where demand and prices are low to those where both are high. Locating cement plants close to terminal facilities and controlling one-third of the international trade in cement have contributed to that company's success as it exploits agglomeration advantages.

- Unpredictable shifts in industry factor costs create dynamic arbitrage opportunities. In wine and other agricultural industries, for example, weather is so unpredictable that crop yields and prices vary substantially from year to year and country to country. A sourcing strategy that flexibly shifts purchases between countries will therefore generate an advantage over a company that is locked into a single country. This is why agribusiness firms diversify production across geographies. ADM, for example, operates facilities in over 75 countries.

The second set of drivers relates to the rate of innovation. A stable industry in which neither products nor production methods change much, such as bone china, will not benefit from dynamic arbitrage in the way that a rapidly evolving technology, like LEDs, will. The inherent technological dynamism of an industry is therefore a factor to consider.[4] Similarly, the extent to which innovations spill over between countries affects the viability of the dynamic arbitrage strategy. A business, like construction, in which most countries are autarkical will not be as amenable to the agglomeration strategy as products sold on the Web to the younger generation, like gangnam style music, where any hit goes viral globally within days.

Two factors limit the ability of firms to exploit dynamic arbitrage opportunities. The first is when there are few or only predictable differences among countries. As countries become more integrated in free trade and currency zones, uncertainty decreases. European producers that could have exploited currency movements between French francs, Italian lire, and Greek drachmas can no longer do so under the common currency. As a result, CPG companies moved to concentrate activity within Europe after the creation of the eurozone.

The second factor includes the usual suspects of barriers to trade – high transport costs etc. Notice, however, that since dynamic arbitrage leverages ideas and innovations, the absence of trade need not prohibit the agglomeration strategy. A fast food restaurant can take a product innovation from one country around the world, as KFC did with Krushers (a milkshake-like drink with confectionery pieces that was developed in India), even though there is no physical movement of fast food around the world.

It is important to notice how this example captures the tension inherent in the transnational strategy. Country subsidiaries have to be sufficiently different in order to support a variety of experiments, but sufficiently similar that any good idea can be replicated everywhere. KFC can apparently take Krushers anywhere around the world, but struggles to transfer the KFC pie, developed in New Zealand, to other countries.

Factors that constrain the dispersion of activities, such as economies of scale and a large share of value added in activities that must be performed locally, also limit the feasibility of dynamic arbitrage strategies.

Overriding all these inhibitors of dynamic arbitrage possibilities are management complexities. If the relevant set of countries that can be exploited includes Mongolia, Congo, and Venezuela, the sheer impracticality of doing business in all three countries could outweigh any potential benefits.

IMPLICATIONS OF CHOICE OF INTERNATIONAL STRATEGY

The drivers of strategic choice outlined above are extensive and hard to quantify. Nevertheless, it is important for every multinational to examine them to get a sense of which sources of international advantage might be exploited in its industry. While not deterministic, assessing where the industry lies along each continuum is necessary input into choosing an international strategy.

The analysis will rarely identify an economic necessity to pursue one specific international strategy. Industries that are at extremes on certain dimensions, such as sausages in business system differences, might support limited strategic choice, but in general the analysis will only provide an indicator of which strategy is most appropriate. Instead we should recognize that the choice of international strategy is **rarely black and white** and that there is a degree of freedom for individual firms to choose the strategy that suits them best.

In addition we must recognize that the choice of strategy, to the extent that it is determined by the underlying **economic structure of the industry**, can vary across **segments** within the industry, and through **time**. Within the accounting industry, for example, large multinational clients probably require a global strategy because of the demand for global consistency. In contrast, the middle market of local retailers and service clients probably requires a multidomestic or transnational strategy as business system differences are substantial. This is why the global accounting firms often struggle to manage operations inside a country because they actually serve two different businesses within a single entity.

Nor is there necessarily an inexorable move toward more integrated strategies within every industry. After WWII the importance of technological developments in design and plant construction economies supported a global strategy in the cryogenic industrial gases business. As the technology matured, the fact that the economic radius of a mes plant was limited led toward the multidomestic strategy and devolution of authority to regional managers. In the last stage, as clients globalized and demanded consistent supplies of a range of gases, the transnational strategy became more attractive. Note that within industrial gases there has always been a segment – distribution of gas cylinders to body shops, welders, etc. – that was local because high transport costs overrode any other driver of international strategy.

At the end of this analysis we then confront the fact that economic determinism does not typically prevail in the choice of international strategy. Rather, international strategy remains a choice variable for many multinational companies. This has two implications.

First, a firm should choose an international strategy as much on the basis of its heritage, skills, and capabilities as on the economics of its industry. Critical to this is the firm's **original competitive advantage** or FSA. If a firm pursues a low-cost strategy in its domestic market, the set of skills it has built will favor international strategies of aggregation and arbitrage. In contrast, a differentiator capable of developing innovative products might be more likely to adapt an augmentation or agglomeration strategy.

Second, companies should not agonize over finding and pursuing the one "right" or "best" strategy, but should **make a choice they are comfortable with**, and then move on to the more important work of ensuring that every tough choice of product, scope, location, and organization is aligned with that strategy. It also implies that looking over your shoulder at what competitors are doing and naively trying to copy them because they have "it right" is probably the worst thing to do.

The choice of international strategy therefore boils down to executives having the courage of their convictions in making a decision they can commit to (although they are encouraged to periodically review its premise), and then moving on to address the issues covered in the next part of the book. Strategy is, after all, simply the guiding direction for the organization. It must always be referred to – hence the generic international strategy grid that lays out the default answers to the four key questions – but it should never be overly deterministic.

NOTES

1. For other drivers of globalization, see Yip, G.S. (2002) *Total Global Strategy*, 2nd edition. Prentice Hall: Englewood Cliffs, NJ.
2. "Clearly we are too European today and that is a big difficulty for us" (Maxime Picat, Director General of Peugeot, quoted in *Business Life*, January 2013, p. 11).
3. Data accessed at http://www.bloomberg.com/slideshow/2012-05-12/highest-cheapest-gas-prices-by-country.html#slide1.
4. Jeffrey Williams introduces three types of industry – slow, standard, and fast cycle – identified by their average rate of price increase/decrease (Williams, J.R. (1992) How sustainable is your competitive advantage? *California Management Review*, Spring, 29–51).

REFERENCES AND FURTHER READING

Gao, Z. and Tisdell, C. (2004) Television production: its changing global location, the product cycle and China. University of Queensland Working paper #26, January.

Harzing, A.-W. (2000) An empirical analysis and extension of the Bartlett and Ghoshal typology of multinational companies. *Journal of International Business Studies*, 31(1), 101–120.

Porter, M.E. (ed.) (1986) *Competition in Global Industries*. Harvard Business School Press: Boston, MA.

Ricart, J.E., Enright, M.J., Ghemawat, P., Hart, S., and Khanna, T. (2004) New frontiers in international strategy. *Journal of International Business Studies*, 35(3), 175–200.

Williams, J. (1992) How sustainable is your competitive advantage? *California Management Review*, Spring, 29–51.

Yip, G.S. (2002) *Total Global Strategy*, 2nd edition. Prentice Hall: Englewood Cliffs, NJ.

PART THREE

Managerial Implications

Multinational executives face tough choices every day in every aspect of their activities. Whether at four in the afternoon when a customer from a new geography asks for a reduced price to seal a deal, or at ten the next morning when a regional plant manager asks for approval to drop some local products, executives are always being tested in the implementation of their strategy. It is here that the rubber hits the road, and if international strategy is to be more than just a nice intellectual concept for senior executives, it has to directly influence such decisions.

The final part of the book, therefore, addresses the managerial implications of international strategy. It provides a toolbox and a set of analytic processes to guide executives as they make each tough strategic decision. While it will be found that the recommended actions are substantially impacted by the firm's international strategy, this part of the book looks through the lens of the individual decision and provides assistance when making those choices. The approaches outlined do not depend on having mastered the previous parts of the book (though it will surely be helpful if you have) as they are designed to function as independent aids to decision making.

All the controversial issues within multinationals can be subsumed under four headings: what product (broadly defined to include positioning, pricing, and processes) to offer around the world, and how much variation to allow between countries; in which countries to compete and how to allocate resources among those countries;

the geographic location and configuration of activities around the world; and how to formally structure the enterprise and support it with appropriate organizational processes, systems, and values.

Each chapter therefore takes up the challenge of providing pragmatic guidance to executives wrestling with one of these four decisions. The intent is to provide analytic processes which both draw on the best practices of contemporary multinationals and can be readily employed. While there are pieces of theory interspersed throughout this part, the focus is on providing tools that can be applied by any executive to their own situation.

The final chapter asks whether there is a single best international strategy, and, if so, what that strategy might look like. If the previous chapters lay out ways to balance advantages and supersede tradeoffs, is there now a dominant international strategy that all multinationals should pursue which combines the best of each separate strategy? Put another way, can we reconcile the pursuit of operational efficiency in every activity, which leads to the exploitation of multiple sources of international advantage, with the recommendation that enterprises pursue a single international strategy? After all, every successful multinational will today operate in many geographies, feature a complex supply chain, encourage empowered subsidiaries to meet many local requirements, and will adopt multifaceted and nuanced administrative procedures.

The concluding chapter argues that there still is a need for every multinational to have a clearly articulated, effectively communicated, and well-understood international strategy. While acknowledging that many decisions can be made on operational efficiency grounds alone, the need for a unifying direction to resolve remaining conflicts and ensure the alignment of every executive's activities and choices demands that, at their core, every multinational pursues a single coherent international strategy.

What Product?

MOTIVATION

Many of you will be familiar with the HSBC advertisements that adorn most of the world's major airports. To support its positioning as "the world's local bank," HSBC demonstrates how the same word or picture can convey entirely different meanings in different parts of the world – a "football" in the US is oval shaped with tapered ends, in the UK is round, and in Australia is oval shaped like a rugby ball with rounded ends – implying that its local knowledge allows it to adapt its product and service offerings to meet the peculiarities of any market. The irony is that HSBC's main product for consumers is a premier account designed for the few cosmopolitan globetrotters that want single source access to a bank account in several different countries and currencies! Yet this example neatly captures the first strategic choice that confronts firms which compete internationally and illustrates the underlying dilemma – do you offer a single product with similar brand positioning everywhere you choose to compete, like the premier account,[1] or do you adapt your product and market positioning to satisfy the idiosyncrasies of different geographic markets?

Look at Exhibit 7.1 and consider the following question (before reading on!): Which company sells the beverages shown in Japan, including the hot coffee, Georgia, available in vending machines throughout the country?

In fact, it is the Coca-Cola Company (Exhibit 7.2)! The company, revered as owning perhaps the most widely recognized brand in the world, actually owns or licenses more than 500 brands globally.[2] And I bet you have never heard of at least three-quarters of them, including "Yoli," a lemon–lime soda available in Acapulco Mexico, and "Lemon and Paeroa" available in New Zealand.

So if even the most "global" company in the world has a profusion of local brands, perhaps we should all learn a lesson and adopt local products? Not so fast. Consider one of the most successful global advertising campaigns – MasterCard's "Priceless"

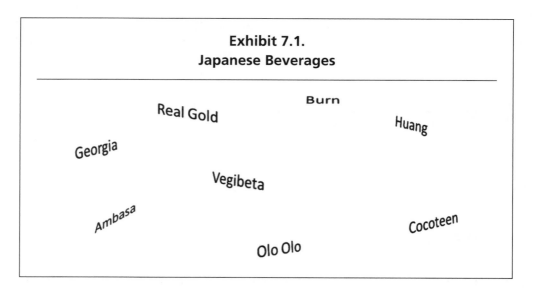

**Exhibit 7.1.
Japanese Beverages**

campaign. Launched in 90 countries and 47 languages, the same positioning – "there are some things money can't buy, for everything else there is MasterCard" – allowed MasterCard to gain 14% market share points relative to Visa in a five-year period in the USA, and had similar success elsewhere. One product, a credit card, sold the same way, everywhere around the world.

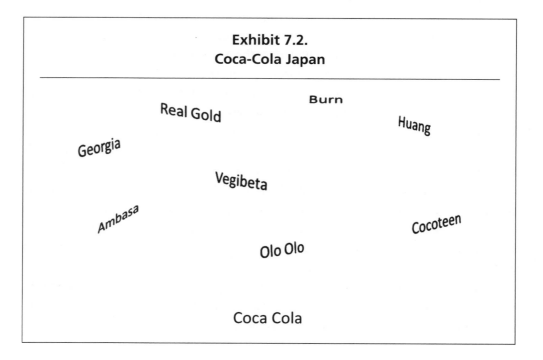

**Exhibit 7.2.
Coca-Cola Japan**

Confronted with these two very different strategies, what is a company to do? How should a company respond to the ever-present differences between countries? When are those differences simply a matter of degree which can be overridden by a single global product, and when are they a matter of substance that requires strategic accommodation to local needs?

Every international executive has confronted this thorny issue of whether to have local product variety or to coordinate on a more globally standardized version. The French subsidiary might want packaging in bold colors to attract attention and dominate shelf space in mass retailers. Germany, in contrast, might want to minimize the cost of packaging in order to compete on price with competitors from lower wage countries, like Hungary, while the regional manufacturing function just wants to standardize the packaging. And all the intense adversarial sessions to hash out the final choice is between well-intentioned executives simply trying to do their best for the company as a whole!

STRATEGIC TRADEOFFS

Given all the differences among countries identified earlier, it is rare that the exact same product can be sold successfully everywhere. Trivial differences, such as language and voltage, abound, but, more often than not, substantive differences arise. Just think of food items like sausages, biscuits (or cookies in the USA), beer, chocolate, and even pizza, and the list goes on.[3] And lest you think it is only consumer goods that vary globally, consider how variations in country regulations affect transportation – driving on the left versus the right, the width of railroad tracks, trucker hours, customs screening processes, and so on.

Even if the product itself is standard around the world, the way it is used, how it is distributed, and cultural perceptions of it can fundamentally differ among countries. Pharmaceuticals, for example, have exactly the same physical effects on every human body in the world, and yet income levels, cultural attitudes toward the body, and the institutional structure of health care are so different around the world that even though the physical product is the same everywhere, the marketing and sales of a drug can be profoundly different. Cholesterol-lowering drugs, like Lipitor, for example, are routinely prescribed to prevent heart attacks in the USA, but can only be economically justified after a patient has suffered a heart attack in Poland.

Faced with these differences, multinationals confront the classic strategic tradeoff in the product market between **local responsiveness and global efficiency** as they consider what product they should sell around the world (and more broadly how they should position, place, price, and promote their products – the 4Ps of traditional marketing). Standardizing the product exploits scale economies, experience, and static arbitrage opportunities, but at the cost of reducing the willingness to pay in every country when the product no longer exactly matches local preferences.

But this choice has implications beyond just the classic product market dichotomy because it directly affects the firm's ability to capitalize on all sources of international advantage. If a firm chooses a single global product it will exploit scale economies from **aggregation** and can readily **arbitrage** factor costs across countries. Yet, if it chooses many products, it can adapt its offering to the needs of individual markets and effectively **augment** the existing product set in every country, and be able to reap the benefits of **agglomeration** as product variation supports more innovation.

This chapter begins by focusing on the physical product itself. We then extend the analysis to other aspects of the marketing mix. By the end we identify approaches that come close to realizing the best of all worlds, by designing products and their associated positioning that potentially supersede the underlying tradeoffs and achieve all four international advantages at the same time!

PRINCIPLES

Economic Significance of International Differences

It is an unchallenged assertion that there are differences among countries. The real question is not whether such differences exist, but how firms should respond to them.

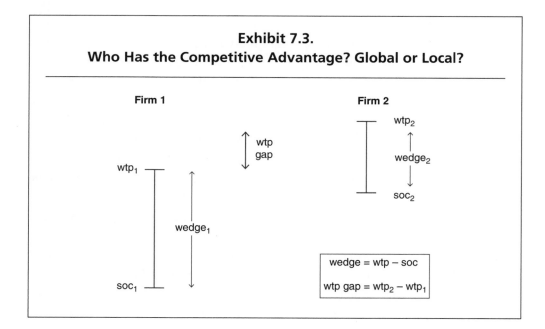

Exhibit 7.3.
Who Has the Competitive Advantage? Global or Local?

Firm 1

Firm 2

wtp_2

wtp gap

$wedge_2$

wtp_1

soc_2

$wedge_1$

$wedge = wtp - soc$

$wtp\ gap = wtp_2 - wtp_1$

soc_1

In particular, are such differences **economically significant** with strategic implications that compel companies to adapt their products to those differences, or are they just a matter of degree that can be easily and cheaply accommodated? It is this question of when the willingness to pay a penalty for the globally standard product is so large that it offsets any cost savings, that underlies the choice of product offering around the world. Exhibit 7.3, repeated from Chapter 2, can now be seen as Firm 2 selling the local product with high willingness to pay and high cost, and Firm 1 the global standard low-cost product, which in this example has the advantage.

Limit to Self-Interested Behavior

One obvious question is why, if a particular configuration of products is optimal for the multinational, can separate country organizations not agree to pursue that product strategy? If it is better to collaborate on developing a single product, why will subsidiaries not reach such an agreement?[4] The answer is that there is a limit to how far self-interest will go (Exhibit 7.4).

Exhibit 7.4.
Joint Profit Maximization

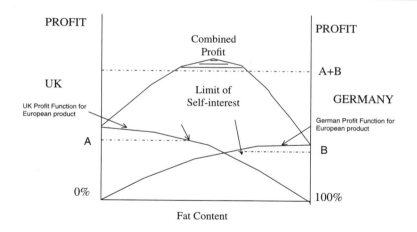

In the classic example of Unilever developing a "butter beater" product for Europe, there was tension between Germany, whose consumers, simplistically, preferred a high-fat product, and the UK, where low-fat spreads were desirable. If the UK developed its own spread it would be a zero-fat product that would make profit A. However, any fat level up to about 40% in a jointly developed European product would still make more money for the UK (the European product profit function starts above A because development and manufacturing costs are now shared). In contrast, Germany would choose a 100% fat

---

spread for itself and would make profit B, while a European product with a fat content above 60% would be profitable for it. The combined profit function, however, shows a maximum at 50% fat, and yet Germany would not agree to this, since it can make more by defecting to develop its own product.

When country managers are rewarded on their own country's performance and have the right (or at least the threat) of unilateral action to design their preferred product, cooperation to arrive at the global optimum will not necessarily occur. The joint profit-maximizing product choice might result in one country benefiting at the expense of another – which would then choose to operate alone. While complicated incentive schemes can be designed to arrive at the global optimum, the fact remains that self-interested behavior by country managers cannot be relied on to achieve this optimum.

PROCESS

Step 1: Characterize Market Differences

The first step in the process of choosing between global standardization and local variety (Exhibit 7.5) is to identify how demand for satisfying the underlying customer need varies among countries. Most executives have a reasonable sense of this, although those intuitions (or prejudices/biases), which are often correct at a first-order level, can lead to errors if not examined in detail. It was believed, for example, that the Chinese would not buy life insurance because they will not discuss death. Repositioning life insurance as a savings product, however, enabled the Chinese company, Ping An, to become one of the most valuable insurance companies in the world.

Exhibit 7.5.
Product Selection Process

WHAT PRODUCT?

Characterize Market Differences
⬇
Global Demand?
Common segment
Satisfy universal needs
⬇
Accommodate Market Differences?
Limited economic significance
Platform product
⬇
If no, then
ADAPT TO LOCAL MARKETS

Indeed, there are many examples of management errors interpreting the extent of country differences and similarities – although the truth is often not as clear as apocryphal stories make out (see box). Any analysis must therefore begin with a careful examination of how the product is bought, used, interpreted, and shared in the countries in which the multinational is active, since without a detailed market and cultural understanding it is easy to exaggerate perceived similarities or variations between countries.

Cultural Mistakes

International business textbooks abound with examples of seemingly basic mistakes made by multinationals when entering foreign markets. Take, for example, Coke's initial entrance into China in the 1920s. Wanting to keep the Coca-Cola name for the Chinese product, the company failed to realize that the phrase "Coca Cola" when translated into Chinese was actually a series of characters meaning "bite the wax tadpole" (Finch, 1986). Similarly, in more modern times, Chevy's Nova is said to have encountered poor sales in Spanish-speaking countries, given that *no va* translates as "does not go" in Spanish.

What may come as a shock is that these and many other examples are, in fact, misleading. There is no evidence to support the truth of either claim, placing both in the realm of urban myths – repeated so frequently over time that they have been taken for fact (Lasswell, 2004). Initially, Coke did not even attempt to devise an official character equivalent for the Coca-Cola brand. And according to Chevy, the Nova actually did very well in Spanish-speaking markets, since *no va* is not how a Spanish speaker would describe a broken car, and the word *nova* conjures a variety of other connotations for many Spanish speakers, including the name of one of Mexico's most popular brands of gasoline.

This does not mean, however, that there are not examples of major companies making such mistakes. In 2001, as Honda was preparing to introduce a new model, now known as the Honda Fit, executives at the company realized that the name under which the car was supposed to be released, Fitta, was a crude reference in Norway and Sweden to a female body part. When the car was finally released in Europe, the name was changed to Jazz to dissociate from the near-blunder.[5] On a similar note, when Parker Pens launched in the Latin American market, a mistranslation of its "Avoid embarrassment—use Parker Pens" slogan led to a promotional campaign encouraging people to avoid pregnancy with Parker Pens (Ricks and Mahajan, 1984).

Translation and naming errors are not the only concern: Microsoft introduced an initial version of its Windows 95 operating system that included a map of India showing Kashmir as an independent territory, despite a heated ongoing dispute with China over the area's status. The blunder led to an eventual recall of over 200,000 units. A similar incident occurred after the Saudi Arabian government took issue with the use of a Koran chant in the soundtrack to a video game released by Microsoft, and another recall had to be issued.[6] Examples of this type of mistake in advertising abound, from an ad by Procter & Gamble in the Japanese market that portrayed a husband entering the room where his wife was bathing (considered an invasion of privacy in Japanese society),[7] to an ad by Mountain Bell in Saudi Arabia depicting an executive talking at a desk with his feet up,

---

showing the soles of his shoes (also considered highly offensive) (Kardes *et al.*, 2010), and Pepsodent's failed marketing campaign for whitening toothpaste in South East Asia, where locals chew nuts to *blacken* their teeth (Burton, 2009).

All of these examples illustrate the need for detailed market research to ensure that cultural sensitivity is taken into account at every level of a business. As Pankaj Ghemawat has emphasized, measures such as cultural education, participation in cross-border teams and projects, immersion experiences and expatriate assignments, dispersion of unit headquarters, and a focus on geographic and cultural diversity in leadership can go a long way toward helping a company adapt appropriately to new cultural environments.

It is also important to note that many of the blunders described above, like the case of the Honda Fit, were caught before products or campaigns were launched, thanks to exactly this kind of caution. Finally, in some cases, it is even possible for companies to cleverly exploit elements of cultural scandal, such as Electrolux's US campaign slogan "Nothing sucks like an Electrolux," which though it may initially seem like a blunder, in actuality was likely a calculated move to bring attention to the company's products through viral marketing.[8]

Having characterized the dimensions that differ between countries, the dilemma over product selection is resolved by answering a sequence of questions. The endpoint of this process identifies whether a product (and its associated positioning) can be designed that is capable of being cheaply and effectively adapted to local needs without compromising its global integrity. If it cannot, we have to acknowledge the demand for local responsiveness and pursue a strategy that supports such variety.

Step 2: Can We Identify or Create Demand for a Global Product?

The second step asks whether there is a **common segment across countries** that is large enough to support the targeted market for a single product? Rolex, for example, only needs to serve perhaps 1% of any market to be profitable. If there is a common segment of 1% of customers around the world then the product need not be altered to appeal to these "global" consumers.

If there is not a common global segment of the right size, can we nevertheless **transform the consumers** so that they will accept and adopt the global product, or **design a product that has universal appeal**? This is the famous Ted Levitt argument about not accepting the world as it is, but having the imagination to educate the consumers and transform their demands to desire your product, or having the insight to identify and then satisfy a latent and unmet universal need. Achieving this goal will obviously require a shift in consumer buying behavior in many countries to overcome the heritage of local preferences and institutions.

(a) Identify and Serve a "Global" Segment

A company can choose to pursue a broad scope and serve most customers, like Walmart, or it can focus on a narrow set of customers and uniquely satisfy their particular needs, like Maytag, which historically sold the most "reliable" laundry equipment. While we assume that every firm has made that choice within its original market to generate a competitive advantage (FSA), when it becomes international the firm faces a similar decision. Can it focus on serving a narrow set of "global" customers that have similar needs around the world, such as expatriate Indians watching Bollywood movies, or does it have to satisfy a broader set of customers whose needs within each country might be different?

Commonly observed differences in consumer demand between countries reflect aggregates. Within every country there are typically many market segments with varying preferences for different attributes. As a result, it is quite possible that even if the majority of demand in a country is not for the particular product under consideration, there might well be a segment of that country's consumers who do value that specific product offering – the target customer for HSBC's premier account mentioned in the introduction, for example. If that product is not currently offered in the market, augmenting the domestic product set with this global product will attract some customers.

Examples of **global market segments** abound. These include industrial goods manufacturers which have similar component requirements everywhere around the world; wealth management services for ultra-high net-worth individuals (defined by firms, such as Citigroup's private client group, as having over $20 million in investable assets) who all seek the same level of personal attention, breadth of investment opportunities, and global coverage; small "dormitory" refrigerators that are sold to students in developed countries, but families in emerging markets because of their low cost; overnight delivery services for documents and spare parts; and smart phones with numerous software applications – although the traditional BlackBerry, rather than the Apple iPhone, is perhaps the better example since it appealed to the corporate road warrior in every country, but had little appeal outside that narrow market segment.

A global segment will typically not be the largest part of the market in any given country. Nor will that global segment necessarily have the same position or market share in every country. Rather, the purchase behavior and customer preferences of that global segment will be the same everywhere, regardless of what the rest of demand looks like in any country. For example, Rolex watches[9] (and this is hypothetical since I do not know the actual structure of demand for this product) might be bought by only the wealthiest 1% of consumers in Pakistan; in the USA that segment might be the broad middle class; while in the UK the only people that buy Rolex watches are the nouveaux riche and WAGs (Wives And Girlfriends of soccer players). Regardless, in every country there is a segment of universal global customers who all value the attributes and associations of Rolex watches, enabling the company to sell exactly the same product everywhere around the world.

As the examples suggest, the origins of the global customer segment can vary. At the very high end (e.g., wealth management and Rolex), it could be that there is a segment of cosmopolitan consumers with the income to afford those investor services and a $20,000 watch. But, again, the specifics of such a luxury segment can vary among countries. In China purchasers of brands such as Louis Vuitton are typically aged between 20 and 40, whereas in the West they are typically over 40 (Chada and Husband, 2007).

It could also be the case that the global segment is, if not at the bottom of the pyramid, at least at the low end of the price range in developed countries. Indeed, the original argument of Ted Levitt was that global efficiencies would drive costs so low that even if the product did not exactly meet local needs, the value proposition would attract consumers everywhere. In this case, as for "dorm" fridges, or the Fiat 500 world car,[10] the global segment will be found at the low end of the market.

But global segments need not just be identified by income level. Much of youth culture today is global. Someone my age would have little interest in Harry Potter, and yet the novels and films have appealed to youngsters everywhere. Mobile phone apps, like "Angry Birds," or online phenomena, like "memes," can quickly take root globally among teens. *Fifty Shades of Grey* has found a female audience around the world. Cultural icons like Princess Diana, in her day, or Kate Middleton (now Duchess of Cambridge) today, can also transcend country boundaries. I watch BBC television programs and, I suspect, there is a similar global segment of (hopefully) educated and intelligent viewers everywhere![11] The BBC television series *Doctor Who* and *The Office*, for example, have now run in 48 and 80 countries, respectively.[12] Indeed, PBS, the highbrow US television producer, has just launched its own channel in the UK, seeing a common customer in that country. Political preferences, religious background, ethnicity – any and all of these dimensions can form the basis for a global market segment if members of those groups are distributed around the world and if that segmentation substantially drives purchase behavior for the product or service in question. In that case, the same product can successfully be sold wherever in the world that segment is found.

(b) Transform Consumer Tastes to a New Global Standard Product

Even if there is not currently a global market with similar preferences in many countries, companies should not give up the attempt to sell the same product around the world. The question becomes how entrenched these heterogeneous customer demands are, and how easy it would be to transform those needs to converge on a common product offering.

Ted Levitt in his seminal article "Globalization of markets" argued that many firms just gave up when confronted by market differences, and, in a failure of the imagination, did not conceive of a way to transform customer needs. Ambitious though his rallying cry was, it remains hard to find many examples of companies that have been able to achieve such a breakthrough. The ones that do come to mind are perhaps memorable because they are rare.

No one would deny, for example, that Steve Jobs was able to develop a series of products with global appeal and so transformed the telecommunications and computing sectors. The iPhone and the iPad have revolutionized the mobile phone and PC markets, respectively, and created global demand for a single product. Canon, with its SLR (Single Lens Reflex) camera, did something similar in the 1970s, incorporating demand patterns across several markets to design a lightweight, compact, easy-to-use, and reasonably priced camera with global appeal (Porter, 1986).

The challenge with the transformation of global consumer tastes is exactly that. How can one firm overcome the legacy of thousands of years of cultural, economic, and institutional country differences? Perhaps a creative genius can identify common characteristics across geographies that define a hitherto unknown or latent product need. Perhaps an aspirational need can be created that overrides previous cultural identities, as when Kim Kardashian sells her perfume around the world. Or perhaps a company can value-engineer a product so that even if it is not exactly what consumers desire, the low price outweighs their historic preferences.

One approach to developing a single global product is to identify the **highest common denominator** among customer needs and preferences around the world. One example is that quoted by Ted Levitt of a washing machine that came as an automatic with a heater and could be sold for less than £100 throughout Europe in 1980.

Product Development Process (A)

The common needs to be captured in the global product design have to be carefully identified through market research and focus groups in all target countries. This takes the involvement of senior managers in every country since the nuances of customer behavior in each country, which are hard to capture in systematic research, have to be accurately represented, and the company has to avoid a single country hijacking the development process and biasing the product to its own country needs.

The ideal development process for finding the highest common denominator is perhaps the heavyweight team (Clark and Wheelwright, 1992). This separately structured team will have the resources and support from senior management necessary to drive consensus across the organization. At Sharp, for example, such teams are called "Gold Badge" because team members are given the gold badge and accompanying authority of the company president. Even if there are lead countries on the team, they must receive input from all the other countries with veto/approval rights at key milestones on the development path.

While appealing – surely there are common sets of underlying needs around the world that any product can satisfy – the practice is much more difficult because of those pesky country differences. Indeed, attempts to design the global product have more often than not foundered for one of four reasons.

First, the risk that seeking the highest common denominator actually degenerates into the *lowest common denominator*! In the attempt to satisfy everyone, the product ends up satisfying no one. Design by committee, which is what is required to ensure that the interests of all countries are adequately represented, leads to compromise and an inferior offering. In the auto industry, for example, everyone wants a car that has an engine, seats, and wheels. Beyond that, it can be hard to agree what exactly are common global requirements at a given price point: leather or vinyl seats? Tight steering or loose suspension? As a result, the product that emerges from the lengthy design process has an engine, seats, and wheels but not much else that is attractive to consumers anywhere. As one GM executive noted of its earlier product strategy, "GM used to have vehicle interiors that were indistinguishable from one another. ... We no longer have to design simply for the lowest common denominator".[13]

The second risk is that the compromise which satisfies every country's particular need goes to the other extreme and produces the *highest common multiple* including every bell and whistle. The result of this is readily apparent – a terrific product that pleases everyone, except that it now costs too much for anyone to afford or is too complicated to use! Microsoft Word 2003, for example, included 31 toolbars and 1,500 separate commands. Similarly, more than two-thirds of smart-phone users would be satisfied with only six or seven of the most common features available.[14]

The third risk is that the attempt to average demand between countries and customers ends up satisfying no one because the product is *"stuck in the middle."* Consider the Tata Nano designed to cost less than 1 lak ($3,000). This would be an automobile that offered more benefits than the $1,000 motorbike – the most common mode of personal transport in India – but which, at one-third of the price of the cheapest car on the market, would also appeal to car buyers. Unfortunately, sales have been limited because the Nano fails to deliver sufficient improvement on the motorbike to justify the price premium, while also failing to meet minimum purchase criteria for most existing car buyers.

The final risk is more insidious because it is antithetical to the whole intent of finding the highest common denominator. It occurs when there simply is no way to square the circle – there simply are *no commonalities between countries* because needs in countries are mutually exclusive.

The classic example, mentioned earlier, was when Unilever tried to develop a new "yellow fat" product to take on butter and margarine in Europe. The concept seemed to be a perfect example of Ted Levitt's global imagination – develop a natural, low-fat, healthy, and tasty spread that would be a "butter beater." And appealing it is – who would not want a great-tasting, healthy, natural, low-fat spread? It has to be a winner. And Unilever invested substantial time, resources, and management effort from major European countries to come up with exactly that product. Unfortunately, there is no way to develop one product that meets those needs across Europe because they are *mutually inconsistent*. Germans and Dutch view butter as natural and healthy, while the British and French see vegetable oil as being healthier because it has a lower fat content. With such conflicting preferences, it is literally impossible to find one product that satisfies the same needs in every country. Country differences really can matter and can prevent there ever being a transcendent product. However appealing the notion of the "global" product, we cannot guarantee that it can be discovered in every case.

Step 3: Can We Efficiently Accommodate Market Differences?

In the third step we ask if we cannot find or create a truly common customer around the world, whether the differences among customers in different countries are a matter of **degree or substance**? Are they trivial differences that either do not radically affect buying behavior and the purchasing process or which can be cheaply accommodated without a fundamental change in the product, or do they compel a firm to substantively alter the product?

If the differences are substantive, it might nevertheless be possible for firms to use the same chassis or **platform** to accommodate different global requirements within the same basic product. While the notion of a global platform is familiar in the auto industry, we will show that this concept is successfully employed across many industry sectors.[15] If, for example, the core of SKII, the very high-end P&G skin care range based on sake brewer's yeast, can be adapted to offer the very different types of facial cleansing demanded by different regions, then essentially the same product can still be used globally. This is the stage at which the broader notion of a product becomes important as we see that the platform can involve aspects beyond just physical characteristics of the product itself.

(a) Determine the Economic Significance of Country Differences

When trying to satisfy somewhat different customer needs across countries, we must determine whether those differences have economic significance. We begin by considering three types of differences that are present, but which will not prevent a firm selling essentially the same product everywhere. Factors that fall into these three categories are a matter of degree rather than substance because they do not have a material effect:

Minimum requirement   To sell a product in any country requires a firm to meet the basic expectations that consumers and regulators have for that product in their country. These become the minimum requirements for doing business in that country. Factors include the language used on packaging materials and manuals; adherence to specific country standards, such as voltage, paper size, the physical configuration of plugs and other interface standards such as the width of railroad tracks, mobile telephony, television systems, etc.; and adherence to legal requirements for content, advertising claims, financial reporting, etc.

Competing in any given country is then a binary decision: either the firm accommodates those differences or it will be excluded from the country. When these minimum requirements are substantive, the firm either defaults to a strategy of local responsiveness, or chooses not to compete in that country. Child car safety seat laws in Europe and the USA, for example, are so different – the one requiring attachment to two metal hooks at the base of the car seatback, while the other uses a top-tether system – that manufacturers like Dorel have been forced to have entirely different models in each region. Some Western software companies originally chose not to develop their programs in 16-bit Asian form and so did not offer their products in countries that could not use 8-bit Western character format. If the decision is to serve that market, minimum requirements have to be met.

Minimal cost adaptation   Many differences are economically trivial because they can be accommodated at very little expense. Printing packaging, labels, and manuals in several languages is obviously necessary to support sales in countries with different languages, but its cost is rarely prohibitive. Indeed, many basic requirements can be met at limited expense and so do not act as a deterrent to competing internationally. One example is the set of manuals in different languages which today come as standard in any electronic product. For only a few cents, all European languages are covered in the inserted manuals – and when starting up the product itself, the consumer is initially asked in which language the on-screen menus should be.

Similarly, PCs now come with a power supply cord and transformer that allows a user to operate in countries regardless of whether the electricity supply is 110 or 220 volts. While not costless, the adaptation can be achieved without pricing the product out of the market.

Products might also differ between countries if the cost penalty of such local adaptation is not exorbitant. Nescafé, the instant coffee powder, for example, has a different taste in some countries. This can be achieved relatively cheaply simply by tweaking the reputed 800 components in the standard product (Gumbel, 2007). In this way, variations in taste are accommodated without a strategic penalty – the same plant, for example, can make all the different varieties on the same production line.

Similarly, Boeing will always customize the inside of its aircraft to accommodate the preferences of the various flag carriers. British Airways, for example, wants a substantial first-class section in its long-haul fleet, while Ryanair squeezes as many seats as it possibly can into its fleet of 737s – and is reputedly looking to take out a set of toilets in order to accommodate more seats.

Minimal willingness to pay variation   Many other differences are economically trivial because they do not dramatically affect consumer willingness to pay. A country's preference for one color over another might, at the margin, affect sales volumes, but will not drastically affect consumer demand. Perhaps Latin countries prefer darker woods in their furniture; Scandinavian countries lighter woods. But the slight differences do not prevent IKEA being successful in Southern Europe with a product range initially developed for Northern Europe.

The three sets of differences described above are probably found in the demand for nearly every product and are ultimately differences of degree, not of substance. To accommodate them is a necessary task for firms that compete internationally and can be referred to as the **localization** of the product. However challenging that task might be administratively and logistically, no substantive change to the product is required to transfer and sustain the firm's advantage. Thus, this commonly observed "localization" – important though it is in the day-to-day management of operations – is not adaptation in the strategic sense. It leads to the minor differences we observe among almost every product everywhere, but does not force companies to make fundamental strategic choices.

(b) Accommodate the Differences Without Compromising the Global Standard

Failing all of these approaches, the last question becomes whether or not the local differences can be accommodated within an appropriately designed global product.

The first approach is to create **common modules** that can be put together in different combinations to meet local needs. The commonality of the modules allows for efficient production. The various combinations allow for localization. In telephone central office switches – the vast computerized hubs that route calls and which replaced operators manually plugging in connections – the country requirements are profoundly different. To accommodate the differences, the Swedish producer, Ericsson, created a modular switch design. Simplistically, if the company produced a total of 125 modules, for country A it would use modules 1, 4, 7, 19, 25, and so on, but in country B, modules 1, 4, 8, 23, 26, etc. Variety was accounted for by having a sufficient set of modules, while the fact that every country's need could be met from a standard set of modules provided economies in R&D and manufacturing.

Accessories can be dealt with in the same manner, somewhat like the "localization" of manuals. An electric razor, for example, will come with an attachment for trimming mustaches in some European countries. A vacuum cleaner can be customized with attachments according to the typical flooring in a country.

The second approach is appropriate for companies that offer a range of products, such as retailers. This can be thought of as the **80/20 rule** since it involves offering a globally standardized 80% of the product range, while allowing each country to choose 20% of the range to satisfy specific local needs. This **core/periphery** approach is adopted by many retailers, such as IKEA, and can also be applied to restaurant menus, like McDonald's or KFC, which, according to a spokesman, has "core items that are consistent around the world, but then we meet the local taste palate wherever we operate" (Lin and Patton, 2013). The majority of the menu is the same everywhere, but countries are allowed to offer a Kiwiburger in New Zealand (not featuring kiwi meat but beetroot!). This approach is obviously only possible when the company is offering a line of items rather than a single item, but it allows for sufficient localization to attract customers while retaining the benefits of global scale economies in the core product line.

A variant is the **90/10 rule**, this time applied to country selection rather than product range. The idea is to recognize that some countries might have such aberrant preferences that it is not worth extending the product offering to satisfy those extreme needs. Instead, the solution is simply not to sell in those countries (as we noted above, when minimum requirements for the product in a country are too different). A product is developed that fits most countries but which simply ignores the requirements of outlier countries. This was the case for Canon in the photocopier business, where the larger Japanese paper size led the company to develop a global product that actually did not fit the Japanese market.

THE PLATFORM SOLUTION

If we cannot discover the one product that satisfies every country's needs, can we nevertheless find a core product that can consciously be designed so that it can cheaply and easily be adapted to meet those varied needs? This is the notion of the **platform product** which is the approach many multinationals have adopted to resolve the trade-off between local adaptation and global efficiency. If you can accommodate local tastes while still capturing global efficiencies, there is no tradeoff. Examples, as we will see, include the world cars of major auto makers, refrigerators, consumer packaged goods, and financial services.

The basic concept of the front/back platform is that there is a core to the product that is the same everywhere, and which supports sufficient variability to accommodate country differences. In the example of a refrigerator, the platform will be the insulated box and the compressor that cools the refrigerant, while the local variability is the racking and layout of the shelves and doors. In New Zealand, for example, there can be a dedicated shelf for butter. In Korea, there is a separate compartment for kimchi, the strong-smelling but ubiquitous pickled cabbage dish. As mentioned earlier, Whirlpool at one time painted a green line on the factory floor to distinguish that part of the production line manufacturing the common core of the product – "behind the green line" – from that part of the line which split to produce local variants.

The Whirlpool example clearly illustrates how the concept of the platform product works. The platform ("behind the green line") contains those elements of the product that:

- do not need to differ between countries;
- are subject to substantial scale economies (such as the engine and the frame in car production, which is why the major auto manufacturers now produce less than 20 car platforms for all their hundreds of models);
- are invisible or irrelevant to consumers, such as the wiring and components under the hood in the automobile, so they do not influence willingness to pay;
- come early in the production process, such as the car frame onto which everything else is assembled.

In contrast, there are those aspects of the product that are not built into the platform itself but which come after the green line and which vary across countries, and that:

- come at the end of the production line. This is why variety in items like manuals and accessories can be so readily accommodated, since the relevant ones can be placed in with the packaging as the last step in production.

- are not subject to economies of scale and so can be manufactured in small lots for each country. Again, printing manuals is not a scale-sensitive operation, so that producing in eight different languages does not incur a substantial cost penalty.

- are apparent to customers, do feature in their purchase criteria, and do vary between countries, such as the steering wheel or dashboard layout. It is these aspects of the product that make it so hard to have the one standard global product. Designing a car that gives tight handling, which Europeans like, will not give the soft ride that Americans like. Instead, a common platform or chassis has to be able to support two different suspension systems, each customized for one region.

Notice that care has to be taken in regard to the current location of a specific activity along the production line. The current manufacturing strategy should not be taken as given. Instead, a sophisticated platform product strategy will involve reengineering the entire production process to ensure that those aspects of the product that need to be altered between countries are moved to the end of the production line. If the dashboard really is critical in customer purchase behavior, then the dashboard should be one of the last items assembled into the automobile. Cleary there are some limits to this reengineering – it might be hard to assemble the dashboard after putting the windscreen in place, and trying to weld the chassis with all the interior assembled might be difficult – but the principle of disaggregating a product's component parts into the back (core) and the front (variants) of the platform according to the above criteria can be enormously powerful in developing a version that achieves the twin goals of local variation and global efficiency. Ford, for example, under the "One Ford" plan introduced by Alan Mulally, switched its line up from regional to global and claimed to have made product development two-thirds more efficient as a result (Groom and Seetharaman, 2012). VW similarly claimed to save 20% on materials and 30% on tooling and facilities by making 44 separate vehicles, including the Polo, Golf, Passat, Tiguan, and Skoda Octavia off a single platform (Neil, 2012).

The above discussion has been couched in terms of a complex engineered product where it is easy to understand the principle of a core platform and the periphery of local variants. Does this platform notion apply to other types of product and service? The answer is that it does carry over into all sorts of items, although the nature of the platform itself differs according to the type of product or service. One way to capture these different approaches is to recognize that the platform can be any combination of three Ps: physical **product,** market **positioning,** and operational **processes.** Thus, although we began the chapter by suggesting the strategic question was about what physical product the multinational should offer around the world, we find that the resolution concerns a much broader conception of "product."

For a *complicated manufactured item*, like a car, plane, or washing machine, the platform is the *physical product* itself. The product is designed as a standard base that can accommodate feature variety. The Boeing 777, for example, can be internally reconfigured so that overhead bins are lower for Japanese airlines in order to be more accessible to their physically shorter customers.

A variant of this within *high-technology products* is that software can provide the localization around a common *hardware* platform. The mobile phone is a good current example of this use of hardware as platform. The same phone can be used in many countries, each of which can have different local standards and carriers, simply through the use of a SIM card with appropriate software.

Similarly for products that do not have a huge number of discrete components, like *consumer packaged goods*, it is still possible to have a physical product platform that allows local adaptation through slight changes to ingredients. Nescafé can alter the mix of flavors by country. Coca-Cola can change the amount of sugar in Coke around the world. Unilever can alter the amount of salt and preservatives in its margarine products. While the core product stays the same, additives can also be altered to local tastes. P&G was able to configure its high-end skin care cosmetic SKII around a base formed from sake brewer's yeast, and yet develop varieties that could whiten skin for Asians and cleanse skin of oils for Europeans (the most important purchase criterion in each market).

In this context, and given the importance of marketing to the success of these products, it can reasonably be asked whether the physical platform remains the key to success. In fact, for most consumer packaged goods it is not. Rather the platform becomes the *brand positioning*, since it is that which remains the same around the world, even as the physical attributes of the product itself vary. For CPG companies, competitive advantage comes from generating novel consumer insights and developing products and their accompanying associations to uniquely satisfy unmet needs. It is the insight, rather than the specifics of the product, which are the firm's valuable resource (or FSA), and it is this insight that functions as the global platform even while its physical manifestation is allowed to vary locally. At L'Oréal, for example, CEO Paul Agon says:

> Imagine that each brand is a box. Each box is really very precisely defined, in that it occupies a very distinct market position. It is sold to a particular type of customer through a particular distribution channel. Our managers around the world know that they can't play with the position of the brands. We don't play with the boxes. The trick is to do innovative things inside of each box.
>
> (Lal and Knoop, 2012)

The shorthand representation of this global platform in CPGs can be thought of as the brand manual which defines the brand name and the key attributes of the product and its market positioning that drive customer purchase behavior. Tchae, for example, a Unilever green-tea drink, captured a positioning of relaxation and Eastern mysticism without being definitive about the actual tea taste – since country preferences differed in that regard. When the high-level brand positioning successfully identifies a set of universal purchase criteria, it can be applied uniformly even while the details of its product form vary.

The brand manual still has the difficult task of defining those aspects of the brand positioning that must be the subject of a global mandate to be the same everywhere, and those that can vary locally. Global mandates fall into two categories: physical attributes and brand associations. With respect to the former, the list will include product criteria – a diaper, for example, must have a certain adhesive strength in its tabs, should offer a specified level of absorbency using a particular gel, but could perhaps be offered in slightly different sizes in different countries – and those relating to the representation of the brand itself – the color and font of the brand logo, layout of packaging, etc.

The latter are more difficult to capture and convey. Some CPG firms capture the associations as text-based descriptions. Others use images and graphics to describe the emotional appeal that the brand is required to convey, such as "Love of Family" for a diaper firm. Again the challenge is how to capture the common theme but allow the manifestation of those associations to be tailored to local markets. The positioning of the Gillette Mach 3 razor, for example, was around speed and power. In the USA this was represented in commercials with NASCAR racing, which is the most popular form of car racing for the target market. In Europe, in contrast, that same message was best captured with Formula One racing – the preferred auto sport in the region. Similarly, while Coke used an American football player (Mean Joe Greene) in a series of US advertisements, it used a soccer player (Diego Maradona) for the comparable series outside the USA. In all cases, it is the essence of the brand that remains the same globally since that has been identified as the unifying factor driving consumer behavior. The specific representation of that platform "essence" can be adapted to local needs.

In *service* businesses the platform often becomes the back office operations, along with the brand positioning. Citibank is a classic example of this approach. It has the same brand and logo in every country in which it operates, and has traditionally relied on the same technology for ATMs, credit card systems, etc., around the world. This means that the specific product offerings can vary by country – not offering credit cards in China, having different terms and conditions on a mortgage to meet local legal requirements – but every country uses the same technology platform and systems. A more humorous example was HSBC, which reputedly offered a bank account in Madagascar whose interest rate was tied to the football results of the English Premier League the previous week! If the common technology platform supports it, country subsidiaries can offer it!

More broadly in service businesses, the platform can be thought of as the common *operational processes* that the multinational employs globally. McDonald's and fast food restaurants fit in this category. The brand is the same throughout the world, and a brand manual describes the restrictions imposed to ensure that restaurants everywhere have the same look and feel of US fast food. Just as importantly, the kitchen layout and restaurant processes are also standardized. With this in place, McDonald's can pursue the 80/20 product rule so that in India it can offer lamb burgers rather than beefburgers to accommodate Hindu preferences, but nowhere does McDonald's offer lobster – not just because of the price point (McDonald's does offer a lobster roll seasonally in the Northeast USA), but because boiling pots of water cannot be accommodated in the McDonald's kitchen. McDonald's therefore has a thick manual of procedures that includes instructions about how often and how to clean toilets, refresh coffee filters, etc. Standardizing the processes for operating a fast food restaurant provides the value to operators across countries (FSAs), and can be enforced globally without being absolutely specific about what the product itself looks like.

Product Development Process (B)

The challenge for the new product development process in developing a platform product is to coordinate the preferences and activities of disparate geographic subsidiaries. This can be thought of as allocating responsibility for design and implementation of the new product to a global function, or to local management (Exhibit 7.6). At one extreme, authority for both activities can be given to each country. This fits with the multidomestic strategy by supporting local product variety. At the other extreme authority would lie with a global function, which would develop a standard global product. The off-diagonals are more interesting. It is when development is global but implementation is local that we are most likely to arrive at a platform product. The global function (or an ad hoc project team drawn from key geographies) identifies the common core for the product, but knowing that local variation will happen in its implementation hopefully crafts a platform on which customization is feasible. When development comes from within countries, but great innovations are rolled out around the world, the multinational is relying on the free market to generate champions who will drive global adoption.

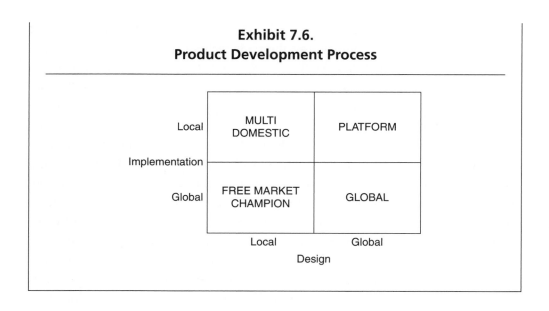

Exhibit 7.6.
Product Development Process

	Local	MULTI DOMESTIC	PLATFORM
Implementation	**Global**	FREE MARKET CHAMPION	GLOBAL
		Local	Global
		Design	

Implementing the Platform Approach

Having identified the front/back platform as a solution to the tradeoff between global standardization and local adaptation, it is important to make clear that this is merely the beginning of the problem. Implementation simply triggers the discussion of what should go behind the green line, and what should go in front of the green line. How do we distinguish activities that are globally standardized from those that are executed locally?

Consider again fast food restaurants, such as KFC. While it might be obvious that pizza does not fit in the kitchen, what products should be allowed locally? Pork? Breakfast? And if the platform is the set of operational standards, what processes should be standardized? And to what specifications? Should KFC specify fresh rather than frozen chicken, or should some restaurants in some countries under some circumstances be able to use frozen chicken?

The real issue with the notion of a platform as business processes in particular,[16] but more generally as regards where to draw the "green line," is the **degree of specificity** of the global standard. The reason is the tradeoff involved in drawing the line (Exhibit 7.7). The more specific the mandate, the more valuable the resource (FSA) being deployed, but the less flexible is that resource (see box). The more generic the global mandate, the more flexible and supportive of adaptation it becomes, but the less competitively superior and sustainable it will be.

Global Platforms

The RBV (Exhibit 7.7) identifies the underlying tension inherent in specifying the global platform, whether product, position, or process. The more that is standardized globally – the more specific the resource being leveraged across countries – the better the firm is able to leverage its experience and drive efficiency for competitive advantage. It also builds a sustainable advantage by making it harder for competitors to imitate those processes. It is therefore ideal for the "exploitation" of a particular way of operating a business. However, that very standardization prevents the experimentation and adaptation to local conditions that produces innovation and continuous improvement. Global standardization therefore undercuts the "exploration" that can create new business ideas and dynamic arbitrage opportunities.

Exhibit 7.7.
Resource-Based View

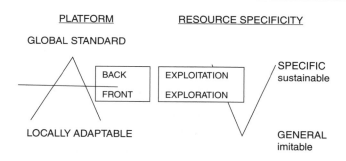

In contrast, if processes are left underspecified – if resources are general – and the value added of the multinational is just a set of general principles, they can be readily adapted to local requirements, which encourages variety and experimentation. However, they are less likely to be distinctive (after all, how hard is it for a hotel chain to deliver "culturally appropriate customer service?") and easier to copy (Friesl and Larty, 2013; Szulanski, 1996).

Imagine a continuum representing the specificity of the product embedded in the platform and being utilized across countries (Exhibit 7.8). "High specificity" would be a set of blueprints concerning raw materials, shape and size of packaging, manufactured in a specific way, etc. "Low specificity" would be a limited set of attributes governing its appearance and presentation to consumers, such as "biologic action" or "does not fade colors." We can think of this calibration as running from a **detailed set of rules to a general set of principles**.

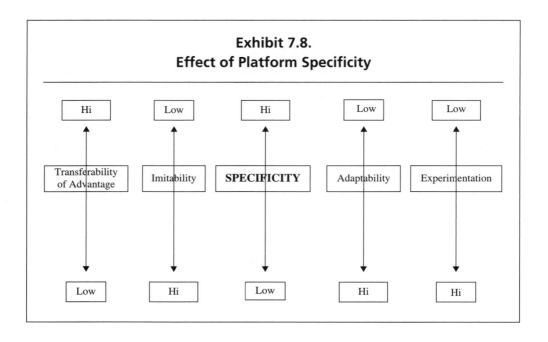

Exhibit 7.8.
Effect of Platform Specificity

Hi	Low	Hi	Low	Low
Transferability of Advantage	Imitability	**SPECIFICITY**	Adaptability	Experimentation
Low	Hi	Low	Hi	Hi

Specifying the product in great detail has wonderful advantages, but also important drawbacks. The advantages are, first, being sure that the competitive advantage is actually replicated in the subsidiary – there is simply no room for error in copying the product. Second, the competitive advantage will be hard for others to copy since the product is so detailed – perhaps if the manufacturing process is not followed, product consistency will suffer – and each minute detail contributes to the overall effectiveness of the product.

The drawback to high specificity is that because the product is so tightly specified, there is no room for local adaptation. To the extent that local variation is required, the process is overspecified and the global mandate will actually be counterproductive. A second drawback is that the tighter the specification, the less experimentation each subsidiary will be able to pursue. If the multinational is to benefit from learning across its subsidiaries, it needs to provide the flexibility to generate innovation variety.

In contrast, those products subject to only broad principles are terrific for accommodating local variation and encouraging local experimentation. However, they end up being so bland – of the "cleans clothes well" type – that they are easy for competitors to copy and do not transfer the skill effectively because they do not tightly specify behaviors.

One aid in the decision of where to draw the line is to differentiate among aspects of the product or service because they do not all need the same degree of specification. At the Hult International Business School, for example, the school uses a 100/80/50 rule to define the degree of standardization of courses among its campuses in Boston, San Francisco, London, Shanghai, and Dubai: 100% of learning outcomes are required to be the same for every version of a course that is taught at each campus; 80% of the topics covered by the faculty have to be the same; but only 50% of the materials must be the same everywhere. This notion of **disaggregation and discrimination** becomes the best way to ensure that a brute force, "one size fits all" platform approach is not adopted, which would prevent a more nuanced drawing of the line.

PRODUCT MORE BROADLY DEFINED

As described above, the platform concept applies to the entire business system, not just the physical product. This raises the issue of **global marketing**. While this topic is properly left to international marketing (Arnold, 2003; Aaker and Joachimsthaler, 1999), and the preface noted that this text would not stray far into the specialized areas, a few words are nevertheless required on how other elements of the marketing mix can be used to achieve the appropriate balance on the local responsiveness/global efficiency frontier. Importantly, this will make clear the distinction between global products, global positioning, global brands, and global advertisements, and note that they can each be designed to support the underlying "platform."

Global Positioning

In fact, physical product is often the least likely of the marketing Ps to be globalized. We mentioned earlier that "positioning" rather than "product" can be the basis of the global platform. Indeed, companies can pursue different combinations of product and positioning commonalities across countries (Exhibit 7.9). The product can be allowed to differ even while the brand positioning is the same everywhere – the meat in McDonald's burgers. In this case the brand not the product becomes the platform. Or the product can be the same but the positioning can vary around the globe – the case of Merck which sold its cholesterol-lowering statin Zocor in very different ways around the world. In addition, the two extremes of the global strategy with the same product and positioning around the world – Intel and Caterpillar – and the multidomestic strategy of varying brand positioning and product specifications to fit the local market – Henkel in detergents in Europe, for example (see box) – can be found.

As described earlier, when the positioning is the platform, the brand manual becomes central to global management. This document will define the attributes – both product and associations – that have to be maintained globally, while other aspects of both are free to accommodate local preferences.

Exhibit 7.9.
Product and Brand Positioning

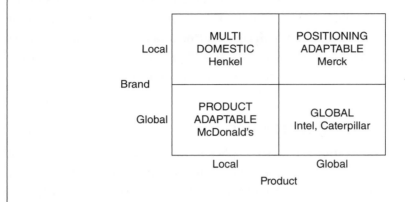

Henkel International Brand Strategy

The example of Henkel's multidomestic strategy requires more examination. In fact, the European detergent company was even more discriminating in its approaches to brand versus product as the platform (Exhibit 7.10). While moving toward more regional integration, Henkel maintained products in all four quadrants of the product/brand matrix.

Exhibit 7.10.
Henkel European Brand Strategy

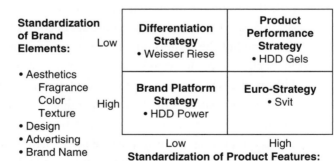

Source: Adapted from Arnold, D., Henkel KGaA: Detergents Division. HBS Case #502-019.

Global Brands

A more specific form of global positioning is to have a common brand name around the world. But what are the benefits of a global brand if it is only the brand, and not the product itself, which is standardized?

Global Brands

One of the main exponents of global brands has been the privately held confectionery, food, and petfood giant, Mars. After sponsoring the Olympics in 1984, Mars undertook to globally standardize its confectionery brands and rein in the local freedom that had allowed for substantial regional variation. This renamed a number of very successful products – the Snickers bar, for example, was actually called Marathon in the UK – and launched coordinated global marketing programs. Today, while having backed off from the more extreme aspects of global branding and marketing, Mars has 16 global brands, including M&Ms, of which 11 are billion dollar-plus brands.

Some cost savings on global brands arise in packaging and advertising production, so credit can be given to the global brand name for those economies of scale. Henkel, for example, at one time estimated that it cost 50,000 euros each time a production line had to be switched to a new stock keeping unit (SKU). However, media purchasing, which is the biggest single marketing cost, occurs in local markets (with limited exceptions, such as satellite television and sponsorship of global events like the Olympics) and is unaffected by the brand name. If the identifiable cost savings behind global brands (as opposed to global products) are therefore limited and rarely sufficient to outweigh the penalty of not being able to customize names and connotations for the local market, why should any firm adopt a global brand?

The answer, surprisingly, is that the argument is not so much about cost efficiency as it is about **market effectiveness**. The benefit is not to the customer but is inside the organization. First, a global brand can drive global innovation, whether in product or positioning and advertising campaigns, more rapidly and effectively than if country managers can object to new ideas by claiming they will not work with "my brand in my country." P&G, for example, asserted that it could roll out innovations for global brands 90% faster than for products that had differing brands around the world. The "not invented here syndrome," invoked when there are unique brands to protect in each country, can be a real impediment to rapid global product development.

Second, concentrating the best global resources of an organization on a few major efforts rather than frittering those resources on an endless series of local adaptations and initiatives will produce more substantive innovations and improve marketplace impact. As Unilever described the product development process, "**less is more**." Rather than every country committing its best talent to incremental changes that make the existing product slightly more desirable in their country, why not combine efforts to develop a breakthrough product that can revolutionize the market? Each country alone does not have the capability to do this. The domestic center of competence lacks the global insight to do so. But combining efforts can develop absolutely the best new product. It is, therefore, managerial rather than production economies that drive global brands today as firms seek to create a culture that optimizes globally rather than protects local self-interest.

Global Advertisements

A less frequent aspect of a global platform is the global advertisement, because that places the most demands for commonalities across countries. Although this has been the holy grail of a number of CPG companies, the actual occurrence of true global advertisements – literally the same commercial used everywhere – has not been widespread. We all think we can list many examples of global advertisements – Coca-Cola, M&M's, Nike, Marlboro, British Airways – but what might seem to be global campaigns often turn out to be not quite so worldwide, and we pretty soon run out of campaigns to list. It is reported that only 16% of the top 10,000 brands in 31 countries were recognized in more than 1 country, and only 3% in more than 7 countries.[17] Even Coca-Cola, for example, believes in "freedom within a framework" for its advertising so as to be "Glocal" and allow the global creative concept to be tailored to regional markets (Wind *et al.*, 2013). The challenge for global advertisements is that differences between countries in market, medium, and message make it inappropriate to use the same commercial everywhere.

The **market** differences we have already dwelled on at length. With respect to advertising, the important market differences include language – to be truly global an advertisement cannot feature actors speaking because you cannot dub different languages onto the same lip movement; culture – humor is difficult to translate across countries, taboos in Arab countries can restrict the ability to use sex to sell in the way that is common in the West; and connotations – red may mean good luck in China, but passion and desire in Western countries; an understated reference to the royal family may be readily understood in the UK, but go completely over the heads of most Philippinos; while the number 4 represents death to Chinese and so will not feature in a commercial, just as no house will be numbered 4, let alone 444.

The differences in **medium** are just as profound: in Germany you cannot claim product superiority – "the best" – unless it can be scientifically proven; billboards are prohibited on major highways in Germany, yet can be a vital trendsetter in California; cigarette and liquor commercials are banned on television in the USA, but not in Poland; and so on. All complicate development of a single global advertising campaign.

And the differences in **message** that are needed to address the different strategic positions of a firm in different countries mean that it is often irrelevant to pursue a global advertisement. British Airways, for example, which paved the way for global advertising with its famous "Manhattan Landing" commercial in 1982, did not follow that with a second global campaign (see box).

Manhattan Landing

Perhaps the first global advertisement – the British Airways "Manhattan Landing" commercial which showed the island of Manhattan (prominently featuring the twin towers of the World Trade Center) coming in to land at night at Heathrow Airport – illustrates the very weakness of the idea. In response to Ted Levitt's appeal, the Saatchi & Saatchi advertising agency, then at the height of its creative and financial prowess, embraced the idea of global advertisements and sold British Airways on the idea in the early 1980s. The exact same commercial was run in over 40 countries, differing only in the voiceover recorded in the local language.

While notable, if only for featuring the precursor to the spaceship in the hit movie *Independence Day*, deconstructing the commercial reveals a lot about the weaknesses of global advertising. One constraint was that no lips are seen moving on the commercial – all the sound was voiceover. This made dubbing the soundtrack in different languages simple, but limited the creative content. Similarly, there is no humor or other culturally contingent theme in the advertisement because these are so hard to translate across borders. Coca-Cola is reputed to have once used a three-part comic strip as an advertisement around the world. The first box showed a bored and lethargic person, the second that person drinking a Coke, and the third, the person in action having fun. Unfortunately, while English speakers read comics from left to right, in Muslim and Asian countries people read from right to left, leaving them with an entirely different take on the benefits of drinking Coke![18] Finally, the tag line of "The World's Favourite Airline" (notice the use of the British spelling of Favorite) is not exactly a compelling value proposition. Yet if an advertisement is to work in so many countries, where BA's competitive position differs so much, it almost has to be limited to the lowest common denominator positioning.

Indeed, when BA looked to do the follow-up campaign, the UK wanted a commercial that demonstrated BA's superior cabin service – a positioning somewhat more specific than the bland "World's Favourite Airline" and which addressed the perception in the UK of poor service levels (a perception that was reality in the early 1980s). US executives merely wanted to let consumers know to which US cities BA flew. The perception in the USA (and the reality) was that BA's service was actually quite good when compared to domestic US airlines. Americans simply did not know if BA flew to their city. The conflict between the different marketing challenges prevented agreement on any further global advertising campaigns.

The difficulty in developing an advertisement that has a powerful effect on consumers around the world leaves the potential benefit of such campaigns as being cost savings. Yet, here again there are real limits. There are few global media that run a single commercial. Most are bought locally so that global purchasing scale is irrelevant. Some small cost savings might be made on advertising production costs – making only a single commercial rather than one for each country – but production costs are typically only a small share, perhaps 10% of the total cost of any campaign. This explains the rarity of global advertising for anything other than truly global products and companies clearly pursuing global strategies, such as luxury brands targeted at the cosmopolitan global consumer, like watchmaker Patek Philippe's "You never actually own a Patek Philippe, you merely look after it for the next generation" commercial.

Global Pricing

Substantial price differences across countries for most products reflect differences in the underlying factor costs, consumer preferences, and competitive conditions among countries. Even the Big Mac price index compiled by *The Economist* shows dramatic price variations of up to 260% between South Africa and Switzerland, or almost 1,000% in terms of Big Macs per hour worked between Canada and India (Ashenfelter, 2012). The same is true for another standard global product, the Macbook, which in 2010 ranged from $1,190 in the USA to $1,760 in South Africa and over $2,000 in Brazil.

In principle, this variation is appropriate because pricing to local market conditions maximizes the capture of consumer surplus. However, price differences create arbitrage opportunities for buying in one country and reselling the product in a higher priced country. The existence of such "gray markets" or "parallel imports" makes the extraction of consumer surplus from each country difficult. While car companies might maximize profitability in the UK by charging prices 20–30% more than on the Continent, parallel imports restrict their ability to do so.

In the case of AIDS drugs, for example, the price in Africa can be one-hundredth of that in developed countries. If everyone paid the African price, there would be insufficient revenue to compensate the manufacturers (let alone recoup the original drug development cost). If everyone paid the US price, millions of Africans would be unable to afford their lifesaving drugs. However, there is enormous profit to be made selling AIDS drugs bought at African prices in high-price developed countries. To prevent this, pharmaceutical manufacturers place restrictions on their wholesalers; introduce irrelevant product differences, like color, in order to at least track the illicit trade;

and closely monitor channel sell-thru and inventories. In spite of this, about 10% of pharmaceuticals are estimated to be illegally traded in the gray market in Europe with higher shares elsewhere.[19]

Firms selling an easily traded global good vulnerable to price arbitrage have the choice of limiting the set of countries in which they sell to those that would support similar prices; trying to enforce limits to trading with different prices; or accepting the lower overall revenue that comes from a single global price.

Global Placement

As we get further away from the product itself, the ability of every multinational to accommodate country differences increases since they have limited effect on scale efficiencies and a big impact on consumer preferences. The channel of distribution, for example, will often vary between countries. Indeed, in some cases, adapting to a unique local distribution structure can be thought of as a minimum requirement of doing business in that country. That certainly used to be the case in Japan, where restrictions on the size of retail outlets had a major impact on the ability of US firms, such as Whirlpool, to sell there, or Toys "R" Us to operate there.

Global Promotion

This is the easiest aspect of the marketing mix to localize. Promotions are typically country specific – Thanksgiving has no role outside the USA (except on a different date in Canada) – and are negotiated and priced without spillover among countries. Thus, most companies devolve responsibility for promotions to the countries, and headquarters does not often attempt global coordination of this activity.

STRATEGIC FIT

At this point we return to the process flow chart and remind ourselves that if we cannot find a way to operationalize the platform concept (and the previous approaches to a standard product have also failed), then we must **adapt** the product to the unique requirements of each market in which we sell. For some products, like sausages, differences are so overwhelming that products have to be allowed to vary if a multinational has a hope of selling in many countries. This should not be accepted grudgingly, but embraced as a fact of doing business around the world.

More generally, the choice of what product, broadly defined, to offer around the world is most readily determined by fit with the international strategy (Exhibit 7.11).

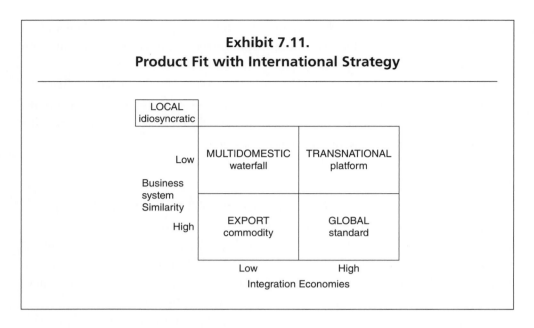

Exhibit 7.11.
Product Fit with International Strategy

	Integration Economies

LOCAL
idiosyncratic

	Low	High
Low	MULTIDOMESTIC waterfall	TRANSNATIONAL platform
High	EXPORT commodity	GLOBAL standard

Business
system
Similarity

Integration Economies

Local

The local strategy capitalizes on idiosyncrasies to celebrate the uniqueness of domestic demand that creates entry barriers to foreign firms. Residential construction, for example, is one of the more local businesses. What passes as a desirable house in Germany is frowned upon in Singapore, and vice versa. Pursuing the local strategy therefore requires companies to be as responsive as possible to local, even sub-regional, product needs. It is their willingness and ability to do so that provides their competitive advantage.

Export

The export strategy simply sells the local product abroad wherever there is demand for that commodity. The strategy exploits the home country's factor cost advantage and the product offered is that which most effectively embodies that factor. An oil producer exports oil. Ukraine exports grain. And China exports low-cost labor embodied in whatever product specification is provided to it.

No attempt is made to alter the product to accommodate the needs of foreign markets, rather the exporter simply makes a "take it or leave it" offer of the standard product. Hollywood does not produce alternative endings for its movies, nor does Bollywood violate Indian norms of kissing and nudity in its movies, and yet both find huge markets outside their home countries. Similarly, the NBA sells rights to its games internationally without changing its product – perhaps by limiting the height of players – to make it more attractive to Europeans to participate in the sport.

Multidomestic

The multidomestic strategy devolves decision rights for product design to the individual country organizations. Historically the strategy was one of adaptation of the original home country product design, rather than each country literally developing its own design from scratch. However, since each country was allowed to evolve toward offering the ideal product for their national customers, the traditional multidomestic strategy was characterized by every major country having the full set of product development activities. These would include market research and marketing, as well as design, if not the capability to undertake basic research.

Indeed, a continuing reliance on leveraging the home country's development capability gave rise to the international product lifecycle. Contemporary versions of the product lifecycle still exist, although not to the extreme of taking decades and waiting for fully depreciated machinery to be available before launching a product outside the home region. The VW Beetle, for example, was still being made in Mexico in 2003, 65 years after its introduction in Germany, 18 years after its manufacture and sale had been discontinued in Europe, and 25 years after ceasing production in the USA.[20]

The modern version of the product lifecycle is characterized by the concentration of product development capability in a center of competence at home, complemented by the presence of those functions – market research, product engineering, etc. – necessary to adapt the original idea to satisfy unique requirements in each country. In this case, the domestic innovation and development capability is the valuable resource that justifies keeping the corporation together once the initial transfer of designs and skills has been accomplished.

Global

The global strategy requires a standardized product to serve the entire world – think Caterpillar bulldozers and Intel chips (although even for these products recognize that there has to be the relevant amount of "localization" to ensure that they pass local customer minimum requirements). Again, the product includes more than just its physical design, covering marketing, branding, and distribution.

The traditional explanation for the advantage of the global strategy came from manufacturing and other cost savings when a single product was sold the same way everywhere around the world. The emphasis was on scale economies and the efficiency with which the strategy could be implemented. In the 1990s, for example, the major cost of variety for Henkel in its European detergent business was a €50,000 set-up cost every time a product formulation was changed in manufacturing (Arnold, 2001).

Transnational

The platform approach described above is employed by the transnational strategy to transcend the tradeoff between local responsiveness and global efficiency. However, an important aspect of the transnational is leveraging innovations from wherever in the world they occur to everywhere in the world the firm operates. This has important implications for the product development process and organization of marketing activities around the world.

Unlike the traditional multidomestic, which concentrated innovative capability in the home country supported by sufficient resources and competence in foreign subsidiaries to adapt those innovations to local needs, the transnational seeks innovative ideas everywhere it operates. It therefore seeks to build capabilities in key subsidiaries (see Chapter 5) since they must be capable of originating innovations themselves.

CONCLUSION

Product is perhaps the one decision where it is possible to see a solution that transcends the underlying strategic tradeoff. In fact, the most profound issue of product choice concerns not what should be the default choice of product strategy, but the extent to which every multinational can strive to achieve the transcendent transnational solution with some form of platform design.

The platform approach, whether using the physical product, its brand positioning, or the processes involved in producing and delivering it, in principle allows a multinational to achieve the best of both worlds – accommodating local variety while still exploiting global efficiencies and leveraging global innovations.

The qualifications and provisos that have been illustrated above in the implementation of the concept should have convinced readers that while aspirational, the platform product is not the solution for everyone. Some industries and some international strategies impose a more straightforward choice between local responsiveness and global efficiency in product design strategy.

NOTES

1. Throughout this chapter the word product refers to both physical products and services.
2. Brands listed on Wikipedia, accessed at http://en.wikipedia.org/wiki/List_of_Coca-Cola_brands. Many of these are sub-brands of the "Diet Cherry Coke" variety.
3. American chocolate has about 10% cocoa solids, UK 20%, and Europe 40% (Purser, E. (2009) The great transatlantic chocolate divide. BBC News, December 15, accessed at http//news.bbc.co.uk/2/hi/uk_news/magazine/8414488.stm); European beers are darker, more alcoholic, and maltier than light American beers; Italian pizzas are thin crust with little sauce, American pizzas thick crust and heavy sauce.

4. The same question can be asked for each of the four strategic decisions. We confront it first here.
5. Auto manufacturers seem to be particularly prone to naming mistakes – Kia's concept car, Provo, caused offence in Northern Ireland; Mazda's LaPuta translates as "the whore"; Nissan's Moco as "booger"; and the Toyota MR2 when pronounced in French sounds like the word "excrement" (Pogatchnik, S. (2013) Kia concept car "Provo" reminds some of IRA terror. *Boston Globe*, March 5).
6. http://www.ln.edu.hk/cultural/visiting%20scholar/articles/essay_AcademicCommons.pdf.
7. http://www.deseretnews.com/article/705371647/Some-international-ads-are-perceived-as-sexist-due-to-different-cultural-norms.html?pg=all.
8. Cited at http://itre.cis.upenn.edu/~myl/languagelog/archives/005097.html.
9. This example is the same as in Chapter 5.
10. Unfortunately for Fiat, with a starting price of $16,000, US consumers did not seem to see the value proposition of the small, if "Sexy," Italian car. Sales in the year of launch in 2011 were only 20,000 units – well below the 50,000 expected by CEO Marchionne, illustrating the difficulties of selling a "world car."
11. In a peak news period, the BBC World Service has a weekly global audience of nearly 250 million (BBC global audience rises by 14 million. BBC website, accessed June 28, 2012).
12. http://www.walesonline.co.uk/news/wales-news/2008/07/13/how-the-daleks-invaded-earth-91466-21331115/ and http://www.slate.com/articles/arts/television/2006/09/foreign_office.html.
13. See Kalogeridis, C. (2004) No more designing for lowest common denominator. Automotive Industries, July, accessed at http://www.ai-online.com/Adv/Previous/show_issue.php?id=505#sthash.fyTznKMY.dpbs.
14. See Rockbridge (2013) Not enough or too many? December 9, accessed at http://www.rockresearch.com/not-enough-or-too-many-using-turf-analysis-to-define-a-short-list-of-features.
15. VW, for example, announced in 2012 a new platform that by 2017 would be used for over 40 models across four brands and types of vehicle and account for over 4 million cars a year.
16. This "product" platform discussion verges into that concerning the platform as a set of business processes in Chapter 9.
17. Millward Brown data cited in Ghemawat, P. (2011) The globalization of firms. IESE Globalization Note Series, accessed at http://www.ghemawat.com/management/files/AcademicResources/GlobalizationofFirms.pdf.
18. Documenting this advertisement has proved difficult. Instead there is evidence for a detergent company that had a similar advertisement featuring three panels from left to right of dirty clothes, detergent, and clean clothes! (See White, M. (2001) *A Short Course in International Marketing Blunders*. World Trade Press: Petaluma, CA. p. 29.)
19. Hospitalpharma.com (2003) Global pharmaceutical parallel trade: can it ever happen? October 15, accessed at http://www.hospitalpharma.com/features/feature.asp?ROW_ID=354.
20. VW Beetle, accessed at http://www.squidoo.com/1967-vw-beetle.

REFERENCES AND FURTHER READING

Aaker, D. and Joachimsthaler, E. (1999) The lure of global branding. *Harvard Business Review*, November/December, 136–146.

Arnold, D. (2001) Henkel KGaA: Detergents Division. Harvard Business School Case #502-019.

Arnold, D. (2003) *The Mirage of Global Markets: How Globalizing Companies Can Succeed as Markets Localize*. Financial Times Press: London.

Ashenfelter, O. (2012) Comparing real wages. Institute for the Study of Labor (IZA), Bonn, Discussion Paper #6500.

Baden-Fuller, C. and Winter, S.G. (2005) Replicating organizational knowledge: principles or templates? *Papers on Economics and Evolution*, No. 0515, Max Planck Institute of Economics, 1–40.

Burton, D. (2009) *Cross-Cultural Marketing: Theory, Practice and Relevance*. Routledge: London.

Chada, R. and Husband, P. (2007) *The Cult of the Luxury Brand: Inside Asia's Love Affair with Luxury*. Nicholas Brealey: London.

Clark, K.B. and Wheelwright, S.C. (1992) Organizing and leading "heavyweight" development teams. *California Management Review*, 34(3), 9–28.

Finch, D. (1986) Eat their words? Without translators, some firms "bite the wax tadpole." *Across the Board*, 5(12), 49.

Friesl, M. and Larty, J. (2013) Replication of routines in organizations. *International Journal of Management Reviews*, 15, 106–122.

Govindarajan, V. and Trimble, C. (2012) *Reverse Innovation*. Harvard Business Review Press: Boston, MA.

Groom, N. and Seetharaman, D. (2012) "One Ford" strategy top focus, says incoming Ford COO. Reuters, November 29.

Gumbel, P. (2007) Taste test: same, but different. *Time*, June 14.

Kardes, F., Cronley, M., and Cline. T. (2010) *Consumer Behavior*. Cengage Learning: New York.

Lal, R. and Knoop, C. (2012) The universalisation of L'Oreal. Harvard Business School Case #513-001, p. 4.

Lasswell, M. (2004) Lost in translation. *Business*, 2.0(7), 68–70.

Levitt, T. (1983) The globalization of markets. *Harvard Business Review*, May/June, 92–102.

Lin, L. and Patton, L. (2013) KFC loses its touch in China, its biggest overseas market. *Business Week*, May 20, p. 21.

Neil, D. (2012) At Geneve, the promise and perils of sharing. *Wall Street Journal*, March 10, p. D9.

Porter, M.E. (ed.) (1986) *Competition in Global Industries*. Harvard Business School Press: Boston, MA.

Prahalad, C.K. and Hart, S. (2002) The fortune at the bottom of the pyramid. *Strategy + Business*, 26(1), 2–14.

Quelch, J. and Jocz, K. (2012) *All Business Is Local*. Penguin: London.

Ricks, D.A. and Mahajan, V. (1984) Blunders in international marketing: fact or fiction? *Long Range Planning*, 17(1), 78–83.

Szulanski, G. (1996) Exploring internal stickiness: impediments to the transfer of best practice within the firm. *Strategic Management Journal*, 17, 27–43.

Vernon, R. (1966) International investment and international trade in the product cycle. *Quarterly Journal of Economics*, 80(2), 190–207.

Wells, L. (1972) *The Product Life Cycle and International Trade*. Harvard Business School Press: Boston, MA.

Wind, J., Sthanunathan, S., and Malcolm, R. (2013) Great advertising is both local and global. *Harvard Business Review Blog*, March 29.

Which Country?

MOTIVATION

Most companies begin life in a single country. This still leaves them with another 192 in which to sell their products.[1] Once they have their feet under them domestically, every firm that wants to expand geographically therefore has to decide in which countries to compete.

Indeed, many companies making their first international move have had to wrestle with a choice, like that described in Chapter 2 facing the small Spanish furniture manufacturer. With limited resources it could pursue either the unexpected, but large, one-time order from Uzbekistan, or make a long-term investment in a showroom and sales representation in France. While one obvious solution would be to go for the larger or faster growing market, decisions made simply on the size and attractiveness of the market ignore differences between countries. Even answers to simple questions, such as whether anyone in the Spanish firm can speak Uzbek, might lead the company to avoid the potentially more attractive option, to say nothing of its concern about the political, and possibly even the personal, risk of doing business in Uzbekistan. How does a company weigh up the relative **merits of different countries as markets**?

Even mature companies that already have a global footprint face the question of how to allocate and prioritize capital and management resources among countries. WebCT, a provider of learning management systems for college students (now merged with BlackBoard), faced enquiries from about 70 countries as it pursued international expansion. Should all its effort be concentrated in one or two countries, or should it spread that effort over many in order to capture the most first-mover advantages? What should its overall geographic portfolio look like, and how should it **allocate resources between countries** in the portfolio?

Nor is selecting the markets in which to compete the end of the strategic decisions confronting an emerging multinational. As a company expands internationally it has to choose whether to establish its own activities abroad rather than simply contracting with domestic firms to provide the necessary local functions. Should WebCT take the leap of hiring its own salespeople in Australia rather than relying on the distributor through whom initial sales were made, or should it establish a full-blown subsidiary with the capability to customize the learning platform for the local market? Thus, every multinational has to consider the appropriate **organizational form** for its foreign activities.

Finally, multinationals confront a question of **timing**. Is it better to enter a country, like Vietnam, before demand has been established, in which case the firm might take losses while it builds first-mover advantages? Or should it wait until a large enough market exists to provide an immediate return on investment, but at the cost of having to confront incumbents who moved earlier?

STRATEGIC TRADEOFFS

Decisions concerning the firm's geographic footprint are problematic because they involve the strategic tradeoff of **simplicity versus scale** that results from the choice of **competing in one (or a few) versus many countries**. The former approach ensures that the selected markets are similar to each other so that **augmentation** is likely to be viable, and coordination straightforward. The latter allows the firm to **aggregate** demand and exploit economies of scale and experience, but at the expense of market diversity threatening the viability of those economies and complicating the management task.

One revealing measure of this tradeoff, drawn from Ghemawat (2007), is Walmart's profitability as a function of geographic distance from Bentonville, Arkansas (Exhibit 8.1). At least to around 2000, the further Walmart went away from its corporate headquarters, the lower its profitability! Other research shows that every additional hour's flight time to its US subsidiary reduces a Japanese company's profit by 7% (Boeh and Beamish, 2011), while student satisfaction at Hult's campuses is negatively correlated with distance from administrative headquarters in London!

PRINCIPLES

Indeed, the reality, suggested by Exhibit 8.1 and described in Chapter 2, is that there is a "**liability of foreignness**." That is to say, the overseas activities of a multinational are less profitable than in its home country. While country-specific factors can make some foreign markets more profitable than the domestic market – every mobile phone company makes more money in Mexico than in their home markets, for example – on average, returns to international activities are lower than at home. In one recent study of 18,000 European multinationals, profit in the home market was 30% higher than in foreign subsidiaries (although that gap has been narrowing over time) (Dischinger

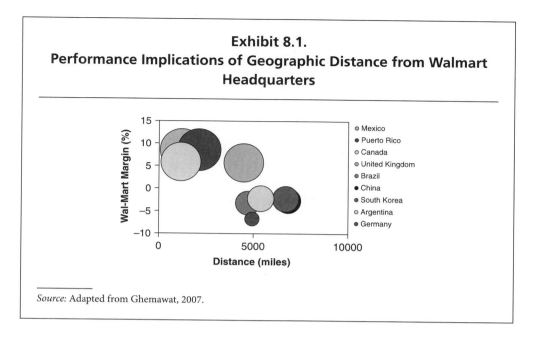

Exhibit 8.1.
Performance Implications of Geographic Distance from Walmart Headquarters

Source: Adapted from Ghemawat, 2007.

and Riedel, 2009). Any firm considering geographic diversification must acknowledge this fact and be clear about how an increase in scope creates value.

Logically the choice of where to compete can be answered, as with all capital budgeting decisions, by selecting the market that will provide the best **long-term return on investment**. To determine where this will occur, a firm needs to know two things about its potential markets: the *long-term attractiveness of each market*, and the *extent of the firm's competitive advantage* (or disadvantage) in each of those markets. While in principle all the same factors that determine market attractiveness and competitive advantage domestically still apply, when competing internationally an additional set of factors that capture the nature and extent of foreign product market differences need to be considered. It is understanding the influence of these factors and how they balance out the traditional determinants of attractiveness and advantage that concern international strategists.

But no firm can treat markets as independent of each other. We must also consider the **portfolio implications** of resource allocation decisions. Prime among these considerations are the overall financial characteristics of the portfolio – cash flow, growth, profitability, and risk – that determine the firm's market value and its access to capital. Given the volatility among countries in economic, political, and technological risk, such portfolio decisions are more complicated in the international arena.

Finally, the firm needs to take into account **strategic interrelationships among markets**. These can be economic, such as accepting lower returns in a large market in

Exhibit 8.2.
Competitive Position Across Countries

Carbonated Soft Drinks 1999 Global Market Shares

COUNTRY	8oz cans per capita consumption	Annual growth rate	Coca-Cola share %	Pepsi Cola share %
Germany	344	−3%	56	8
UK	370	7%	43	12
France	158	3%	60	8
Russia	52	na	26	12
Brazil	276	12%	51	7
Venezuela	290	na	70	30
China	22	8%	34	16
Thailand	114	5%	52	45
India	6	na	56	44
Pakistan	14	na	25	71
South Africa	207	na	97	0
Saudi Arabia	229	na	24	76
USA	768	2%	44	31
Worldwide	125	na	53	21

Source: Cola Wars Continue HBS case #702-442.

order to exploit scale economies and reduce overall costs, or they can be competitive – acknowledging multimarket interactions with the same competitor. Consider Pepsi Cola (Exhibit 8.2). Should Pepsi concentrate its efforts in markets where Coke is weak and share gains possibly easy, or should it invest to restrain Coke's dominance in large markets? Global competitive interactions must also shape a firm's geographic scope and resource allocation decisions among countries.

With regard to the mode of entry or the organizational form that a firm chooses in markets where it competes, the underlying principles of **organizational economics** apply. Firms must possess an internalization advantage (ownership advantage) over the market form of organization if they are to justify incorporating a foreign activity inside the hierarchy. This will depend on the critical *resources and capabilities* that are being leveraged into a country and on the *governance costs* surrounding their deployment within the firm hierarchy or across firm boundaries.

Finally, the timing of investment in a country will depend on the **length of commitment** to that investment, and on the **option value** created by retaining certain future courses of action.

PROCESS

We now apply these overarching principles to the specific issues embedded in the decision of where a multinational should compete (Exhibit 8.3):

Which countries should we compete in?

What should be the allocation of resources among countries in which we compete?
How should we enter a particular country?

What should be the organizational form of our presence in a country?
When should we enter a given country?

What should be the size, timing, and sequencing of the investment commitment to a country?

Not surprisingly, we will find at the end of the analysis that the answers to these three main questions depend on the firm's international strategy.

Step 1: Geographic Scope

(a) Standalone Country Attractiveness

The traditional approach to any diversification decision is the infamous two-by-two matrix beloved of consultants. This captures the dimensions of **market attractiveness** and **competitive advantage** (Exhibit 8.4). Its implications are never to invest in the lower left quadrant; to invest in every market in the top right quadrant; and to think

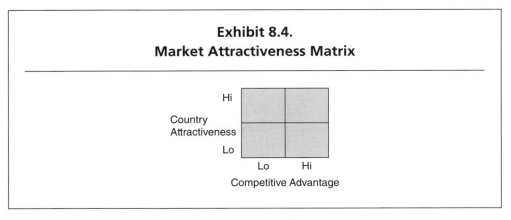

Exhibit 8.4.
Market Attractiveness Matrix

Country Attractiveness (Hi / Lo)

Competitive Advantage (Lo / Hi)

carefully before committing to any markets in the off-diagonals – the top left might be very risky, while the bottom right threatens to produce inadequate returns.

The choice of which countries to diversify into is no different, and every multinational will have applied some version of this matrix when making portfolio choices and resource allocation decisions across countries. Recently, Wendy's, fresh off its success surpassing Burger King to become the second largest US hamburger chain, had to decide where to expand outside the USA, which in 2010 had generated 92% of its revenue. It identified three large and growing markets, namely, China, Brazil, and Japan, as potential opportunities, but in the end committed to Japan, not so much because it was the second largest fast food market in the world, but because Wendy's past experience operating there increased the likelihood of success. The application of the two dimensions produced a plan to grow to 700 restaurants in Japan, and included selling a $16 burger topped with goose-liver pate and truffles![2]

While the factors that underpin industry attractiveness and competitive position are well known, the complication comes in understanding how country differences play into the evaluation of those two dimensions. We will outline an approach to this problem as if the task was to choose the next country to enter, and then will describe how to use it when making resource allocation decisions across an existing geographic footprint.

It is important to recognize that this analysis typically begins with a quick screening of a large number of countries on a limited number of key variables, such as market size and country risk. The process can then concentrate on a more complete examination of the narrower set of countries which are plausible candidates for entry.[3] Often, a back of the envelope calculation about the size of the addressable market in a country will quickly rule out many geographies. A large life insurance company, for example, will probably not want to consider entering Nepal, as the limited market potential will likely be outweighed by the cost of doing business there as a foreign firm and by the overhead cost incorporating, even that small entity, into global operations. In fact, an exact calculation of the served market is often not required (or even possible to determine). Rather, the firm might simply choose to place a lower bound, say a market size of $100 million, below which it will not consider entry. Confirming that a country does not yet have that market potential is all that is required to drop it from further consideration.

Country attractiveness is determined by two factors: the attributes that make the nation state as a whole a more or less desirable country in which to compete; and the size and attractiveness of the specific industry within the country.

Country Attributes

FUTURE ECONOMIC PERFORMANCE AND COUNTRY RISK   There are many determinants of the future economic performance of a country ranging from institutional infrastructure to cultural heritage and political stability. Most companies generate a long list of such factors under a few broad headings and consider the risk and volatility inherent in each (Table 8.1).[4]

Typically, the first category is *economic performance* captured in variables like GDP per capita levels and growth rates. More advanced measures might include the share of the target market – typically the middle class – since economic growth might be more rapid for those consumers. As many developing countries go through spurts of growth and crises of economic decline, the standard deviation of GDP growth might be included as a measure of volatility.

The second category is the *institutional structure* and the risk posed by any perceived instability or variability in the enforcement of rules and regulations. Included

---

Table 8.1   Factors Determining Country Attractiveness

Factor	Typical metrics	Risk and volatility metrics
Economic	GDP growth GDP per capita Percentage middle class	Standard deviation of growth rate
Institutional	Political system Minority representation	Likelihood of coup
	Legal system	Likelihood of expropriation Intellectual property protection
Cultural	Religion Language Colonial heritage	Immigration rate
Technology	Broadband infrastructure Miles of road and rail network	

here are regime stability and the legitimacy of the government and political process; absorption of minorities of all types into the political process; and the extent to which the rule of law is applied and will, for example, enforce property rights over intellectual capital. Also included would be the level of corruption. Russia, for example, is listed as 127th out of 177 nations for "transparency" with an estimated $300 billion a year in bribe-taking.[5] As a result, IKEA halted its Russian expansion in 2009 because of the "unpredictable character of administrative procedures" (Stott, 2010). Similarly, the lack of patent protection, and restrictions on freedom from censorship in China have led some companies, like GoDaddy, not to operate in that country.

Third, there are *cultural* factors that perhaps drive the longer term performance of the economy – the dominant religion, colonial heritage, and so on. South Korea, for example, has one of the most vibrant video-game user populations. Because of its predominant youth culture and technology "savviness," it also has one of the highest Internet penetration rates in the world.

Fourth, there is the *technology and logistics infrastructure*. Many African countries have actually done a good job in this regard, at least with respect to wireless communication. In 2010, for example, wireless penetration was 45.2% higher in Gabon than the USA in 2004, and South Africa actually has more mobile phone subscriptions per 100 people (135) than the USA (98).[6] In contrast, the transport infrastructure might be outdated and ineffective as, for example, is the railroad system in Mozambique where only one main line and three small branch lines are in occasional operation.[7] In an example that involves a stark juxtaposition, India has higher household penetration of mobile phones (75%) than toilets (53%) (Doron and Jeffrey, 2013).

The intent of all these variables, and it has to be acknowledged that the list of potentially relevant measures is enormous, is to identify those that predict the long-term potential growth of the country, and that capture non-market factors which could lead to financial, strategic, or even personnel losses if the firm chose to compete in that country. No list can be exhaustive, and each firm should pull together the most relevant and accessible data or turn to outside analysts, like the Economist Intelligence Unit's country reports (see box).

Framework for Country Analysis

A number of frameworks from consulting firms have been advanced for country analysis. Perhaps the most comprehensive is PEST and its many derivatives.[8]

Political Analysis

- Type of economic system in countries of operation
- Government intervention in the free market

- Comparative advantages of host country
- Exchange rates and stability of host country currency
- Efficiency of financial markets
- Infrastructure quality
- Skill level of workforce
- Labor costs
- Business cycle stage (e.g., prosperity, recession, recovery)
- Economic growth rate
- Discretionary income
- Unemployment rate
- Inflation rate
- Interest rates.

Economic Analysis

- Political stability
- Risk of military invasion
- Legal framework for contract enforcement
- Intellectual property protection
- Trade regulations and tariffs
- Favored trading partners
- Anti-trust laws
- Pricing regulations
- Taxation – tax rates and incentives
- Wage legislation – minimum wage and overtime
- Work week
- Mandatory employee benefits
- Industrial safety regulations
- Product labeling requirements.

Social Analysis

- Demographics
- Class structure
- Education
- Culture (gender roles etc.)
- Entrepreneurial spirit
- Attitudes (health, environmental consciousness, etc.)
- Leisure interests.

"DISTANCE" FROM THE DOMESTIC ECONOMY   While the factors identified above are country specific, their impact on an individual firm will depend on that firm's background and heritage. A rapidly growing economy ruled by a theocratic regime, for example, might not be a desirable location for a Western firm even if it posed no issues for companies from certain countries. To capture this measure of **bilateral fit**, Ghemawat (2001) introduced the CAGE framework.

Taking the economic literature on the determinants of global trade – in particular, gravity models, which seek to explain the difference in trade volumes between countries that cannot be accounted for simply by the relative size of their economies – Ghemawat identified **four types of "distance"** that affect the attractiveness of a particular country for any given firm: cultural, administrative, geographic, and economic (CAGE). Essentially, he takes a PEST-like set of variables and shows the effect that differences on those dimensions have on the magnitude of international trade between countries (Exhibit 8.5).

Because many of the variables in the CAGE framework are based on economic research, it is even possible to quantify their impact. As an example, the biggest single explanatory factor for trade between two countries remains geographic distance! An increase from 1,000 to 5,000 miles (1,600 to 8,000 km) between countries decreases the expected volume of trade by about 80% (Frankel and Romer, 1999). Similarly, large effects come from language differences (trade is 42% larger between countries that share a common language); colonial ties (trade is 188% more likely between countries that have a colonial tie); a common land border (125% higher); regional trading bloc membership (47%); and common currency (114%) (Ghemawat, 2007).

Ghemawat applies the framework to a US fast food company considering where to expand its international activities. A team put together its best estimates of market size and growth rates for the fast food business in a number of countries, but could not come up with a compelling case for any single country. When management overlaid

Exhibit 8.5.
The CAGE Framework

	Cultural Distance	Administrative Distance	Geographic Distance	Economic Distance
Country-level bilateral	- Different languages - Different ethnicities; lack of connective ethnic or social networks - Different religions - Different values, norms and dispositions	- Lack of colonial ties - Lack of shared regional trading bloc - Lack of common currency - Political hostility	- Physical distance - Lack of land border - Differences in climates/disease environments	- Rich/poor differences - Other diff. in factor endowments (including infrastr., advanced factors)
Country-level unilateral (isolation)	- Insularity - Traditionalism	- Non-market/closed economy (home bias vs. foreign bias) - Lack of membership in intl. organizations - Weak institutions; corruption	- Land lockedness - Lack of internal navigability - Geographic size - Geographic remoteness	- Economic size - Low per capita income - Low level of monetization

the CAGE measures that predicted the effect of "distance," one country – Mexico – stood out because of its ties with and geographic proximity to the US market.

While this analysis is perhaps more quantitative than necessary, it does illustrate the importance of considering the bilateral fit between a firm and a market, and not just the underlying characteristics of the country itself when choosing where to compete.

Industry Attractiveness   The second set of factors determining market potential is those affecting the size and structural attractiveness of the specific industry in each country. These determine the expected long-run profitability of the business and set the base expectation for the firm's return in that country.

MARKET OPPORTUNITY: SIZE AND GROWTH OF ADDRESSABLE MARKET   When analyzing in detail the market potential of a limited number of countries, the size and future growth of the addressable market must be accurately assessed. If the firm is already active in the country, data might be easily available from local experience and contacts. If this is the first time the country has been considered, data is usually accessible through an industry association or government statistics. Care does, however, need to be taken to estimate the future of the **served market** for the firm's products or services. Just because the overall market looks substantial, country differences might conceal large variations in demand for the particular segment the firm serves. Russia, for example, has one of the highest penetrations of mobile phone subscriptions in the world (168 per 100 people). However, the market for smart phones is a much lower share of that market (just

Exhibit 8.6.
Differences in Profitability Across Industries

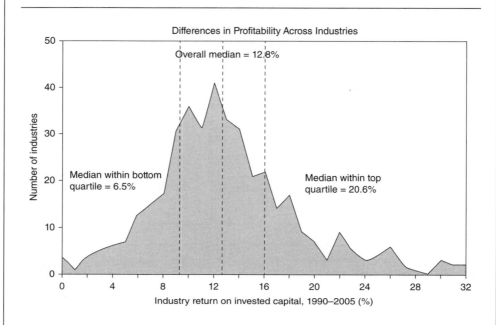

Differences in Profitability Across Industries

Overall median = 12.8%

Median within bottom quartile = 6.5%

Median within top quartile = 20.6%

Number of industries

Industry return on invested capital, 1990–2005 (%)

Source: Standard & Poor's Compustat, author's calculations.
Note: Return on invested capital is calculated as earnings before interest and taxes divided by the sum of long-term debt, total equity, and minority interest.

over 10%) than it is in other developed countries, like France where it is over 30% (Sterling, 2011). In contrast, the growth rate for smart phones might well be higher in African countries than it is in developed countries. Indeed, South Africa has had the fourth highest growth rate for mobile communications in the world in recent years.

One important proviso to this analysis is in order. It is easy for companies to be seduced by the size of a market opportunity. And yet profitability is not always correlated with market size, as any number of firms that rushed into China or Russia have found to their cost. A large market often only serves to attract a large number of entrants and competitors, leaving smaller countries with less competition as more profitable locations. If we imagine that there is a minimum scale of operation for a business, choosing to compete in a country where perhaps only a few competitors will pass that hurdle is often preferred to a larger country where many can compete effectively. Size alone is rarely the determinant of whether a market opportunity is worth exploiting. The Chinese auto market is now the largest in the world, selling over 18 million cars in 2011. Unfortunately, with 171 local manufacturers returns are hard to make (Yin, 2012).

INDUSTRY STRUCTURAL ATTRACTIVENESS   The framework for the analysis of industry attractiveness is the traditional Five Forces model of Porter (2008). The premise for this is the fact, intensively studied by industrial organization economics, that all industries are not created equal – some are inherently more profitable than others and show superior long-term industry average profitability (Exhibit 8.6). Porter's Five Forces has been taught in every MBA program for the last 30 years and is a fundamental building block of all strategic analysis (see box).

Industry Structure

The foundation of industry structural analysis is an extended view of competition in an industry (Exhibit 8.7). This goes beyond just direct rivals to include the set of players that limit or fight for a share of the value created by an industry – customers and suppliers who seek to extract value, and substitutes and entry barriers that limit value creation. Note that many strategists now consider the framework to include a sixth force, namely complements, which are the opposite of substitutes in that they increase demand for or the value of the product itself.[10]

Exhibit 8.7.
The Five Forces

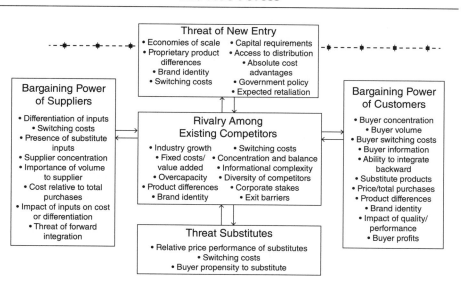

Well-documented across a broad array of industries, time periods, and performance measures, sustained intra-industry differences in profitability are found within all countries. The interesting observation is that there remain substantial differences in the long-term attractiveness of the same industry in different countries. Khanna and Rivkin (2001), for example, showed that the average correlation of industry profitability across countries was only 0.095 (see Exhibit 8.8).

The important implication of this research is that the analysis of industry structural attractiveness has to be conducted separately for each country. Just because the industry is profitable in one country does not imply that it will necessarily generate above-average returns in another country. The reason for this is obvious since many of the determinants of industry attractiveness vary between countries. Consider the cement industry where market profitability in the high fixed-cost, cyclic industry is critically affected by the level of industry concentration. Just because CEMEX makes exceptional returns in its domestic market, where the top three players have a 92% market share, will not ensure that the business is anywhere near as profitable in countries like Egypt, where the top six players only have a combined 77% market share (Betts and Crimes, 2004).

Competitive Advantage

The second dimension of the attractiveness matrix concerns the ability of the firm to win in a given market – whether it can overcome the liability of foreignness and still have a competitive advantage. This dimension can be divided into two broad sets of determinants. The first is the multinational's underlying competitive position in the country. The second is the ability of management to execute in that particular country.

COMPETITIVE POSITION   The tools used to understand competitive advantage – relative cost analysis, conjoint analysis etc. – are those taught in every MBA class and widely applied in domestic strategy formulation. We will not dwell on those tools here. What we can observe is that an initial estimate of competitive position in a new country cannot be as sophisticated as when developing a full-blown strategy. Instead, simple heuristics or surrogate measures are often deployed.

One obvious measure, if the firm is already present in the country, is current financial performance – a higher return on invested capital is a good indicator of strong competitive position. Another is relative market share, the presumption being that this correlates with competitive advantage and financial performance. For a new entrant, one relevant metric is probably the combined market share of the largest three incumbents, with the belief that a more fragmented market will allow for easier entry. Potential entrants also have to consider the likely response of competitors to their entry. This

Exhibit 8.8.
Cross-Country Correlations in Industry Profitability

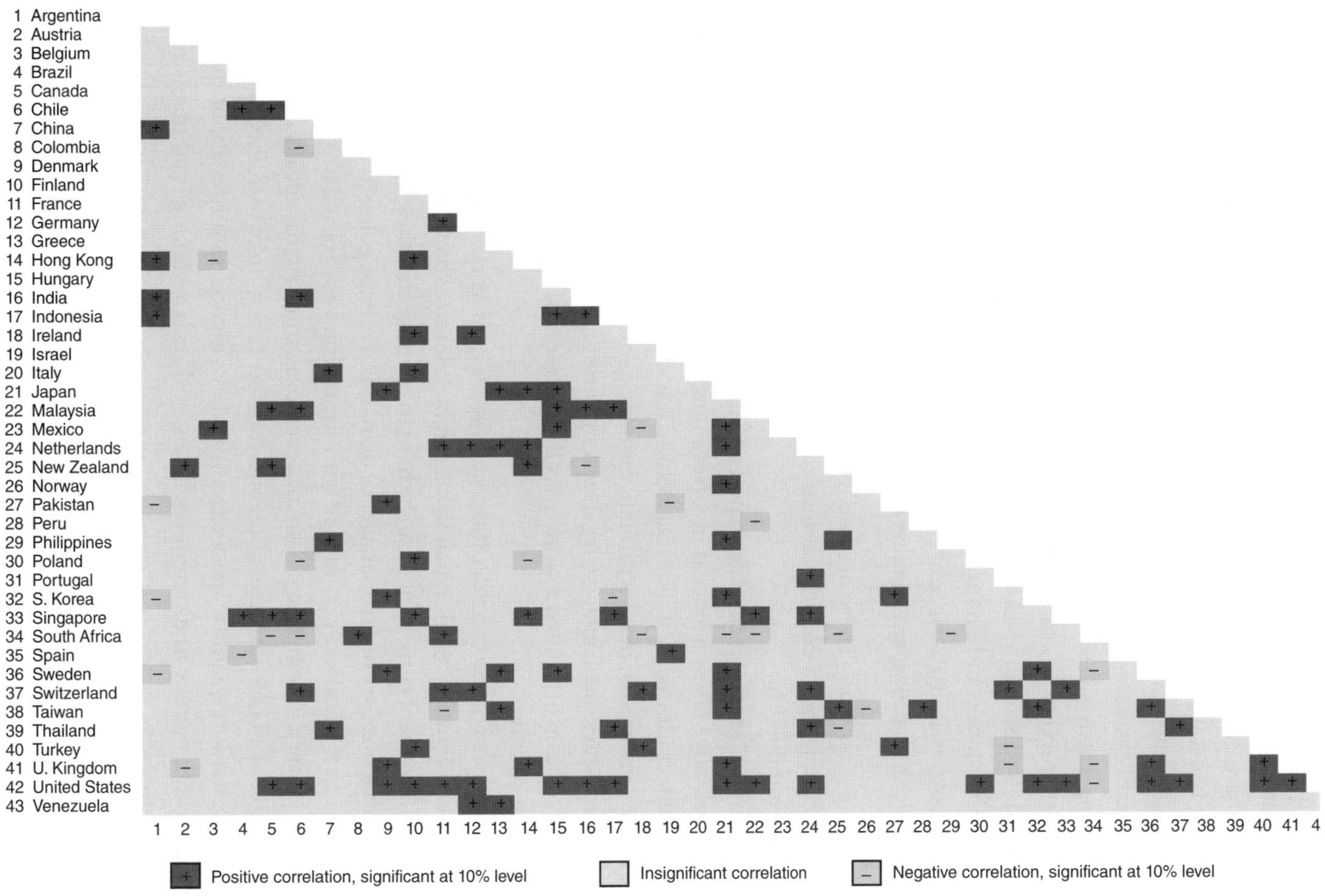

1 Argentina
2 Austria
3 Belgium
4 Brazil
5 Canada
6 Chile
7 China
8 Colombia
9 Denmark
10 Finland
11 France
12 Germany
13 Greece
14 Hong Kong
15 Hungary
16 India
17 Indonesia
18 Ireland
19 Israel
20 Italy
21 Japan
22 Malaysia
23 Mexico
24 Netherlands
25 New Zealand
26 Norway
27 Pakistan
28 Peru
29 Philippines
30 Poland
31 Portugal
32 S. Korea
33 Singapore
34 South Africa
35 Spain
36 Sweden
37 Switzerland
38 Taiwan
39 Thailand
40 Turkey
41 U. Kingdom
42 United States
43 Venezuela
1 2 3 4 5 6 7 8 9 10 11 12 13 14 15 16 17 18 19 20 21 22 23 24 25 26 27 28 29 30 31 32 33 34 35 36 37 38 39 40 41 4
Positive correlation, significant at 10% level
Insignificant correlation
Negative correlation, significant at 10% level

Source: Khanna and Rivkin, 2001.
Reproduced with permission of Jan Rivkin.

involves some estimation of incumbents' commitment to the market. An entrenched local family-owned firm, for example, is more likely to react aggressively to entry than a multinational that is performing poorly in that geography, even if both have the same market share. None of these measures is a perfect indicator of competitive advantage, thus care has to be taken in using such simplistic measures, even if they are often the only ones readily available on a comparable basis across countries.

Alternatively, some firms choose to qualitatively assess competitive position by comparing themselves to incumbents on what they identify as being the critical resources (FSAs) or key success factors in the business. These might include an assessment of brand strength; technological capability; production scale economies, first-mover advantages; and so on. While more directly related to competitive position, these measures are typically only assessed qualitatively and so have all the limitations and biases that accompany managerial judgment (Exhibit 8.9).

ABILITY TO EXECUTE   There are two determinants of a company's ability to successfully execute within a country: country compatibility, and the firm's managerial and resource bandwidth.

The first of these echoes Ghemawat's CAGE framework, although this time in a more qualitative fashion since it involves managerial "distance" rather than the more quantifiable trade distance. The idea behind it is similar – to highlight differences with the home country that make it difficult for management to operate in the subject country. Again, issues like language, legal system, time zone, and culture come to the fore, and have to be incorporated into an overall assessment of management's ability to operate in that country.

The firm also has to consider how much spare managerial capacity it has to deploy in any given country. While small firms can be keen to expand internationally, if they face a management constraint it can be hard to envisage that they will be successful in a country that imposes heavy managerial demands. Perhaps going to a more developed market, even if it is already populated with strong competitors, is a better solution than trying to create a new market in a small developing country that speaks a different language and has poor communication and transportation links with the home market. Although hard to quantify, most executives have a good intuition about their firm's willingness to operate in different countries, and such a ranking is all that is required before combining factors to arrive at an overall assessment of a firm's "ability to win" in a given market (Exhibit 8.9).

Weighting

With a long list of factors underpinning the two dimensions of country attractiveness and ability to win, a key question is how to weight them in deriving a single, aggregate

Exhibit 8.9.
Market Selection

Legend: ● Attractive/good position ○ Moderately attractive/medium position ◑ Least attractive/weak position

Markets	Market attractiveness					Ability to win			
	Size	"New Normal Growth"	"New Normal Profitability"	Structure	Overall	Share	Trend	Capabilities	Overall
A	●	○	○	○	○	●	●	○	●
B	○	○	○	○	○	○	○	●	○
C	○	○	◑	○	◑	○	○	◑	○
D	●	○	○	○	○	○	○	○	○
E	○	○	○	○	○	○	○	○	○
F	●	◑	●	○	○	●	●	○	○
G	●	◑	●	●	●	●	○	●	○
H	●	◑	○	○	○	●	●	○	●
I	○	○	○	○	○	●	○	○	●
J	●	○	○	○	◑	●	●	○	○
K	●	○	○	◑	◑	○	○	●	●
L	○	●	○	○	○	●	●	●	●
M	◑	○	○	○	◑	○	●	●	●
N	◑	○	○	○	○	○	●	○	●
O	○	○	○	●	●	●	●	●	●
P	◑	○	●	○	●	●	○	●	○
Q	◑	◑	◑	◑	◑	●	○	○	○
R	●	●	○	○	○	○	○	○	○
S	○	◑	○	●	○	●	○	○	○
T	○	●	○	○	○	●	○	○	●
U	●	○	○	○	○	○	○	●	○
V	○	○	○	○	○	○	○	●	○
W	○	○	○	○	○	○	○	○	○
X	●	●	○	◑	○	○	●	○	○
Y	●	○	◑	○	◑	○	●	○	○
Z	●	○	○	◑	○	●	○	●	●
A1	●	○	○	○	●	◑	○	○	◑
B1	●	◑	○	○	○	◑	○	○	◑
C1	○	◑	○	●	◑	○	●	○	○

88

metric which can be used to prioritize country selection. A number of approaches are feasible.

The first, which is often used in the initial screening process, is a **binary** decision rule. For some criteria, a country must be above a certain level, or it is simply removed from consideration. An example might be the level of corruption in a country. If a firm is not convinced that activities in that country will pass the test of the Foreign Corrupt Practices Act, it will simply be excluded from further analysis. The earlier example of requiring the market potential to be above $100 million is another such binary rule.[11]

Next, the hierarchy of factors can be ranked in **lexicographic order**. The process thus orders the individual criteria, and passes countries through each filter in turn until only one is left standing. This process would say that a country with a market potential over $100 million is preferred to all others, regardless of how it ranks on other criteria. The next filter might be political stability, and so on.

If the process wants to account for all factors rather than address them sequentially, there is, unfortunately, no good way to weight the list. Some firms use a simple **high, medium, low ranking** for each element and then attribute different arithmetic weights to each (see Exhibit 8.9), but, in practice, the entire process often incorporates a degree of judgment and, to be honest, **personal preference**! There is no way round this. Perhaps the main consolation is that fiddling the weights so that the CEO's desire to visit Paris ranks France high on the list of possible markets at least reflects a likelihood that the firm will be a success in that country because senior management will be happy to travel there. Regardless, the value of detailed analysis is in stimulating the appropriate conversations, and confronting facts that validate or rebut initial managerial beliefs.

The output of this analysis explains the traditional expansionary paths followed by multinationals, and gives particular credence to the importance of the similarity dimension. Historically, multinationals first entered large, culturally and economically similar, and physically adjacent markets. Thus, US firms went to Canada and then the UK. British firms went to the USA and the wealthier Commonwealth countries, like Australia and New Zealand. European firms tended to expand into their contiguous neighbors. Only later in the sequence of expansions did multinationals begin to enter "distant" countries, whether in terms of lower incomes, smaller size, or alien cultures.

(b) Resource Allocation and Portfolio Balance
Existing Footprint

When the issue is managing resource allocation across an existing global footprint, the same dimensions can be applied to derive a matrix of market attractiveness and ability to win. With the size of each bubble being some measure of sales or assets in the various countries (or potential market size when considering new entry), the matrix reveals the relative attractiveness of different countries (Exhibit 8.10).

Most executives in multinationals will have been exposed to some variant of this tool as an input into resource allocation decisions across a portfolio of current countries and businesses. Simple though it is, the matrix has power to sort through a complicated set of variables and come up with straightforward recommendations.

In the portfolio in Exhibit 8.11, the recommendation would be to invest in the two larger businesses on the right, while withdrawing from the small businesses on the far left and minimizing investment in the large business at the top of the matrix – even

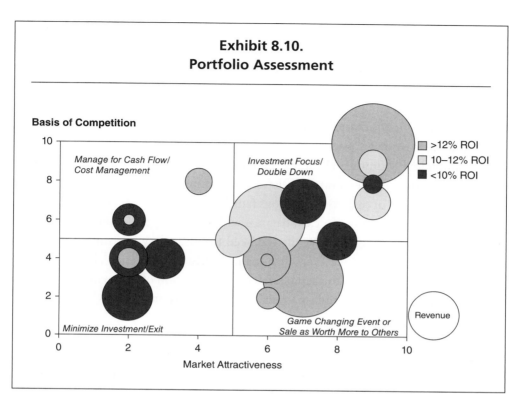

Exhibit 8.10.
Portfolio Assessment

Basis of Competition

- Manage for Cash Flow/ Cost Management
- Investment Focus/ Double Down
- Minimize Investment/Exit
- Game Changing Event or Sale as Worth More to Others

>12% ROI
10–12% ROI
<10% ROI

Revenue

Market Attractiveness

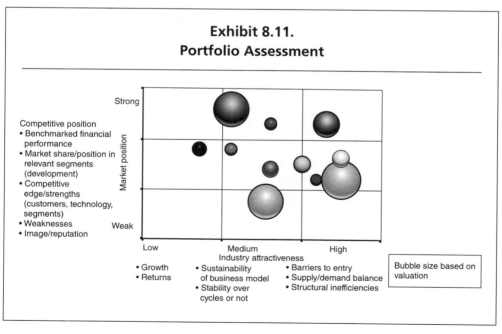

Exhibit 8.11.
Portfolio Assessment

Competitive position
- Benchmarked financial performance
- Market share/position in relevant segments (development)
- Competitive edge/strengths (customers, technology, segments)
- Weaknesses
- Image/reputation

Strong

Weak

Market position

Low   Medium   High
Industry attractiveness

- Growth
- Returns

- Sustainability of business model
- Stability over cycles or not

- Barriers to entry
- Supply/demand balance
- Structural inefficiencies

Bubble size based on valuation

if that has a strong market position, the unfavorable industry structure will probably result in destruction of shareholder value. While never intended to be definitive, the matrix does provide a useful default prescription for resource allocation among countries.

Portfolio Diversification and Balance

Until now we have been portraying the decision of where to compete as a choice among individual countries. However, we must now go beyond standalone country attractiveness and consider strategic relationships among markets. The original BCG growth/share matrix of cash cows and dogs fame emphasized internal corporate funding and focused on achieving a cash balance within the corporate portfolio between cash users and cash generators. While the need to fund every investment internally has declined over time (since every firm can, in principle, finance any net present value positive investment in the capital markets), the notion of achieving balance has become entrenched in many multinational portfolio decisions.

GROWTH AND RETURN   One particularly salient form of geographic balance that many multinationals seek is between growth and profitability. The capital markets reward companies that are able to grow while earning above their cost of capital. While it might be hard to have every individual country deliver high return on equity and high growth, many multinationals reach this combination through portfolio diversification. Some countries, possibly mature markets where the firm has a strong competitive position, will generate profit but less growth. Other countries, possibly developing countries, will require substantial investment to grow rapidly while providing limited returns. On their own, neither provides the performance that is attractive to the capital markets. Together, with each country playing a different role, the portfolio offers both growth and return.

In the example in Exhibit 8.12, the implication of the matrix is to invest in the Iberia business which is high growth (this example predates the recent financial crisis!), if it can be balanced by investment in Benelux. The high returns there offset the investment and lower margins required to grow the Iberian business.

Note that shareholders can diversify themselves to achieve this balance by making separate investments in developing and developed countries. However, capital market imperfections lead most multinationals to feel the need to achieve portfolio balance with respect to growth and return – if not with respect to completely balancing cash flow internally. The implication is that many multinationals allocate different roles in the portfolio to different country subsidiaries, Typically, this is to support strategic growth countries, like India and Brazil, by not expecting them to deliver short-term

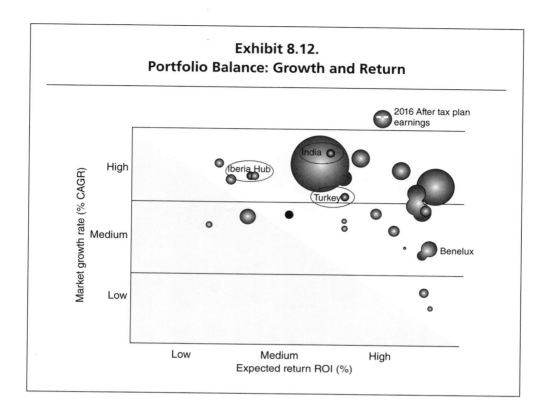

Exhibit 8.12.
Portfolio Balance: Growth and Return

earnings, while limiting investment in mature geographies in order to maximize their returns. Country managers in many multinationals will be familiar with being allocated such a role to play in the portfolio, along with a corresponding priority for capital investment and talent. Country managers will also be familiar with other implications of portfolio planning as the metrics they are held accountable for vary with the strategic goal for their operation. Perhaps one country will be given an ROI target, another a market share goal.

RISK AND RETURN   Every company has to consider the overall risk of its geographic portfolio. While economists debate how coupled the economies of the world have become, there is still sufficient divergence in their economic performance to warrant some diversification. A portfolio that is constructed of businesses whose financial performance is negatively correlated creates more value than one in which country performance is correlated. This suggests that if, for example, Peru is a high-risk and volatile country, but that performance is negatively correlated with Japan (and the multinational has a large Japanese operation), then Peru has a value in the portfolio over and above its standalone potential.

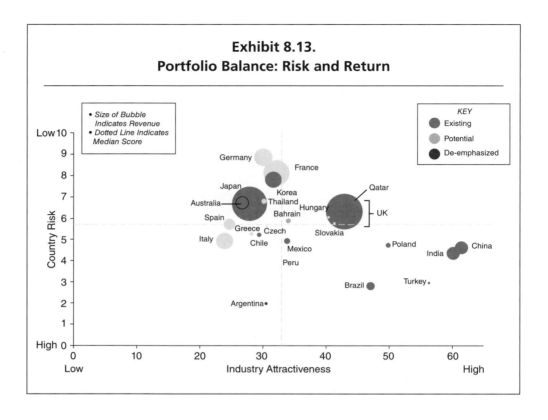

Exhibit 8.13.
Portfolio Balance: Risk and Return

Risk also applies to the likelihood of success in a country. China, for example, is a large and growing market that attracts many competitors. It might therefore rank high on country attractiveness, but low on competitive position for a Mexican multinational entering such an alien market. This suggests that any investment in China for that firm is high risk, if potentially high return. While on a standalone basis this might be too much risk to bear, if the portfolio contains other, lower risk investments, it might be possible to justify the Chinese opportunity. Having a "degree of difficulty 10 dive" somewhere in the portfolio is often appropriate when allocating resources to ensure long-term sustainable growth, if balanced by other, more secure investments.

In the example in Exhibit 8.13, the implication of the matrix is to minimize investment in Argentina, commit to the UK, and investigate the potential of at least two additional countries – Germany and France. China and India are the big question marks for the portfolio – both attractive markets, but each with a degree of risk. Perhaps the answer is to choose one of those high-risk/high-return markets to achieve the desired portfolio risk balance.

One result of the desire to achieve diversification with respect to risk, growth, and return is that multinationals typically look to build a balanced portfolio between

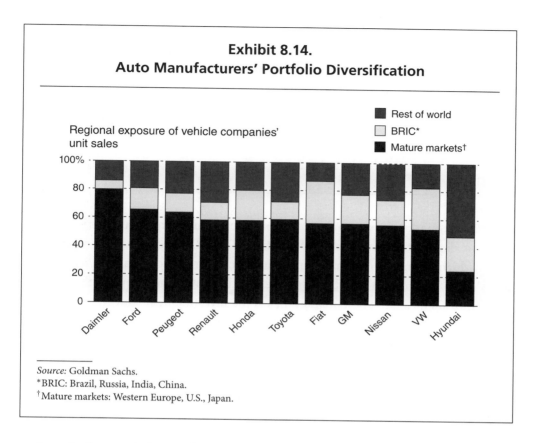

Exhibit 8.14.
Auto Manufacturers' Portfolio Diversification

Regional exposure of vehicle companies' unit sales

Legend:
- Rest of world
- BRIC*
- Mature markets†

Source: Goldman Sachs.
*BRIC: Brazil, Russia, India, China.
†Mature markets: Western Europe, U.S., Japan.

regions. In the auto industry, for example, GM, for all its faults and recent travails, and VW are given credit for having built a more balanced portfolio of sales than many of their competitors (Exhibit 8.14). Today this results in multinationals having a Triad presence with substantial operations in each of the three regions – Europe, America, and Asia – and distributed between developed and emerging markets in each of those regions (Ohmae, 2002).

Competitive Interaction

A second overlay determining a multinational's global resource allocation is its interaction with major competitors. Earlier, we alluded to the challenge that Pepsi Cola faces as it competes globally with Coca-Cola. More generally, many companies in oligopolistic industries have to include competitive interaction in their resource allocation decisions (Carr and Collis, 2011).

This sort of interaction has given rise to a number of strategic suggestions as to how companies that meet each other in many markets should behave. One recommendation is that each firm should be sure to have a small presence in the other's

Table 8.2 Bearing Company: Global Market Shares (Estimated)

| | 2010 Market Share (%)[12] | | |
COUNTRY	SKF (Sweden)	Timken (USA)	NSK (Japan)
USA	21%	34%	12%
Japan	7%	7%	35%
Europe	31%	7%	7%

home/major market to maintain a deterrent threat. Indeed, many industries, such as bearings, demonstrate this sort of interaction (Table 8.2). I call this the **80/20** strategy in which, even if it is actually unprofitable on a standalone basis to have only a 20% share of the competitor's home market, the benefit of the deterrent threat to the competitor's 80% share home market makes the investment worthwhile. Others call this strategy building **footholds** in competitors' bases, and point out that if a competitor makes a move in one country, firms will often **cross-parry** by making a similar move in a different country to reestablish parity. It is important to note that the resulting geographic footprint might not be justified on the standalone attractiveness of the countries in question but is justified by the competitive interaction.

Other strategies that have been identified include **cross-subsidy,** which was the reputed strategy of many Japanese firms in the 1980s as they took profits from the protected Japanese domestic market to gain share in the open US market. Another is **mimetic diversification** whereby companies copy the market presence of competitors, regardless of whether that footprint makes sense or not (Fligstein and Dauber, 1989). The argument is that replicating the competitor's geographic footprint reduces risk since the competitor will not have preferential access to unique ideas or opportunities. A more sophisticated argument points to managerial incentives when compensation is tied to relative performance. Consider when Firm A enters Vietnam, but Firm B, believing that is not an attractive market, does not. If Vietnam actually turns out to be a good market, Firm B's executives look bad and their compensation falls. If, however, Firm B had gone to Vietnam in spite of its own estimation of market attractiveness, it would also perform well. And what if Vietnam turns out to be a failure? Well, no one can blame Firm B because Firm A went there as well! This skewed incentive structure, it is argued, leads to mimetic diversification. Whether it is observed in practice is debatable, although it is hard to deny the pressure placed on a CEO by the Board and the capital markets if a competitor is making substantial investments in countries the CEO chooses not to enter.

Answering the more general question of optimal resource allocation comes back to finding where the marginal ROI is highest. Simple though it is to state, calculating those returns is nearly impossible. As a result, there are no *a priori* answers to questions such as whether to shore up a home base against attack from the global competitor; attack a competitor in its strong markets; or seek to be a first mover in countries where neither is yet present because the market is immature. The way to play the global competitive game does, however, depend on the extent of **market interdependencies**.

If there are no economic linkages between markets, then, absent the mutual deterrence discussion above, multinationals should treat each market as economically discrete. In practice that would mean looking at the ROI in each country on a standalone basis. This, after all, was the presumption behind the multidomestic strategy. With no linkages between markets, multinationals should only compete in those countries in which they make a current profit. A US industrial gases company that is losing money in Europe can safely exit the region without detriment to its competitive position in the USA.

In contrast, if there are linkages among markets, competitive parries and ripostes make sense since performance in one market has consequential repercussions in other markets. Boeing cannot allow Airbus free reign in Europe, even if it struggles to be profitable there, since allowing Airbus the scale and cash flow from an uncontested European market would damage Boeing's ability to compete in the USA. Firms that compete across economically related markets, therefore, need to be concerned about their **relative not absolute performance** in every market. If I do poorly in one market, it does not matter if my presence there damages my global competitor more. With interrelated markets the globe has to be treated as a single entity, and resources have to be allocated recognizing spillovers between countries.

Strategic Importance

The last factor determining a multinational's global footprint is the importance some markets can take, over and above their standalone attractiveness. Particularly in businesses where there are linkages across markets and companies seek to exploit aggregation and agglomeration advantages, multinationals must factor in the global contribution of a market when deciding where to compete.

SCALE   If a firm is pursuing an international strategy whose advantage comes in part from exploiting global scale, then the **absolute size of a market** must play an important role in determining where to compete. In this regard, the earlier advice not to be seduced by the size of the market opportunity is inappropriate. To return to the Boeing example, in an industry where global scale matters, Boeing must attempt to build a market presence in every large country, or it will have no hope of success. Even if it loses money in China, the incremental benefit from spreading fixed costs over additional volume is worthwhile. Put another way, the marginal cost of a sale in China will be substantially lower than the full cost – thus justifying Boeing's presence even if it makes a loss there.

DEMANDING CUSTOMERS AND INNOVATION Similarly, multinationals pursuing an agglomeration strategy that seeks to leverage product and process innovations around the world cannot afford to be absent from geographies that are at the **leading edge of innovation** or have the **most demanding customers**. Any video-game company will have to sell in South Korea and Japan if it is to have an insider's insight and ability to sense and respond to innovations in those cutting edge markets. Again, this would be true even if the firm was losing money in those markets, or even if the market was small. New Zealand, for example, is a tiny, distant market, but because it is a driver of yacht design, many leading yacht manufacturers have a sales presence there. Indeed, the argument can be extended to the need to be present in any market where a **key competitor** is based, since the company must closely monitor the competitor's activities.

Strategic Fit

These last factors of market importance and interrelationships begin to point out how the choice of geographic scope is affected by international strategy. Every multinational will seek to compete in attractive markets where it can build a competitive advantage – those in the top right of the original matrix. Beyond those, the decision on geographic scope has to be aligned with the generic international strategy.

LOCAL By definition, the local strategy does not have to confront the choice of where to compete outside the domestic market. Predicated on the advantage of satisfying idiosyncratic local demand, such a strategy supports a presence in only one market.

EXPORT The export strategy that leverages a country-based advantage is also relatively indifferent to the choice of foreign markets. Since the strategy involves little in the way of investment and commitment to foreign markets, it can enter and leave markets at relatively low cost. Not seeking to exploit any linkages between markets, the strategy can freely respond to opportunities on their standalone attractiveness as they arise. To return to the example of the Spanish furniture manufacturer, if the firm chose to be an exporter, it could happily take the one-time Uzbekistan order – provided it had the management capability and bandwidth to execute the deal.

MULTIDOMESTIC The underlying presumption of the multidomestic strategy is that there are no interdependencies between countries. Rather, the competitive advantage comes from augmenting the product or capability set available in each country. In this case, market selection is primarily driven by the standalone attractiveness of each country, perhaps with a portfolio overlay to ensure an overall growth/return balance.

GLOBAL   The global strategy seeks to aggregate demand worldwide in order to exploit scale economies and views market selection from the perspective of overall contribution to the portfolio, rather than just standalone attractiveness. As we suggested above, this means that large markets and those where important competitors have a strong presence have to be included in the portfolio regardless of profitability.

REGIONAL   Rather than competing everywhere, the regional strategy limits market presence to countries that are similar. Indeed, Rugman noted how common this approach has been among multinationals. The Triad variant divides the multinational into three, almost separate, regional entities that are able to capitalize on similarities within regions, while allowing differentiation among the Triad regions. This balances the multidomestic and global strategies and perhaps partially supersedes the trade-off between the simplicity of competing in similar markets and extending geographic scope to gain scale.

TRANSNATIONAL   As with the global strategy, the transnational exploits linkages among markets and so has to consider interrelationships among the portfolio of countries. In this case the markets that must be included are those that feature demanding customers, leading edge innovations, and critical competitors. Regardless of the attractiveness of those countries, firms pursuing the transnational strategy have to allocate resources to them or risk losing preferential access to the future innovations and learning that underpin the agglomeration advantage.

Step 2: Entry Mode
The second question to address when expanding a geographic footprint is what organizational form to adopt in new markets. The firm does not have to undertake foreign direct investment in order to compete in a new country. It can always contract with third parties for the provision of the services needed to market, sell, distribute, and service its product. Indeed, to become a multinational, the firm has to have an "internalization" advantage over market contracts to justify subsuming those activities within the corporate hierarchy.

Alternative Organizational Arrangements
The set of organizational arrangements available when selling in a country can be arrayed along a continuum from contractual to hierarchical, according to the extent to which they rely on market exchange rather than administrative control (Exhibit 8.15). At one end of that continuum is the simplest form of spot contract – responding to

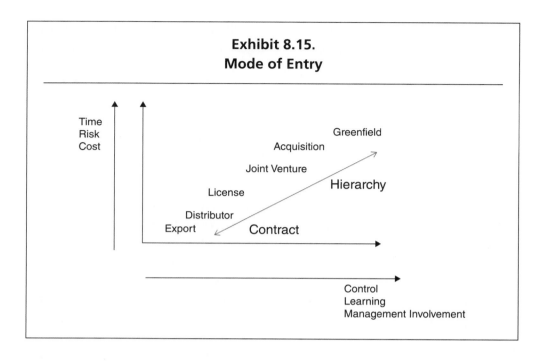

Exhibit 8.15.
Mode of Entry

a single order from a foreign country by exporting to that country while letting the customer perform all local work. Next along the continuum is finding a distributor or agent who will represent the firm on a regular basis in the country. The length of that relationship can vary, with shorter terms less likely to involve mutual investment. Then there would be a license or franchise agreement (perhaps including contract manufacturing), which implies a longer contractual term and begins to specify obligations on both sides, going beyond the simple terms and conditions of individual trades to perhaps include advertising, quality checks, and other reputational factors. Next, there would be a joint venture or some form of alliance in which partial control rights are passed to the multinational. Extending those rights to majority ownership or acquisition finally internalizes the local entity within the multinational. Last, and most difficult, is establishing the firm's own greenfield operations in the new country, with every activity now carried out within the firm's hierarchy.

Strategic Tradeoffs

Traditionally the choice between these alternative arrangements for the governance of transactions has been portrayed as depending on the tradeoff between the need for **control** and the **risk** associated with making an (irreversible) investment in the country (Kim and Hwang, 1992; Agarwal and Ramaswami, 1992; Anderson and Gatignon, 1986). However, the mode of entry depends on other tradeoffs, particularly that between needing **local knowledge and relationships**, and hence a local partner to overcome the liability of foreignness, **versus the inability to contract** effectively with those local entities. On the one hand, a new entrant needs to quickly access the complementary resources required to access distribution, acquire local market knowledge, develop contacts with regulators, and so on. Such resources can be more readily accessed through a local partner. On the other hand, it can be difficult to write a contract that effectively protects the interests of the multinational against intellectual property theft, or that ensures adequate investment by both parties. In the presence of such high transaction costs, the multinational would have to make the investment itself and retain the activities inside the corporate hierarchy.

A more detailed analysis of tradeoffs, and therefore the pros and cons of each mode of entry, follows this **localization versus internalization** argument. Those organizational arrangements at the contractual end of the continuum will most rapidly and effectively access local resources at the lowest cost. In contrast, toward the hierarchical end of the continuum, multinationals will need time and investment to acquire or build the required local capabilities. They will also incur far more risk since investments may be sunk in the country and lost if the entry strategy fails.

Conversely, at the contractual end of the continuum, the multinational will have limited control of the local operations and so will not be able to directly set policies or make decisions itself. Nor will it be easily able to internalize learning about market demand, or protect its resources and capabilities from potential expropriation by its contract partner. Those drawbacks disappear at the other end of the continuum when all activities are contained within the hierarchy.

Joint ventures should be recognized as an intermediate organizational form that have some of the benefits and some of the weaknesses of both extremes (see boxes).

Joint Ventures

As an intermediate organizational form, joint ventures are typically employed when each party brings a distinctive resource to the entity which is difficult to contract over. Ben Gomes-Casseres, for example, classifies joint ventures according to the asset being provided by each party, and finds four common types (Exhibit 8.16) (Gomes-Casseres, 1996). The first two are supply joint ventures in which one party manufactures product for a firm with a distinctive technology or design – the case of Boeing using joint ventures to produce critical parts for its planes, or when, in the other direction, a multinational supplies technology to a local partner for local production. The third is market access, as when Coca-Cola and IBM were required to take on a joint venture partner if they were to sell in India, or when Otis joint ventured with local municipalities in China. The fourth is when firms have complementary technologies and need each other to bring a product to market. These joint ventures tend to be more contentious since there is an element of

---

competitive learning in the relationships that engenders every interaction with a degree of suspicion (Hamel *et al.*, 1989). Hennart's (1991) list of joint venture types – supply, market entry, learning, and scale – is similar, with the addition of the potential for additional volume as the motivator for the partnership.

Exhibit 8.16.
Generic Types of International Joint Venture

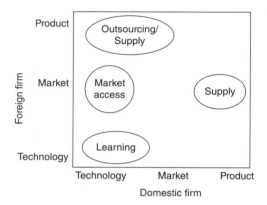

Regardless of the motivation for the joint venture, this mode of exchange typically exists when there is not an obvious transaction cost justification for using either the hierarchy or a contract.[13]

How to Manage a Joint Venture

Jim Austin outlined a useful stages model for effective management of an international joint venture (Austin, 1990).

Identify the logic for collaboration:

- "know yourself" to understand in advance your objective for the outcome of the joint venture and your definition of success;

- "assess needs complementarity" to understand what resources you are missing and are looking for in the joint venture partner;

- "look for goal congruency" so that both parties will have a common purpose for the entity.

Select the partner:

- "know your partner" by performing a detailed analysis to predict its behavior by empathizing with its motivations, aspirations, and expectations. It is critical to develop your own interpretation of what the partner wants from the joint venture rather than relying on its (self-serving) statements.

Structure the alliance contract:

- "control creatively" by acknowledging that there is no standard format for a joint venture. Each will have its own contractual peculiarities addressing the specific needs of the venture and partners.

- "identify conflict points" so that areas where there is likely to be disagreement can be addressed in advance, and processes to resolve them identified before the venture is operational.

- "make clear rules" for those items and issues that are fundamental to each side. Thus, the use and provision of "hard currency" by one partner might be laid out in detail within the agreement. Similarly, the number of Board members from each side; the parent from which key executives should come; and other governance and personnel issues might be clearly structured. Other aspects of the contract have to be left to agreement on broad principles since it is impossible to contract around every imaginable eventuality (and all those you never anticipated usually come to pass!). The most important insight about a joint venture is that signing the contract is not the end, but the beginning, of discussions of how to run the entity. If partners are continually looking for contractual terms to tell them how to operate, the venture is likely to fail. As a friend who ran such an entity once said, "the contract is merely the framework for a lawsuit!"

- "make transactions transparent" so that dealings between the joint venture and the parent organizations are visible to both parties. This prevents either side having surreptitious interactions with the joint venture that could undermine the relationship.

Manage alliance dynamics:

- "communicate often and clearly" to prevent any issues escalating or festering without the other side being aware and able to respond;

- "share gain and pain equitably" so that neither side harbors a grudge or feels that they are being exploited by the other;

- "be flexible" as a spirit of trust and openness would suggest;

- "review and revise" give and take for the duration of the joint venture, which requires the willingness to revisit features of the initial agreement if they are an obstacle to the venture's continuation.

Conclude alliance:

- "know when to exit" when the initial objective has been met, or when it becomes apparent that continuation no longer satisfies current strategic goals;

- "closure is not a failure." Perhaps the second most important lesson for joint ventures is that they have a natural lifespan. Ending the partnership is often a consequence of its success – perhaps the multinational now understands the local market and feels able to compete on its own, while the local partner wants to move on to other businesses. It was found, for example, that while about 40% of joint ventures close, many of those were actually successes (Gomes-Casseres, 1987).

Choice of Mode of Entry

The choice of mode of entry depends on balancing the strategic tradeoffs and so depends on a set of determinants, including country factors, company position, and the nature of the product or service itself.

Country factors

Country-specific laws and regulations can have an enormous impact on a multinational's mode of entry. Many nations have policy restrictions that limit foreign competition and protect indigenous firms. India, for example, before embarking on a policy of liberalization, only allowed foreign firms to operate as minority owners. China still insists on multinationals having local partners, and some governments require foreign firms to locate manufacturing in their country as a condition of market entry. Poland, for example, required pharmaceutical companies to manufacture locally if they wanted to sell locally. Similarly, some governments demand export offsets when a multinational sells in their country. Indeed, quotas or high import tariffs can force a firm that wants to take advantage of a market to locate manufacturing there.

Faced with such demands, which are more likely to be imposed in sensitive or nationally important industries, like defense, telecommunications, and financial services, potential entrants can either agree to the host country's terms or choose not to compete in that country. Coca-Cola, for example, chose for a long time not to be present in India because of the requirement to have a majority local partner. When it did reenter in 1993, five years after Pepsi (both had left in 1977), it struggled to regain market share, and Pepsi still outsells Coke by almost 2:1 today (Gulati and Ahmed, 2012).

More generally, country factors can affect the willingness of multinationals to adopt a mode of entry toward the hierarchical end of the continuum because it entails a longer commitment and therefore more risk. If a company believes that the risk factors (captured in the analysis described earlier) are sufficiently high, it might only compete in that country through short-term contractual arrangements. Similarly, the "distance" from the domestic market, particularly the extent of managerial fit and ability to execute within a country, can matter. Without the capability to speak Uzbek, for example, the Spanish furniture manufacturer would not set up its own sales operation, and would have to rely on export or distribution agreement to sell there.

Company position

The resources and managerial capabilities of the firm can therefore have a substantial impact on its mode of market entry. Small firms, for example, will struggle to support a greenfield investment and are more likely to rely on contractual arrangements, such as distributorships. Culturally distant economies will also be more likely to be entered with a contractual arrangement.

The state of competition in a market can also determine the appropriate entry mode. If entry involves adding capacity to an already overbuilt market, acquisition is often the preferred entry mode. CEMEX, for example, enters new cement markets through acquisition because it does not want to build additional capacity. Something similar happens in retailing in mature markets where there are few new store locations available. Walmart's successful international expansions, like in the UK, have therefore come from the acquisition of players already owning desirable store locations.

Nature of product or service

Since the drawbacks of contractual arrangements concern their transaction costs, the nature of the business has an important impact on the preferred mode of entry. Market failures typically arise when one party is unwilling to commit appropriate resources because it is vulnerable to opportunistic behavior by the other. In the international context this could be the unwillingness of a distributor to invest adequately in marketing a product because it fears the multinational will go direct to its customers in the future. Or it could be the failure of the multinational to provide enough personnel and expertise to support the local partner because it worries that transferring too much knowledge will allow the local partner to compete at a later date.

While all transactions are potentially vulnerable to opportunistic behavior, such failures are more likely to occur when the valuable resources (FSAs) being deployed in the new country are intangible rather than tangible (Chapter 2). Contracting for the sale of soft toys, for example, is much easier than for the provision of professional services. As a result, in service industries multinationals typically enter at the hierarchical end of the organizational continuum as they try to both leverage and preserve valuable knowledge inside the firm. Consultants, private equity firms, hedge funds, and investment banks, for example, often expand internationally either by finding an existing partner willing to champion the expansion and live in the new country, or by acquiring a local firm. Contractual agreements are more fraught and have tended to be less successful modes of entry for such firms.

In product businesses it is those involving transfers of knowledge and those requiring relationship-specific investment that are most at risk. That is why MetLife but not Disney enters countries with a high control mode of governance.

Internationalization Process

Integrating the factors that determine the mode of entry produces a **lifecycle** view of a multinational's commitment to a market that progresses along the continuum and which is borne out in the historical evidence (see box). This suggests a logical sequence to the adoption of governance modes that applies both to a firm's commitment within a single country and to that firm's choice in additional markets as it learns from its prior internationalization experience (Johanson and Vahlne, 1977; Melin, 1992).

J & P Coats in the USA

Scottish textile manufacturer J & P Coats entered the cotton-thread business in the USA in the early 1830s, prompted by its weak position in the domestic market. At first, the company exported through local merchants, depending on a single US wholesaler – Parsons, Canning of New York – but the relationship quickly soured as Parsons, Canning began to struggle and failed to send payment back to Scotland. By 1840, Coats had moved to exporting through a network of agents in Boston, New York, and Philadelphia, headed by a general agent Andrew Coats (younger brother of the company's founders). Threads were branded with the Coats name, as opposed to previously, when Parsons, Canning placed its name on all products. In 1869, Coats began local manufacturing after purchasing the Conant Thread Company of Rhode Island. Finally, in 1891, Coats established a US subsidiary, Coats Thread Company, to handle US sales with a new management hierarchy to oversee the growing business in the USA (Dong-Woon, 1998).

In the early stages of a firm's involvement in a country, or when it is smaller, the firm typically relies on exports prior to establishing a formal distribution agreement. As its comfort with operating in the market increases, it either acquires the distributor or establishes its own operation. Either way, as time passes the firm shifts to a hierarchical form of organization as both the risk and cost of localization decrease.

Similarly, while early international moves are more likely to involve contractual arrangements, as the firm's global experience increases, later market entries are more likely to be internalized within the firm. Others disagree, arguing that if a firm learns how to operate in a particular way in one country, it will replicate that mechanism in other countries to reduce risk. Either way, there is a strong sense that multinationals learn over time about their preferred entry mode into countries (Kogut and Zander, 1993).

Born Global

Today there is an argument that firms can be **born global** – competing anywhere and accessing whatever resources they need from everywhere around the world through flexible contracts and a "networked" organization (Kerr, 2013a,b). While the Internet and modern communications enhance a company's ability to do this, the drawbacks of using even sophisticated contractual forms to govern transactions in foreign countries remain and limit the viability of such a strategy.

Strategic Fit

As with the selection of country in which to compete, the choice of mode of entry can be traced back to the need for alignment with the chosen generic international strategy (Harzing, 2002).

The **local** and **export** strategies essentially earn rents from their domestic activities and do not need to control what happens in foreign countries. Indeed, to the extent to which they operate internationally, they will pursue contractual relationships. The **multidomestic** strategy is the most capable of adapting to local regulation and institutions because the firm's operations in one market are relatively independent of what goes on elsewhere. It is multidomestic firms that are, therefore, most likely to operate in countries that impose onerous conditions on entry, such as local equity participation, and for whom the mode of entry will differ the most between countries. The **global** strategy requires high control arrangements since working with local partners, each of whom have their own interests and incentives, can prevent or slow the global standardization which is its key to international advantage. Thus, these multinationals will typically own subsidiaries abroad. An exception would seem to be Caterpillar, which operates through dealerships around the world. However, Caterpillar's dealers have very long-term relationships with the firm – often over 50 years – and, with their fates tied exclusively to the firm, they almost become part of the company.[14] Similarly, the **transnational** strategy requires high-control forms for the governance of foreign activities, since it must retain the ability to quickly and easily arbitrage ideas and opportunities across its global footprint. Local partners can too readily impede the coordination and flexibility that is the hallmark of a transnational's advantage.

Step 3: Timing of Entry

The third issue of market entry concerns not whether investment should be made in a country, but when that investment should occur. This is important since carefully sequencing investment can reduce the risk of hierarchical modes of entry.

Consider the Chinese market in industries like electric vehicles and shale gas, which today are still nascent, but which presumably will be substantial in the future. Should a firm move now to establish the relationships that are so important to success in that culture, and be willing to hold on for the long term, even in the face of the inevitable hiccups and roadblocks for the sake of proving commitment to the Chinese? Or should it wait until the market has been established, the necessary infrastructure to support the business is in place, and uncertainties over the protection of intellectual property rights resolved? Many companies, like eBay and Home Depot, and the Italian appliance manufacturer Indesit, felt the pressure to go to China in the 1990s believing it to be a golden opportunity, only to leave after years of losses when they recognized that later

Exhibit 8.17.
Timing of Entry

EARLY →→→→→→→→→→→→→→→→→→→→→→→→→→→→→ LATE

FAVORED WHEN:

First mover advantage	Rapid/easy imitation
Flexible adaptation	Rigidity / Inertia
Certainty	Ambiguity

entry would be feasible and might actually be lower cost (Barboza and Stone, 2010; Macleod, 2011). Kellogg's, the breakfast cereal company, for example, only entered China in 2012. Entering a nascent market, however huge it may become, is not necessarily the optimal timing decision.

The choice of early or late entry to a new market gives rise to three tradeoffs: moving before or after market demand is established; before or after competitors have entered; and before or after uncertainties about market structure have been resolved. In each case, moving early involves higher risk, but offers higher rewards; moving late is less risky but potentially less rewarding (Exhibit 8.17).

Consulting firms entering an emerging market, for example, have to decide between flying consultants into the country to meet occasional early demand, or bearing the fixed cost of a local office when there is insufficient demand to keep employees fully billed. Similarly, while consultants benefit from being a first mover in a new market by establishing a local social network, building capacity ahead of demand is risky given the many uncertainties about the form of the new business in that country. Moving before these uncertainties have been resolved might lock a firm into an inappropriate business model. In the first Internet bubble several startups chose to align with portals, like Netscape and Yahoo, believing that control of the consumer would lie with these hubs. As search engines and open access replaced a portal's "walled garden," those companies which had paid large sums for the right to be carried exclusively by these portals suffered badly. Similarly, a life insurer which invested in building an agency force in a developing country would lose heavily if banc-assurance later became the preferred distribution channel.

The tradeoff in these cases is relatively simple. When there are substantial first-mover advantages, such as in businesses, like auction sites, with network externalities; when demand growth and market format are relatively certain, as occurs when a product already has a history in other countries; and if firms can easily adapt to changing market conditions – the risk of moving early is reduced. Conversely, it is better to delay if rapid imitation is easy, as appears to be the case today for online coupon sites which have no underlying scale economies or network effects to favor first movers; if there is enormous uncertainty about future market size and structure; or if there is rigidity and lock-in to the initial entry strategy.

One principle that can mitigate these tradeoffs is to maximize the **option value** of entry by sequencing investments in a country. Gradually escalating the level of investment, rather than committing all the investment at once, maximizes value by restricting investment to the minimum necessary to maintain the right to make the next investment. If, for example, an oil company is negotiating to invest in offshore exploration in a new country, it will phase the commitment to purchase drill rigs in line with the passage of certain milestones in the contract process.

The principles regarding the size and timing of investment suggested by an options perspective are:

- Break down any project into incremental phases.
- Delay every commitment as long as possible.
- Only invest in order to reserve the right to play at the next stage.

Strategic Fit

As usual there is a strategic overlay to the timing decision. The local and export strategy is essentially opportunistic in its presence in foreign countries. With no need to commit to any given market, firms pursuing such strategies can enter and leave markets according to current conditions, thus favoring later moves. The multidomestic strategy's perspective on timing really does come down to the value of the first-mover advantage. Many CPG companies, like Colgate and Gillette, built long-term sustainable advantages around the world by being first movers in many countries. Similarly, Pepsi Cola was able to beat Coca-Cola in markets like Russia, India, and Saudi Arabia because it took the economic and reputational risk to enter those countries before they had become recognized participants in the global economy.[15] Firms pursuing global strategies probably need to be early movers if only to preempt other global competitors. Transnational firms are also likely to move early as the strategy is predicated on exploiting uncertainty and unpredictability.

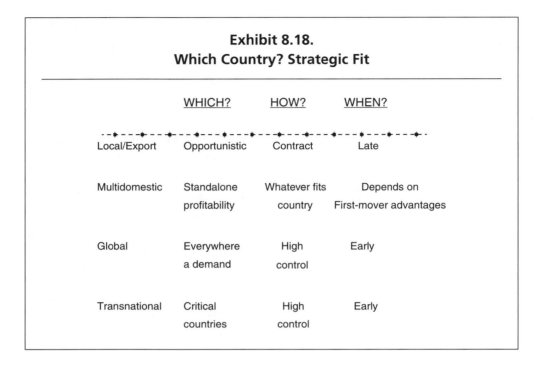

Exhibit 8.18.
Which Country? Strategic Fit

	WHICH?	HOW?	WHEN?
Local/Export	Opportunistic	Contract	Late
Multidomestic	Standalone profitability	Whatever fits country	Depends on First-mover advantages
Global	Everywhere a demand	High control	Early
Transnational	Critical countries	High control	Early

SUMMARY: STRATEGIC FIT

We conclude the chapter with the admonition that, however difficult the choice and however complicated the analysis, the related set of decisions about where to compete, how to enter a market, and when to invest, can be determined by their alignment with the generic international strategy. Indeed, we have been giving interim summaries to that effect at the conclusion of each step in the process.

The outcome of the decision process will not provide the definitive answer to the choices. However, the strategy will provide a default, or bias, as to how to make those decisions in an internally consistent way (Exhibit 8.18).

The **local** and **export** strategies treat foreign markets as opportunistic and so are best accessed through contractual arrangements, such as agency and distribution deals, and can be moved into and out of at will. The **multidomestic** strategy only competes in a country where it can be profitable on a standalone basis. The entry mode will be adaptable to match local regulations or requirements, and the timing of the investment will depend on the importance of first-mover advantages to long-term success. The **global** strategy will seek to enter any market where there is substantial and reliable demand, and will adopt a high-control mode of governance in order to maintain global standardization. The emphasis will be on early entry to preempt competition and gain scale from the additional market. Similarly, the **transnational** strategy, although now choosing to compete in all critical countries (in the sense of being the location of leading customers, innovations, or major competitors), will also seek to maintain activities inside the corporate hierarchy and be an early entrant into new markets.

In fact, the demands of the international strategy to be in a particular country can even drive other choices. Deutsche Bank, for example, tried for a long time to enter the US investment banking business because it viewed that market as critical to its overall strategy. It first acquired the British merchant bank Morgan Grenfell as a step to building its investment banking capability, and then used that vehicle to enter the USA. After that initiative's failure, Deutsche Bank hired US bankers with huge guaranteed bonuses to bring on board the necessary talent. When that failed, Deutsche Bank bit the bullet and acquired Bankers Trust, since no other entry mode gave it the US presence which, at that time, it felt its strategy demanded.

NOTES

1. Currently there are 193 nations recognized by the United Nations (http://www.un.org/en/members/index.shtml). Even the Latin American online auction site, DeRemate, which must have set a world record by operating in nine countries within five months of its founding in 2000, ran just in its home market, Argentina, for six weeks.
2. *Boston Globe* (2011) Wendy's burgers go up-scale. December 29, accessed at http://www.boston.com/business/articles/2011/12/29/wendys_adds_16_foie_gras_burger_in_japan/.
3. When the process involves auditing a current geographic portfolio in order to make resource allocation decisions, every country, in principle, needs to be analyzed in some detail.
4. Note that many of the ideas captured in this section regarding the choice of country in which to sell products and services are the same as those that govern the choice of country in which to locate the performance of an activity (see Chapter 9).
5. Transparency International Corruption Perceptions Index 2013, accessed at http://cpi.transparency.org/cpi2013/results/.
6. The World Bank, accessed at http://data.worldbank.org/indicator/IT.CEL.SETS.P2.
7. O'Carroll, S. (2012) Private sector driving infrastructure development in Mozambique. Frost & Sullivan, March 27, accessed at http://www.frost.com/prod/servlet/market-insight-top.pag?Src=RSS&docid=256606512.
8. Rugman, A. and Collinson, S. (2010) *International Business*. Pearson Education: Harlow. Other forms of PEST are: PESTLE/PESTEL: Political, Economic, Sociological, Technological, Legal, Environmental; PESTLIED: Political, Economic, Social, Technological, Legal, International, Environmental, Demographic; STEEPLE(D): Social/Demographic, Technological, Economic, Environmental, Political, Legal, Ethical; and SLEPT: Social, Legal, Economic, Political, Technological.
9. Transparency International Corruption Perceptions Index 2013, accessed at http://cpi.transparency.org/cpi2013/results/.
10. Examples include software as a complement for hardware, roads as a complement for automobiles, or golf resorts as a complement to airlines (Brandenburger, A. and Nalebuff, B. (1997) *Co-opetition*. Doubleday: New York).
11. Note that some analysts put the two dimensions of country attractiveness and risk on separate dimensions and screen out countries that fall on the low side of either dimension. Similarly, some analysts portray industry attractiveness and growth on two dimensions in order to eliminate candidates which are low on either measure.

12. Japan Bearing Industrial Association shares estimated by *Nikkei Business Daily*, July 30, 2011, and information from former industry executives.
13. It is important to recognize that "joint ventures" cover a wide range of alliances and contractual forms with differing ownership structures and contractual provisions. The subject is therefore wider and more complicated than described above (Todeva, E. and Knoke, D. (2005) Strategic alliances and models of collaboration. *Management Decision*, 43(1), 123–148).
14. The oldest Cat dealer in the USA dates from 1914.
15. Pepsi famously exchanged syrup for Stolichnaya vodka and tankers in the 1980s, while Coca-Cola waited until the fall of the Iron Curtain before entering the country. Coke's reentry into Saudi Arabia in 1988, from which it had been absent for 25 years because of the Arab boycott of companies operating in Israel, was known for its selling "red Pepsi."

REFERENCES AND FURTHER READING

Agarwal, S. and Ramaswami, S.N. (1992) Choice of foreign market entry mode: impact of ownership, location and internalization factors. *Journal of International Business Studies*, 23(1), 1–27.

Anderson, E. and Gatignon, H. (1986) Modes of foreign entry: a transaction cost analysis and propositions. *Journal of International Business Studies*, 17(3), 1–26.

Austin, J.E. (1990) *Managing in Developing Countries: Strategic Analysis and Operating Techniques*. Free Press: New York.

Barboza, D. and Stone, B. (2010) China, where US internet companies often fail. *New York Times*, January 15.

Barkema, H.G. and Vermeulen, F. (1998) International expansion through start-up or acquisition: a learning perspective. *Academy of Management Journal*, 41(1), 7–26.

Betts, M. and Crimes, R. (2004) Construction and building materials sector. JP Morgan European Equity Research, August 16.

Boeh, K. and Beamish, P. (2011) *Connecting flights: the time sink that kills profits*. Harvard Business Review, December.

Brandenburger, A. and Nalebuff, B. (1997) *Co-opetition*. Doubleday: New York.

Brouthers, K.D. and Brouthers, L.E. (2000) Acquisition or greenfield start-up? Institutional, cultural and transaction cost influences. *Strategic Management Journal*, 21(1), 89–97.

Brouthers, K.D., Brouthers, L.E., and Werner, S. (2008) Real options, international entry mode choice and performance. *Journal of Management Studies*, 45(5), 936–960.

Buckley, P.J. and Casson, M. (1981) The optimal timing of a foreign direct investment. *Economic Journal*, 91(361), 75–87.

Carr, C. and Collis, D. (2011) Should you have a global strategy? *MIT Sloan Management Review*, 53 (1), 21–24.

Cavusgil, S.T. and Knight, G. (2009) *Born Global Firms: A New International Enterprise*. Business Expert Press: New York.

Chang, S.-J. and Rosenzweig, P.M. (2001) The choice of entry mode in sequential foreign direct investment. *Strategic Management Journal*, 22(8), 747–776.

Dischinger, M. and Riedel, N. (2009) There's no place like home: the profitability gap between headquarters and their foreign subsidiaries. CESifo Working Paper No. 2866.

Dong-Woon, K. (1998) The British multinational enterprise in the United States before 1914: the case of J. & P. Coats. *Business History Review*, 72(4), 523–551.

Doron, A. and Jeffrey, R. (2013) *The Great Indian Phone Book*. Harvard University Press: Cambridge, MA.

Fligstein, N. and Dauber, K. (1989) Structural change in corporate organization. *Annual Review of Sociology*, 15, 73–96.

Frankel, J. and Romer, D. (1999) Does trade cause growth? *American Economic Review*, 89, 379–399.

Gao, G.Y. and Pan, Y. (2010) The pace of MNEs' sequential entries: cumulative entry experience and the dynamic process. *Journal of International Business Studies*, 41(9), 1572–1580.

Geringer, J.M. and Hebert, L. (1989) Control and performance of international joint ventures. *Journal of International Business Studies*, 20(2), 235–254.

Geringer, J.M. and Hebert, L. (1991) Measuring performance of international joint ventures. *Journal of International Business Studies*, 22(2), 249–263.

Ghemawat, P. (2001) Distance still matters: the hard reality of global expansion. *Harvard Business Review*, 79(8), 137–147.

Ghemawat, P. (2007) *Redefining Global Strategy*. Harvard Business School Press: Boston, MA, Exhibit 2-1, p. 36.

Gomes-Casseres, B. (1987) Joint venture instability: is it a problem? *Columbia Journal of World Business*, 22, 97–102.

Gomes-Casseres, B. (1996) *The Alliance Revolution*. Harvard Business School Press: Boston, MA.

Gulati, N. and Ahmed, R. (2012) India has 1.2 billion people but not enough drink Coke. *Wall Street Journal*, July 13.

Hamel, G., Doz, Y., and Prahalad, C. (1989) Collaborate with your competitors—and win. *Harvard Business Review*, January/February, 133–139.

Harzing, A.-W. (2002) Acquisitions versus greenfield investments: international strategy and management of entry modes. *Strategic Management Journal*, 23(3), 211–227.

Hennart, J. (1991) A transaction cost theory of joint ventures: an empirical study of Japanese subsidiaries in the United States. *Management Science*, 37, 483–497.

Hennart, J.F. (1993) Explaining the swollen middle: why most transactions are a mix of "market" and "hierarchy." *Organization Science*, 4(4), 529–547.

Johanson, J. and Vahlne, J. (1977) The internationalization process of the firm: a model of knowledge development and increasing foreign market commitments. *Journal of International Business Studies*, 8, 23–32.

Kale, P. and Singh, H. (2009) Managing strategic alliances: what do we know now, and where do we go from here? *Academy of Management Perspectives*, 23(3), 45–62.

Karnani, A. and Wernerfelt, B. (1985) Multiple point competition. *Strategic Management Journal*, 6(1), 87–96.

Kerr, W.R. (2013a) *Launching global ventures: business models*. Harvard Business School #813-161, March.

Kerr, W.R. (2013b) *Launching global ventures: location choices*. Harvard Business School #813-160, March.

Khanna, T. and Rivkin, J. (2001) The structure of profitability around the world. Harvard Business School Working Paper, No. 01-056.

Kim, W.C. and Hwang, P. (1992) Global strategy and multinationals' entry mode choice. *Journal of International Business Studies*, 23(1), 29–53.

Kogut, B. and Singh, H. (1988) The effect of national culture on the choice of entry mode. *Journal of International Business Studies*, 19(3), 411–432.

Kogut, B. and Zander, U. (1993) Knowledge of the firm and the evolutionary theory of the multinational corporation. *Journal of International Business Studies*, 24(4), 625–645.

Li, J. and Li, Y. (2010) Flexibility versus commitment: MNEs' ownership strategy in China. *Journal of International Business Studies*, 41(9), 1550–1571.

Macleod, C. (2011) Best Buy, Home Depot find China market a tough sell. *USA Today*, February 23.

Melin, L. (1992) Internationalisation as a strategic process. *Strategic Management Journal*, 13, 99–118.

Ohmae, K. (2002) *Triad Power*. Free Press: New York.

Porter, M.E. (2008) The five competitive forces that shape strategy. *Harvard Business Review*, 86(1), 78–93.

Rugman, A.M. and Collinson, S. (2010) *International Business*, 6th edition. Pearson Education: Harlow.

Scott, J.T. (1982) Multimarket contract and economic performance. *Review of Economics and Statistics*, 64(3), 368–375.

Slangen, A.H.L. (2013) Greenfield or acquisition entry? The roles of policy uncertainty and MNE legitimacy in host countries. *Global Strategy Journal*, 3(3), 262–280.

Sterling, B. (2011) 42 Major countries ranked by smartphone penetration rates. *Wired*, December 16.

Stott, M. (2010) Russia corruption "may force Western firms to quit". Reuters, March 15.

Todeva, E. and Knoke, D. (2005) Strategic alliances and models of collaboration. *Management Decision*, 43(1), 123–148.

Yin, T. (2012) China's plans for its own car brands stall. *Business Week*, September 3, p. 21.

Where to Locate?

MOTIVATION

I began research for this book in the late 1990s. At that time China had barely appeared on any multinational's radar screen (Exhibit 9.1 shows market shares of global exports – the best measure of a country's presence in international competition). As a result, when I am asked what has been the biggest recent change in the global arena, my response is simple, "China." China has emerged on the global landscape in the last two decades, in a dramatic way, by opening new markets and new locations for multinationals and triggering repercussions around the world. We covered product market issues in the previous chapter. Here we consider countries like China as locations for a multinational's activities and address the factor market issues underpinning international competition.

The chart in Exhibit 9.2 shows the impact China had on global manufacturing in the first decade of the twenty-first century. In 2004 there was seen to be a huge labor cost advantage to be arbitraged by relocating manufacturing to China. Even after allowing for all the additional overhead and coordination costs of managing operations in a country as foreign as China, it was expected that the landed cost into the USA or Europe would be at least 25% lower than if the item was made domestically. At the same time as such analyses were making China the preferred location for manufacturing and replacing Japan as the country to fear for the "hollowing out" of manufacturing, India was being touted as the preferred location for services, like software development and call centers, for similar reasons (Exhibit 9.3).

But what a difference a decade makes! Today, if you talk to many executives with experience of operating in China, they will explain that it is oversold as a manufacturing location, as India is for software development and call centers.[1] The backlash has begun. A survey, for example, found one-fifth of German manufacturing companies, including the teddy bear company Steiff, planning to exit their Chinese operations

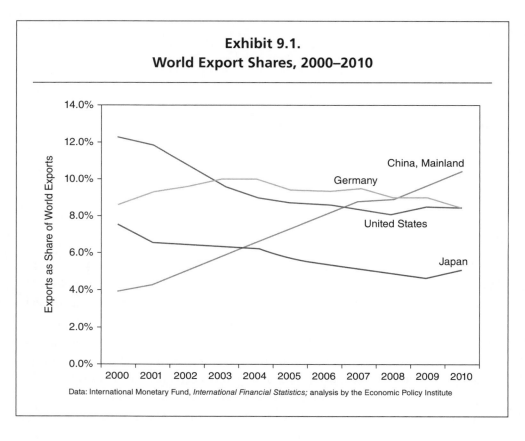

Exhibit 9.1.
World Export Shares, 2000–2010

China, Mainland

Germany

United States

Japan

Data: International Monetary Fund, *International Financial Statistics;* analysis by the Economic Policy Institute

(Westall, 2008). Similarly, the US leather goods company Coach announced in 2011 that it was decreasing Chinese production from 85% to 40% of its total, and Caterpillar, among other heavy goods manufacturers, said it would move production of some large machines back to the USA.[2] By 2012, even Apple was proposing to move some iPhone manufacturing back to the USA, and BCG was projecting that, by 2015, China would only have a 5% manufacturing cost advantage against the USA (Sirkin *et al.,* 2011).

Real wages are rising so quickly in China that its labor cost advantage is being eroded by newer developing economies, such as Vietnam[3] (Exhibit 9.4). Labor turnover is possibly even more of an issue, by some accounts averaging over 30% pa (Rein, 2012). The managerial complications of coordinating activities in China have been more onerous than ever imagined. And dealings with the Chinese government, which is actually not a single government but multiple constituencies including the central (Beijing), State, Municipality, and State-Owned Enterprise levels, are hard to manage. And all of this before concerns about the inadequate protection of intellectual copyright in the country – exemplified by the recent discovery of fake Apple Stores.[4]

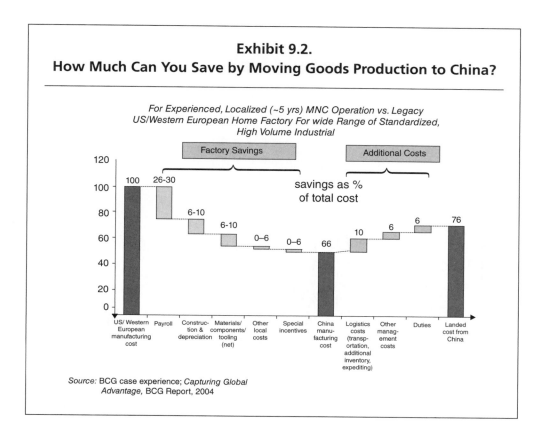

Exhibit 9.2.
How Much Can You Save by Moving Goods Production to China?

For Experienced, Localized (~5 yrs) MNC Operation vs. Legacy US/Western European Home Factory For wide Range of Standardized, High Volume Industrial

Source: BCG case experience; *Capturing Global Advantage*, BCG Report, 2004

Now, China is not going to be replaced as an important location for manufacturing operations any time soon. Rather, it will continue to grow its share of global manufacturing. However, its history over only 15 years does illustrate that the choice of where multinationals should locate their activities is more complicated than simply going to what appears to be the current low-cost location. In fact, there is a process to determine the optimal configuration of a firm's activities which answers the third fundamental question of international strategy – where to locate? – and which only begins by understanding current factor cost differences between countries.[5]

Indeed, operating a dispersed geographic footprint with a complex and differentiated supply chain is what we associate with effective international strategy since the contemporary multinational is almost defined by having distributed its activities around the world. Today, one expects to see a multinational with R&D located in one country, manufacturing in another set of countries, and marketing headquartered in yet another place. Delta, a $1 billion revenue Israeli textile company, for

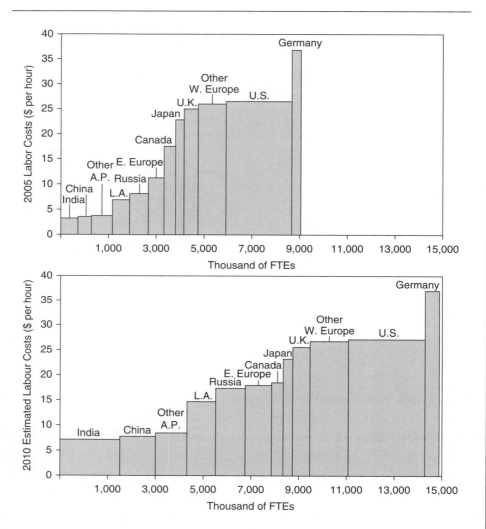

Exhibit #4 (pg. 20) "Evolution of Global Skilled Workforce (Hourly Labor Cost versus Thousands of FTEs)" from the "Tata Consultancy Services: Selling Certainty" Case #PG0-004. Reprinted by permission of Pankaj Ghemawat. From Case "Tata Consultancy Services: Selling Certainty", by Pankaj Ghemawat and Steven A. Altman. Copyright © 2010, Pankaj Ghemawat; all rights reserved.

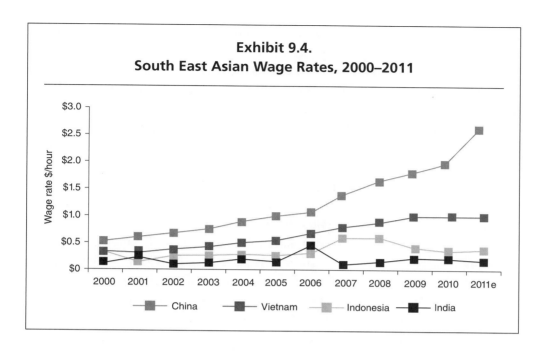

Exhibit 9.4.
South East Asian Wage Rates, 2000–2011

Legend: China — Vietnam — Indonesia — India

example, sources cotton in Egypt, manufactures in Israel, Turkey, India, and the Dominican Republic among other locations, while having sales organizations in the USA (for Victoria's Secret) and the UK (for Marks & Spencer).[6]

And lest you think that the location decision only matters for manufacturing, GE today has substantial R&D facilities that make real contributions to the global product line of its advanced medical electronics business in China and India. Indeed, in 2011 it announced the relocation of the headquarters for its important X-ray business from Wisconsin to China.[7] Similarly, Procter & Gamble moved its beauty and baby care business to Singapore, while Johnson & Johnson moved headquarters of its baby care business to Shanghai in order to have insider access to that country's young generation and capitalize on their trends and innovations (Neff, 2012).

Even smaller companies might wrestle with the issue of where to place their new Asian headquarters, or in which country to look for software developers. That is why location decisions that seek to exploit CSAs are critical to every multinational's international strategy.

STRATEGIC TRADEOFF

The decision of where to locate an activity, and the related question of the overall number and configuration of those activities, is non-trivial, not just because of the difficulty of identifying the ideal country, but also because it confronts another strategic tradeoff – between **one and many locations** that support either **static or dynamic efficiency**.

If a multinational chooses to concentrate an activity, think manufacturing, in one location it can exploit several advantages. It can, in principle, locate in the one country which is currently the low-cost location for the performance of this activity and so benefit from that country's factor cost advantages (CSAs). It will also be able to exploit scale and experience economies by concentrating operations in the single location.

However, there are risks to concentrating activity in a single location. First, as firms that compete in "footloose" industries have learnt, the optimal location for the performance of an activity can shift rapidly. Li & Fung, for example, the huge Hong Kong trading company, sources from 240 offices in 40 countries among 15,000 suppliers (McFarlan *et al.*, 2012), and will regularly relocate much of its purchases between countries as exchange rates, economic activity, and wage rates alter. A company that commits to a single location leaves itself vulnerable to risks, including not just unpredictable economic performance, but also the classic exogenous events like floods, fires, and wars which are typically excluded from insurance policies.

Second, a single location limits the multinational's learning from innovations occurring elsewhere in the world. Indeed, while it might be possible to access the ideas driving innovation and process improvement from afar, the belief is that firms have to be "insiders" – co-located with competitors, suppliers, and customers in "clusters" – to capitalize on them in real time. It is also only with multiple locations for the same activity that a multinational can operate different experiments contingent on each country's unique factor market conditions. Any of these slight adaptations then has the potential to be leveraged into a system-wide improvement that continually advances the firm's productivity frontier. In effect, while a single location favors the **exploitation strategy,** multiple locations support an **exploration strategy**.

If these arguments appear to suggest the advantage of diversifying risk and creating option value by having the flexibility to move operations and learning across a diversified geographic footprint, such dynamic optimization comes at the expense of the static optimization that a single, optimally located activity provides.

PRINCIPLES

A firm is a collection of activities that are undertaken under the hierarchical authority of a legal entity. Beyond these boundaries every firm contracts with numerous parties for the performance of the remaining activities required to actually design, develop, produce, distribute, market, and sell its products or services to final consumers. Every firm must, therefore, make decisions about which activities to keep within the firm and which to allow others to fulfill; that is, what is the appropriate level of **vertical integration** – forward along the value chain into distribution and marketing, and backward along the value chain into component manufacturing and basic research? Apple, for example, has had enormous recent success forward integrating into the operation of Apple Stores. In contrast, the PC manufacturer Gateway failed partly because it opened its own retail stores.

Answering the decision as to where the boundary of the firm should lie won Ronald Coase the Nobel Prize in Economics and is acknowledged to be a fundamental strategic choice for all firms – domestic or multinational. When companies are considering the location for their activities, a prior question therefore has to be whether that activity should even be included within the firm hierarchy. Should it simply avoid the locational question by outsourcing the activity, or otherwise access it through some contractual arrangement?

In practice, as we will see by the end of the process outlined below, decisions about outsourcing and location are often made concurrently (Exhibit 9.5; see also box).

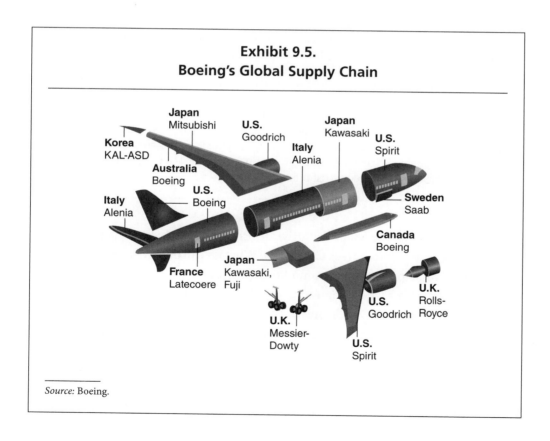

Exhibit 9.5.
Boeing's Global Supply Chain

Source: Boeing.

We cannot cover all the issues that drive decisions about which activities to undertake inside the firm hierarchy (see Chapter 2). What we can observe is that outsourced activities tend to be pedestrian, commodity processes for which there exist competitive and liquid markets where contracts can be written with low transaction costs. In contrast, activities retained inside the firm relate to a distinctive resource or core competence which the firm itself has an advantage in performing, or for which there would be substantial transaction costs involved in market contracting. While at the end of the process outlined below companies should understand how the decision to outsource activities can be aligned with their international strategy, for the purposes of the analysis, we will assume that the boundaries of the firm have already been established.

Two other principles should be noted. First, while we treat activities as analytically equivalent, a key factor in the location decision is the **length of commitment**. If a firm is considering where to place a new R&D center for which it will have to build laboratory facilities, hire scientists with appropriate skills from a limited pool, and then wait five to ten years for any research programs to bear fruit, the location decision will be affected by many more factors than if the firm is placing a six-month contract for raw materials. The latter is regularly renegotiated and so can simply be based on current price quotations from vendors in each country.

Second, because there are huge uncertainties involved in the decision, there is enormous scope for **personal preference and bias** to play an important role. Gravity models of trade showing language, colonial ties, and distance as key drivers of the volume of trade between countries are one indication of this. I know of many location choices, even within the USA, that were made because the CEO wanted to be able to frequent that city or because his or her country house was close by. Do not underestimate the power of personal preference in this process!

PROCESS

The process of deciding where to locate an activity, which we can think of as where to build a new manufacturing facility, follows discrete steps (Exhibit 9.6). Although discussed here sequentially, the best way to proceed in the real world is to quickly iterate through the entire process with whatever limited information is at hand to narrow the options, and then focus detailed analysis on the prime targets that have been identified. It might turn out, for example, that the firm already has production within Europe and Asia but not in the Americas. All analysis can then be focused on

Exhibit 9.6.
Where to Locate Process

INTERNATIONAL STRATEGY

- DISAGGREGATE VALUE CHAIN
- LOCATION
  - Static optimization
  - Dynamic optimization
- CONFIGURATION
  - Number of locations
- DEGREE OF LOCAL ADAPTATION

choosing a location within that region, since the optimal configuration to accord with the firm's international strategy has to include an Americas facility. Cycling through the decision process this way can simplify the required analysis.

Step 1: Activity Selection

(a) Activity Definition

The first step is to disaggregate the set of activities which lie within the firm hierarchy and which are typically represented in the **value chain**. At least in principle, the optimal location of each "activity" can then be derived independently.

While it is easy to separate activities at the aggregate level – R&D, manufacturing, and so on – when it comes to the detail within each of those categories the task can become problematic.[8] A firm deciding to offshore software development, for example, can break that activity into many parts, such as coding and project planning (Exhibit 9.7). While there is no limit to the number of steps in a value chain, business process reengineering has provided ways to approach the task of disaggregating any activity into a manageable number of steps – typically 15 or fewer.

Exhibit 9.7.
Disaggregated Activities (RM = Relationship Manager;
CSM = Client Service Manager; SIM = Software
Implementation Manager)

Service Delivery (Ongoing)
    Client Facing (RMs, CSMs)
    Participant Facing (Phones, some C/S)
    Back Office (C/S, FinOps, C&E)

Implementation & Corporate Actions
    Client Facing (Project Mgrs., SIMs)
    Back Office (Configuration, data)

Systems
    Development
    Testing (All areas)
    Support (All areas)

Other
    Sales/Marketing
    Finance
    HR/SDU
    Business/Product Development
    Risk/Compliance/Control
    Other

Once an activity has been broken into discrete steps, the firm must still identify which of those steps, although conceptually discrete, have to be **co-located** and which can be separated and potentially located in different countries. In many cases the solution is often one of two extremes. Either only a minimal number of sub-activities that are mundane and clearly separable, like manufacturing commodity components, will be offshored, or the majority of activities, including managerial functions, are offshored.

When offshoring software development, for example, firms typically end up either moving only applications, whose output can be well specified and independent of other blocks of code, or, acknowledging the need to maintain effective coordination of the entire process, moving most of the function. A leading financial services firm, for example, ultimately chose to move most of its development activity, including senior managers and project planners, to India, since moving only basic development did not produce adequate savings, and trying to move an intermediate level of activities would lead to excessive coordination and logistical costs as domestically based leaders struggled to control geographically distant activities.

(b) Activity Mobility

Having identified the activity sets that can be treated as separable for location purposes, it has to be recognized that many of those activities are not footloose in the sense of allowing multinationals the free choice of where to locate the activity. Indeed, many activities leave no discretion as to where the activity can take place. Physical practicalities (haircutting), the economics of transport costs (dry cleaning), or infrastructure requirements often force a multinational to conduct certain activities wherever it sells the product or service.[9] Most service, marketing, and many sales functions have to be performed in the country where the customer is found – although there are always exceptions. Aircraft operated by domestic US airlines, for example, can be serviced in Latin America since the asset is mobile. The Internet is now facilitating remote location of activities in the sales process. Nevertheless, the safest jobs in developed countries today are probably skilled workers in the service sector, such as plumbers and carpenters, because these activities have to be done on-site[10] (see box).

The Threat to US Jobs from Offshoring

The Princeton economist Alan Blinder used a labor department list of over 800 job categories to determine the threat posed to US domestic employment by offshoring. You too can use this list to judge the threat and see how vulnerable your job is.[11] Among Harvard Business School students the results were predictable, but still interesting. Unlike

---

Blinder, who estimated that between 22% and 29% of US jobs could potentially be sent offshore, MBA students suggested that 21% to 41% of jobs were vulnerable (Smith and Rivkin, 2008). Their biggest fear was that "analysts" would be offshored (i.e., that their jobs would go overseas!).

The division of activities that best captures the extent of geographic mobility is the upstream/downstream categorization. Upstream activities like R&D and component manufacturing, which are farther from the customer, are typically viewed as footloose, while downstream activities, like selling and service, are seen as relatively immobile. The upstream activities also tend to be those that are scale sensitive and so are more likely to be concentrated in a few locations than downstream activities that need to be localized for the end customer. Obviously it is only the footloose activities where a multinational has discretion over their location that need be the subject of further analysis.

Step 2: Location

The decision process for a single activity that will be retained inside the corporate hierarchy and is geographically mobile – say R&D (Exhibit 9.8) – remains complicated. It would be relatively simple to calculate which country appears to be the **current low-cost location**, but as the earlier story of China illustrates, that would be shortsighted. Clearly we need to incorporate some measure of **longer term country competitiveness** if we are considering a long-term commitment or investment for that particular activity. But even then, we need to acknowledge that an incremental location decision has to fit with the existing portfolio – its overall **configuration of facilities**. Even if we were to identify Vietnam as the ideal long-term location, perhaps we would already have too much risk from concentrating manufacturing in South East Asia, and so choose to locate in Mexico instead.

Those three steps make up an effective process for identifying where to locate a footloose activity. The first can be thought of as solving the linear program for most efficient current location. The second is dynamic and considers that innovation and productivity improvements can make some currently less efficient locations competitive. The third derives the optimal configuration given the existing portfolio of locations and recognizes that, given economic volatility and the inevitable uncertainties of international activity, any decision will have a legacy that outlives our ability to usefully predict many of the variables involved. As a result, configuration is ultimately driven more by strategic fit than by operations research calculations.

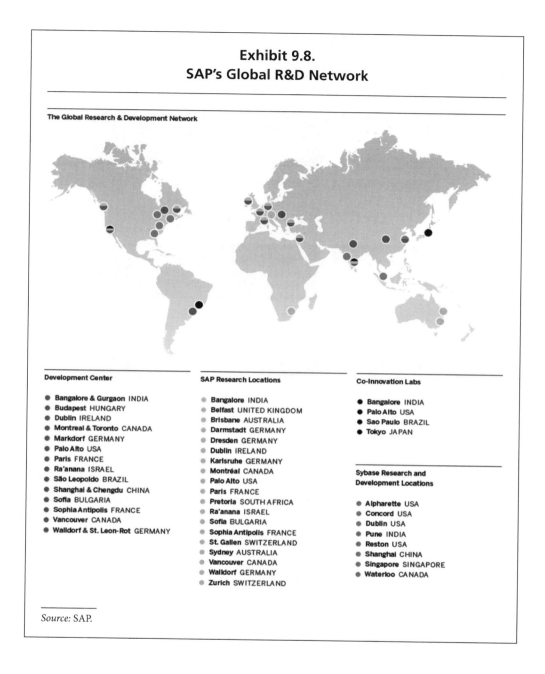

Exhibit 9.8.
SAP's Global R&D Network

The Global Research & Development Network

Development Center

- Bangalore & Gurgaon INDIA
- Budapest HUNGARY
- Dublin IRELAND
- Montreal & Toronto CANADA
- Markdorf GERMANY
- Palo Alto USA
- Paris FRANCE
- Ra'anana ISRAEL
- São Leopoldo BRAZIL
- Shanghai & Chengdu CHINA
- Sofia BULGARIA
- Sophia Antipolis FRANCE
- Vancouver CANADA
- Walldorf & St. Leon-Rot GERMANY

SAP Research Locations

- Bangalore INDIA
- Belfast UNITED KINGDOM
- Brisbane AUSTRALIA
- Darmstadt GERMANY
- Dresden GERMANY
- Dublin IRELAND
- Karlsruhe GERMANY
- Montréal CANADA
- Palo Alto USA
- Paris FRANCE
- Pretoria SOUTH AFRICA
- Ra'anana ISRAEL
- Sofia BULGARIA
- Sophia Antipolis FRANCE
- St. Gallen SWITZERLAND
- Sydney AUSTRALIA
- Vancouver CANADA
- Walldorf GERMANY
- Zurich SWITZERLAND

Co-Innovation Labs

- Bangalore INDIA
- Palo Alto USA
- Sao Paulo BRAZIL
- Tokyo JAPAN

Sybase Research and Development Locations

- Alpharette USA
- Concord USA
- Dublin USA
- Pune INDIA
- Reston USA
- Shanghai CHINA
- Singapore SINGAPORE
- Waterloo CANADA

Source: SAP.

(a) Shortlist

No analysis should consider all 193 countries listed by the UN as candidates for the location of a given activity. Thus, the first step in a location process is to quickly winnow out countries that do not deserve further analysis. One of these filters might

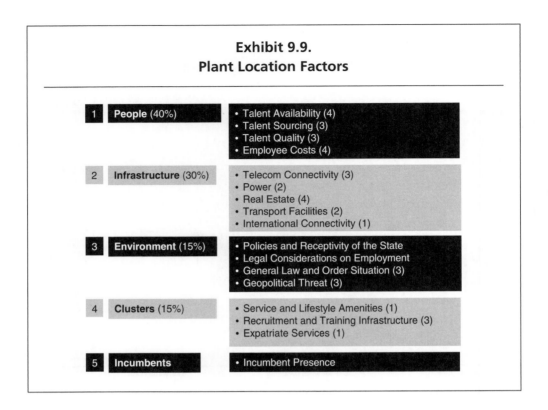

Exhibit 9.9.
Plant Location Factors

1	**People** (40%)	• Talent Availability (4) • Talent Sourcing (3) • Talent Quality (3) • Employee Costs (4)
2	**Infrastructure** (30%)	• Telecom Connectivity (3) • Power (2) • Real Estate (4) • Transport Facilities (2) • International Connectivity (1)
3	**Environment** (15%)	• Policies and Receptivity of the State • Legal Considerations on Employment • General Law and Order Situation (3) • Geopolitical Threat (3)
4	**Clusters** (15%)	• Service and Lifestyle Amenities (1) • Recruitment and Training Infrastructure (3) • Expatriate Services (1)
5	**Incumbents**	• Incumbent Presence

well be fit with the international strategy, but other filters can narrow the set of possible locations. One approach would be to use a readily available set of rankings such as the Global Competitiveness Survey published by the World Economic Forum, which ranks countries annually according to their likely future long-term productivity growth.

While this may be useful, companies often prefer to customize the analysis by compiling their own list of relevant criteria (Exhibit 9.9).

These criteria typically include those that relate to the **feasibility** of actually performing the activity in the country.[12] Does the country have the physical infrastructure to support the business? The lack of suitable port facilities or reliable electricity supplies, for example, might prevent the opening of a cement plant in Mozambique. Does it have an adequate supply of skilled labor? Many companies feel unable to operate high-tech facilities outside a narrow set of developed countries for this reason, and such operations therefore tend to cluster in limited geographies, like biotechnology in Massachusetts. Is there a sufficient pool of local executives that can manage an MNC's operations? Doing business in the former Eastern Europe was initially very difficult because few former bureaucrats from state-owned enterprises had experience with

Western accounting or even the notion of cost of capital. Does the government and regulation allow the business to operate? The Australian mining company Lynas, for example, was denied a permit by the Malaysian government to operate a rare earth processing facility because of environmental concerns that had already forced the company to relocate the plant away from its mine in Western Australia.

A second set of factors relate to the **willingness** of the firm to locate there and revolve around whether staff would be comfortable operating in that environment. This obviously covers factors like physical safety (no one will relocate to Somalia today), lifestyle, weather, culture (which deters some corporations from moving to Middle Eastern countries that strictly enforce Muslim laws), language, ethics and the expectation of illegal behavior (so that one well-known private equity firm refuses to do business in Russia because it is viewed as a "kleptocracy"), geographic distance from home office, and, to be honest, personal preference.

A third set of factors concern the uncertainties that inevitably accompany international activity and include a broad set of **political and economic risks**. Is there a possibility of future expropriation? How volatile will economic growth be? How substantial is the political risk? Notice that country risk is not necessarily company risk because it is specific to each firm and industry. If, for example, Argentina's high country risk leads to periodic rapid currency depreciations, some businesses might flourish because they can export from there. This was the case for the Argentinian candy company Arcor, which actually benefited from the country's economic woes since a substantial proportion of its production was exported.

In practice, companies compile a list of the factors they think are relevant to their business – typically about 40 items within a few broad categories – score each country on those items on a scale of 1 to 5, and then weight each category (Exhibit 9.9). When compiled on an Excel spreadsheet it is easy to conduct sensitivity analysis by altering the scores for, and weights of, each variable.

At the very best, with each country assessed on the various dimensions and weighted in some sensible fashion, this exercise can end up as a powerful screen for identifying a limited set of countries for further detailed analysis. Unfortunately, such a process can add a veneer of rigor and objectivity to what is essentially a qualitative exercise since many of the factors, such as infrastructure, technology, and managerial capabilities, can only be arbitrarily assessed. There is no rational way to quantify many of these variables, and certainly no rigorous way to weight the various categories. At the very worst, therefore, this process can add an air of respectability through spurious quantification to the preconceptions of senior executives. Indeed, I once attended a presentation by a consulting firm of its findings on where to locate an activity. Management clearly disagreed with the recommendations, and as the consultants became

Exhibit 9.10.
Manufacturing Costs at Different Kodak Plant Locations

	Rochester	Malaysia	Mexico	Ireland	Virginia
Net Operating Cost after Tax					
Materials*	1056	1077	993	1288	1056
Labor*	239	98	75	221	193
Depreciation*	-	51	36	74	75
Distribution	6	15	13	16	7
Duty	40	95	95	55	40
Overhead*	625	503	467	694	583
Expat. Support	-	112	69	121	63
Complexity	-	119	119	131	71
					-
TOTAL	1966	2070	1867	2600	2088

*Taxed at local rate, all other at US rate

Source: Adapted from Kodak Business Imaging Systems Division HBS Case #693-043

increasingly uncomfortable, they plaintively asked "What do you want the answer to be?" since they could easily change scores and weights to produce any answer management wanted!

(b) Current Cost

Once a shortlist of countries that are credible locations for the activity has been identified – most likely between four and six locations – a detailed analysis of those locations can be conducted.

This begins by calculating the relative cost of production in each country to identify the current low-cost location (Exhibit 9.10). This is primarily a static analysis, although it can involve projecting cash flows for a number of years, and essentially addresses the situation with respect to existing factor market conditions. Think of it as an operations research approach to find the most efficient location. For shorter lived investments this might be the only step that is required.

This step is conducted like any **relative cost analysis** by identifying and then quantifying the cost elements involved in fulfilling the activity at local factor prices (Halaburda and Rivkin, 2009). The first step is to develop the **cost structure** for performing the activity, divided into those elements with differing cost drivers. For a manufacturing plant this would identify direct costs, including labor costs at the various skill levels, raw material and component costs, taxes, utilities, capital and depreciation costs, and the costs of shipping, tariffs, etc., involved in delivering the product to end-use geographies. In addition, there is usually a more difficult set of managerial overhead costs associated with headquarters coordination and oversight, including expatriate managers' expenses and the airfares and time of executives traveling to the overseas location.

The unit of analysis might be the factory – what would be the total cost of building and operating a plant capable of a certain annual output level? Or it could be a specific product – what is the cost of manufacturing and delivering one wooden table of a certain specification from this location? The choice depends on the particular decision.

Having identified the separate line items, the analysis quantifies the **factor costs** of performing those activities in each country – finding per kilowatt hour electricity rates in local currency, wage rates by skill level, local material costs, railroad shipping costs per tonne mile, and so on. This analysis can become very detailed so the focus should be on large cost elements and those that show substantial differences across countries. Inordinate focus on quantifying numbers that are readily available, such as airfares from headquarters to each country, can be misplaced. It is often the assumptions, made with a finger in the air, that coordination costs are, say, 5% of the total that are incorrect, and not the assumption that senior executives fly only once a year in first class on British Airways at $12,738 a roundtrip, which makes the difference in the analysis.

Ideally all the data for this static comparative cost analysis will come from detailed local information in each country. This requires fieldwork including making calls to Rhine barge captains to acquire shipping rates for 1,000 tonnes on a Wednesday afternoon from Basle to Strasbourg, or to Eon, the German electricity utility, for quotes on the kWh cost for a peak load of 500 MW in a certain municipality etc. Failing this, macroeconomic equivalents can be found that describe relevant economy-wide measures of wage rates, tax rates, etc.

What can be more difficult, but just as important, is getting a handle on **productivity differences** between countries. The usual assumption in relative cost analysis is that firms have the same efficiency levels when performing an activity unless there is a structural explanation, such as choice of technology, for differences. However, in the case of comparing costs across geographic locations, even though the plant will be operated by the same company and may well employ the same technology, there are usually substantial productivity differences between countries.[13]

Surprising though this is, substantial inter-country productivity differences do arise from sources including differing labor practices, cultural attitudes, and managerial oversight limitations (Bloom *et al.*, 2012). Particularly with respect to labor productivity, therefore, an adjustment has to be made which acknowledges that some locations will be less efficient. Ideally, data for this adjustment will come from company-specific analysis across a firm's existing locations, or sector-specific productivity comparisons. Failing this, aggregate country labor productivity data can be used to correct for these underlying efficiency differences.

A final thought is that the calculation should not just address costs, if there is a substantial location effect on **willingness to pay**. The primary reason that Zara keeps manufacturing in Galicia is to support its fast fashion strategy. The rapid inventory replenishment cycle allows Zara to quickly adjust to market preferences and limits the expense of markdowns on slow-moving stock. The result is increased price realizations relative to clothing manufactured in more distant locations. Thus, a complete static analysis has to factor in demand-side consequences of location choice. Indeed, two of the main reasons that BCG found that 37% of US manufacturing firms were intending to bring manufacturing home were the desire (a) to bring products to market faster and (b) to increase customer responsiveness i.e., demand rather than cost advantages (Sirkin *et al.*, 2011).

Intimidating though this exhaustive analysis appears, with modern technology it is actually not that challenging,[14] and will certainly identify an optimal location (Exhibit 9.10). Interpreting that result depends on the robustness of the analysis and its sensitivity to changing assumptions. While the focus of sensitivity analysis should be on the larger items of cost and those that have the potential for larger differences among countries, there is a simpler way to understand how the result was derived, rather than checking each and every line item.

The cost of performing an activity can be divided into three categories. The first category includes items that are **globally traded** and whose cost will therefore not vary by location. This might include oil (before considering local taxes), or major components like electric motors and PCs. The second category includes costs incurred **independent of the location** of this particular activity, like the cost of corporate headquarters. It is only the third category of cost items, those that **vary with location**, which actually affects the location decision.

In practice, this last category can be relatively small (Exhibit 9.11). In manufacturing industries today, for example, the average direct labor content (the most obvious factor driving location choices) is about 9% of total cost. If components and purchased parts that average close to 35% of the cost structure are bought at global prices, the variance between countries will therefore be limited to only a small part of the total cost.

While US manufacturers do feel the threat of low-wage economies, if the advantage of developing countries operates on a relatively small part of the cost structure (2.5% in Exhibit 9.11), that threat is actually limited. Even with free labor the foreign

Exhibit 9.11.
US Retail Clothing Cost Structure

US retailer		Chinese factory	
• Store labor	$3.50	• Materials (includes imported U.S. leather)	$10.96
• Store rent	$4.50	• Factory overhead, miscellaneous	$1.88
• Advertising, marketing and promotion, storage, transportation	$5.25	• Factory labor	$1.30
• Selling, general and administrative costs merchant fees	$5.75	• Boxes and labels	$0.52
• Mark-downs, close-outs, theft, inventory errors	$10.75	• Factory profit before interest and taxes	$0.65
• Store profit before interest and taxes	$3.46	• Cross-Pacific shipping and duty	$1.48
TOTAL	$33.21	TOTAL	$16.79

Retail costs based on industry averages for U.S retail stores
Sources: Forsan (factory and shipping costs), Kurt Salmon Associates (U.S. retailer costs)

country would only have a 2.5% cost advantage! This is why many US firms today are feeling more confident about their US manufacturing base, particularly since the overhead cost of manufacturing, which increases with global coordination, now averages between 150 and 250% of direct labor costs.

More likely to move to low-wage economies are activities that are labor intensive. Most of the cost for clinical trials of new drugs, for example, are labor related, and 13 of the top 20 pharmaceutical companies have established R&D centers in China since 2006 to reduce cost (and, to be honest, to have easier access to human trials).[15]

This logic also illustrates why corporate tax rates are one of the more important drivers of location decisions today. First, tax rates operate on the profit margin, so when that margin is large relative to other location-bound cost items, it can be the largest, single, location-specific cost item. Second, the cross-country variation in tax rates can be more extreme than labor rates. When some countries offer extended tax holidays and others charge rates as high as 40%, the difference becomes substantial! The simple, though exaggerated, example in the box, supports this argument.

The Importance of Tax Rates in Location Decisions

| | Configuration Across Countries | | | |
| | 1 | 2 | | |
	Country A	Country A	and	B
Sales	100	100		70
Cost	40	70		40
Profit	60	30		30
Tax@ 50%	30	15	@ 0%	0
Net profit	30	15		30
Total profit	30		45	

In column 1, all production takes place in country A where profits are taxed at 50%. In the second case, all manufacturing (the 40 of cost in column 1) is relocated to country B. In country B manufacturing costs at 40 are exactly the same as in A; however, the corporate tax rate is 0%. If the transfer price between country B and A is arbitrarily set at 70, the second configuration generates 50% higher profit (15 more) simply by exploiting the lower tax rate in country B.

The fact that so many countries and development zones offer tax breaks as an incentive for multinationals to locate there only illustrates the effectiveness of the practice. While the policy consequence might be a "zero sum" race to the bottom among countries, the pragmatic effect on location decisions cannot be denied. Corporate tax rates now vary between 41% in Japan and 40% in the USA, down to 8% in Switzerland, 13% in Ireland, and 15% in Iceland,[16] and many companies, including Kodak, did indeed move activities to Ireland to exploit that country's favorable tax structure.[17]

(c) Future Competitiveness

As the introduction on the role of China as a manufacturing location suggests, location decisions cannot simply be driven by a comparison of current factor costs. Rather, firms need to consider the potential of each country over the lifetime of the investment in that activity.

One way to calculate that long-term potential is simply to forecast future costs in each location over the project lifetime. I have seen examples where 20-year cash flows have been projected using each country's wage inflation calculated from a reliable

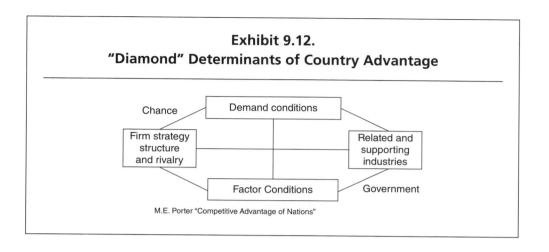

Exhibit 9.12.
"Diamond" Determinants of Country Advantage

M.E. Porter "Competitive Advantage of Nations"

source, such as the Economist Intelligence Unit; some estimate of utility cost inflation; and so on. Having gone to great lengths to calculate future costs in the local currency, those numbers then have to be translated into a common currency, such as US dollars. This is where such analyses typically break down. Either an economist's estimate of the future appreciation or depreciation of the currency is taken that is inconsistent with separate assumptions made about macroeconomic variables, such as inflation; or the currency is adjusted by the differential inflation rate between countries, which simply offsets the initial inflation assumptions. The end result is either a projection which is wildly skewed by the assumption about one metric (which would be offset in the real world by the general equilibrium behavior of the economy), or one that merely increases current costs at some common rate and so does not generate any difference between the short- and long-term difference in cost among countries.

Moreover, for many activities the choice of location should not be driven simply by factor costs. Michael Porter argued that it is long-term productivity growth that makes a country the best location for particular industries. Although his research sought to explain the comparative advantage of nations, the framework he developed – **the diamond** (Exhibit 9.12) – can also be applied to the location of a multinational's activities (Porter, 1998). While not a detailed forecast of factor costs, the diamond can identify the most innovative geographical areas over the long term.[18] It can, therefore, suggest where to locate a regional marketing headquarters, a manufacturing facility, or an R&D center. It is, however, less useful in the location decision for minor activities or generic functions, like basic metal bending, which are present in most economies.

Competitive Advantage of Nations

Seeking to explain why only a limited number of regions dominated the global market shares of many industries, such as Hollywood in movies, Holland in tulips, the UK in auction houses, and Denmark in insulin, and drawing on an older literature concerning the benefits of **agglomeration**[19] – the benefits of being collocated with other enterprises – Porter argued that industrial success comes from the creation of a vibrant and aligned system in a location – what he refers to as a "diamond' and others call an "ecosystem" (Moore, 1996) – of four factors. If each of the factors is favorable for innovation, there is a strong likelihood that the country will host a viable industry "**cluster**" and will be a location for successful firms.

The first factor is the **demand conditions** that generate pressure from customers to improve efficiency and innovate. Porter argues that it is local customers who are in daily contact, and among whom firms live and share the same experiences, rather than distant foreign buyers that drive innovation. If domestic customers are large, growing, leading edge, and demanding in their needs, they will compel the subject industry to continuously upgrade its products or services. Industrial customers, for example, look to close linkages with their local suppliers for support in eliminating process bottlenecks. The success of Japanese car, motorbike, and ship manufacturers in the 1970s and 1980s, for example, drove demand for advanced machine tools and contributed to the success of firms such as Mori Seiki and the numerical controls producer Fanuc. Similarly, it is only when experiencing the same consumer trends as their customers that firms can successfully capture the latest end consumer ideas and innovations.

The second element is **factor conditions**, including not only the traditional factors of labor, land, and capital, but, more importantly, advanced factors of production related to the specific industry.

The global wine industry, for example, has undergone a more dramatic shift in global market shares in the last three decades than most manufacturing industries as the "New World" countries, including the USA, Australia, New Zealand, and Argentina, gained share at the expense of the "Old World" countries, such as France and Germany. Indeed, the share of world exports coming from Europe has declined from 95% in 1980 to below 70% in 2005 (Parcero and Villanueva, 2011). Filling the gap, Australia alone has gone from nowhere to being the second largest exporter of wine to the UK – the largest market for wine imports in the world.

While traditional factors of production, such as the cost of land, which can be one-sixth the cost of the Old World in the New World (see box below), and labor – about 20% of French cost in Chile, for example – can partially explain the success of the New World vineyards, there are also specialized research institutes and university courses for oenologists in Australia that have driven enormous improvements in grape cultivation and wine production. Screw caps (that save the one in ten bottles that spoil when the cork fails), drip irrigation, mechanical harvesters, and stainless steel vats have all changed the industry in the New World to a modern industrial scientific orientation away from its traditional agricultural craft basis in the Old World.

Factor Cost Differences

Consider the cost of land in Switzerland compared to Australia (see Exhibit 9.13). Increasing land under cultivation in the former country would involve carving out new terraces on a mountain side. In Australia it simply requires extending drip irrigation to another hectare of empty land!

Exhibit 9.13.
Vineyards in Switzerland and Australia

Credit/Copyright Attribution: "Natali Glado/Shutterstock"

© Koolstock/Masterfile

In other industries the presence of advanced research programs, tailored university courses, and specialized laboratory facilities all create specialized skills and advanced technology that drive industry innovation. In contrast, general factors of production, such as college graduates or machine tools, can be found in most advanced countries and do not differentially contribute to their success. They are a necessary, but not sufficient condition for industrial success.

The third element of the diamond is the **structure of the industry and the strategies of incumbent firms**. Porter is a great believer in the importance of intense competition as a driver of efficiency and innovation. Thus, he argues that a competitive industry with many equivalent-size firms struggling for market leadership is the most dynamic structure. In contrast to the industrial policy practiced in many Western countries in the last half of the twentieth century, which focused on supporting national champions with the scale to compete internationally, Porter observed that most vibrant industrial clusters featured intensely competitive firms. Even in Japan, which some had seen as the best exponent of a national policy of picking winners, Porter noted the proliferation of firms within successful industries (Table 9.1).

Table 9.1 Number of Domestic Competitors in Successful Japanese Industries (1987)

Audio equipment	25	Automobiles	9	Cameras	15
Copiers	14	Machine tools	112	Motorcycles	4
Television sets	15	Trucks	11		

Source: Porter (1998)

Firm strategy also makes a contribution to an industry's success in a country. Although Porter does not believe that there is one best strategy, rather each industry's economic structure will determine which strategies are most viable, he recognizes the importance of firms' choosing and executing against a clearly articulated international strategy if they are to succeed.

The fourth factor concerns the **related and supporting industries** that form the industry's ecosystem. Consistent with his notion that it is a system of economic entities that creates competitive advantage, Porter looks to the presence of successful firms in the broader value net as an important determinant of industry success – a "cluster" or group of industries that are related along the value chain – which co-locate in a region and which mutually support and improve other participants in the cluster. His examples include the biomedical sector in Massachusetts, including teaching hospitals, biotechnology companies, and universities, and the movie industry in Hollywood with screenwriters, directors, video equipment manufacturers, and so on. In each case, it is not a single, narrowly defined industry that succeeds, but a group of companies in overlapping and linked industries which succeed.

Porter adds in two other factors – luck and government policy – as contributors to the overall success of an industry. A classic example of luck accounts for the location of the carpet industry in Dalton, Georgia which is today still responsible for 90% of all the functional carpet made in the world. Apparently, the origin of this business can be traced back to a single woman, Catherine Evans, and the tufted bedspread she made as a wedding present in 1895 by copying (and improving) an older candlewick method (Krugman, 1991)! Such accidents of history, Porter argues, can often be found as the original reason why an industry began, or got a lead, in a certain location.

Government too has an important role to play in the success of an industry, not in the classic industrial policy sense of picking winners and channeling resources and support to a national champion, but, in the way in which Porter powerfully advocates, as a promoter of all the elements of the cluster, and a catalyst for the synergistic interaction among the full set of players in the ecosystem (Porter, 1998).

New Zealand Wins The America's Cup

In 1995 *Black Magic*, a yacht from New Zealand, a country with a population of only 3.5 million, managed to win the America's Cup – the premier yachting prize – against teams from the USA and Australia, some of whom spent over $100 million in the campaign (Enright and Capriles, 1996). What accounted for this unlikely success? Porter's diamond framework characterizes the underlying conditions that contributed to *Black Magic*'s success and illustrates how the framework can even be applied in a non-commercial setting:

- *Demand Conditions*: New Zealand is an island nation where no one lives farther than 90 miles (145 km) from the ocean. The main city, Auckland, is built on a natural harbor, and the subtropical weather encourages year-round outdoor activity. Indeed, one-third of Auckland households own boats. The interest of the nation in the America's Cup was such that over 1.5 million Kiwis (one-quarter of the entire population) bought red socks – the emblem of the *Black Magic* team – and raised over $15 million for *Black Magic*, which on a per capita basis would enable the USA to raise $1.5 billion to support a single national team! On the night that *Black Magic* actually won the America's Cup, over 92% of the New Zealand population was watching the event on television!

- *Firm Strategy and Structure*: Coming from a sporting nation that values successful athletes, such as All Black rugby players, and fosters good-natured competitiveness, Kiwi sailors regularly compete with each other and strive to outperform their peers. This rivalry enhances the skills of all concerned and produces world-class sailors from a young age. Since a spell overseas was traditionally seen as an alternative to a university education, many young New Zealanders spend time touring the world before settling into careers, and good Kiwi sailors are in demand as crew on race yachts everywhere. In fact, New Zealand yachtsmen have won Olympic medals and several, such as Peter Blake and Russell Coutts, the captain and helmsman of *Black Magic*, respectively, were acknowledged to be among the best sailors in the world.

- *Factor Conditions*: As mentioned above, the physical characteristics of New Zealand – climate and geography – create conditions that encourage sailing. Despite its small land mass, the country has the ninth longest coastline of any country in the world.

- *Related and Supporting Industries*: Winning the America's Cup requires not only great sailors, but also a superior boat design. New Zealand has a globally successful yacht-building and marine industry, including market leaders in winches, masts, and sails. A number of the leading boat designers are also New Zealanders. The country has dozens of sailing magazines, a number of yachting research institutes are related to universities, and several long-established yachting organizations exist, including the Royal New Zealand Yacht Club. As a result, there was a vibrant community of companies and individuals who could work together to push the envelope of boat design, and provide the resources and talent necessary to support the program.

These factors created a vibrant cluster of interrelated individuals and firms that collectively drove the performance of the yacht called *Black Magic*. As can be seen, they are so interrelated that it is often hard to know whether to classify a cause as a demand or a factor condition. This merely reinforces Porter's belief that the explanation for an industry's success is derived from the entire "cluster."

A couple of provisos give pause for thought about the predictive power of the framework. First, New Zealand had competed in earlier America's Cup competitions and lost. Therefore, it could not be the diamond alone that contributed to the success of *Black Magic* or the country would have won on its first outing. The way that this particular team was organized and managed also made a contribution to its success. Peter Blake, who spearheaded the challenge, was known as a charismatic leader. The team built two very similar boats to be raced against each other in preparation for the competition. Careful testing of any changes could then be made by treating one boat as the control.[20] Indeed, there always have to be such firm-specific factors present to explain which company from an advantaged country will win in global competition. Without this, we would have no way of explaining why one firm located in a favorable cluster would outperform any other based in that location.

Second, in 2006 the winning America's Cup team came from Switzerland – a landlocked nation. Obviously the diamond cannot explain every successful firm or identify every desirable location!

While Porter's argument has been powerfully applied as an *ex post* rationalization to explain industrial location, whether it can be predictive is more uncertain. In Porter's analysis factor conditions lead to success either because they are favorable for an industry (e.g., low wages for textiles in China), or because they are lacking, in which case the struggle to overcome adversity forces the industry to innovate. The classic example of the absence of factors of production leading to success is the Dutch tulip industry. Since Holland lacks land and sunshine you would not expect it to be successful in any agricultural business, yet it dominates the world tulip business. Porter argues that because Holland lacked land and sunshine it developed innovative methods, such as greenhouses and genetics, to efficiently cultivate tulips. However, if a country can win in an industry either because it has the underlying factor conditions, or because it does not, the predictive power of the framework is weakened.

The second issue with the framework is whether foreign firms can access a viable diamond by maintaining some presence in that country. If that is possible, then domicile will not be a determinant of success, since firms based in any country will be able to leverage any other country's diamond. In some sense this is the argument being made in this book. I might be a French video-game producer, but if I place a marketing function in Korea, I can capitalize on the bleeding edge demand in the country with the fourth largest market for video games in the world (Cross, 2011), with over half of Koreans reporting they regularly play video games, and higher (83%) Internet penetration than the USA.[21] More generally, international strategy is premised on a belief that foreign firms can exploit foreign CSAs. If they cannot, they should give up because only firms based in the appropriate country will ever win.[22]

Porter himself argues that firms have to be **"insiders" in a locality** to be able to fully tap into the cluster and capitalize on a region's positive externalities. A foreign firm hiring from that location, for example, might still find geographic distance preventing it from acting on the latest ideas in its home country. While the notion that geographic distance still matters in an age of instantaneous electronic communication seems outdated, evidence suggests that it remains an important determinant of social relations.[23]

In fact, Porter argues that a firm must relocate its headquarters and senior executives to the appropriate location if it is to win in global competition. While some firms have done this – Ciba Vision relocated its headquarters from Basle, Switzerland to Duluth, Georgia for such reasons – it does seem to be the case that locating certain key activities, such as R&D, marketing, and advanced types of manufacturing, in foreign countries does allow multinationals to capitalize on those locations as insiders (Alcácer and Chung, 2013).

What is clear is that simply placing a few expatriates in a desirable location does not provide access to the full benefit of that cluster. This implies that a multinational has to establish a substantial presence in the country of choice; that it hires sufficient locals with access to the domestic social networks to be able to capitalize on those networks; and that it ensures the local activity is closely tied to the rest of the global enterprise and has influence over global decisions rather than becoming an outpost with limited interaction with other parts of the multinational. Indeed, many firms pursue this approach including, for example, Novartis, which has located its newest R&D facility employing over 2,000 scientists in the Boston area to capitalize on the Massachusetts biomedical cluster. Similarly, Shire, a major player in the generic pharmaceutical industry, has built its US headquarters outside Boston.

Strategic Fit

Despite these provisos, it is clear that Porter's diamond framework is a useful tool for identifying the location with the best long-term potential. It can, therefore, suggest the optimal location for a critical activity.

If the static and dynamic analyses coincide in their location recommendation, it is obvious where to place the activity. If there is conflict between their results, the multinational faces head on the tradeoff between static and dynamic efficiency. Should we locate in the currently preferred (low-cost) location, or should we sacrifice short-term advantages to ensure we exploit the optimal long-term location?

While there is no general rule to decide whether to favor the now over the future, one principle identified earlier is relevant – the **length of commitment** represented by investing in the location. The shorter the commitment, the more likely the answer is to go with the current low-cost location. The longer the commitment, the more likely the more innovative location is to be ideal. This is why operational efficiency often provides the answer for many location decisions, independent of the strategy. Optimizing the material supply chain, for example, will typically involve sourcing from many countries and production of components or assembly in many other countries. Such a configuration takes value chain decomposition and country specialization as a given and produces a complex and ever-changing picture that can accompany any one of the international strategies.

Note that this suggests another solution – to reshape the investment itself, perhaps by reducing the size or length of commitment, to make the argument in favor of one location more compelling. GE, for example, built a local supply base in India to support its medical system's manufacturing facility, in order to avoid additional investment that would have been stranded if and when it relocated the actual manufacturing plant to a different, lower cost location.

Otherwise, the **international strategy** will be an important determinant of the choice. In particular, the transnational strategy that pursues an agglomeration advantage is most likely to favor the dynamically preferred location. In contrast, the global strategy with its emphasis on static economies would favor the currently favored location.

Step 3: Configuration

Whether explicitly or implicitly, every firm that competes internationally generates a risk profile from the configuration of locations for each of its activities. A company that only has manufacturing in its home market is essentially placing a bet that future economic conditions will favor that country as a long-term location. In contrast, a firm that consciously distributes manufacturing plants across several countries, and has perhaps balanced the production capacity in every region with its sales in each region, has gone some way toward hedging risk – although trading off the benefit of concentrating production in a single low-cost location.

This choice of overall geographic configuration – or what one can think of as the number of locations for each activity – is the third step in the process of deciding where to locate key activities. Rather than simply optimizing the location of the latest facility, firms must understand how that location fits into the overall **geographic portfolio**.[24]

Consider the classic case of competition in the earth-moving equipment business between Caterpillar and Komatsu (Bartlett, 1986). Caterpillar had built a dominant global position after WWII following in the steps of US Army engineers who had seeded Caterpillar's ubiquitous yellow bulldozers around the globe during the war. As economies recovered, Caterpillar supplied the heavy equipment necessary to rebuild infrastructure and support economic growth in nearly all major economies. Most of this equipment came from Caterpillar's manufacturing facilities in Peoria, Illinois – its home base and very much a company town. Until the late 1980s over 85% of Caterpillar production came from the USA. Similarly, Caterpillar's most feared rival from the 1970s onwards, Komatsu, supplied all its rapid postwar international growth and expansion from Japanese plants. It had over 90% of its production in Japan until the late 1980s. Essentially, a US producer competed with a Japanese producer as the pair captured nearly 60% of the entire world sales of earth-moving equipment (Exhibit 9.14).

While Komatsu initially benefited from low wages and steel prices, by the early 1980s it was an efficient manufacturer and designer of quality equipment that could compete with Caterpillar globally – at least at an exchange rate of 200 yen to the dollar. Fortunately for Komatsu, in 1980 President Reagan and the Federal Reserve introduced economic policies to curtail inflation that raised US interest rates and strengthened the US dollar. As a result, the yen depreciated to a low of nearly 250 yen to the dollar in 1982. This allowed Komatsu to gain global market share while Caterpillar lost nearly 20% of its global market. When the dollar dramatically reversed course in 1986, collapsing to 150 yen to the dollar, the effect on global market shares was obvious given the concentrated production configuration of the two firms.

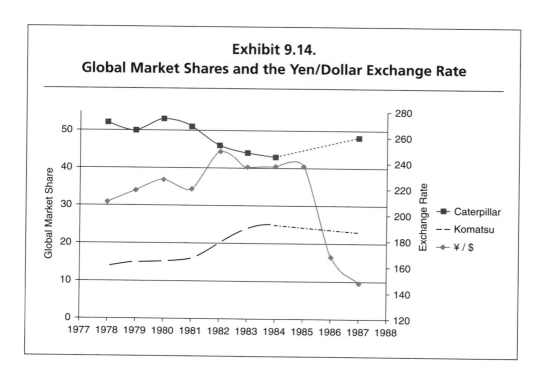

Exhibit 9.14.
Global Market Shares and the Yen/Dollar Exchange Rate

Komatsu's market share began to fall, and Caterpillar was able to regain much of its recently lost market share.

If firms place all their eggs in one basket, as Caterpillar and Komatsu had done, they are vulnerable to unpredictable shifts in the economic, political, and technological factors that characterize international competition. As we saw in Chapter 3, although a one-year depreciation of the exchange rate by almost a third (which is what happened to the USA in 1986) is unusual, shifts of 7% per year are the norm. This is why companies must consider the risk profile of their global portfolio of activities as they optimize the location of the incremental facility, and is why Caterpillar and Komatsu rebalanced global production in the 1990s, relocating between one-quarter and one-half of production outside their home countries.

Lest we think that global configuration is only a defensive concern to minimize risk, we must acknowledge that wise companies can turn volatility into an advantage. Becton Dickinson, for example, the leading producer of blood containers, has manufacturing plants spread around the world with excess capacity in each. When economic conditions favor producing in one location, that facility works flat out to supply globally until a shift in exchange rates, wage rates, demand, or some other unexpected event makes another plant lower cost. With a conscious strategy to continually reallocate production, Becton Dickinson capitalizes on the option value of a geographically dispersed manufacturing configuration. Indeed, many multinationals today, like NCR, maintain at least two facilities for manufacturing each of their key products. This diversifies risk but, more importantly, allows them to dynamically arbitrage factor costs by continually reallocating production between the two facilities according to, in NCR's case, weekly cost differences.

These examples establish the two extremes of geographic configuration – betting everything on a single location and flexibly reallocating production among a dispersed, but coordinated set of facilities. Somewhere in the middle lies a third configuration that seeks to hedge risk, perhaps by balancing supply and demand within each region (Exhibit 9.15).

Notice that this phenomenon of managing the global configuration of activities is absent in the domestic context. If Boeing relocates its headquarters from Seattle to Chicago, or Electrolux closes a US facility and shifts production to another North American plant, there are no major strategic consequences since all are subject to the same US institutional environment. It is only the volatility and unpredictability of international activity that causes firms to have to assess their overall geographic portfolio.

Notice also that the importance of geographic diversification of activities varies by industry. When the product is the same around the world and demand is price elastic,

Exhibit 9.15.
Dell's Regional Manufacturing Hubs, 2001

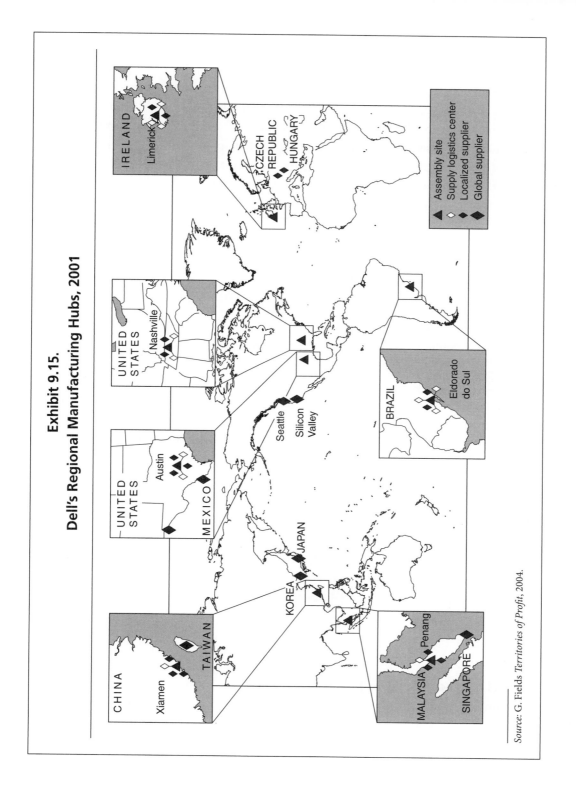

Source: G. Fields *Territories of Profit*, 2004.

the choice of configuration is more relevant. If, in contrast, the product is highly differentiated and demand is price inelastic, firms have more ability to cope with external shocks. Shiseido, for example, the Japanese cosmetics manufacturer, is more insulated than Komatsu from a dramatic yen appreciation because it can more easily absorb a price increase. Shiseido also has more of its cost structure incurred in its end markets. The correspondingly lower share of cost accounted for by its Japanese manufacturing cost means that the risk of a concentrated manufacturing configuration is reduced.

Disaggregated Global Supply Chains

One effect of disaggregating a firm's activities and optimally locating each one has been the emergence of complex global supply chains within industries. As different countries become specialists in certain activities, a multinational will be coordinating logistics between many locations. One benefit of this configuration is a degree of risk diversification since all activity is not concentrated in a single country.

The tradeoff for such increasingly common supply chains is the administrative cost of coordination and the vulnerability to shocks. US auto plants, even those of US car companies, were temporarily closed after the Japanese earthquake in 2011 as supplies of key components made only in Japan were disrupted. Thus, a global supply chain does not, of itself, hedge risk. Only if the locations of each activity are hedged will the multinational realize that objective.

Alternative Configurations

Concentrate   An obvious geographic configuration is to **concentrate** the activity in a single country. This has the benefit of focusing the activity in the optimal location, capitalizing on the location's CSAs, and exploiting scale economies in a single facility. The tradeoff for this configuration is that concentration essentially "bets it all" on that location. The firm becomes extremely vulnerable to the occurrence of any unpredictable event, such as an earthquake or a political coup in that country, and to shifting economic conditions.

Hedge

Financial Hedge   Many will argue that the best way to manage the risk of a single location is a financial hedge. If Caterpillar is vulnerable to exchange rate movements because it only produces in the USA, why not lock in the current exchange rate by selling forward future yen revenues? When Caterpillar receives yen from selling its bulldozers in Japan in a year's time, it has guaranteed itself a certain dollar income to match the US dollar expenses it will be incurring. While there will be a cost associated with the hedge – a discount on the forward exchange rate and financial transaction costs – Caterpillar will have hedged the financial risk of its concentrated configuration.

This is an attractive option and many firms do indeed use financial hedges to offset exchange rate risk. However, there is a limit to how far a hedge can be employed. In principle, a company would need to hedge the value of all future foreign sales over the lifetime of the facility. A simple rolling hedge – hedging next year's output at today's rate – which is what most firms practice, does not lock in today's rate forever. A variant of this would be to use a balance sheet hedge. If Caterpillar took out yen-denominated debt to match all its expected future yen revenue streams, when the yen depreciated, which would hurt its dollar revenues, the dollar value of its debt would fall by an offsetting amount.

The limit to a financial hedge is then the ability of the firm either to find a 20-year futures market for the yen/dollar exchange rate – which simply does not exist – or to leverage the balance sheet with yen-denominated liabilities that match all the expected future yen revenues – which could result in an unsustainably high debt/equity capital structure. Thus, financial hedges, while an intrinsic part of the short-term activities of international firms, cannot overcome the risk of concentrating long-lived investments in a single country.[25]

PHYSICAL HEDGE   A physical hedge is a more direct way to offset risk. In fact, the multidomestic strategy with a self-contained subsidiary in each country has the geographic configuration that provides such a physical hedge. When each subsidiary matches what it produces in the country to what it sells in that country, a firm's operations are physically hedged. The tradeoff with this dispersed configuration is, of course, the inability to exploit scale economies across multiple locations, and the acceptance that local production is not going to exploit the lowest global factor costs.

Note that while there are no foreign sales by subsidiaries that are vulnerable to exchange rate risk, there is still a competitive risk for each subsidiary. A competitor based in a country experiencing a favorable shock would still be able to exploit that shift to gain market share elsewhere. Similarly, a fire in its factory would leave the subsidiary's customers in the lurch.

Less extreme is the configuration that many CPG manufacturers have adopted of being physically hedged within each of the Triad regions. A firm with this geographic configuration balances supply and demand within a region, but has limited product flows between regions. If this configuration has a single facility in the optimal location within each region, it can exploit some scale economies and capitalize on some CSAs. Particularly when each region includes countries whose exchange rates and economic performance are correlated (which one expects within a Triad region), but which are less correlated with other regions, this configuration also achieves some risk reduction.

The Triad configuration still leaves a firm vulnerable to competitive risk. In fact, the only strategy that entirely eliminates this risk and so offers the optimal physical hedge is to emulate the competitor's footprint by exactly matching its geographic configuration. While this is feasible for a firm in competition with only one other firm, the breadth of international competition faced by most firms makes this impossible. The optimal physical hedge in this instance would require a configuration matched to that of the entire competitive set. In practice, the Triad strategy probably gets closest to this configuration.

Flexibility   The third approach to portfolio configuration is not to be concerned with risk management by adopting a conservative and defensive posture, but to turn uncertainty and volatility on its head and use it offensively. This was the example above of Becton Dickinson exploiting the option value of a **dispersed but coordinated network** of manufacturing locations.

The value of such a configuration applies both to physical production and to the sourcing of innovations. Becton Dickinson holding excess capacity inside each of three Triad regions with the coordinative capacity to switch between plants as exogenous events alter the low-cost location is an example of the former. CEMEX encouraging each cement plant manager to improve efficiency by responding to local factor market conditions and bottlenecks in his or her operations is an example of the latter. Once CEMEX's IT system tracking individual plant performance demonstrates that an innovation has improved efficiency, the practice is rapidly replicated in other facilities, either by a plant manager asking to implement the new practice, or when the company's SWAT team shows up for what has become at least a triennial visit to every plant.

There is also enormous value to a dispersed but coordinated configuration of locations for product innovation. Häagen-Dazs was able to leverage the dulce de leche ice cream flavor, popular in Argentina, around the globe because it was willing to look for innovation everywhere and did not rely, as had so many traditional CPG firms, on the headquarters country as the sole source of new ideas. Similarly, Fremantle Media, the originators of shows like … *Idol*, looks to source new program ideas from around the world. *Idol* came from the UK, *Big Brother* from the Netherlands, and *Survivor* originally from Sweden. Each of these approaches exploits the option value that comes from the flexibility afforded by a dispersed but coordinated geographic configuration.

The Triad configuration blurs into this approach as a multinational with operations within each of the three major regions begins to coordinate across regions. As a result, this configuration is perhaps becoming the most common arrangement for critical multinational functions. Google's data center configuration, for example, includes seven in the USA, Finland, Belgium, and Ireland while it is adding centers in Singapore and Taiwan.[26]

Outsourcing the activity is the last way to achieve flexibility. When the activity is not performed inside the firm hierarchy but accessed through market contracts, the firm has minimized its commitment and maximized its flexibility. Rather than having invested in a plant that will last 20 years, the firm now has short-term contracts that allow it to relocate suppliers at each, perhaps annual, renewal. The result is a complex global supply chain that utilizes specialized players at each stage of the value chain, often in emerging markets (Lessard, 2013).

At this point we have come full circle back to the original decision concerning which activities to retain inside the firm hierarchy. We must acknowledge that to exploit the benefits of flexibility, a firm might ultimately choose to outsource an activity that it would otherwise have kept within the hierarchy. The sports goods companies, like Nike, for example, have outsourced nearly all their manufacturing of trainers, clothing, and equipment, which allows them, in principle, to rely on producers in Thailand one year, the Philippines the next year, and Vietnam the year after.

Choice of Configuration

How does a firm choose among these different global configurations for each of its activities? The answer depends on the value of dynamic versus static efficiency in the industry (see box).

To Concentrate or Disperse?

Consider a firm facing the choice to concentrate production in a single facility or to disperse production among three different locations so that it can continually reallocate production to the current low-cost location. If we assume there are fixed costs, is it worth adopting the dispersed location?

		Concentrate	Flexibility
A	Fixed cost	10	30 (3 plants, each with excess capacity)
	Variable cost	90	90
	Total cost	100	120 (at current exchange rates)
B			
	Cost incurred in local currency (@60% of total cost)	60	72
	Cost incurred at global prices	40	48
	Total cost (after 30% exchange rate depreciation in one country)	100	$98.4 = 72 \times .7 + 48$

At first glance the answer is obviously no (panel A), since the total production cost would be higher: 120 compared to 100 because three plants have more fixed cost. However, if we assume that 60% of the total cost is incurred in local currency (panel B) we can assert that a 30% shift in exchange rate in favor of one country would make the dispersed strategy lower cost (98.4 compared to 100). Note that this assumes all production is switched to the preferred location. If, as is more likely, the switch is only marginal, the benefit would be accordingly smaller.

This simple illustration shows the limitation of the flexibility strategy, and suggests that it will only be feasible in a business with low fixed costs, high factor price volatility, and high local content. It also explains why, as economic volatility across a region, such as Europe, decreases, firms look to rationalize their activities and concentrate them in a few locations. Indeed, this is what occurred in Europe after the introduction of the euro ended exchange rate volatility among countries sharing the new currency, and, at least in the short term, limited the variation in economic performance between countries.

The benefits of concentrating an activity in a limited number of locations fall into three categories (Table 9.2). The first are factors favoring a single facility rather than multiple facilities. The second are factors that make one country the dominant location for the performance of the activity by a wide margin. The third are the administrative cost savings and motivational enhancements arising from simpler management of a single facility.

In the first category, benefits include scale economies and site-specific learning and experience that cannot be readily transferred across locations. In the second category, factors that favor operating in one country include large differences in

Table 9.2 Concentrate for Static Efficiency versus Dispersion for Dynamic Efficiency

	Pro/Concentrate	Con/Disperse
Single facility	Scale economies (high fixed costs)	High transport costs
	Site-specific learning	Big share of location-independent value added
Dominant location	Large variance in current factor costs	High tariffs
	Big share of local value added	Big share of global value added
		Unpredictability of optimal location
Administrative costs	Only one site	Bureaucracy to coordinate
		Loss of high-powered incentives

factor costs between countries which gives a substantial cost advantage to the currently optimal location, and a large part of the cost structure accounted for by local value added, rather than by globally traded inputs whose cost does not vary between countries.

The third category favoring concentration is the administrative costs of coordination. As a multinational's activities become dispersed across many countries and facilities, managing the logistics network becomes problematic. GE Medical Systems, for example, had to coordinate the movement of 2 million parts across countries while delivering 95% of them within 72 hours of a request being made. Complex global supply chains are hard to manage.

In contrast, dispersing activities among multiple locations is favored when limits to trade, including high transport costs and substantial tariffs, are important, and when there is no penalty to placing activity away from the "optimal" location.[27] If a high percentage of the cost structure is accounted for by globally traded inputs, costs in different locations will be more equal, as will be the case when a large share of costs is incurred independent of the focal activity's location. Dispersion is also more advantageous when there are dramatic and unpredictable exogenous shocks, affecting factor prices or innovations, to be exploited.

Strategic Fit

As with all strategic decisions the choice of configuration often ultimately depends on the international strategy. Indeed, Porter's configuration and coordination matrix (see Chapter 4) makes this link explicit:

		COORDINATION	
		Low	High
CONFIGURATION	Dispersed	Global	Export/import
	Concentrated	Multidomestic	Transnational
		Local	

By definition, the local strategy requires all activities that the firm retains inside the hierarchy to be performed domestically. These are necessarily concentrated in the single geography.

Export/Import   A firm that concentrates its activities and has little activity outside its home country pursues the export (or import) strategy. A natural resource company, like the iron ore mining giant Fortescue, only operates mines in Western Australia. Its main customers are in China, but its activities in that country are limited to sales. Other than arranging the shipping of the ore to Chinese ports, Fortescue has a limited presence outside Australia to coordinate.

Global   The global strategy will be biased toward the concentration of key activities (even if the supply chain is dispersed) in order to drive static efficiency. The classic story of Komatsu's success, leveraging a concentrated configuration of activities to threaten Caterpillar's market dominance, illustrates that strategy. With manufacturing and R&D concentrated in Japan, Komatsu had a tightly coordinated strategy that controlled sales, marketing, and service operations distributed around the world, and which sequentially entered geographies in a long-term global rollout. Unlike the export strategy, Komatsu's global strategy required tight integration between domestic headquarters and subsidiaries.

Multidomestic   A CPG company pursuing the classic multidomestic strategy had a dispersed geographic configuration, replicating most of its activities in every country in which it chose to operate. This network of activities was, however, not coordinated in any systematic way. Instead, each subsidiary was encouraged to pursue its own course, adapting to local market conditions. This configuration represents the classic physical hedge with each country responsible for all the activities in its territory and with no reliance on other parts of the enterprise. The modern variant of this, which many CPG firms have pursued, is the Triad strategy where a region, rather than the single country, functions as a self-contained entity.

Transnational   Finally, a company like Becton Dickinson, pursuing a transnational strategy, creates advantage through the coordination of a globally distributed network of activities to exploit the benefits of agglomeration.

Step 4: Degree of Adaptation

Just as with product design, multinationals that operate facilities in many countries must choose how much local adaptation to allow in those facilities. They can, like Crown Cork and Seal, send old production equipment manufacturing previous generation products to emerging markets, while utilizing the latest machinery in developed markets. Or they can, like Intel, NCR, and CEMEX, use the most modern equipment in every facility, regardless of its location, in order to manufacture state-of-the-art products as efficiently as possible everywhere. What then should be the appropriate amount of local variation in the performance of an activity, particularly given that local management always tries to optimize for local conditions?

At some level, the question of the degree of process adaptation is intrinsically tied to the degree of product variation. As a result, much of the discussion on adaptation in Chapter 7 is relevant here. If the product is to be customized to the local market, then the production process will have to vary accordingly. If the product is a global standard, then the extent to which the production process can alter between facilities will be limited. Nevertheless, even a multinational pursuing a global strategy still has some freedom to vary local production processes. At Federal Express, for example, the degree of automation at a local station where packages are sorted for local delivery, or at the airport hub, can vary. In China, where wage rates are low and political correctness requires extensive employment, facilities will be less automated than when performing exactly the same task in the USA. Thus, it is relevant to ask how much adaptation should be allowed in the production process, independent of the extent of product variation across the multinational.

Answering this question raises again the tradeoff between global standardization and local responsiveness. If processes are standardized, best practices can be readily transferred between facilities, and global sharing of activities, such as purchasing or component manufacturing, is enabled. If processes are localized, local management can adapt to factor cost differences and so optimize production costs on a country-by-country basis.

To make this discussion tangible, think again of FedEx's express delivery business – a standard global product. The set of procedures employed in that business includes logistics – sorting and transporting the packages – and client-facing protocols in package pickup. FedEx essentially has to construct a playbook that specifies how to operate around the world, but still wants to allow managers to choose policies which best fit their country.

A first observation is that local operating procedures always have to **meet local legal requirements**. In China, for example, local labor laws require that employees must be full time, working a minimum number of hours each week. Unlike in the USA, therefore, FedEx cannot use part-time labor to accommodate the peak workloads that occur when planes arrive and leave within a narrow window of time at the end of the work day (outbound) and early in the morning (inbound). Instead, in Shanghai employees will be engaged to complete 40 hours within the week, although their schedules will be arranged across peak demand times. Similarly, as was alluded to above, requirements to demonstrate commitment to the local government will lead to employment of, what in the USA would be seen as, large numbers of redundant security personnel.

FedEx in China also has to violate one of its key process design tenets. The government refused it a license to operate commercial vehicles for local pickup and delivery. Instead, FedEx must use refitted passenger vans. The vehicles that perform the core of the FedEx business are therefore completely different in China than everywhere else!

Similarly, all companies must operate within local environmental laws. Often, such regulations are less onerous in foreign markets than in the home country, so it is possible to operate at lower standards overseas. The extent to which a multinational chooses to take advantage of such flexibility is partly up to the ethics and values of the organization, and partly an economic decision. Should Nike allow subcontractors to employ child laborers if that is acceptable in certain countries? Should Union Carbide be willing to "pollute" the local water supply given that it is legal to operate at these lower standards in many countries (see Chapter 1, "Race to the Bottom")?

A second observation is that altering operating processes to optimize local factor costs is appropriate when such differences can be accommodated without strategic tradeoffs. In other words, local choices that simply drive **local operational efficiency** should always be allowed. I remember one classic example in a Chinese soft drinks bottling factory, when the solution to empty bottles on a conveyor belt falling over on the way into a filling machine appeared not to be cutting the width of the conveyor so that the bottles were tightly confined, but a SWAT team whose only job was to rush between spills to right fallen bottles!

Determining exactly which decisions affect operational efficiency without strategic tradeoffs is difficult. FedEx uses more labor in its Chinese sort facility since calculations have shown that some aspects of automation only become economic when compensation passes $60,000 per annum. Replacing equipment in China with manual labor then makes economic sense, as does allowing drivers to spend more time with customers. However, such decisions gradually begin to compromise the FedEx strategy of rapid, reliable delivery. At the margin, less automation and longer pickups do not conflict with the strategy, but as processing becomes more manual and drivers engage in more chat with customers, the entire system begins to lose its focus on throughput speed and elimination of human error.

Cultural differences also have to be accommodated. Many customers in China struggle to fill out the FedEx waybill that accompanies a package. While the document is in Chinese and English, completing all the lines often requires advice from the FedEx driver. Moreover, Chinese culture has the expectation that you go to the customer, rather than that the customer goes to the provider, and so the driver/client interaction has to be more extensive than in the USA. As a result, while getting the driver in and out of the client's location as fast as possible is critical in the USA, in China drivers are allowed five minutes for each pickup.

In other service businesses, like hotels and restaurants, interactions with customers are also critical to delivering a quality experience. But what is understood as good customer service varies by country. In Western countries busy executives typically want the breakfast bill before the meal has ended in order to expedite payment. In other cultures, even during the early morning rush, it would be considered rude to present a bill before it was requested since guests would interpret the action as being asked to leave the restaurant. In this situation, presumably the hotel would want to allow the definition of good customer service to vary between countries.

But as such local variation is allowed, it becomes increasingly difficult for a company to maintain the global procedures and standards that ensure consistency and support the transfer of FSAs embedded in those processes. How can the Four Seasons deliver its exceptional personalized customer service across its eighty-nine hotels if it is impossible to define what exactly that service level looks like?

More generally, the multinational is confronted with the difficult task of choosing where to draw the line in the rules that govern production processes and service delivery around the world (Exhibit 9.16[28] and Chapter 7). Neither is detailed specification of thousands of **specific guidelines** feasible since many of those will not be appropriate in every country. Nor will a few **general principles** be effective since they degenerate into vacuous, and therefore meaningless, generalities, such as "provide excellent customer service."

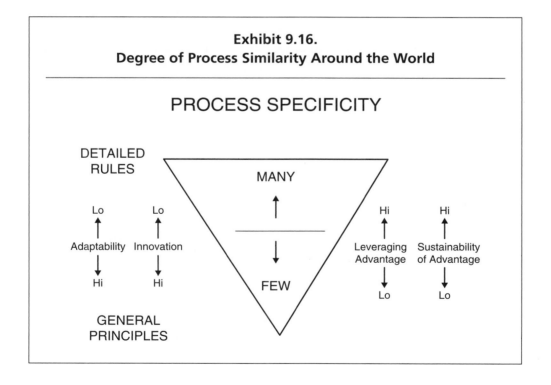

Exhibit 9.16.
Degree of Process Similarity Around the World

PROCESS SPECIFICITY

DETAILED RULES

Adaptability — Lo / Hi

Innovation — Lo / Hi

MANY / FEW

Leveraging Advantage — Hi / Lo

Sustainability of Advantage — Hi / Lo

GENERAL PRINCIPLES

A good example arises in the fast food business. All the multinational chains, like McDonald's and Yum (which operates KFC, Pizza Hut, and Taco Bell), have standard operating processes for their kitchens around the world which can support local food items. Sounds good. But what exactly are those standard processes? Is it a 764-page manual that dictates "defrosting 3 inch strips of frozen chicken from our global supplier for 2 minutes and 17 seconds at 7 a.m. each morning?" Or is it simply a one-page description that specifies "good food in a clean environment?" The latter can clearly accommodate local variety, but where is the global value added? The former promulgates global standards that presumably have been found to be effective, but where does that leave the local freedom to purchase fresh chicken if it is cheaper or preferred by local customers?

The answer is to find that mid-level specification of core standards and procedures that have real bite, but still allow local flexibility. Drawing that line to get the balance between transferability and sustainability of the underlying competitive advantage, and meeting local needs and encouraging local variety and experimentation, are among the toughest tasks when designing global operating processes.[29]

Many companies cycle between the extremes of specification during their internationalization experience. When Tesco, for example, first went international, it maintained tight control over processes in its foreign operations and failed badly in France. It then backed off and allowed countries more local autonomy provided they remained consistent with the "Tesco Way" and core principles, such as loyalty programs. This led to success in Asia, though with a slightly different business model. The real payoff came later. When the UK operation began to perform poorly, executives were brought back from Asia to suggest changes. Because they operated in slightly different ways, but still according to the guiding principles and values of the company, these Asian managers were able to diagnose problems and offer solutions that had escaped UK management but were applicable to the Tesco model.

Other companies go through a different cycle, starting with local freedom and a minimum number of constraints on operating behavior. This is useful for getting a foothold in new geographies but requires a gradual tightening of control and imposition of standards to effectively leverage the global organization. Alico, for example, the international life insurance arm of AIG, "planted the flag" starting in the 1980s, and grew to include a presence in more than 40 countries by 2010, with a "do whatever it takes to get started" philosophy. Stories abound of AIG executives choosing which country to enter next by looking out the window during a transcontinental flight! And of executives arriving in a new country with literally only a suitcase to start the business! In such an environment there were few processes or controls on country managers, a problem which began to haunt Alico as competition from later movers appeared. Acquisition by MetLife provided the structure and systems needed to rein in extreme local variety and leverage global efficiencies by adoption of an appropriate set of global process requirements.

SUMMARY: STRATEGIC FIT

It is useful to summarize the entire location decision process by illustrating how its components are determined by the international strategy. While not definitive, and at the level of overall configuration not explicit about which countries will be chosen, we reach the conclusion that the multinational's location decision is determined by its international strategy:

Int strategy	What activity?	Which country?	How many (config.)?	What process variation?
Local	All	Domestic	Concentrated	None
Export	All (except some selling)	Domestic	Concentrated	None
Multidomestic	Most	Everywhere	Dispersed, physically hedged	Adaptable, as required
Global	Each separate	Current low cost	Concentrated, bet	Limited
Transnational	Each separate	Long-term innovation	Dispersed, option value	Careful discrimination

Strategies that feature limited activities outside the home country – local, export, and import – have restricted location choices since nearly every activity is conducted within the home market. The multidomestic strategy is similarly straightforward since most activities are located in every country in which it competes. Almost by definition, multidomestic companies will therefore have a dispersed and physically hedged configuration, and will allow substantial local variation in the performance of activities. In contrast, the global strategy will disaggregate the value chain and choose optimal locations for each activity separately. It will concentrate each activity in a limited number of locations – probably only one or two – and constrain the extent of process variation around the world.[30] The transnational strategy is the one that favors locations that have the best potential to support long-term innovation in the activity, and will have multiple sites around the world to exploit the volatility and unpredictability of their differences. It is this international strategy that has the biggest challenge drawing the line between general principles and detailed rules for each activity. As a result, the transnational carefully discriminates among processes when drawing that line in order to balance their advantages.

NOTES

1. Arakali, H. and Munroe, T. (2013) The end of Indian IT staffing as we know it. Reuters, March 26. In 2010 the Philippines actually passed India in call center revenues (reported in Everest Group (2010) Manila's banter beats Bangalore call-centre race. *Business Standard*, December 4, accessed at http://www.business-standard.com/article/technology/manila-s-banter-beats-bangalore-call-centre-race-110120400053_1.html).

2. Gapper, J. and Jopson, B. (2011) Coach to shift manufacturing from China. *Financial Times*, May 12, accessed at http://www.ft.com/cms/s/0/e01b1796-7cb6-11e0-994d-00144feabdc0.html#axzz2s5wJ13Fv; Rapoza, K. (2012) US factories leaving China. Forbes, July 25, accessed at http://www.forbes.com/sites/kenrapoza/2012/07/25/u-s-factories-leaving-china/.

3. In 2013 monthly minimum wages varied between $23 in Bangladesh, through $113 in Vietnam, to $212 in Guandong Province, China (Core Solutions (2013) Wage increases continue in low cost sourcing countries, accessed at http://www.coresolutions.com/wage-increases-continue-in-low-cost-sourcing-countries/).

4. In one city, Kunming, 22 fake Apple Stores were unearthed. Apparently, employees in many of those stores "genuinely thought they worked for Apple"; see Lee, M. (2001) Fake Apple Store in China even fools staff. Reuters, July 21, accessed at http://www.reuters.com/article/2011/07/21/us-china-apple-fake-idUSTRE76K1SU20110721.

5. What makes the location decision even more problematic is that the decision to go to India, for example, is just the beginning of an analysis to choose the optimal location within that country from among the many possible sub-regions, like Mumbai, or Chennai.

6. Delta Home Page, accessed at http://www.deltagalil.com/global-presence-overview.aspx.

7. *Boston Globe* (2011) GE X-ray leaders move to China. July 27, accessed at http://www.boston.com/business/technology/articles/2011/07/26/ge_moving_x_ray_business_to_china/.

8. Even at this level of aggregation care has to be taken when differentially locating activities. When US television set manufacturers offshored manufacturing to Taiwan in the 1970s, they retained product design and process engineering in the USA. The resulting disconnect between the manufacturing plant and these functions partly contributed to their failure as they automated production at a slower rate than competitors, such as Matsushita, which collocated these functions in Japan so that engineers could quickly test product and process innovations.

9. A 2008 study by the Bureau of Economic Analysis showed that production-enhancing factors such as "the proximity to suppliers, the availability of highly skilled workers, and the presence of an extensive transportation infrastructure" were more important in the location choices of multinationals than production cost attributes like the availability of cheap labor (Mataloni, R. (2008) Foreign location choices by US multinational companies. Research Spotlight Bureau of Economic Analysis, March, accessed at http://www.bea.gov/scb/pdf/2008/03%20March/0308_locations.pdf).

10. Note, however, that immigration can put pressure on wages in these trades. Skilled UK construction workers found this out to their cost after the EU allowed free movement of labor and thousands of Polish tradesmen entered the UK. Substitutes, such as prefabricated houses, that can be manufactured outside a country potentially also threaten the security of these jobs.

11. Blinder, A. (2007) How many US jobs might be offshorable? Princeton University CEPS Working Paper No. 142, accessed through the O*NET database at http://online.onetcenter.org/.

12. This section overlaps with Chapter 8. In particular, the PEST framework for country analysis is as relevant for deciding whether to locate an activity in a particular country as it is for whether to compete in that country.

13. This is X-efficiency: see Liebenstein, H. (1966) Allocative efficiency vs X-efficiency. *American Economic Review,* 56(3), 392–415; Garvin, D. (1983) Quality on the line. *Harvard Business Review,* 61, September/October.

14. Unlike when I was a consultant in the early 1980s and performed a similar analysis without the aid of Excel or any computer program – updating any information required by rubbing out every relevant number and recalculating the entire spreadsheet for every location by hand!

15. McKinsey study reported by Thomas, K. (2013) Drug research in China falls under a cloud. *New York Times,* July 22, accessed at http://www.nytimes.com/2013/07/23/business/global/drug-research-in-china-falls-under-a-cloud.html.

16. Bloomberg Business (slideshow). Corporate tax rates around the world, accessed at http://images.businessweek.com/ss/09/09/0909_tax_countries/2.htm; Houlder, V. (2013) Unsafe offshore. *Financial Times,* January 14, p. 9.

17. This analysis only concerns real location choices. Simply moving profits on the books by shifting the legal location of subsidiaries and transfer payments might well achieve many of the benefits of tax havens but is not considered here.

18. Indices of global innovation and competitiveness can also be helpful, although they refer to countries in general and not for a specific industry (e.g., INSEAD's Global Innovation Index, accessed at http://www.globalinnovationindex.org/content.aspx?page=GII-Home).

19. See Marshall, A. (1991) *Principles of Economics.* Macmillan: London, Chapter 4, and more recent economic geographers, such as Krugman, P. (1991) *Geography and Trade.* MIT Press: Cambridge, MA (for which he won the Nobel Prize in Economics). The usage of the term agglomeration here accords with economists' past terminology and is not the same as the agglomeration advantage as described in this text.

20. Previous teams had a single boat. Other competitors chose to try out two very different designs of boats in the hope of finding the one that worked best in the particular waters and winds of San Diego where the races took place. Since weather conditions are never the same, unless there is direct competition with a control boat, any improvement in performance cannot be directly attributed to the change made to the subject boat that day.

21. Internet World Stats, accessed at http://www.internetworldstats.com/top25.htm.

22. The irony is that because location matters to firm success, location does not matter! Outside firms, knowing how important it is to be an insider in an advantaged location, relocate key activities there and overcome the disadvantages of their domestic location.

23. Analysis of social networks suggests that geographic distance still matters. The networks of personal relationships that individuals build are directly related to their distance apart – even to the extent that office locations near an exit or toilet, which presumably increase the frequency of personal interactions, shape patterns of cooperation.

24. Note that this step in the process is often invoked first when narrowing down the set of locations for detailed analysis to those that fulfill an appropriate role in the firm's global footprint.

25. Firms that use exchange rate predictions to determine when and when not to hedge currency risk are merely acting as speculators.

26. Google data centers, accessed at http://www.google.com/about/datacenters/inside/locations/.

27. International trade theory discusses the proximity–concentration tradeoff (see Brainard, S.L. (1993) A simple theory of multinational corporations and trade with a trade-off between proximity and concentration. NBER Working Paper No. 4269; Yeaple, S. (2013) The multinational firm. *Annual Review of Economics,* 5, 193–217): many plants minimize transport costs, but lose scale economies. While relevant, optimal configuration depends on more than these two factors.

28. This is the same figure as in Chapter 7.

29. A useful extension is to consider the extent to which processes are tacit and contextually dependent as determinants of how easily they can be transferred across geographies; see Brannen, M.Y. and Voisey, C.J. (2012) Global strategy formulation and learning from the field. *Global Strategy Journal,* 2(1), 51–70.
30. If the minimum efficient scale allows for several plants, the global strategy is more likely to disperse operations in order to achieve some degree of risk reduction.

REFERENCES AND FURTHER READING

Alcácer, J. and Chung, W. (2013) Location strategies for agglomeration economies. *Strategic Management Journal.* DOI: 10.1002/smj.2186.

Alcácer, J., Dezso, C.L., and Zhao, M. (2013) Firm rivalry, knowledge accumulation, and MNE location choices. *Journal of International Business Studies*, 44(5), 504–520.

Allen, L. and Pantzalis, C. (1996) Valuation of the operating flexibility of multinational operations. *Journal of International Business Studies*, 27(4), 633–653.

Asmussen, C.G., Benito, G.R.G., and Petersen, B. (2009) Organizing foreign market activities: from entry mode choice to configuration decisions. *International Business Review*, 18(2), 145–155.

Bartlett, C. (1986) Caterpillar–Komatsu in 1986. Harvard Business School Case #387-095.

Birkinshaw, J.M., Braunerhelm, P., Holm, U., and Terjesen, S.A. (2006) Why do some multinational corporations relocate their headquarters overseas? *Strategic Management Journal*, 27(7), 681–700.

Blinder, A. (2009) How many US jobs might be offshorable? *World Economics*, 10(2), 4–78.

Bloom, N., Genakos, C., Sadun, R., and Van Reenen, J. (2012) Management practices across firms and countries. *Academy of Management Perspectives*, 26(1), 12–33.

Brannen, M.Y. and Voisey, C.J. (2012) Global strategy formulation and learning from the field. *Global Strategy Journal*, 2(1), 51–70.

Connelly, B.L., Ketchen, D.J., and Hult, T.M. (2013) Global supply chain management: toward a theoretically driven research agenda. *Global Strategy Journal*, 3(3), 227–243.

Cross, T. (2011) All the world's a game. *The Economist*, December 10.

Enright, M. and Capriles, A. (1996) Black Magic and the America's Cup: the victory. Harvard Business School Case #796-187.

Fisch, J.H. and Zschoche, M. (2012) The role of operational flexibility in the expansion of international production networks. *Strategic Management Journal*, 33(13), 1540–1556.

Flores, R.G. and Aguilera, R.V. (2007) Globalization and location choice: an analysis of US multinational firms in 1980 and 2000. *Journal of International Business Studies*, 38(7), 1187–1210.

Friesl, M. and Larty, J. (2013) Replication of routines in organizations: existing literature and new perspectives. *International Journal of Management Reviews*, 15(1), 106–122.

Ghemawat, P. and Nueno, J. (2003) Zara: fast fashion. Harvard Business School Case #703-497.

Halaburda, H. and Rivkin, J. (2009) Analyzing relative costs. Harvard Business School Note #708-462.

Hennart, J.F. (2014) The accidental internationalists: a theory of born globals. *Entrepreneurship Theory and Practice*, 31(1), 117–135.

Jaehne, D.M., Li, M., Riedel, R., and Mueller, E. (2009) Configuring and operating global production networks. *International Journal of Production Research*, 47(8), 2013–2030.

Jensen, R.J. and Szulanski, G. (2004) Stickiness and the adaptation of organizational practices in cross-border knowledge transfers. *Journal of International Business Studies*, 35(6), 508–523.

Jensen, R.J. and Szulanski, G. (2007) Template use and the effectiveness of knowledge transfer. *Management Science*, 53(11), 1716–1730.

Krugman, P. (1991) Increasing returns and economic geography. *Journal of Political Economy*, 99(3), 483–499.

Lessard, D. (2013) Uncertainty and risk in global supply chains. MIT Sloan Research Paper No. 4991-13.

Madsen, T.K. and Servais, P. (1997) The internationalization of born globals: an evolutionary process? *International Business Review*, 6(6), 561–583.

Marshall, A. (1892) *Elements of Economics of Industry: Being the First Volume of Elements of Economics*. Macmillan: London.

McFarlan, F.W., Kirby, W., and Manty, T. (2007) Li & Fung: 2006. Harvard Business School Case #307-077.

McFarlan, F., Chen, M., and Wong, K. (2012) Li & Fung in 2012. Harvard Business School Case #312-102.

Minbaeva, D., Pedersen, T., Björkman, I., and Fey, C.F. (2014) A retrospective on: MNC knowledge transfer, subsidiary absorptive capacity, and HRM. *Journal of International Business Studies*, 45(1), 52–62.

Moore, J. (1996) *The Death of Competition: Leadership & Strategy in the Age of Business Ecosystems*. HarperBusiness: New York.

Neff, J. (2012) From Cincy to Singapore: why P&G, others are moving key HQs. *Advertising Age*, June 11.

Parcero, O. and Villanueva, E. (2011) World wine exports. American Association of Wine Economists Working Paper #87.

Porter, M.E. (1998) *The Competitive Advantage of Nations*. Free Press: New York.

Rein, S. (2012) *The End of Cheap China: Economic and Cultural Trends that Will Disrupt the World*. John Wiley & Sons, Inc.: Hoboken, NJ.

Sirkin, H., Zinser, M., and Hohner, D. (2011) Made in America, again why manufacturing will return to the US. Boston Consulting Group Perspectives, August 25.

Smith, T. and Rivkin, J. (2008) A replication study of Alan Blinder's "How Many U.S. Jobs Might Be Offshorable?" Harvard Business School Working Paper #08-104.

Westall, S. (2008) For some, "Made in China" doesn't fit. *New York Times*, July 14.

How to Organize?

MOTIVATION

A recent student was looking forward to her future career as an international executive.[1] Excited by the opportunity, she came to ask what she should do to perform well in her new position. As we talked, the role became clear – she was to run a manufacturing facility in South Africa producing components for a key product that was sold to a few large multinationals. One of the first questions I asked was, "Who do you report to?" After a long pause, the student admitted that she was not sure – it could be the global head of manufacturing who was responsible for optimizing the corporation's global supply chain; it could be the president of the business unit to whom the product line reported; it could be the South African country manager in whose subsidiary she was based; or it could even be the corporate vice president of marketing in charge of global accounts. As I pointed out, "if you don't know who you report to, it's going to be hard to do a really good job for anyone!"

This anecdote illustrates the challenge, familiar to all global executives, of designing an organization capable of balancing the competing perspectives intrinsic to international competition. Indeed, organizational issues are often the most prominent concerns of international executives. Many is the time I have heard country managers complain how a local initiative, such as the design of new packaging, has been overruled by the global business unit head – "if only we could get them out of the packaging decision!" Conversely, headquarters can be frustrated by the inability of country managers to agree to rationalize regional production – "we could cut cost by 8% if only I could tell the countries to accept a standard package!" While every executive can readily identify the weaknesses of their organization, within companies that compete internationally unique tensions exacerbate the conflicts of every hierarchical organization.

STRATEGIC TRADEOFF

Traditionally the organizational tension within multinationals has been described as that between local autonomy and global coordination – local managers need the freedom to adapt the company's strategy to their particular country needs, but global headquarters must still control overall resource allocation, monitor and reward performance, and drive efficiency and learning across countries. We can think of this as the tradeoff of **delegating authority to many organizational units versus centralizing authority in one unit**. The benefit of delegation is that incentives can be put in place to motivate country managers to optimize local performance. The benefit of centralization is the coordination that improves global performance. Thus, the organizational tradeoff is **motivation versus coordination**.

The complication in the global context is that coordination has to take place across several dimensions, each of which has a claim to be represented in determining the global optimum – business unit, function, and geography[2] (Exhibit 10.1).[3]

Optimization of performance along each dimension requires making different choices to realize different advantages (Exhibit 10.2). The countries want local autonomy to adapt products and processes to the needs of their market (local responsiveness). The business unit wants to rationalize operations across geographies (global efficiency and static arbitrage), and the function wants to continuously improve and leverage its expertise around the globe and across businesses (dynamic arbitrage).

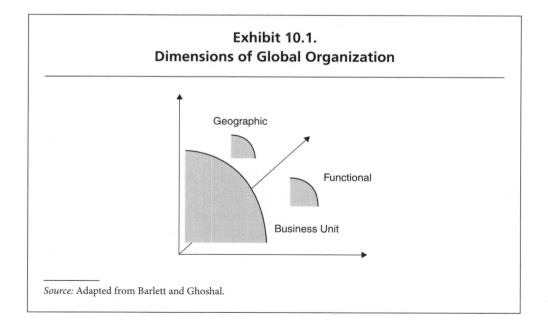

Exhibit 10.1.
Dimensions of Global Organization

Source: Adapted from Barlett and Ghoshal.

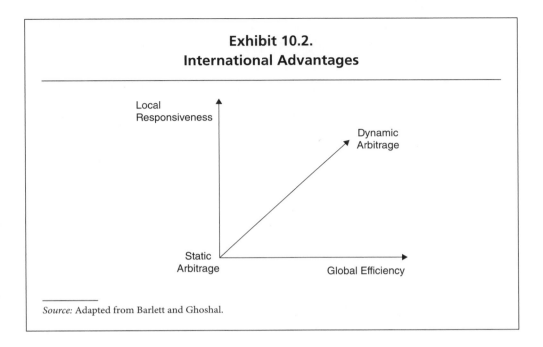

Exhibit 10.2.
International Advantages

Source: Adapted from Barlett and Ghoshal.

How to balance, or even supersede, the tradeoffs within a hierarchical organization is the subject of this chapter. We start by examining structural solutions, but move to a perspective that resolves the tradeoffs through informal organizational processes.

PRINCIPLES

We cannot address all issues of organization design. However, we will take up the challenge of applying organizational economics to the unique issues surrounding international competition. These flow from the fundamental challenge of achieving both **differentiation and integration** within any complex organization (Lawrence and Lorsch, 1967). In confronting this hierarchy, organizations face two tasks: controlling delegated decision making in discrete units and coordinating activities across those units.

The first task facing headquarters executives in multinationals is to **control delegated decision making**. This can be thought of as overseeing the **vertical** lines of accountability in the formal hierarchy which allocates decision rights to one of the three dimensions of geography, business, or function (see next section). Having chosen that line of reporting, the multinational must still minimize agency costs by establishing the appropriate control, monitoring, and incentive systems for those to whom decision-making authority has been delegated. We will say little on this topic since it is a problem facing every organization (but see the box).

Control Systems

Every organization seeks to empower front line employees and move the locus of decision making as close as possible to those possessing current local information. However, organizations must minimize the **agency costs** of lower level executives making decisions in their own self-interest. The solution is to design monitoring and reward schemes that provide incentives to empowered executives to behave, as closely as possible, in the interests of the entire entity. This is achieved by choosing between **outcome, behavior, and clan control** (Eisenhardt, 1985; Ouchi, 1979). The most common choice between behavior and outcome control (see later for clan control) depends on the extent to which behavior, as opposed to outputs, can be accurately monitored (favoring behavior control), and the degree to which executives' influence on performance can be accurately assessed, because they have authority over all relevant activities (favoring outcome control).

Instead, we concentrate on the second organizational task of **coordinating activities across discrete units**. This is achieved by deploying the full suite of organization design levers to design an **administrative context** that supports the chosen international strategy. The intent is to find ways to integrate the activities of differentiated and specialized organizational units.

We divide those levers into two categories: hard and soft. The former, to introduce an architectural metaphor, are the walls, plumbing, and electrics of the building the company represents. The latter have more to do with the occupants of the building than its physical reality. The hard elements of organization design can, in turn, be divided into the formal structure, and the systems and processes that overlay the lines of authority. The soft elements are the people, and the purpose and values of the organization. While any effective organization needs to employ both these **formalization** and **socialization** levers, it is ultimately the softer side of organization design that makes the greatest contribution to effective execution of international strategy.[4]

DESIGN LEVERS

(a) Structure

The solution that most managers traditionally turned to when managing across borders was the design of the firm's organization structure – the boxes and reporting lines on the organization chart. Indeed, one very visible implication of the complexity of international management has been the trauma of regular organizational restructurings that many multinationals experienced. Chris Bartlett once famously argued that firms should "get off the organizational merry go round" because the knee jerk reaction to difficulties coordinating international activities was to reorganize the company (Bartlett, 1983). This reflected a strongly held, if rarely articulated, belief that somewhere out there was *the* one right organization structure that would miraculously solve all problems and resolve all tensions within the multinational.[5]

Put that way, it is obvious why structure alone cannot solve the organizational challenge of international strategy. How can a one-dimensional structure balance the requirements of the country, business, and function? Structure alone will not make international management simple. In fact, its complexity will always challenge managers, and multinationals will always have to deploy a wide range of additional processes and policy overlays. Nevertheless, structure remains a necessary feature of every company and a review of the various structural alternatives is valuable. This also allows us to track the evolution of organization structure over time and suggests how a multinational's organizational heritage leaves a legacy imprinted on its culture.

Principles

The fundamental premise of structural design is to minimize communication cost, maximize the use of information and knowledge, and optimize accountability (Child *et al.*, 2002). This is achieved when discrete units are **specialized**, and responsible for a set of closely related tasks. As noted earlier, in the multinational these specialized units could be countries, business units, or functions.

Regardless of how the firm is divided, each unit should:

Match authority with responsibility so that an executive is only held accountable for actions that are under his or her control. This design rule suggests that units contain all the operations and activities that determine their performance and are, as far as possible, unaffected by decisions outside the unit.

Group together activities and processes that have a high degree of similarity and connection. This suggests that activities that are tightly integrated with each other, in terms of either product flows or expertise, should be within the same unit under a single decision maker.

Adopt hierarchies within each unit so that decision-making authority and reporting lines are transparent.

Ultimately, since strategy determines the task environment within the organization we will find that the chosen "structure should follow strategy" – the conclusion of Al Chandler's seminal work on the history of multibusiness organizations (Chandler, 1964).

Structural Alternatives

Given these design rules we can follow the structures that multinationals have historically deployed. Each gives authority to function, geography, or business unit and so optimizes for one source of international advantage.

Functional When large-scale organizations first emerged within industrializing nations, they adopted a functional structure. Units were created that were responsible for discrete activities, so that marketing and sales would be separated from manufacturing, and each function could specialize on a unique task. This structure drives **functional effectiveness** but creates all sorts of coordination problems between functions so that customers are typically shortchanged. Today the functional structure is used primarily in single business entities or where some functions, such as IT in banking, are central to the organization.

International As companies began to go overseas, the natural adjunct to a functional domestic structure was to add another specialist unit that dealt with foreign activities – the international department. Most activities remained in the home market, and goods exported to the foreign markets were the responsibility of an international department which sold to local distributors or agents in foreign countries. In this structure, many of the tasks for the international department were logistical – arranging shipping, taking orders, providing customer service, etc.

While this description sounds almost preindustrial, in fact it remains representative of many companies that have **limited international activities**. Even today, smaller software companies, for example, are often organized this way, with an international department dealing with licensing and sales queries from foreign markets.

Geographic As companies extended their international scope and began to build their own operations abroad, they created separate subsidiaries for each country. Particularly when communications were slower and transport costs higher, these subsidiaries replicated most of the activities performed in the home country and became "clones" of the domestic operations – the classic multidomestic strategy. Such a structure has the merit of maximizing **local autonomy**, since every country manager is held accountable for the performance of his or her country and is given full authority over most activities necessary to deliver that performance.

Global Business Units Other multinationals that began with a more global strategy, such as Caterpillar, chose to optimize on the **global efficiency** dimension and adopted a business unit structure with authority over all global operations. This places the country manager in a subordinate role since authority for key decisions, such as plant location and product design, lie with the global business unit head.

Matrix Since the global business unit merely replaces optimization on one dimension with that of another dimension, the natural inclination was to find a structure

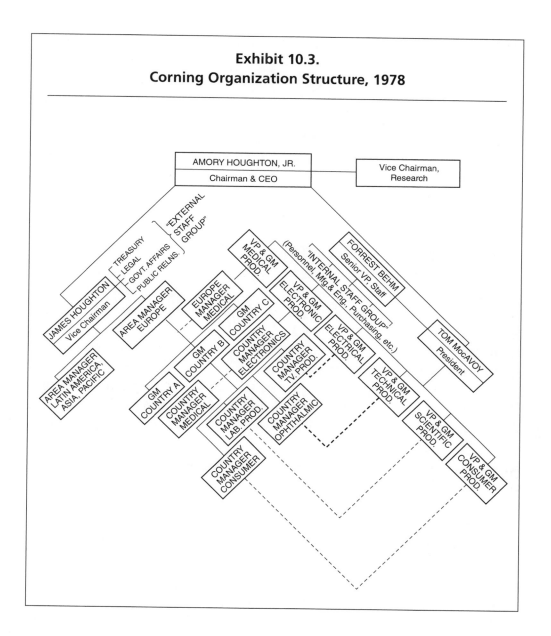

Exhibit 10.3.
Corning Organization Structure, 1978

that balances the two. This is the goal of the matrix structure (see Exhibits 10.3 and 10.4 for examples of a classic matrix at Corning in 1978 and a modern matrix at P&G in 2006).

The matrix organization has each executive report to multiple bosses – traditionally, as at Corning, to a country manager and a global business unit head. The intent is for every executive to balance the conflicting demands of geography and business

Exhibit 10.4.
P&G Organization Structure, 2006

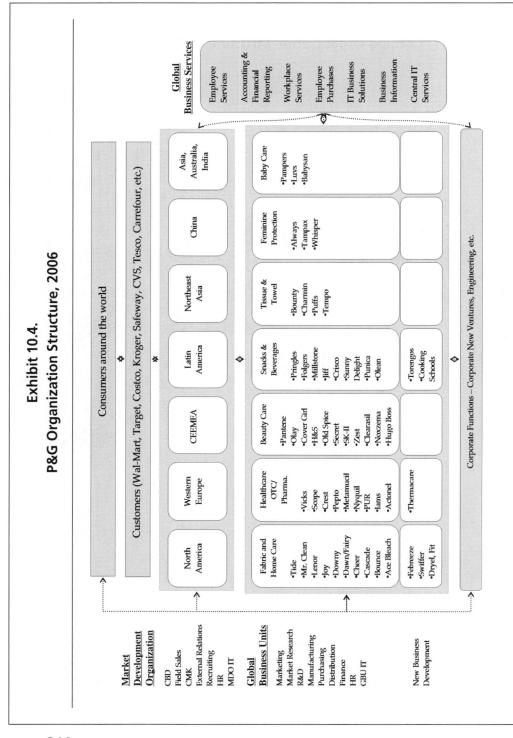

1: Exhibit #5 (pg. 15) "Organization 2005 Structure, 1999" from Case Study "Procter & Gamble: Organization 2005" #9-707-519. Reprinted by permission of Harvard Business School Publishing. Copyright © 2005 by the President and Fellows of Harvard College. Harvard Business School Case #9-707-519. The Case was prepared by Piskorski *et al.* as the basis of class discussion rather than to illustrate either effective or ineffective handling of an administrative situation.

themselves because they are personally accountable for both dimensions. This would be the case for the student described at the opening of this chapter.

Notice that the opening highlighted the obvious weakness of this structure. With no single superior, it is hard for an individual to know how to behave. Readers who have worked inside a matrix organization will know the frustration of reporting to many bosses, each of whom wants to be informed of your activities and each of whom tries to direct your behavior – and that is a polite way of describing the stresses of managing in a matrix!

While there are ways to make the matrix more effective than just described, the fixes lead us into a discussion of other organizational levers. Simply giving managers multiple lines of reporting upward does not, by itself, solve the challenge of organizing for international advantage.

Network   A new organization design has recently been touted that takes advantage of improvements in communication to do away with much of the traditional hierarchy (Nohria and Ghoshal, 1997). The network organization blurs the boundaries of the organization and so is entwined with decisions about which activities should be undertaken by the firm itself (Chapter 9).

Masquerading under various names – network, virtual, "born global" – the principle of the new structure is to maximize flexibility by creating an ever-changing set of relationships, many of which cross the traditional boundary of the firm. Rather than having formal and rigid reporting structures, units are self-organizing as they pull in resources as required and just as swiftly discard those no longer needed. An ever-changing and overlapping set of teams based on personal relationships and short-term contracts then becomes the structure – if indeed we can even consider these structured in a traditional sense. Examples include Wikipedia, many startup firms, and parts of Aventis, a large French conglomerate focusing on pharmaceuticals and agriculture. When formed through a merger of two European companies in 1999, Aventis's US engineering department was poorly organized and highly dispersed, reporting to different subsidiaries with little centralized coordination. In order to solve this problem, the company created six technical service groups, structured around process technologies and customer needs rather than geographic divisions. These virtual organizations allowed engineers to work from anywhere, did not require a traditional expensive management hierarchy, and encouraged the flexible sharing of innovation and best practice information.[6]

While appealing, the issue of accountability comes to the fore in a structure where no one has direct authority over the team. Failures can occur anywhere, and with limited recourse other than ending the relationship and moving on to another partner, those with responsibility for delivering a final product are vulnerable to team members failing to deliver what they promised on time, within budget, and to the requisite quality. Contracting and recontracting can also be a nightmare unless **trust** substitutes for the more traditional methods of shaping and monitoring behavior. We are, therefore, still awaiting the verdict on such structures and exactly what role they can play in the modern multinational.

Evolutionary Paths and Administrative Heritage

As these brief descriptions have suggested, there is a sense of historical **evolution** in MNC organization design, and earlier writers captured this dynamic (Exhibit 10.5) (Stopford and Wells, 1972). Most companies start out with limited foreign sales and few products sold internationally and so create the international department. As they grow their international activities, multinationals adopt either a geographic structure or a global business unit structure according to their international strategy. Either way, they historically ended up with a matrix organization.

Importantly, at every stage predictable conflicts arise within the organization as the weaknesses of the current structure come to the fore and are "exploited" by those who have power in that structure. At Corning, for example, the international structure failed because it did not have sufficient weight within the company to attract the resources necessary to drive global expansion. About 20 years after WWII, therefore, a shift to a geographic structure was made that enabled international sales to

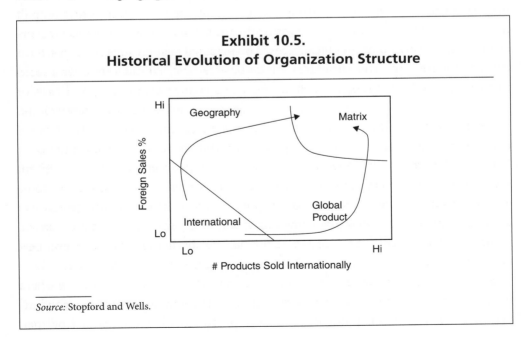

Exhibit 10.5.
Historical Evolution of Organization Structure

Source: Stopford and Wells.

expand tenfold in a decade until pressures to transfer technology between countries and to coordinate global marketing led to a number of interim positions, like "business manager," and committees, like "World Boards." Then, in 1975 a McKinsey-designed matrix structure was introduced along with emphasis on design levers other than formal structure (Yoshino and Bartlett, 1986). Issues around a lack of timely data that aggregated worldwide performance, and continuing confusion about roles and responsibilities, then led to the adoption of worldwide business units by the 1980s.

While an accurate description of the evolution of many multinationals, this path is not deterministic. Indeed, there are many who argue today that even entrepreneurial ventures can and should be "born global" in strategy and structure. However, it has been a path taken by many firms, and the legacy of such an experience leaves an imprint, or what Bartlett and Ghoshal call an "**administrative heritage**" (see box). Knowing where your organization has come from and the attitudes and beliefs generated in those various structures can offer powerful insight into the behaviors of its members.

Administrative Heritage

Bartlett and Ghoshal (1998) identified a **regional** pattern in the structuring of multinationals. They observed that European multinationals historically tended to pursue a multidomestic strategy and therefore adopted a geographic structure managed as a decentralized federation; Japanese companies had a global strategy with a centralized hub structure; and US firms an international strategy with a coordinated federal configuration.

I support the notion of national differences in organization structure (Collis *et al.*, 2012). I vividly remember one summer when I worked in turn with a European, US, and Japanese company, each of which was active in many lines of business and across many countries. I was struck by how much the identifier on an individual's name badge revealed about the heritage of his or her company. Unilever identified managers by the country in which they worked, Honeywell identified them by their business unit, and Sharp by their hierarchical rank! The European firm still drew on its heritage as a country-based organization, the US firm its global business unit structure, and the Japanese firm its hierarchical structure.

Whether true or not, the importance of this observation reinforces the value of understanding the history of organization structure in your company. That evolutionary path has a lasting influence on the perceptions and attitudes adopted by participants within the organization.

Strategic Fit

From this brief discussion, it should be apparent that no formal organization structure alone can ever create an administrative context that resolves the inherent tradeoffs and tensions within a firm that competes across borders. By aligning authority with only one dimension, or by confusing managers with multiple lines of reporting, structure is too blunt an instrument with which to balance the competing claims of each management axis. There is a fit between structure and some simple multinational forms and some international strategies, like export. However, the complexity of representing the multiple interests of a multinational limits the contribution of, though not the need for, a structural solution to organization design.

How then should a multinational design its formal structure since every corporation has to have one? We begin by promulgating a principle that should be apparent from the discussion so far – **every organization structure is sub-optimal**. That simple fact leads to a number of valuable observations:

Do not view organizational restructuring as the solution to the challenge of managing a multinational. As Chris Bartlett pointed out, continually reorganizing in the hope of finding the perfect structure is counterproductive because of the enormous disruption wrought as managers struggle to fill new roles, build new relationships, and master new processes. Rather than seeking the nirvana of an optimal structure, accept that one does not exist, and concentrate instead on making the one you currently have work.

This was nowhere better exemplified than when A.G. Lafley took over from Dirk Jager as CEO of P&G in 2001, after the latter's failed attempt to introduce a new organization structure (the matrix of Exhibit 10.4). One of the first announcements Lafley made was that he was not going to change the structure, even though that was acknowledged as one of the causes of Jager's replacement. Instead, he would make it work by adding new processes, and allowing the company the time to go through what he called "repetitions," within the new structure.

Do not respond to mutterings within the company about the flaws in the current structure. Since every structure has its weaknesses and will always appear to be ineffective to some participants, responding to every complaint will lead to continual reorganizations.

Put in place the best structure for the firm at this point in time – the one that addresses more of the current problems than any other – and recognize that it is not optimal; communicate that message to the organization; and then, like Lafley, move on to make that structure work by deploying other organization design levers.

The default organization structure depends on the international strategy being pursued. As the discussion to date has illustrated, structures have to be "fit for purpose." For us, the bias as to the fit between international strategy and structure matches accountability and responsibility to the intended source of international advantage:

- Local will have a functional structure.
- Export will have an international structure.
- Multidomestic will have a geographic structure for local responsiveness.
- Global will have a business unit structure for static efficiency.
- Transnational will have a matrix structure for coordination and dynamic efficiency.

However, these relationships are merely guidelines. It is not a requirement that a particular international strategy should always have the indicated structure.
Periodically restructure the organization. Given that no structure solves all problems and that the negative aspects of any structure will gradually come to the fore, every so often it will be necessary to make a change. How often this change should take place given the stresses it invokes is debatable, but it is probably true that about every decade any multinational requires a change to its formal structure to rejuvenate the organization.

(b) Processes

The second organization design lever involves the processes that are placed around the frame of the formal structure. These include a broad set of systems and policies from capital budgeting and financial reporting to the project teams and committees that cut across the allocation of authority in the hierarchy. Our concern is with the processes that provide the **horizontal overlay** to offset or mitigate the failure of hierarchical flows of information and resources to support optimization on more than one dimension. It is these mechanisms that multinationals use to integrate the activities of differentiated and dispersed entities.[7]

Principles

Nothing as simple as an organization chart can represent the complex tensions and tradeoffs within a firm that competes across borders. Instead, multinationals adopt more nuanced approaches to representing the legitimate demands of the various organizational dimensions. To reflect that complexity, these processes should be **differentiated and flexible**.

More specifically, the tools adopted should vary across the organization, and over time. They should vary across the organization to be customized for specific needs and situations. And, as the particular failures of any organization structure evolve over time, so the processes used to remedy them must adapt to solve the most pertinent current problems. The success of one process, for example, might produce a momentum to push further initiatives, or it might be institutionalized in a more formal policy. Other processes might be allowed to wither and die as their original purpose passes, or as their learnings become embedded in the firm's culture and behaviors.

Our initial impulse is to design processes with a clear intent and obvious application. Yet the detail can be hard to specify in advance, and the more transparent the process, the more obvious it is who wins and loses from its introduction. Visibility can, therefore, create defensiveness and even obstruction to the implementation of the process. Alternatively, processes can be designed that are initially indistinct in the allocation of responsibilities. One result of this messiness is that in the struggle to deal with ambiguity, the organization itself refines and customizes the process and finds its own way to an endpoint that was never quite clear in the beginning. It is in this sense that the **journey matters** – the experiences of the organization along the way become as important to the effective implementation of any process as the endpoint itself. Even if executives know how they want the process to work, it is sometimes better to allow those charged with its execution to reach that conclusion themselves.

One classic example concerns Ray Gilmartin, the CEO of Becton Dickinson, and then of Merck & Co. When Gilmartin took over as CEO of Becton Dickinson, he confronted a geographic organization structure that was unable to develop effective global strategies. As a result, he created a Worldwide Business Strategy Team (WBST) for each product that cut across geographies, with the intent that these entities would be responsible for strategy setting.

When first established, the WBSTs were not given a clear charter of responsibilities, nor were they given authority over any specific decisions within Becton Dickinson. Neither were they told how often they should meet, how much time commitment they required, and so on. To make matters worse, many of the original members of these WBSTs were neither very senior, nor were they executives with day-to-day involvement in the business on whose team they were placed. Naturally, these teams struggled to articulate their purpose and to get any traction influencing strategy development.

Despite a year or so of widely expressed frustration, the teams did make progress towards identifying an agenda for the WBSTs. Gilmartin then shifted personnel so that executives on any given WBST had a day job within that business, and was able, for the first time, to get agreement on the broad outline of responsibilities for the WBSTs.

A year later, and after the WBSTs had begun to demonstrate their value by improving the quality of strategic discussions, changes were made to place senior executives from each business on the corresponding WBST, and which spelt out in detail the activities and authority of the WBST. Within a year these policies were functioning effectively and were acknowledged as drivers of improved performance.

Notice that the entire process took three years of struggle and frustration, but that, at the end of that time, members of the WBSTs fully supported their role and understood the value the teams brought to the firm. In contrast, had Gilmartin imposed the structure that he perhaps imagined from the very beginning, no one would have been on board and all would have resisted what they saw as a loss of authority.

The real punchline to the story, however, occurred when Gilmartin took over as CEO of Merck & Co. Again confronted by a company that had a regional structure with limited global strategic thinking, he chose to create WBSTs within Merck. But which design did he adopt for these WBSTs? The final version that had emerged after three years at Becton Dickinson and for which there now existed clear templates describing authority, agenda, membership, etc.? Or the original ambiguous and clearly inferior version that was initially introduced at Becton Dickinson, and which would likely lead to three years of frustration as Merck executives wrestled with exactly the same questions that their predecessors had faced?

In spite of the fact that Gilmartin now had a good sense of the answer he wanted – he had a clear vision of the endpoint – he chose the latter option. For three years Merck executives struggled and complained about the ambiguity of the role of the WBSTs. For three years they asked for clarity and for Gilmartin to tell them what he wanted the WBSTs to look like. And at the end of the three years, the version of WBST they arrived at was not that different from the one that emerged at Becton Dickinson! Why did Gilmartin not short-circuit all the stress and frustration by imposing that version of the WBST at the start? Because if he had, the organization would have rejected it! Only by allowing executives to go through the struggle themselves, to find what worked and what did not, to see what benefits the teams could bring – that led them to ask for more authority for the WBST – to take the journey themselves, did the process work.

Hard though it is to see an organization struggle (particularly if you think that you know the answer), however tough it is to watch "sausages being made," it is often better to let executives experience and learn from the pain themselves than to dictate an answer they instinctively reject. To truly embed a horizontal overlay into a company's culture can involve a shared journey from ambiguity to clarity.

Tools

Allocation of Decision Rights   Organization structure allocates decision rights with formal reporting lines identifying who has authority for each decision. However, this implies that there is a single decision maker at each stage in the hierarchy. In practice, decision making within multinationals demands a more nuanced allocation of decision rights if it is to optimize across multiple dimensions. This recognizes that more than one person should influence each decision, and that there are important roles to be played in the process other than just having final authority over the decision.

This belief that there needs to be **disaggregation and discrimination in the allocation of roles and responsibilities** gives rise to a more refined approach to decision making. The consulting firms have their own names for this – McKinsey the "Decision Grid" and Bain the "Decision Driven Organization." Whatever it is called, the intent is to complement the formal organization structure by specifying: (a) a list of important decisions that are to be made by the organization and (b) a variety of roles that can be involved in making a decision, from having final authority, through making recommendations, to providing information relevant to the decision; and identifying (c) which managers are involved in each decision and (d) what role they are assigned in each decision.

The net result is that rather than a simple vertical hierarchy, decisions are thoughtfully distributed throughout the organization to balance relevant perspectives.

In the example shown in Exhibit 10.6, drawn from Corning Glass, executives can be allocated one of eight different roles in a decision from "Authority to make the decision" to "Business concurrence" and "Information provider." The role of each manager will then vary across nearly a hundred decisions that range from "location of new manufacturing facility" to "price of new product introduction." Bain's decision-driven organization approach similarly focuses on the question of "Who gets the D?" – who is given authority to make a specific decision among the other roles in the RAPID (Recommend, Agree, Perform, Input, and Decide) framework (Rogers and Blenko, 2006).

To introduce the decision grid to an organization typically requires extended discussions among relevant managers about exactly who plays which role in what decision. The result of these meetings is a grid (similar to that in Exhibit 10.6) which defines the allocation of responsibilities for each decision.

As you can imagine, if there are 30 or so executives and 100 decisions involved in developing a decision grid, these are not easy or short meetings. Moreover, the resulting document is never regularly used, in the sense that at 4 p.m. on Thursday when a country manager is debating with a global vice president of marketing about who has the right to decide promotional Christmas prices, each pulls out the book to find out who "has the D" for this specific decision. Indeed, when first shown this tool most executives and students make fun of the spurious exactitude it offers in a process that all recognize cannot be precisely defined. What, for example, does "business concurrence" actually mean? Is it the right to veto the decision? To make a point of view known to the decision maker?

Exhibit 10.6.
Decision Rights for Corning's TV Business

Legend:
D — Decides
A — Approves
R — Recommends
BC — Business concurrence
C — Concurs
IP — Initiates
TC — Technical concurrence
IP — Inputs
* For U.S. decisions only

Worldwide Resource Allocation	U.S. Electrical Products Division					European Area — Sorvel								CGIBA							Worldwide Management				Finance			Corporate Staffs								
	Bus. Dev. Liscomb	Controller Russell	TV Bus. Mgr. Galley	Mfg. Mgr. Fralley	Gen. Mgr. Dawson	TV Div./Plant Controller Hollack	TV Production Timbal	TV Sales & Mktg. Prestal	TV Div. Mgr. Picot	Tech. Dir. Ayotte	Head of Staff Maurice	President Regis	Gen. Mgr. CEE McCann	Planning Mgr. Winkler	Licensing Roederer	Socialist Countries Roederer	Financial Mgr. Hamer	Gen. Sales Mgr. Stoff	Deputy Area Mgr. Wuench	Gen. Mgr. Dulude	Staff Mktg. & Bus. Dev.	Staff Mfg. & Eng.	Control & Planning	Worldwide Mgr. Dawson	Treasury	Control	Bus. & Fin. Planning	Mfg. & Eng.	Technical Staffs	Purchasing	Mfg. Services	Industrial Relations	Manpower Dev.	Public Relations	Legal	Govt. Affairs
1. Recommend allocation of resources to major new product development programs	R₁	IP	R₁	R₁	R₂	IP	R₁	R₁	R₂	IP	IP	BC				C		IP		BC	BC R₃	IP	IP	D		TC	IP	R/TC	R/TC				IP/TC		TC	
2. Recommend allocation of resources to major process development programs	IP	IP	IP	R₁	R₂	IP	R₁	IP	R₂	IP	IP	BC				C		IP		BC	BC IP	R₃	IP	D		TC	IP	R/TC	R/TC				IP/TC		TC	
3. Recommend allocation of resources for major cost reduction programs	IP	IP	IP	R₁	R₂	IP	R₁	IP	R₂	R₁	IP	BC				C		IP	C	BC	BC IP	R₃	IP	D		TC	IP	R/TC	R/TC				IP/TC		C	
4. Determine need, location, and timing for adding or reducing plant capacity	IP	IP	IP	R₁	D*	IP	R₁	IP	R₃	IP	R₂	D*				R	IP	IP		D*	D* IP	R	IP	D*		TC	IP	R					IP/TC		TC	C*
5. Decide management of production work force (expansion, contraction, assignment)		IP		D	C	IP	R₁		R₃		R₂	D	D						C	C				C												
6. Decide on interarea sourcing	IP	IP	IP	R₁	R₂	IP	R₁	IP	R₃	IP	R₁	BC	R₂			R₁	IP	IP		BC	BC IP	R	R₃	D	TC	TC	IP					TC*	R	IP	TC C*	C
7. Decide who maintains existing technologies (e.g., black-and-white, spinning)			IP	R	R	IP	R	IP	R	IP	BC				R	R'	R		IP	BC							IP	R/TC								
8. Assign specialized people resources to temporary assignments (e.g., to implement special three month project)																																				
a. Assign operating personnel (e.g., marketing, manufacturing) to another area		R	R	R	D/BC	R	R	R	D/BC	D	C	R			R	R	R₂	IP	BC	BC	BC	C	BC	BC					D				R		C	C
b. Assign technical staff and M&E personnel		R	R	R	R	R	R	R	R			R			R	R	R			BC	BC	R		BC				D					R			

Source: McKinsey-prepared form as filled out during a decision grid meeting.

The value to the process is, of course, not the actual grid, but the **conversation** among managers that led to its creation. Most companies never confront the question of exactly who should be involved in a particular decision, or who really has authority to make that decision. While these responsibilities can never be exactly defined or distributed, at least having the discussion independent of making the actual decision can alert participants to the perspectives and vested interests of others. It is the mutual airing and sharing of these points of view far from the heat of a particular instance that creates value by allowing parties to empathize with others when a real decision arrives.

While it is clear that a full-blown application of the decision grid will produce a very, perhaps too, nuanced allocation of decision rights within the firm, a simpler version captures many of the same benefits. Corning Glass, for example, acknowledged that each of its three main businesses (Consumer, Television, and Scientific) required a different balance between local and global authority over decisions (Exhibit 10.7). Consumer glass – the traditional CorningWare product – was a more local business than scientific glass – test tubes and beakers – which was a more standardized product and needed to be managed on a global basis. Across activities within any given business, R&D was the one activity which most benefited from global scale and so required the most centralized decision making. In contrast, sales took place on a local level and were best left to the country organization. Even within a broadly defined activity, such as marketing, specific activities required a differentiated allocation of decision rights. The brand had to be consistent around the world, so decisions concerning the logo,

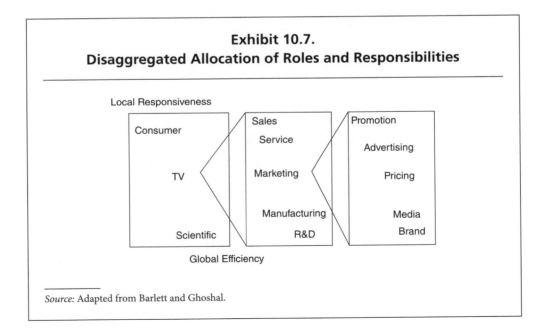

**Exhibit 10.7.
Disaggregated Allocation of Roles and Responsibilities**

Local Responsiveness

Consumer

TV

Scientific

Sales

Service

Marketing

Manufacturing

R&D

Promotion

Advertising

Pricing

Media

Brand

Global Efficiency

Source: Adapted from Barlett and Ghoshal.

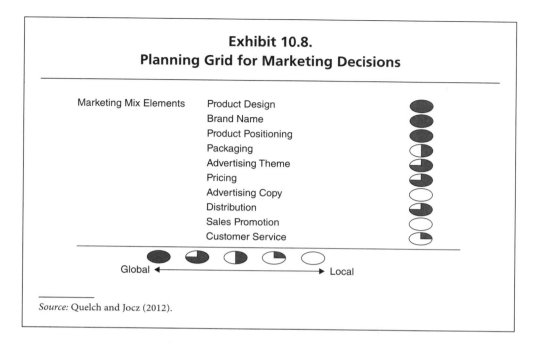

Exhibit 10.8.
Planning Grid for Marketing Decisions

Marketing Mix Elements
- Product Design
- Brand Name
- Product Positioning
- Packaging
- Advertising Theme
- Pricing
- Advertising Copy
- Distribution
- Sales Promotion
- Customer Service

Global ⟵⟶ Local

Source: Quelch and Jocz (2012).

names, and overall positioning had to be decided globally. However, promotional decisions – whether to offer a deal on President's Day in the USA – were obviously a local decision.[8] The result is a much simpler description of where the balance of power lies (Exhibit 10.8). Partitioning decisions in this way and allocating authority differentially within the organization are absolutely critical to mitigating the intrinsic weakness of the formal structure at cooperating across dimensions.

Beyond decision rights, we cannot cover all the systems and processes, such as transfer prices, employed inside multinationals, although we repeat that their design should be situation specific, and vary over time as they seek to balance the primary decision-making dimension of the formal structure. What we can do is highlight the two key processes supporting global coordination and integration: **sharing activities** across discrete units (in order to achieve the benefits of aggregation and arbitrage), and **transferring learning** across units (in order to achieve the benefits of augmentation and agglomeration).

Sharing Activities

It is when an activity is shared between units and does not serve one master that conflict occurs. When a production facility is under the formal authority of the global head of manufacturing, how can a country manager be convinced to accept regional packaging that is not ideal for his or her nation's consumers? When sharing activities, the formal structure alone cannot produce the desired coordination. Instead that has

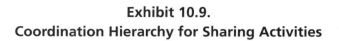

Exhibit 10.9.
Coordination Hierarchy for Sharing Activities

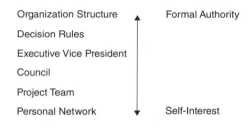

Organization Structure	Formal Authority
Decision Rules	
Executive Vice President	
Council	
Project Team	
Personal Network	Self-Interest

Source: Collis and Montgomery (2005).

to be complemented by horizontal mechanisms that lie on a hierarchy extending from the least to the most formal processes (Galbraith and Kazanjian, 1986) (Exhibit 10.9).

At the lowest level on the hierarchy lie the personal relationships that form outside the formal structure. Managers invariably interact with peers elsewhere in the firm and with managers outside their formal lines of authority, and these networks do allow other points of view to be informally considered. Perhaps a business unit manager does not push his or her authority to the limit in the design of new regional packaging because he or she expects a quid pro quo from country managers on a decision for which they have formal authority. These trades go on all the time inside every organization and represent the natural give and take among managers converging on a joint maximizing outcome, even while pursuing their own self-interest.

The next step on the hierarchy would be the creation of an ad hoc project team with authority to make a particular decision, say the location of a new shared manufacturing plant. With representation from all relevant parties, the resulting choice, although still hard to arrive at consensus, will at least have considered all points of view and so hopefully have reached the global optimum.

Above this would be a standing committee with a defined set of responsibilities, such as a global purchasing council with a remit to reduce cost in the supply chain. While the council might begin with no formal authority, if it includes representatives from all countries it can provide the forum to identify savings that require mutual agreement. Just as the project team can be formalized into a council, the council itself can perhaps gradually be given more authority as it demonstrates its value and achieves buy-in from all constituencies. Notice that this sequencing is reminiscent of the evolution of the WBSTs at Becton Dickinson and Merck & Co. All parts of the organization willingly embrace the concession of decision rights to others when they see how it improves overall performance.

At some stage, the organization might choose to create the position of an executive vice president, say, in charge of global purchasing. This position typically comes with responsibility but no authority and with only a minimal staff, so the task requires influence and persuasion rather than the use of diktat. However, the degree of authority in the position can gradually be increased as the organization comes to recognize its benefits. AP Moller Maersk's global group purchasing unit, for example, has grown in a decade from 3 to 800 people and now covers 80% of all purchases by demonstrating – with the cost savings signed off by the operating units – how it reduced cost in the supply chain.

The next step up the coordination hierarchy is the formalization of decisions in a set of rules that cut across the hierarchical structure. It might be decided, for example, that any purchase over $500,000 has to be approved by the purchasing EVP, or that plant locations must always be consistent with a Triad configuration.

Finally, the company might change the formal organization structure and invert the lines of reporting. Rather than a geographic structure, the company might switch to global business units. While this solves one set of problems, it clearly just starts the process all over again, since countries will now be the underrepresented dimension in decision making.

Management can support the move up this hierarchy by rewarding progress, drawing attention to successes, formalizing each process once it has been demonstrated to be valuable, and occasionally taking symbolic actions to legitimate an action – such as visibly firing a high-performing executive who perhaps did not achieve consensus with his or her peers on a critical action.

All multinationals deploy some subset of these processes with the intent of ensuring the adequate involvement of individuals with an interest in a decision, but who lie outside the formal line of authority. The extent to which they are used depends on the demand for coordination to realize the company's international advantage, and the extent to which activities are shared between discrete organizational units.

Leveraging Learning

Unlike sharing activities, every part of an organization is able to employ knowledge and learning within its own domain without compromising its application elsewhere in the company. However, decisions still have to be made as to who should be responsible for originating new ideas, and to what extent each unit has the freedom to adopt, adapt, or resist newly developed policies. Should new product development be concentrated in global headquarters, or will individual countries have the right to

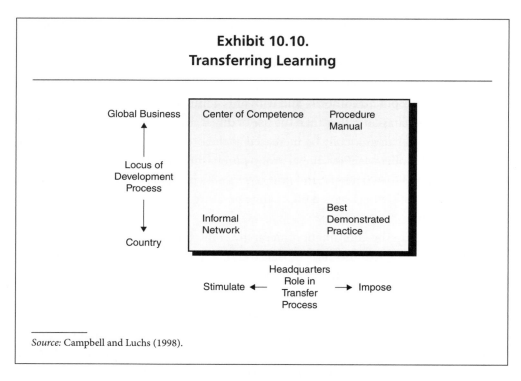

Exhibit 10.10.
Transferring Learning

Global Business

Center of Competence

Procedure Manual

Locus of
Development
Process

Informal
Network

Best
Demonstrated
Practice

Country

Headquarters
Role in
Transfer
Process

Stimulate ← → Impose

Source: Campbell and Luchs (1998).

originate their own ideas? And if they do, who has the responsibility to roll out successful innovations to additional geographies?

Such a choice can be represented in a matrix (Exhibit 10.10) that describes the locus of responsibility for developing and adopting an innovation. On each dimension the choice can be thought of as between countries and the headquarters (or global business unit). The four cells therefore capture four different approaches to arbitraging learning across countries.

In the top right-hand quadrant is where a headquarters function, perhaps within the global business unit, is responsible both for originating new ideas, processes, and products and for imposing them on country subsidiaries. This would be the case, for example, if global manufacturing were responsible for the specification and operation of all plants, and wrote extensive manuals detailing procedures to be followed around the globe whose application it then audited. This design choice has the advantages of specialization and scale (static efficiency), since only a single entity develops the process, and every unit adopts the policies. These are the benefits accruing to centralization and were the arguments behind the historic role of headquarters staff controlling global operations.

Today, the faults of a large bureaucratic staff have limited the frequency of this choice. While it has to be retained for activities that bear on the fundamental integrity of the company – typically the finance function, and perhaps safety, health, and environmental – for other functions the headquarters staff role has been substantially reduced.

The lower left quadrant is where each country develops its own ideas and each chooses whether or not to adopt ideas developed elsewhere. The company therefore gets the benefits of decentralization. Ideas will be originating in many countries, while countries that voluntarily adopt a new practice or product will be more likely to make it a success than when it is imposed on them. However, its drawbacks are the lack of a centralized development process able to concentrate on big ideas, and the lack of a formal mechanism to alert countries to developments elsewhere in the organization. The transfer depends only on informal flows of information.

If this approach is deemed too ad hoc, the company might move toward the right and use a company magazine or website to provide information about what is happening elsewhere in the company. Other tools of knowledge management can be employed here. Danone, for example, which believes that decentralization to its 70 CBUs (Country Business Units) is critical to its strategy, developed a series of best practice transfer processes designed to create a "Networking Attitude" (Edmondson and Lane, 2012). Among the approaches it adopted were "marketplace" presentations of ideas during other conferences or meetings; "Little Books" that compiled examples as stories; and a "Who's Who" internal directory of people and ideas to share. The philosophy throughout according to the EVP of HR was that "headquarters can suggest options, but cannot impose conditions." Further to the right would be an arrangement whereby a council shared ideas developed by the countries – again leaving countries with the freedom to adopt those ideas or not. The next move might involve the unit that originated the idea making itself available to countries that wanted to replicate the idea. Perhaps a SWAT team of experts is formed that can travel to countries seeking to adopt the new process. This is the notion behind the "pitcher–catcher" approach employed at GE. When a process is to be transferred from one country to another, GE identifies the experts in the process (the pitcher), and designates the team in the receiving country that is tasked with applying the new process (the catcher). In this way, good ideas, wherever they originate, can quickly and effectively be transferred throughout the globe.

Further still to the right would be best demonstrated practices that become mandated requirements around the world. While the innovations could come from anywhere, once headquarters understands their value and applicability, it has the authority to mandate their adoption. Jack Welch adopted this approach when as CEO of GE he visited a European business unit and was surprised to find the president of the unit being "mentored" by a junior employee on the uses of the Internet. Impressed with the idea, he insisted that every senior GE executive establish such a mentee relationship.

In the top left quadrant is the role that headquarters staff often seek to play today as a **center of competence**. In this role, the corporate manufacturing unit is tasked with developing new processes, but can only influence and encourage countries to adopt those policies. Without formal authority to mandate adoption they have to become recognized experts from whom countries are keen to learn since they respect their knowledge. Such units need not be large, but have to be staffed by world-class domain experts operating as internal consultants who persuade geographies to adopt their ideas. Unlike traditional staffs they lack authority and must view operating units as their customers. In this regard they are "partners" of, rather than "policemen" for those units (Gulati, 2010).

Role of Corporate Headquarters

The above discussion questions the role that headquarters staff should play in the modern multinational (Andersson and Holm, 2010). The days are long gone when, for example, a global manufacturing staff dictated factory policies around the world in thousand-page manuals and audited subsidiary adherence to those standards. Instead, headquarters staff are today more likely to be seen as centers of excellence, comprising a few senior executives who command the respect of the entire organization and who view their role as coaching and consulting operating companies, rather than dictating and mandating policies.

More generally, there are three roles played by headquarters in a multinational, which shape the size and authority of the various functions performed there. These are similar to those in any multibusiness company (Exhibit 10.11) (Collis *et al.*, 2012).

Exhibit 10.11.
Roles of the Corporate Headquarters

Corporate Functions	Number of FTEs	Role	Typical Activity	Assessment Methodology
Core	# # #	Guardian: Compliance and Authority	Examples: • Corporate Executives • Financial Reporting • Mgmt Reporting	• Measure against external benchmarks and statistics
VALUE ADDED	# # #	Advisor: Education of Client	Examples: • Human Development • Strategic Planning • Business Development • Globalization • Innovation	• Develop a strategy statement for each function • Measure performance against the deliverable
SHARED SERVICES	# # #	Implementer: Order Taker Service to the Business	Examples: • IT • Pension Administration	• Develop a service-level agreement • Use a "market test" (likelihood of being outsourced)

The first role is that of the public company functions required of headquarters acting as representatives of the legal entity. These include external reporting to the financial, legal, and tax authorities, which requires aggregating data worldwide, and performing internal activities that are management's responsibility as agents of the shareholders, such as preventing fraud and monitoring delegated decision making. These latter are typically related to management accounting and the operation of control and incentive systems that minimize agency costs throughout the enterprise.

The second set of headquarters activities are shared services provided to the geographies and businesses. Typically these relate to administrative activities – payroll processing, pension administration, financial accounting – that have to be performed by operating units but which are aggregated and delivered centrally because of scale economies. The location of these tasks is determined solely on the basis of efficiency – they could potentially be outsourced to a third-party specialist or even be performed on behalf of the entire multinational by one of the operating units. Their presence at headquarters is in some sense discretionary.

The third group of activities performed at headquarters are those central to value creation across geographies – that realize the multinational's international advantage. These critical tasks will obviously vary according to the resources (FSAs) the company is leveraging across markets. This role is about making adequate investment in the multinational's resources, and then deploying them across the geographies. It is here that headquarters functions can be key players in coordinating activities across subsidiaries, whether by supervising the sharing of activities or being the conduit for transferring learning throughout the organization.

The trick to designing multinational headquarters is to recognize that every staff function will be performing a mix of the three tasks, each of which has a different driver and requires a different level of authority over the operating units. HR, for example, might provide global employee benefits administration as a shared service in which it is held accountable to a market test and a service level agreement. It can also be monitoring and auditing compensation levels in the geographies with the authority to mandate, for example, that pay should be set according to the second quintile of peer companies in that market. Finally, headquarters HR can be managing the pool of corporate executives on behalf of the CEO in order to ensure an adequate supply of the talent that is the firm's most valuable asset while also advising country subsidiaries on their talent development activities.

(c) People

As the preceding sections should have made clear, making decisions that are best for the company as whole, as opposed to that which is best for the particular unit that possesses decision authority, ultimately comes down to the behavior of the individuals involved. In that sense, the best way to manage the multinational is through its people. What does this imply in practice?

Principles

This is not an exhaustive treatment of human resources in the international context. Instead, we focus on key aspects of human resource management in multinationals, particularly those that allow a company to create a cadre of senior managers who can adopt multiple perspectives, internalize the interests of different organizational entities, and balance them to make decisions in the best interests of the firm as a whole. Those are attributes of a **geocentric general manager** who has mastered the talents required of the three main roles inside a multinational (also see box):

Country manager who is responsible for representing local interests in the implementation of the chosen strategy within his or her geography, while being aware of opportunities in the local environment that could be leveraged globally.

Business unit head who is responsible for the global efficiency of the business's operations and coordination of the international strategy.

Functional head who can transfer learning and ideas around the world while driving innovation in his or her particular domain.

Geocentric Manager

Bartlett and Ghoshal (2003) summarized the task of the geocentric manager in a series of articles in the *Harvard Business Review*. They argued that such rare birds needed to have the skills of a strategist, architect, coordinator, sensor, builder, contributor, scanner, cross-pollinator, and champion. That is an ambitious target. It is also the challenge and opportunity for the individual – a demanding and high-pressure, intense but rewarding, ever-changing, never easy role that I hope every reader aspires to hold.

Tools

HR Policies   While some perspectives of the geocentric manager come with longevity – if I have been in the company a long time, most experiences will have come my way – multinationals are usually more proactive in managing senior executive careers. This means the **corporate HR group** becomes responsible for hiring, training, transferring, incentivizing, and promoting a group of executives who have long-term international careers within the organization. The size of this group can vary, but typically about 5% of executives will belong to, and have their careers managed by the corporate HR group and the "C" suite.[9]

Examples include HSBC, which for years relied on IMs ("International Managers") for its leadership. These individuals, often sons of ministers or military officers, were recruited out of universities (often Scottish), and sent to Hong Kong for three years of training. There they lived in dormitories (no women were hired into the program until the late 1970s) to learn the HSBC way of doing things, until sent to a subsidiary where they remained under the careful watch of their elders and betters – IMs required permission to marry, and their potential wives were vetted until the 1980s! IM contracts stated (as they still do) that HSBC could transfer IMs anywhere in the world with six weeks' notice since they were used as troubleshooters and loyal representatives of the HSBC culture. Compensation for IMs was (and is still) set on a global basis with benefits, such as trips home and private education for children, provided to make frequent international relocation manageable.

Extreme though this sounds today – and even HSBC has toned down the program and now looks beyond the ranks of IMs for potential leaders – the example reflects many aspects of a successful multinational HR development program.

HIRING AND SELECTION   Recruits into these programs are chosen as potential **high performers** and typically drawn from a limited number of institutions believed to produce the desired characteristics. Prime among these attributes, in addition to the standard academic and leadership skills, is a cosmopolitan mindset (see box).

Global Mindset

Those interested in seeing if you have the characteristics required to be an effective international manager can test yourselves at http://www.thunderbird.edu/knowledge _network/ctrs_excellence/global_mindset_leadership_institute/global_mindset_inventory/ index.htm.

The Thunderbird questionnaire is looking for your competence at and interest in qualities like global business savvy, cosmopolitan outlook, passion for diversity, adventurous nature, self-assurance, intercultural empathy, and interpersonal and diplomatic skills (Javidan and Walker, 2013). You should know that I scored low on this test, so either I have my doubts about its reliability, or I have chosen the wrong subject to write on!

Typically one thinks of the recruiting process as the firm choosing among candidates. It is, however, important to realize that an effective hiring process is as much about the candidate choosing the firm. To allow individuals to self-select into the organization, it is therefore vital for a company to be honest and transparent about its values and its expectations for managers. A company like Lincoln Electric, which has a unique performance-driven culture in which every worker is paid a piece rate that is never altered and has no limit to their income, is very explicit about these policies in its hiring process. After weeding out those that do not fit within a short probation period, Lincoln Electric has blue-collar turnover below 6% pa. Similarly, a multinational that expects managers to rotate jobs and countries for an extended part of their career needs to make this transparent in the recruiting process.

SUCCESSION PLANNING, CAREER PATHS, AND DEVELOPMENT   As standard bearers of the company culture and drivers of its strategy, geocentric executives must be exposed to all aspects of the business and evaluated as much on their adherence to desired behaviors as on their performance (see later). Companies like GE, which believe people are their greatest asset and which seek to create a distinctive culture, therefore, rely heavily on **internal promotions**. Typically, corporate HR will expect there to be internal candidates identified for every position above a certain level in the company. Reviewing candidates and planning appropriate experiences for executives in the corporate talent pool to ensure sufficient organizational depth then becomes one of the most critical senior management tasks.

The intent is to develop executives who understand and are able to represent all dimensions of the organization. This means they must spend years operating in country subsidiaries, global business units, and corporate functions. It is only when experiencing these roles that a manager can truly comprehend their perspectives and empathize with all sides of a debate.

To provide managers with this range of experiences requires **frequent transfers**. Previously, some companies, like Pepsico, were notorious for the frequency of executive moves. Roger Enrico, onetime CEO of Pepsico, talked of having seven different jobs within his first 11 years in the company. While variety is important, it is clear that no executive can be effective in a job that lasts less than 18 months – to say nothing of the impact on the executive's work/life balance. Indeed, the risk is that managers adopt counterproductive behaviors – making decisions that yield short-term results, while avoiding any long-term consequences by being two jobs removed from any mess they left behind. Today, most multinationals will expect an executive to be in a position for at least three years, unless some truly unforeseen circumstance arises.

Even if the frequency of moves has declined, the importance of **international experience** has increased for managers. Gone are the days when a CEO was appointed who never had a substantive role outside the domestic operation. Indeed, today three-quarters of Fortune 500 CEOs have spent at least two years working abroad, up from only about a half a decade ago.[10] Although, as Ghemawat notes, today 73% of S&P 500 directors still have no international work experience![11] This implies that every young manager who aspires to be a leader in such organizations needs to be willing, indeed should be enthusiastic, about working internationally. While mastering English can just about suffice for language skills today (and is probably required in multinationals that are domiciled in non-English-speaking countries), having spent no time in foreign subsidiaries will no longer be acceptable.[12]

The corporate HR function has the responsibility to develop and so manage the rotations of its cadre of future leaders. At one level this simply involves matching opportunities to the needs of the candidate, and ensuring there is a good position waiting for the candidate at the end of the three-year assignment abroad (which addresses the greatest fear of managers sent overseas that "out of sight means out of mind" and a loss of relative position). However, it is not just the perspective of the individual that matters. The receiving organization also has to be willing to embrace the transferred manager.

One way to calibrate this concern is to reflect on how often an executive asks for "the worst person you have" to fill an empty position. Managers only want the best possible candidate for the job, and they will only willingly give up a terrific executive to fill a job elsewhere in the company if they believe they will get back someone even better. This implies that HR has to ensure that every international executive has the set of skills expected at their particular level. As a result, HR typically develops **competence profiles for each executive tier** that specify a set of capabilities against which candidates are assessed and evaluated. Training programs, membership of teams, and project assignments are then chosen for each executive to ensure they develop these competences.

There are three problems with this approach to career development. The first is simply the expense of managing, training, and compensating these individuals. The second is the resentment that can arise among those managers (the majority in the firm) who are not being fast-tracked. Hopefully the interpersonal skills of those managers, with appropriate guidance from corporate HR, can overcome some of the defensiveness of an organization that views outsiders as only interested in furthering their own career. However, the more difficult problem concerns whether the international executive is really the best person for the job.

The intent of international transfers is to give managers the full range of experiences so they internalize the multiple perspectives vital to making geocentric decisions. However, this implies that the executive is moved into a position where he or she has limited experience – rather than contributing, the executive is in the position to learn. While sensible for the individual, the question is whether this is the best outcome for the receiving entity. What happens when the new head of marketing in Vietnam is an executive with limited marketing experience, and no experience of South East Asia? Similarly, while locals know their own country, are typically less expensive than expatriates, and are committed to the country for the long haul, expatriates fail on all these dimensions. It is these drawbacks that constrain the size of the pool of internationally mobile executives who quickly advance through a number of different positions.

COMPENSATION AND INCENTIVES   One obvious way to encourage managers to work together to achieve the global optimum is to alter the compensation and incentive scheme to **reward global rather than local performance**. If a country manager is held responsible only for the performance of his or her own country, it is natural to protect those interests. Basing part of the manager's compensation on overall corporate performance alters his or her incentives and makes him or her willing to sacrifice for the greater good. While simple in intent, the drawback to such global metrics is the weakened incentive to maximize the manager's own organization's performance. The more the incentive is tilted toward corporate performance, the weaker the local performance incentives and the greater the agency costs.

Most multinationals tie some share of incentive compensation for senior executives to global performance. The debate is always over the weight that should be on the global, as opposed to the local, component. Typically that balance shifts as executives ascend the hierarchy and their involvement in activities and decisions that affect global performance increases. Junior executives in a country, for example, will have nearly all incentive compensation tied to local performance. A country manager might have 20% tied to global performance, and a regional head perhaps 50%.

Diversity

If a multinational is to become truly geocentric, it should be capable of coping with the diversity of individual backgrounds and country cultures. Indeed, diversity can be **one of the benefits of agglomeration** that multinationals can exploit. Certainly no firm can, like Boeing only 15 years ago, succeed with less than 2% of its senior management being non-American.

While national stereotypes abound and are the fount of many ill-directed jokes, much research has examined the nature and extent of cultural differences around the world.[13] There are substantive debates about the dimensions on which cultures differ, the magnitude of those differences, and the importance of national differences to individual behavior. This last qualification is particularly relevant. Because individuals are multifaceted, their behavior is influenced by many aspects of their background other than nationality, including gender, marital status, religion, profession, and even the values of the entity they work for. As usual, we do not dwell on those debates, but focus on the pragmatic implications of what is generally accepted.

Dimensions, Extent, and Implications of Cultural Differences   All countries have different cultures. The question is whether there are predictable regularities in those differences, and whether they exert such an influence on behavior that executives must act and lead in fundamentally different ways when managing in those different cultures. Put simply, are the ever-present cultural differences merely a **matter of degree** – norms that have to be respected and adhered to when working in a foreign culture – or a **matter of substance,** which cause the nature of the managerial task itself to change?

At one extreme, of course, when I am in Japan I will carry business cards with my name in Japanese to present at meetings; I will not put my feet on the table in Arab countries since showing the soles of your shoes is offensive to Muslims; and so on. These overt manifestations of culture, important though they are when working in different countries, at some level only require sensitivity training in order to raise awareness and allow managers to follow the mantra "when in Rome, do as the Romans do." Indeed, most companies typically give an "onboarding" introduction to local norms and behaviors when a foreign manager arrives in a new country so that he or she never inadvertently violates such expectations.

At the other extreme are fundamental differences in attitudes to authority or hierarchy that demand different leadership styles in foreign countries. Such substantive differences might influence how you negotiate in different cultures, the appropriate organization structure, the skills required for managers in different positions, and even the layout of offices.[14] If they exist, there would be a real need for global managers to learn more than just the basics of sensitivity training.

In fact, there is sufficient evidence of systematic cultural differences on enough important dimensions to be concerned that managing across cultures does require more than cursory adjustments to local norms. Although researchers have used many different instruments and sought to measure many different, if related, dimensions of culture, there is a consensus that **culture matters** because at least some important behaviors are not universal but are culturally contingent.

Perhaps the best known study is the World Values Survey. As with most such research, respondents in many countries are asked a series of questions that typically ask them to rank or rate certain items on a scale – "how important is EQUALITY (equal opportunity for all) as a guiding principle in your life?" Answers position a nationality on a number of dimensions that are believed to correlate with underlying psychological or sociological phenomena. In work by Schwartz, for example, the cultural orientations identified vary from harmony – "fitting into the world as it is, trying to understand and appreciate rather than to change, direct, or to exploit" – to hierarchy – in which "people are socialized to take the hierarchical distribution of roles for granted and to comply with the obligations and rules attached to their roles".[15]

These dimensions are then aggregated to categorize nations into a limited number of distinct types. The World Values Survey (Exhibit 10.12), for example, finds that two dimensions – survival versus self expression, and traditional versus secular–rational values – effectively map differences between cultures.[16] Another study by Andre Laurent argues for the existence of a Blue and a Green culture within Europe (reported in Schneider and Barsoux, 2002). Blue types are goal directed, wanting little oversight, and have a clear sense of time. Green types are much looser on punctuality, more

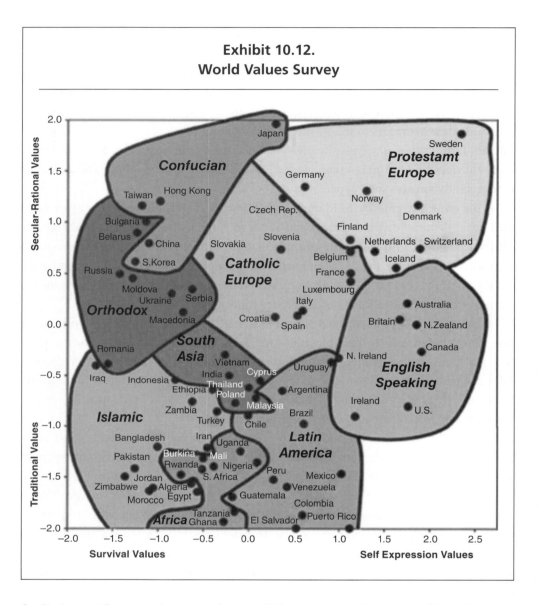

Exhibit 10.12.
World Values Survey

fatalistic, avoid uncertainty… and so on (I leave you to place yourself, and various European countries, among the two categories!).

The aggregate dimensions do not directly translate into managerially relevant factors, even though they were compiled from questions that probed behaviors and beliefs at the micro-level. In fact, perhaps the easier way to understand why leadership should be contingent on culture is to examine cultural differences in specific work-related behaviors. One example (Exhibit 10.13) resonates with discussions of cross-cultural experience that I have been involved in.

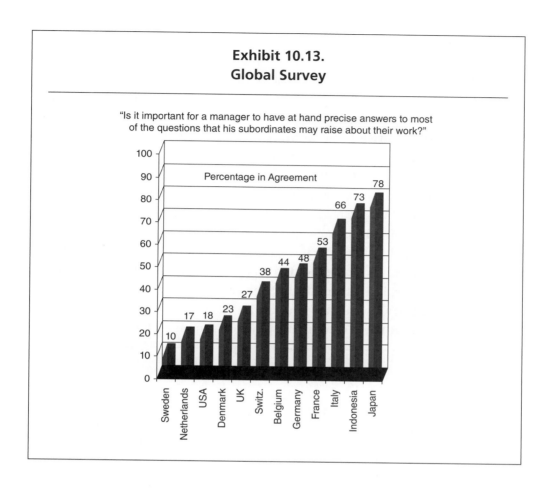

**Exhibit 10.13.
Global Survey**

"Is it important for a manager to have at hand precise answers to most of the questions that his subordinates may raise about their work?"

Percentage in Agreement

Sweden 10, Netherlands 17, USA 18, Denmark 23, UK 27, Switz. 38, Belgium 44, Germany 48, France 53, Italy 66, Indonesia 73, Japan 78

Andre Laurent explicitly probed whether there were systematic differences in national attitudes to the importance of hierarchical superiors being qualified as technical experts in their field. He found that the USA and UK were accepting of bosses who were not masters of the subject for which they were responsible. Japan and Italy, however, demanded bosses who knew their stuff. I remember one heated class discussion where an Italian made exactly this argument to explain why a multinational should not place an American expatriate with an MBA but no manufacturing background as a plant manager in Italy. The American and British students begged to differ. Here is a real example of why cultural differences matter. If it is unacceptable in Italy to have a generalist in a senior functional position, multinationals cannot pursue the sort of career rotation described above in their Italian subsidiary. When fundamental management decisions have to be made differently in different countries, cultural heterogeneity has strategic implications.

(d) Purpose

Principles

The previous section stressed the importance of geocentric managers pursuing the global interests of the firm rather than parochial self-interest. To truly embed the ability to balance strategic tradeoffs in a multinational requires the dissemination of a distinctive corporate **purpose** that describes, communicates, celebrates, and rewards such values and behaviors (Ghoshal and Bartlett, 1999).

It is trite these days to talk of the importance of having a corporate vision and a shared sense of mission for all employees.[17] However, the easiest way to run an organization is when members act, not because they are incentivized to do so, but because they have fully internalized the firm's interests. While a little frightening, the principle of shared purpose leading to corporate success is compelling (see box). The ultimate goal for a multinational is to create **the matrix in people's minds** (Ghoshal and Bartlett, 1999). If this can be achieved, then all other elements of organization design are moot, since every individual will voluntarily internalize the tradeoffs inherent in competing across borders to make the best decision for the company as a whole.

Clan Control

Earlier we mentioned that organization design can employ behavior, outcome, or clan control of delegated decision making. The first two of those mechanisms are commonly found in large multinational corporations. However, we should not underestimate the potential of **clan control** to drive behavior in the global corporate interest. The intent is to have members of the organization internalize the values and objectives of the entity to the extent that they subordinate their self-interest to the good of the whole. Although this sounds spooky – being redolent of cults – when people identify their ego with organizational goals (think how football club supporters feel after their team loses), the management process does become simpler. Indeed, many corporations, typically those that feature a charismatic founder, like Apple, benefit from a lighter version of clan control – "I get such personal fulfillment and psychic benefit from telling people that I work for Apple that I do everything I can to make the company successful, even if it comes at personal cost, like working twenty hours a day."

This purpose describes the values and behaviors required to create a **global mindset** in every employee whose attributes can best be described as:

- "How does leveraging the company's international presence give me an unfair advantage in my country?"

- "How can I accommodate my country differences with the least sacrifice to the company's system-wide advantages?"

The former is obvious and easy for any manager to buy into. An example was AT&T's international wireless business that shamelessly leveraged experience, reputation, and even people from the USA when entering new countries.

The latter is much harder, and its presence is almost the acid test of having built a global purpose throughout the organization. A classic example was the photocopier business of Canon. A global team was put together, based in Japan and with ultimate responsibility lying with the Japanese R&D group, to develop a new global copier. However, paper size varies around the world, and Japan's standard is for a longer page than the US letter size. After much discussion, the team agreed that the new global copier would not actually be large enough for Japanese paper! Rather than veto the copier, the Japanese members got creative about how they could use that machine. By adding an attachment they turned it into a successful copier for business cards – which we all know are central to doing business in Japan (Porter and Ishikura, 1983). That is the sort of attitude engendered by having a global purpose – not just a willingness to sacrifice self-interest, but an ability to turn the apparent liabilities of the global organization into opportunities.

The most important lesson about purpose is that, unlike processes, it has to be **consistently and continually communicated**. The only way to effectively embed a unifying purpose is to repeat the same simple message until it is rooted in everything the firm does. Percy Barnevik, who in his time was celebrated as the creator of the "transnational" organization ABB, was reputed to manage this way. Chris Bartlett tells a revealing story in this regard. He visited Mr Barnevik in the low-rise (three-story) corporate headquarters of ABB in Zurich, Switzerland. On asking Barnevik the secret of his success, Chris was surprised to hear Barnevik's response in his lilting Swedish accent that it was all due to "overhead!" This was at a time when Barnevik was making a name for himself as the proponent of a 30/30/30 approach to reducing headquarters overhead – 30% of every overhead function's activities should be stopped, 30% outsourced, and 30% delegated to the business units. What Chris quickly realized was that Barnevik was referring to a case full of overheads – the transparencies that were used in presentations before the advent of LCD projectors! Barnevik viewed his primary task as repeating the same vision over and over again to every part of the organization, in order to inculcate a shared sense of purpose.

As important as the message is the behavior of senior management. If senior executives do not walk the talk and represent the values they articulate in every action, the organization will never accept the message. Senior executives in multinationals therefore have to be the embodiment of the firm's purpose or everything else will fail. This is why modern evaluation systems typically monitor progress against the twin dimensions of what was achieved (performance) and how it was achieved (behavior and values), with **promotion and compensation** typically conditional on meeting a minimum standard on the latter, not the former dimension.[18]

STRATEGIC FIT/CHOICE

While many of the ideas and suggestions described above are relevant to every multinational, the specific form that each design element should take must match the underlying international strategy.

Local

Other than observing that a purely local firm will have a functional structure, there is little interesting to be said apropos organization design since the underlying strategic tradeoffs are not present.

Export

This strategy involves a limited foreign presence with most activity outside the home market conducted by third parties. Accordingly, a functional domestic structure can be supplemented by an international department that independently administers global sales. Transfers to foreign markets from domestic operations will take place at full cost, and the international department will be treated as a profit center rewarded on the standalone profitability of its activities. Foreign pricing will, therefore, be the responsibility of the international head as there are no interdependencies with domestic operations. Similarly, it will be the international department that determines the optimal form of contractual relations in each foreign market, whether agency, distributor, etc. Perhaps the only important coordination issues concern demand forecasting, since the home production unit needs input into its capacity-scheduling system. Thus, integrating international and domestic order management systems may be necessary.

Multidomestic

The multidomestic strategy requires local responsiveness, so multinationals pursuing that strategy typically adopt a geographic structure. Country managers reign supreme and are given autonomy to act as necessary within their market.

To benefit from the company's knowhow (FSAs) and to continue to leverage ideas and processes, the geographic structure requires the ongoing transfer of skills and knowledge. Since these are vested in individuals, multidomestic firms extensively employ expatriates in senior positions and require every key headquarters executive, such as a global head of marketing, to have rotated outside the home country. This policy is enhanced by regular cross-country meetings at the functional level to support knowledge transfer, and typically involves operational data being available around the world to facilitate benchmarking of new methods and new policies. Nevertheless, these processes will tend to be informal and lower down the coordination hierarchy because decision rights remain with country management.

The multidomestic must also maintain a flow of new products. Traditionally these would have originated in the home country and then cascaded throughout the world on a timetable corresponding to "distance," broadly defined, from the home country. Today, even the multidomestic will look for new ideas everywhere around the world. If, by chance, a successful development appears somewhere, the loose coordinative role played by the global business unit can facilitate its transfer and so continue to augment the product offering in every geography.

Coordination conflicts for the multidomestic strategy primarily concern replication of functions, R&D and manufacturing in particular, throughout the globe rather than concentrating them in a limited number of locations. To limit this inefficiency, informal processes and coordination devices will be employed, including personal networks and ad hoc teams addressing specific issues, such as the location of the next plant. Again, these processes will be among the lower rungs of the coordination hierarchy, perhaps featuring at most a worldwide business strategy team that has responsibility, but not authority, for resolving conflicts between countries and functions.

Compensation will primarily be tied to country performance, since authority for most decisions is granted to the country manager. Transfer prices, to the extent that they are necessary because of limited product flows between countries, would be at market or negotiated prices.

Global

The preferred structure to achieve the efficiency of the global strategy is global product divisions with the global business head accountable for profitability and given authority over country and functional management. It is the head's responsibility to maximize global performance and she will have decision rights over plant location, product development strategy, and so on. In this structure the relatively common transfers along the coordinated global supply chain would be at cost, so no issues of double marginalization prevent reaching the global optimum.

Country-based management is subordinate to the global business unit headquarters in the strategy, and local executives will not move frequently between countries. Instead, they are likely to be hired into the business locally, perhaps trained at headquarters, before being transferred back to their domicile for the rest of their career where their local knowledge gives them an advantage.

In this structure, coordination is required across two dimensions: across activities within a country, and across functions, such as R&D. To remedy the first problem, the country manager will have responsibility for a set of activities, such as government relations, labor relations, communications, and PR that benefit from intra-country coordination. Country managers might also establish central service units for back office functions, like payroll, IT, and real estate, that could profitably be shared across businesses in their country. To address coordination at the functional level – to prevent there being, as I once discovered, seven LCD development initiatives within Honeywell – there will be some use of coordination processes, such as functional committees, that cut across businesses.

Regional/Triad

The essence of the regional or Triad strategy is to be "global" within a region and "multidomestic" between regions. The resulting organization structure should reflect this goal with a regional structure overseeing country operations, while global headquarters ensures that knowledge and ideas and innovations are transferred across regions.

The result will be a small global headquarters which focuses on developing and transferring valuable corporate skills and capabilities around the world. Regional headquarters will be more substantive since they have operational responsibility for country performance. The degree to which they centralize activities within their regions will then depend on the benefit of such policies in their area.

Within this structure, HR policies are set more within the region than globally and most personnel transfers will occur within regions. A cadre of corporate executives might well move across regions in order to transfer knowledge and retain some degree of control over regional operations, but most careers will be within a region. Culture will probably differ between the regions. Some professional service firms, for example, particularly those that are partnerships, will have cultures that differ between geographies. Others, like McKinsey, try to create a shared purpose that unifies and distinguishes the firm globally and through time.

Transnational

It is this international strategy that places most emphasis on balancing the three dimensions or axes of management. As such, it is for this strategy that the notion of a structure alone being able to solve all management tensions is least tenable. Accordingly, a transnational should adopt the formal structure that is most appropriate at that point in time and that best fits with the company's administrative heritage. The challenge is then to layer on the processes, people, and purpose to create the matrix in managers' minds. Most of the discussion in the previous sections is therefore relevant as it outlined ideas for achieving this goal. None of them is *the* solution. All of them are ingredients in a solution, but employing them in the right mix at every point in time is hard.[19] This is why, however appealing the advantages of the transnational, the complexity of its management challenge will inevitably lead some multinationals to prefer a simpler organizational solution, even if it has less ambition as to the advantages it might exploit. For some companies, more effectively implementing a less sophisticated strategy might be the preferred approach!

NOTES

1. This anecdote is a composite of interactions with several students.
2. This sets aside the customer dimension mentioned in the motivation, which can be important for some firms, such as consultants and accounting firms, or those with global clients.
3. See the original literature on the tradeoff between differentiation and integration in Lawrence, P. and Lorsch, J. (1967) Differentiation and integration in complex organizations. *Administrative Science Quarterly*, 12, 1–30.
4. This is a recategorization of categories in the typology – centralization, formalization, informational, and socialization.
5. When I went to business school in the late 1970s, that solution was inevitably the matrix organization.
6. See Pang, L. (2001) Understanding virtual organizations. IASCA Journal, accessed at http://www .isaca.org/Journal/Past-Issues/2001/Volume-6/Pages/Understanding-Virtual-Organizations.aspx.
7. We cannot cover all of the processes employed in multinationals, like capital budgeting, that are found in any hierarchy, but focus on those that are particularly salient in the international context.
8. Notice how the allocation of decision rights overlaps with the discussion of the platform product in Chapter 5. Drawing the line between the front and the back of the platform has to be paralleled by an appropriate allocation of authority for different aspects of the marketing mix.
9. Ghemawat notes that perhaps 1% of executives in large multinationals are on expatriate assignment at any one time (Ghemawat, P. (2011) The globalization of firms. IESE Globalization Note Series.)
10. HCR Group (2012) 75% of CEOs have it: the key to career progression. May 23, accessed at https:// www.hcr.co.uk/?page=BlogandNews&article=251.
11. See Ghemawat, P. (2011) The globalization of firms. IESE Globalization Note Series, accessed at http://www.ghemawat.com/management/files/AcademicResources/GlobalizationofFirms.pdf, where he refers to the Egon Zehnder study.
12. Lenovo, the Chinese PC manufacturer, for example, has English as its official language; see *The Economist* (2013) From guard shack to global giant. January 12, p. 56. Also Neeley, T. (2012) Global business speaks English: why you need a language strategy now. *Harvard Business Review*, 90(5), 116–124.
13. See, for example, Hofstede, G., Hofstede, J., and Minkov, M. (2010) *Cultures and Organizations: Software of the Mind*, 3rd edition. McGraw-Hill: New York; Laurent, A. (1983) The cultural diversity of western conceptions of management. *International Studies of Management and Organisation*, 13(1–2), 75–96; and World Values Survey, accessed at http://www.worldvaluessurvey.org/.
14. Steelcase plans to use its research on cultural differences in the design of its office furniture, see Larson, C. (2013) Office cultures: a global guide. *Business Week*, June 13, p. 15.
15. Schwartz, S. (2006) A theory of cultural value orientation: explication and application. *Comparative Sociology*, 5(2–3), 137–182.

16. Welzel, C. (2006) A human development view on value change, accessed at http://www.worldval uessurvey.org/wvs/articles/folder_published/article_base_83.
17. Indeed, studies of successful firms that find a common theme in the strong vision they adhered to overlook "survivor bias." Even unsuccessful firms probably had a grandiose vision – they just failed to deliver on it.
18. As Jack Welch said, "your values are the ticket that get you into the game."
19. A good description by Zander and Matthews summarized the original idea of Gunnar Hedlund's "hypermodern MNC – a heterarchy" as "multicentered and differentiated internal structures, significantly enhanced strategic roles of foreign subsidiaries, lateral information flows, integration primarily through normative control, flexibility in organizational tasks and governance mechanisms" (Zander, I. and Mathews, J.A. (2010) Beyond heterarchy – emerging futures of the "hypermodern" MNC. In U. Andersson and U. Holm (eds.) *Managing the Contemporary Multinational*. Edward Elgar: Cheltenham, p. 35).

REFERENCES AND FURTHER READING

Aghion, P. and Tirole, P. (1997) Formal and real authority in organizations. *Journal of Political Economy*, 105(1), 1–29.

Alonso, R., Dessein, W., and Matouschek, N. (2008) When does coordination require centralization? *American Economic Review*, 98(1), 145–179.

Anand, J. (2011) Permeability to inter- and intrafirm knowledge flows: the role of coordination and hierarchy in MNEs. *Global Strategy Journal*, 1(3/4), 283–300.

Andersson, U. and Holm, U. (2010) *Managing the Contemporary Multinational: The Role of Headquarters*. Edward Elgar: Cheltenham.

Baiman, S., Larcker, D.F., and Rajan, M.V. (1995) Organizational design for business units. *Journal of Accounting Research*, 33(2), 205–229.

Bartlett, C. (1983) Get off the organisational merry go round. *Harvard Business Review*, 61(2), 138–146.

Bartlett, C.A. and Ghoshal, S. (1998) *Managing Across Borders: The Transnational Solution*. Harvard Business School Press: Cambridge, MA.

Bartlett, C.A. and Ghoshal, S. (2003) What is a global manager? *Harvard Business Review*, 81(8), 101–108.

Benito, G.R.G., Lunnan, R., and Tomassen, S. (2011) Distant encounters of the third kind: multinational companies locating divisional headquarters abroad. *Journal of Management Studies*, 28(20), 373–394.

Björkman, I., Barner-Rasmussen, W., and Li, L. (2004) Management knowledge transfer in MNCs: the impact of headquarters control mechanisms. *Journal of International Business Studies*, 35(5), 443–455.

Campbell, A. and Luchs, K. (eds.) (1998) *Strategic Synergy*. International Thomson Business Press: London.

Chandler, Jr., A.D. (1962) *Strategy and Structure: Chapters in the History of the American Industrial Enterprise*. MIT Press: Cambridge, MA.

Child, D., Goold, M., and Campbell, A. (2002) *Designing Effective Organisations*. Thomson: London.

Ciabuschi, F., Dellestrand, H., and Holm, U. (2012) The role of headquarters in the contemporary MNC. *Journal of International Management*, 18(3), 213–223.

Collis, D. and Goold, M. (2005) Benchmarking your staff. *Harvard Business Review*, 83(9), 28–30.

Collis, D., Goold, M., and Young, D. (2007) The size, structure, and performance of corporate headquarters. *Strategic Management Journal*, 28(4), 383–405.

Collis, D., Goold, M., and Young, D. (2012) The size and composition of corporate headquarters in multinational companies: empirical evidence. *Journal of International Management*, 18(3), 260–275.

Collis, D. and Montgomery, C. (2005) *Corporate Strategy: A Resource-based Approach*, 2nd edition. McGraw-Hill Irwin: Boston, MA.

Edmondson, A. and Lane, D. (2012) *Global knowledge management at Danone (A) abridged*. Harvard Business School Case #613-003.

Egelhoff, W.G. (1982) Strategy and structure in multinational corporations: an information processing approach. *Administrative Science Quarterly*, 27(3), 435–458.

Egelhoff, W.G. (2010) How the parent headquarters adds value to an MNC. *Management International Review*, 50(4), 413–431.

Egelhoff, W.G., Wolf, J., and Adzic, M. (2013) Designing matrix structures to fit MNC strategy. *Global Strategy Journal*, 3(3), 205–226.

Eisenhardt, K. (1985) Control: organizational and economic approaches. *Management Science*, 31(2), 134–149.

Enright, M.J. (2005) The roles of regional management centers. *Management International Review*, 45(1), 83–102.

Foss, N. (1997) On the rationales of corporate headquarters. *Industrial and Corporate Change*, 6(2), 313–338.

Frost, T., Birkinshaw, J.M., and Ensign, P. (2002) Centers of excellence in multinational corporations. *Strategic Management Journal*, 23(11), 997–1018.

Galbraith, J.R. (2000) *Designing the Global Corporation*. Jossey-Bass: San Francisco.

Galbraith, J.R. (2008) *Designing Matrix Organizations that Actually Work: How IBM, Procter & Gamble and Others Design for Success*. Jossey-Bass: San Francisco.

Galbraith, J. and Kazanjian, R. (1986) *Strategy Implementation: Structure, Systems, and Process*. West Publishing: St. Paul, MN.

Ghoshal, S. and Bartlett, C. (1999) *The Individualized Corporation: A Fundamentally New Approach to Management*. HarperBusiness: New York.

Ghoshal, S. and Nohria, N. (1993) Horses for courses: organizational forms for multinational corporations. *MIT Sloan Management Review*, 34(2), 23–35.

Gulati, R. (2010) *Reorganize for Resilience: Putting Customers at the Center of Your Organization*. Harvard Business School Press: Boston, MA.

Hedlund, G. (1986) The hypermodern MNC—a heterarchy? *Human Resource Management*, 25(1), 9–35.

Hofstede, G. (1983) The cultural relativity of organizational practices and theories. *Journal of International Business Studies*, 14(2), 75–89.

Hofstede, G. (1988) *Culture's Consequences: International Differences in Work-Related Values*. Sage: Thousand Oaks, CA.

Javidan, M. and Walker, J. (2013) *Developing Your Global Mindset*. Beaver's Pond Press: Edina, MN.

Laurent, A. (1983) The cultural diversity of western conceptions of management. *International Studies of Management and Organisation*, 13(1–2), 75–96.

Lawrence, P.R. and Lorsch, J.W. (1967) *Organization and Environment: Managing Differentiation and Integration*. Harvard Business School Press: Boston, MA.

March, J.G. (1991) Exploration and exploitation in organizational learning. *Organization Science*, 2(1), 71–87.

Mudambi, R. (2011) Hierarchy, coordination, and innovation in the multinational enterprise. *Global Strategy Journal*, 1(3/4), 317–323.

Nell, P.C. and Ambos, B. (2013) Parenting advantage in the MNC: an embeddedness perspective on the value added by headquarters. *Strategic Management Journal*, 34(9), 1086–1103.

Nohria, N. and Ghoshal, S. (1997) *The Differentiated Network: Organizing Multinational Corporations for Value Creation*. Jossey Bass: San Francisco.

Ouchi, W.G. (1979) A conceptual framework for the design of organizational control mechanisms. *Management Science*, 25(9), 833–848.

Perlmutter, H.V. (1969) The tortuous evolution of the multinational corporation. *Columbia Journal of World Business*, 4(1), 9–18.

Porter, M. and Ishikura, Y. (1983) *Canon Inc.: worldwide copier strategy*. Harvard Business School Case #384-151.

Punnett, B. (2013) *International Perspectives on Organizational Behavior and Human Resource Management*, 3rd edition. M. E. Sharpe: Armonk, NY.

Quelch, J. and Jocz, K. (2012) *All Business is Local: Why Place Matters More Than Ever in a Global, Virtual World*. Portfolio/Penguin: New York.

Roberts, J. (2004) *The Modern Firm: Organizational Design for Performance and Growth*. Oxford University Press: Oxford.

Rogers, P. and Blenko, M. (2006) Who has the D? How clear decision roles enhance organizational performance. *Harvard Business Review*, 84(1), 53–56.

Schneider, S. and Barsoux, J.-L. (2002) *Managing Across Cultures*, 2nd edition. Prentice Hall: New York.

Schwartz, S. (2006) A theory of cultural value orientations: explication and application. *Comparative Sociology*, 5(2–3), 137–182.

Shenkar, O. (2001) Cultural distance revisited: towards a more rigorous conceptualization and measurement of cultural differences. *Journal of International Business Studies*, 32(3), 519–535.

Stopford, J.M. and Wells, L.T. (1972) *Managing the Multinational Enterprise: Organization of the Firm and Ownership of the Subsidiaries*. Basic Books: New York.

Tallman, S. and Koza, M.P. (2010) Keeping the global in mind: the evolution of the headquarters' role in global multi-business firms. *Management International Review*, 50(4), 433–448.

Verbeke, A. and Kenworthy, T.P. (2008) Multidivisional vs metanational governance of the multinational enterprise. *Journal of International Business Studies*, 39(6), 940–956.

Yoshino, M. and Bartlett, C. (1986) Corning Glassworks International (A). Harvard Business School Case #381-160.

The Modern Multinational
Is There One Best Strategy?
Are We All Transnational Now?

MOTIVATION

The preface began with a story about three books on global strategy. I conclude with three examples from recent Harvard Business School cases describing developments at ostensibly similar and successful FMCG multinationals – Danone, Unilever, and L'Oréal. And yet when you peel away the veneer of superficially similar global operations you see three very different approaches to competing internationally. Three different answers to the observation at Unilever that "you always have local consumers and you have the (product) categories – the question is not whether the tension is good or bad; the tension is good. The question is how you manage the tension."[1]

Danone believes that decentralization is essential to its **multidomestic** strategy. As the head of HR observed, "we think there are more disadvantages than advantages in looking for synergies, and the success of our decentralized management can be seen in our local brands." "At Danone a managing director who is in charge of an activity in a country is the decision maker with P&L responsibility. Headquarters can merely suggest options to him, but cannot impose conditions."[2]

Consistent with its heritage of a flexible – *jeu de jambe*[3] – approach to management, Danone is moving "from a Western European company into an international organization with operations worldwide" so that "we can launch in 3 months while it takes Nestlé an average of 12–18 months to get a new product to the market." However, identifying and promoting adoption of global best practices remains problematic within Danone, and cross-functional teams cooperating to launch a new regional product found that "the work was done on top of their normal job. You needed to convince a local general manager to support it because people have other things to do."

Unilever, while ostensibly moving toward "One Unilever," was pursuing a **Triad or regional** strategy: "I'm looking for the sweet spot where I'm better than the global guy because I have the local connectivity, but I'm better than the local guy because I have technological innovations and knowledge coming into my country that he can't replicate."[4] While moving from 70 to 10 operating companies worldwide, the number of factories was cut from 90 to 65, distribution centers from 600 to 300, and the number of brands reduced. However, planning was done on a regional basis so that reduced product complexity across countries, built around a supply chain that could flexibly respond to individual country needs, rewarded regional approaches to product development.

Before the regional consolidation, individual country directors managed the end-to-end supply chain for their market. Afterward, factories reported to a regional supply chain manager who could make impartial decisions regarding capital allocation. This reduced the incentive for country directors to introduce market-specific products because they now paid a price when violating European scale economies. As the head of supply chain noted, "if you can piggyback on another product it will be cheaper to produce. If you decide not to harmonize it means the peculiarity of your market is worth the extra money."[5] As a result, the Knorr soup brand, for example, which had been nearly identical in terms of packaging and value proposition but had 64 different European tomato soup varieties customized for different tastes, was rationalized to less than 24 variants.

P&L responsibility within Unilever Europe remained at the country group level (a related set of individual countries), but now bonuses were partially tied to European performance. But all of this activity involved very little integration outside the region. The attempt of a senior executive to bring "The Perfect Store" concept from Asia, for example, was initially rejected because it was not obvious that it would work in Europe.

L'Oréal, in contrast, is pursuing a **transnational** strategy it calls "universalization" – careful organizational orchestration, ability to transfer learning across geographies, a deep understanding of customer needs across regions, and speed to market. The intent is to have global brands, "you need a global brand, which is then adapted to the key markets in order to offer consumers the right and relevant products, which is what universalization is about,"[6] so that international brand managers "imagine that each brand is a box. … Our managers around the world know that they can't play with the position of the brands, We don't play with the boxes. The trick is to do innovative things inside of each box." In contrast, "decentralized consumer goods companies with many brands can fracture into as many little parts if somebody isn't pulling it back the other way the whole time with a central vision."[7]

A matrix organization at L'Oréal leaves P&L responsibility with countries, with regional zones bridging between them and the Direction Marketing International. However, competences are distributed to certain subsidiaries: "we have now localized in the big markets marketing competence and laboratories that use local raw materials and analyze how products work in local skin and hair."[8] Product development depends on global coordination since "teams made up of diverse profiles cover any issue from multiple angles and thus come up with more holistic approaches."[9] However, "some innovation is done locally. Some flexibility in the mindset is needed and headquarters needs to give some freedom to local management" (note the careful use of the qualifier "some" by a local manager!).

P&G, to squeeze in a fourth example, is pursuing the most **globally** coordinated approach – as A.G. Lafley stated, "One thing we've worked on real hard in the last 5– 10 years is becoming a truly global company" – although its manifestation is closer to the transnational strategy. A global purpose, value, and principles (PVP), initially written in 1987, unifies the company since "the more international and the larger we become, the more important the PVP is because it's the center post."[10] The company's history of promoting from within creates a sense of community and a familial loyalty among so-called "proctoids." That culture, which focuses on ensuring the future of the company as a whole, unifies the organization. Similarly, the extensive transfer of many executives around the world ensures integration and cooperation, even though only three of the original seven Global Business Units are now at Cincinnati headquarters. P&G's 2005 matrix organization (pictured in Chapter 10) only reinforces this collective philosophy.

Thus, three different strategies in the same sector – all of which have been successful. At the end of the book, we can therefore reinforce the message that success in international competition comes from choosing one generic international strategy and effectively implementing that by aligning choices about products, geographic scope, configuration of activities, and organization design with the chosen source of international advantage.

SHOULD WE ALL BE TRANSNATIONAL NOW?

But perhaps the reader is struggling to reconcile the conclusion that there is no one right international strategy with a couple of other ideas expressed in the text. First, that there is a dominant or "best" international strategy which all firms should aspire to pursue – the transnational. From a combination of policies identified in Part 3, this answers the four fundamental decisions in a way that transcends their underlying strategic tradeoffs and delivers all four international advantages. Indeed, this was the argument of perhaps the most influential book on international strategy by Bartlett and Ghoshal in 2002.

The second tension is between the assertion that multinationals must make a discrete choice among a set of mutually exclusive generic international strategies – a company cannot be both multidomestic and global at the same time since that would introduce inconsistencies into its strategic choices – and the possibility that splitting the value chain and pursuing the best strategy for each part of the chain – perhaps arbitraging input purchases, globalizing R&D, and localizing sales and service – create a mixed strategy that improves overall performance. Indeed, this is a large part of the transnational strategy – carefully differentiating the configuration of activities to realize the most relevant international advantage for each one.

The text has postponed to last these two transcendent questions: Is there one "best" strategy? Do companies have to choose one strategy? To answer these we will outline what the "best" strategy might look like, but then argue that even this approach, which appears to combine multiple strategies, has its limits and ultimately requires the multinational to make a discrete choice among international strategies.

What Would the One "Best" Strategy Look Like?

If we believe there is a single best strategy, it is surely the transnational strategy, introduced by Bartlett and Ghoshal and outlined in Chapter 5. After looking in detail at each of the four critical decisions that multinationals confront, we can now revisit the specifics of that strategy to elucidate what appears to be the ideal approach to international competition.

First, we convey the power of the transnational strategy by describing the international advantages it can exploit. Second, we outline the approach taken to each of the four critical choices that enables the transnational to realize those advantages. Then we point out why this solution remains so hard to implement, and therefore why many firms are better off pursuing a less managerially demanding international strategy.

International Advantage

The first advantage of the transnational is the ability to **augment** product space in countries around the world. Replicating a successful and well-established product and positioning in countries that lacked such an offering was the advantage that the traditional horizontal multinational exploited. The transnational is no different in that regard. However, the transnational now goes beyond this by leveraging its coordinated global network of operations to continually introduce innovative products and processes from wherever they originate to everywhere throughout the globe.

The second advantage of the transnational strategy is its ability to **arbitrage** factor cost differences between countries. This was the traditional benefit exploited by the vertical multinational as it sourced inputs from the most favorable locations around the world. Similarly, the transnational will search the world to identify the optimal country in which to locate different activities and source its inputs. But the transnational even improves on this advantage by continually reoptimizing among a coordinated network of dispersed operations.

The third advantage the transnational can exploit is the scale and experience that come from **aggregation.** The ability to drive efficiency by selling a single product around the world is what gave the original proponents of the global strategy their advantage. The transnational achieves this by standardizing those aspects of the business model and activities that truly benefit from scale economies, while allowing those aspects which differ between countries and substantially affect customers' willingness to pay, to vary between countries.

The fourth advantage exploited by the transnational is the **agglomeration** benefit accruing to a dispersed but coordinated global network of operations. Dynamic efficiency is the distinctive contribution of the transnational strategy to international competition as it introduces learning and innovation into the armory of multinational advantages. With locations throughout the globe and an organization capable of integrating those dispersed activities, the transnational ensures it makes the most of continually changing arbitrage opportunities, and leverages its knowledge, whether product or process, throughout the entire company from wherever in the world that learning may originate.[11]

Critical Decisions

Appealing though the transnational sounds in its ability to exploit all four international advantages, its challenge lies in being able to realize those four advantages at the same time. After all, the argument is that exploiting each advantage requires making incompatible choices. While strategy gurus have achieved fame by suggesting that a choice between "either/or" can be replaced with "and" so as to get the best of both worlds, superseding a tradeoff remains difficult. Can the transnational strike a balance regarding the number of products, countries, locations, and organizational units that allows it to achieve all advantages, or will that lead to a failure to configure itself to exploit any one advantage?

Product The platform approach described in Chapter 7 ostensibly allows for the exploitation of the efficiencies of product standardization along with the ability to adapt products to local requirements. The key to doing so is to carefully separate out those components of the product or service that truly benefit from scale economies from those that are critical to local acceptance. While this is simple to say, as we suggested in Chapter 7, it is hard to achieve. Stating that a "green line" exists between the globally standardized and locally variable elements of the "product" only begins the discussion of where to draw that line. In those often acrimonious debates, the entire tradeoff between global efficiency and local responsiveness gets played out without any easy or obvious resolution. Indeed, it might turn out, for example, that since it is demand for the car's engine which varies by country, but the engine is the only component that is scale sensitive, there is simply no way to square the circle and have large-volume output of an adaptable engine! Thus, while the platform product concept remains valuable to all multinationals, it is not a silver bullet that can always transcend the tradeoff between local responsiveness and global efficiency.

Compete The transnational resolves the tradeoff between the efficiency of global scope and the simplicity of serving homogeneous markets by competing in all strategically important countries – whether important because of their size, or by virtue of their being the domicile of a key competitor, or a leading source of product or process innovation. Competing in those countries (and all others that are inherently similar to the company's core geography) ensures that it will have adequate scale and an insider's presence in leading edge markets without spreading its footprint into geographies requiring a very different business model. However, notice the weakness in this argument. What if one of the large and leading edge countries, such as China, is really different than the domestic market? Pursuing global scale would lead to a different prescription regarding a Chinese presence than pursuing simplicity. Again, while sounding good, there can be occasions when the "strategically important" mandate simply cannot be implemented in a way that avoids conflicts with the "similar" markets requirement.

Location The transnational's configuration of activities seeks to resolve the tradeoff between concentrating activities in a single location, which is optimal for exploiting scale economies and static factor cost advantages, and having multiple locations that allow for dynamic optimization and the continuous transfer of learning across the organization. One way to achieve this is the Triad configuration, featuring relatively discrete operations in each of the three major regions but a more concentrated set of facilities inside each region. This configuration should achieve the best of both worlds by combining efficiency within a region with variety and dynamic arbitrage across regions.

While good as far as it goes, the Triad solution is only a middle course. It does not go as far as a global strategy and so concedes some scale benefits. Nor does it go to the extreme of the multidomestic strategy and so is not as locally adaptive as that strategy. As an in-between configuration, it runs the risk of losing advantage to strategies pursuing the more extreme choices.

Organization The final decision for the transnational concerns its organization design. The dilemma can be characterized as choosing between multiple units (typically with one in each country to maximize high-powered incentives) and a more unitary design that centralizes and coordinates activities across geographies. The transnational reconciles this tradeoff, possibly by adopting a matrix structure that balances competing organizational dimensions,[12] but more generally by creating a unifying corporate purpose and a "matrix in the mind" of its key executives, as described at P&G. Rather than viewing structure as the solution, the transnational emphasizes people and processes, developing a cadre of geocentric executives and utilizing cross-cutting horizontal systems and teams to offset the vertical dimension of whatever hierarchical structure is chosen.

The widespread dissatisfaction executives express when working within a matrix shows how hard it is for them to internalize the irreconcilable tradeoffs. Merely moving decisions to the front line and providing the experience, support, and incentives necessary for executives to consider the best interests of the enterprise in their evaluation do not ensure the effective resolution of the decisions. Thus, even though many of the softer organization design elements of the transnational have been adopted by leading multinationals, they do not transcend the inherent conflicts.

Summary

When we introduced the transnational strategy in Chapter 5, we made much of the importance of **balance** when making each of the strategic choices. But that just illustrates how hard this strategy is to implement. It does not provide simple solutions for every decision. Rather, it requires a nuanced and differentiated approach that fluctuates over time and across activities and geographies. This complexity is what makes managing the integrated network so challenging and why it is so easy to get wrong. Binary decisions are replaced by ambiguity and variability. This confuses and misleads executives who find it easier to operate with clearer direction and accountability. While some will flourish in the transnational (and implementing that strategy requires recruiting and developing such managers), other organizations will find greater success with a less ambitious strategy that pursues only one international advantage.

CAN YOU PURSUE MORE THAN ONE INTERNATIONAL STRATEGY AT A TIME?

The second way to reconcile the inherent strategic tradeoffs involved in international competition would not be to seek a single best strategy. Rather, multiple strategies would be pursued and multiple sources of advantage exploited at the same time by splitting the value chain into component activities, and selecting the optimal strategy for each part of the chain. Purchasing would be done globally, service performed locally, and so on. Indeed, one of the merits of the transnational design is that it strives for exactly this decomposition of the value chain (see box). Is this the solution for all multinationals? And does it enable the multinational to transcend the strategic tradeoffs?

Operational Efficiency Through Value Chain Decomposition

Consider a cryogenic industrial gases company that competes in many countries around the world and in several different businesses: on-site facilities to supply gases for manufacturing processes, such as steel; wholesale delivery of bulk liquid atmospheric gases; and local delivery of cylinder gases.[13]

In this multinational, the R&D and plant design groups might be centralized at headquarters with new plant construction contracted to a single global supplier. Production and purchasing might be regionalized so that plant locations are optimized and competitive interactions managed within contiguous geographies. Sales and marketing functions would be divided between businesses: at one extreme, the cylinder gas business would be managed locally; at the other extreme, key account managers would be in charge of global customers, like semiconductor manufacturers. The result is a company that can take advantage of scale in R&D, optimize manufacturing within regions, and yet still respond to local pricing and customer needs.

The good news is that the argument is partially correct. The bad news is that even this approach ultimately cannot reconcile all the strategic tradeoffs and so requires commitment to a single strategy.

Benefits

It is correct that today most multinationals pursue some version of value chain decomposition and optimize the strategy for each element of that chain. It is therefore clear that for many multinationals this "disaggregate and discriminate" approach is appropriate for much of what goes on inside the firm.

However, this approach can be thought of as the analog to **operational efficiency** in business unit strategy. If it makes sense to have a global purchasing group that optimizes raw material and component prices by sourcing around the world, then, of course, a firm should adopt that policy. In fact, we can go further and assert that multinationals that do not at least consider the merits of coordinated purchasing of important globally traded inputs will be far from operationally efficient. But even here there is a limit to how far global coordination should go, and which items should be bought centrally. At the extremes the balance of power is obvious – radio spots should be bought locally, while commodities, like copper, must be purchased globally. But as with all these decisions, the devil is in the detail, and there will always be a range of inputs for which there is no obvious solution. Should auto manufacturers source paint globally to leverage their scale, or should it be bought locally so that delivery and service can be interfaced with local assembly plants?

Every aspect of each activity cannot be cleanly decided on analytic grounds alone. While 80% of what goes on inside multinationals can be optimized according to obvious operational efficiencies, there will always be debates over that last 20% of decisions that require judgment to reconcile compelling arguments from both sides of a strategic tradeoff. No matter how careful the dissection of the value chain, a strategy is needed to resolve that set of contentious issues which frustrate even well-intentioned executives.

Drawbacks

As with competitive strategy a company should push to exploit as many advantages as it can. Even a differentiator cannot ignore cost. A low-cost competitor cannot offer a product that does not meet minimum customer requirements. The same is true in international competition. A firm can pursue operational efficiency as far as it can,[14] **but it ultimately has to adhere to one strategy** for two reasons.

First, as was suggested above, there are always elements of every activity that cannot be easily resolved by operational effectiveness alone – should a particular component be bought locally or sourced globally? Do we need a manufacturing facility in Africa to fill in the global footprint even if it is higher cost? Second, allowing each activity to be independently optimized will not yield the global optimum when conflicts emerge. A multinational cannot, for example, seek to consolidate the number of brands around the world while at the same time leaving marketing authority in geographic subsidiaries. Decisions that are interdependent must be decided jointly and according to the same criterion. That, after all, is the value and purpose of having a strategy – to align and integrate differentiated units. An overall strategic posture is needed to provide the unifying direction for decisions which, if solved independently or remaining a bone of contention between different constituencies within the multinational, will derail successful execution.

Summary

It is important to note that the chosen strategy does not mechanistically produce the answer to every tough decision, but it does provide a bias as to how to resolve every conflict. If nothing else, the strategy places the **onus of proof on why the default choice should be violated**, rather than on why it should be adopted. A multinational pursuing a multidomestic strategy, for example, is not prohibited from rationalizing production in a regional facility. However, it does require a compelling case to be made for that configuration. If the weight of evidence cannot demonstrate the superiority of the single facility, then the strategy would default to the geographies' preference for multiple plants.

At the end of the day, when the simple and obvious choices that drive operational efficiency without introducing a strategic tradeoff have been made – global purchasing of commodities, centralization of R&D, localization of sales and service, or whatever – there will always remain many hard choices (e.g., is paint to be bought globally or locally? Should we have an African facility?) whose resolution must revert to the overall strategy or require the weight of evidence to override the default selection.

That is why it remains so important to have agreed upon and communicated a clear statement of international strategy to act as the magnet aligning the tough choices that face empowered executives throughout the company every day. That is why in the final analysis every multinational does need to have committed to one or other of the generic international strategies.

SUCCESS IN INTERNATIONAL COMPETITION

So where does success in international competition come from? I think there are two components to the successful modern multinational.

Operational Efficiency

The first is ensuring that the firm drives operational efficiency. Following the recommendations in the chapters of Part 3 of this book should enable you to make choices for each of the four key decisions that, as far as possible, optimize performance of those different activities. This can be done regardless of which international strategy is being pursued. That is why many aspects of multinationals superficially appear to be the same. Everyone will have a global purchasing unit (though its scope of responsibility will vary according to the strategy). Everyone will have a "platform" approach to its product offering (though the proportion of the product that is standardized will vary by strategy). Everyone may have regionalized production (though the degree of local product adaptation will vary by strategy). All will have corporate HR groups striving to define a corporate purpose (although that vision will vary according to the strategy). And so on.

Employing all the tools and techniques outlined in this part should enable every multinational to approach the efficiency frontier. Doing so is a requirement of competing internationally, and all multinationals must strive to adopt best practices in those areas if they are to continuously improve. As Porter noted, the pursuit of operational efficiency is the race that never ends. But then ...

One International Strategy

Second, success ultimately comes from choosing, communicating, and implementing a coherent international strategy that allows each and every part of the organization to push to the productivity frontier, confident in the knowledge that it does so in a way that reinforces the decisions of the rest of the multinational.

There is typically not one best strategy to pursue in any given industry (with some obvious exceptions, like semiconductors). This implies that multinationals should not try to identify the best strategy, or, even worse, emulate other multinationals currently identified by gurus as having the latest and greatest strategy. Indeed, the denigration of strategy is to naively copy another's competitive advantage. It is, therefore, important to choose one strategy – the one that best fits your industry, business model, segment, administrative heritage, talent, competitive set, willingness to change, etc. – and spend your time and effort ensuring that you consistently align the actions of every part of the organization to realize the chosen international advantage.

That is why a succinct description of the international strategy, captured as a statement that describes the strategic objective, the scope of the core business model, and the advantage the firm seeks to exploit by virtue of its international activities and the constraints imposed on the four key configuration choices, is so important.

I hope that, in some small way, reading this text enables each and every one of you to accomplish this a little more effectively. I wish you well on that journey.

NOTES

1. J. Zijderveld, President Unilever Europe, quoted in Siegel, J. (2013) Unilever's new recipe for growth. Harvard Business School Case #713-418.
2. F. Mougin, EVP HR at Danone, quoted in Edmondson, A. and Lane, D. (2012) Global knowledge management at Danone. Harvard Business School Case #613-003.
3. Dribbling as a soccer or basketball player does during a game.
4. J. Zijderveld, President Unilever Europe, quoted in Siegel, J. (2013) Unilever's new recipe for growth. Harvard Business School Case #713-418.
5. N. Humphry, SVP Supply Chain, quoted in Edmondson, A. and Lane, D. (2012) Global knowledge management at Danone. Harvard Business School Case #613-003.

6. J.P. Agon, CEO, quoted in Lal, R. and Knoop, C. (2012) The universalization of L'Oreal. Harvard Business School Case #513-001.
7. L. Owen-Jones, former CEO, ibid.
8. J.J. Lebel, Worldwide President Consumer Products, ibid.
9. J.P. Agon, ibid.
10. B. McDonald, COO, ibid.
11. Indeed, to quote one of the best thinkers about international strategy, Julian Birkinshaw, "Today there is a broad consensus that an MNC is an international network that creates, accesses, integrates and applies knowledge in multiple locations. The integration of the knowledge of the MNC on a worldwide basis, although difficult, is what enables MNCs to reap the incremental value of being multinational."
12. However, research identified that only 11% of multinationals operating in three continents adopted the matrix structure (Collis, D.J., Young, D., and Goold, M. (2012) The size and composition of corporate headquarters in multinational companies: empirical evidence. *Journal of International Management*, 18(3), 260–275).
13. This is a hypothetical example drawn from real-world experience.
14. In the famous words of Evelyn Waugh's novel *Scoop*, they can be pursued "up to a point."

REFERENCES AND FURTHER READING

Bartlett, C.A. and Ghoshal, S. (2002) *Managing Across Borders: The Transnational Solution*. Harvard Business School Press: Boston, MA.

ABOUT THE AUTHOR

For the past 25 years David J. Collis has been a Professor at the Harvard Business School, where he is the Thomas Henry Carroll Ford Foundation Adjunct Professor of Business Administration within the Strategy Unit – only the second full-time Adjunct Professor appointed at HBS. Previously, he was the MBA Class of 1958 Senior Lecturer and an Associate Professor in the Strategy Group at HBS, having also completed five years as the Frederick Frank Adjunct Professor of International Business Administration at the Yale School of Management and two years as a Professor at Columbia Business School. The winner of the 50th Anniversary McKinsey Award for the best article in the *Harvard Business Review* in 2008, and a *Harvard Business Review* best-selling author, he is an expert on corporate strategy and global competition, and is the author of the recent books *Corporate Strategy* (with Cynthia Montgomery) and *Corporate Headquarters* (with Michael Goold and David Young), and the present book

International Strategy. Professor Collis is on the faculty for several HBS Executive Education programs, and chairs the programs Global Strategic Management and Corporate Level Strategy. As the author of over 25 articles and book chapters, his work has been frequently published in the *Harvard Business Review*, *Academy of Management Journal*, *Strategic Management Journal*, and in many books including *Managing the Multibusiness Company*, *International Competitiveness*, and *Beyond Free Trade*. The more than 50 cases he has authored have sold over 1 million copies worldwide and his articles over a quarter of a million copies with nearly 7,000 citations.

David Collis received an MA (1976) with a Double First from Cambridge University where he was the Wrenbury Scholar of the University. He graduated as a Baker Scholar from HBSl, MBA (1978), and received a PhD (1986) in Business Economics at Harvard University where he was a Dean's Doctoral Fellow. From 1978 to 1982 he worked for the Boston Consulting Group in London. He is currently a consultant to several major corporations, and on the Board of Trustees of the Hult International Business School, and the Advisory Boards of Vivaldi Partners, and formerly of PICIS, Ocean Spray, and WebCT. He is also the cofounder of the e-learning company E-Edge and the advisory firm Ludlow Partners.

INDEX